THE PSYCHOLOGY OF LEARNING AND MOTIVATION

Advances in Research and Theory

VOLUME 44

THE PSYCHOLOGY OF LEARNING AND MOTIVATION

Advances in Research and Theory

Edited by BRIAN H. ROSS

> BECKMAN INSTITUTE AND
> DEPARTMENT OF PSYCHOLOGY
> UNIVERSITY OF ILLINOIS AT URBANA-CHAMPAIGN
> URBANA, ILLINOIS

Volume 44

ELSEVIER
ACADEMIC
PRESS

AMSTERDAM • BOSTON • HEIDELBERG • LONDON
NEW YORK • OXFORD • PARIS • SAN DIEGO
SAN FRANCISCO • SINGAPORE • SYDNEY • TOKYO

Academic Press is an imprint of Elsevier

Elsevier Academic Press
525 B Street, Suite 1900, San Diego, California 92101-4495, USA
84 Theobald's Road, London WC1X 8RR, UK

This book is printed on acid-free paper.

Copyright © 2004, Elsevier Inc. All Rights Reserved.

No part of this publication may be reproduced or transmitted in any form or by any means, electronic or mechanical, including photocopy, recording, or any information storage and retrieval system, without permission in writing from the Publisher.

The appearance of the code at the bottom of the first page of a chapter in this book indicates the Publisher's consent that copies of the chapter may be made for personal or internal use of specific clients. This consent is given on the condition, however, that the copier pay the stated per copy fee through the Copyright Clearance Center, Inc. (www.copyright.com), for copying beyond that permitted by Sections 107 or 108 of the U.S. Copyright Law. This consent does not extend to other kinds of copying, such as copying for general distribution, for advertising or promotional purposes, for creating new collective works, or for resale.
Copy fees for pre-2004 chapters are as shown on the title pages. If no fee code appears on the title page, the copy fee is the same as for current chapters.
0079-7421/2004 $35.00

Permissions may be sought directly from Elsevier's Science & Technology Rights Department in Oxford, UK: phone: (+44) 1865 843830, fax: (+44) 1865 853333, e-mail: permissions@elsevier.com.uk. You may also complete your request on-line via the Elsevier homepage (http://elsevier.com), by selecting "Customer Support" and then "Obtaining Permissions."

For all information on all Academic Press Publications
visit our Web site at www.academicpress.com

ISBN: 0-12-543344-1

PRINTED IN THE UNITED STATES OF AMERICA
04 05 06 07 08   9 8 7 6 5 4 3 2 1

CONTENTS

Contributors ix

GOAL-BASED ACCESSIBILITY OF ENTITIES WITHIN SITUATION MODELS
Mike Rinck and Gordon H. Bower

I. Introduction 1
II. Activation Caused by Goal Relevance and Spatial Distance in Situation Models 12
III. Activation Caused by Goal Relevance, Spatial Distance, and Semantic Association 16
IV. Activation Caused by Active, Completed, and Postponed Goals 18
V. Delayed Effects of Active, Completed, and Postponed Goals 21
VI. The Time Course of Activation Caused by Active, Completed, and Postponed Goals 23
VII. General Discussion 26
References 30

THE IMMERSED EXPERIENCER: TOWARD AN EMBODIED THEORY OF LANGUAGE COMPREHENSION
Rolf A. Zwaan

I. Introduction 35
II. Comparison with Other Frameworks 37
III. Components of the Comprehension Process 38

IV.	Activation	39
V.	Construal	40
VI.	Integration	46
VII.	Empirical Evidence Consistent with the IEF	51
VIII.	Accounting for Propositional Findings	55
IX.	Accounting for Abstract Language	57
X.	Conclusions	57
	References	58

SPEECH ERRORS AND LANGUAGE PRODUCTION: NEUROPSYCHOLOGICAL AND CONNECTIONIST PERSPECTIVES

Gary S. Dell and Jason M. Sullivan

I.	Introduction	63
II.	Speech Errors and Processing Levels in Production	64
III.	Spreading Activation and Lexical-Phonological Feedback	67
IV.	The Function-Content Distinction and Connectionist Learning Theory	91
V.	Summary and Conclusions	101
	References	102

PSYCHOLINGUISTICALLY SPEAKING: SOME MATTERS OF MEANING, MARKING, AND MORPHING

Kathryn Bock

I.	Introduction	109
II.	Reaching Agreement	114
III.	Conclusions	137
	References	141

EXECUTIVE ATTENTION, WORKING MEMORY CAPACITY, AND A TWO-FACTOR THEORY OF COGNITIVE CONTROL

Randall W. Engle and Michael J. Kane

I.	Introduction	145
II.	The Measurement of WMC	150
III.	Alternative Explanations of the WMC × Higher-Order Cognition Correlation	156

IV.	Macroanalytic Studies of WMC: Its Generality and Relation to Other Constructs	167
V.	Microanalytic Studies of WMC: Its Relation to Executive Attentional Control	180
VI.	A Two-Factor Theory of Executive Control	185
VII.	Implementation of WMC in the Brain	190
VIII.	Conclusions	192
	References	193

RELATIONAL PERCEPTION AND COGNITION: IMPLICATIONS FOR COGNITIVE ARCHITECTURE AND THE PERCEPTUAL–COGNITIVE INTERFACE

Collin Green and John E. Hummel

I.	Introduction	201
II.	Bridging the Gaps: Relating Symbols to Neurons and Cognition to Perception	202
III.	Relational Perception and Thinking	203
IV.	From Images to Objects in Relations	206
V.	Toward a Model of Scene Comprehension	217
VI.	Conclusions	222
	References	223

AN EXEMPLAR MODEL FOR PERCEPTUAL CATEGORIZATION OF EVENTS

Koen Lamberts

I.	Introduction	227
II.	Representation of Events	229
III.	Similarity of Events	231
IV.	Categorization of Events	232
V.	Initial Tests of Event Similarity	239
VI.	Trajectories as a Basis for Event Categorization	247
VII.	Conclusions	255
	References	257

ON THE PERCEPTION OF CONSISTENCY
Yaakov Kareev

I. Introduction	261
II. The Statistical Argument	263
III. Experimental Evidence	265
IV. Summary and Implications	283
References	284

CAUSAL INVARIANCE IN REASONING AND LEARNING
Steven Sloman and David A. Lagnado

I. The Information Is in the Invariants	287
II. What Is a Cause?	291
III. Counterfactual and Probabilistic Judgment	297
IV. Language Use	305
V. Induction	308
VI. Learning	312
VII. Discussion	320
References	320

Index	327
Contents of Previous Volumes	339

CONTRIBUTORS

Numbers in parentheses indicate the pages on which the authors' contributions begin.

Kathryn Bock (109), Beckman Institute, University of Illinois at Urbana-Champaign, Urbana, Illinois 61801

Gordon H. Bower (1), Stanford University, Stanford, California 94305

Gary S. Dell (63), Beckman Institute, University of Illinois at Urbana-Champaign, Urbana, Illinois 61801

Randall W. Engle (145), School of Psychology, Georgia Institute of Technology, Atlanta, 30332

Collin Green (201), Department of Psychology, University of California, Los Angeles, California 90095

John E. Hummel (201), Department of Psychology, University of California, Los Angeles, California 90095

Michael J. Kane (145), Department of Psychology, University of North Carolina at Greensboro, Greensboro, North Carolina 27402

Yaakov Kareev (261), School of Education and Center for Rationality, The Hebrew University of Jerusalem, Jerusalem 91905, Israel

David A. Lagnado (287), Department of Psychology, University College, London WC1E 6BT, United Kingdom

Koen Lamberts (227), Department of Psychology, University of Warwick, Coventry CV4 7AL, United Kingdom

Mike Rinck (1), Dresden University of Technology, General Psychology, Dresden D-01062 FR, Germany

Steven Sloman (287), Cognitive and Linguistic Sciences, Brown University, Providence, Rhode Island 02912

Jason M. Sullivan (63), Beckman Institute, University of Illinois at Urbana-Champaign, Urbana, Illinois 61801

Rolf A. Zwaan (35), Department of Psychology, Florida State University, Tallahassee, Florida 32306

GOAL-BASED ACCESSIBILITY OF ENTITIES WITHIN SITUATION MODELS

Mike Rinck and Gordon H. Bower

I. Introduction

One goal of cognitive science is to gain a better understanding of text comprehension. The consensus is that reading requires many cognitive components that are active concurrently and in coordination—encoding words, grouping words into surface grammatical constituents to extract initial meaning, retrieving from short-term memory concepts and entities mentioned in the recent text, and retrieving from long-term memory information about the topic under discussion (e.g., Gernsbacher, 1994; Glenberg & Langston, 1992; Johnson-Laird, 1983; Kintsch, 1988, 1998; van Dijk & Kintsch, 1983; Zwaan, Langston, & Graesser, 1995). One view is that the information extracted from a text can be partitioned into three coordinated levels: (1) the surface structure of the text on the page; (2) the encoded propositional base which contains the asserted logical relations among the concepts, predicates, and arguments; and (3) the referential representation (often called the mental model or situation model) that the reader constructs, characterizing what the text is referring to and what it is about (van Dijk & Kintsch, 1983; Zwaan & Radvansky, 1998).

The mental model constructed by the reader connects the concepts of the text to things in the real world (e.g., in a news article) or an imaginary one (e.g., in narrative fiction). The model can be used to integrate information about co-referring expressions (e.g., "The first United States' President" and

"George Washington"). In addition, the model establishes the framework of time and space within which the activities described in the text occur. The model is used for deriving inferences, for interpreting the text, for supplying what the text may describe in only a cryptic manner, and for evaluating statements (e.g., as contradicting earlier knowledge). Statements in the text serve as cues for updating or altering the entities and their relationships in the model. The situational model is important because it is largely what people remember about a text. They remember not what the author wrote but what he or she wrote about—the gist of the text.

A. Components of a Narrative

Most recent research on situational models has used simple narratives as the experimental materials (e.g., Bower & Morrow, 1990; Gernsbacher, 1994; Graesser, Singer, & Trabasso, 1994; Graesser, Millis, & Zwaan, 1997; Schank & Abelson, 1977). These materials have several advantages for experimental purposes: (1) They are intrinsically interesting to subjects; (2) their composition can be easily varied to arrange whatever textual variations are to be compared in a counterbalanced manner; and (3) narratives typically use concepts and describe situations and human affairs that are familiar to nearly all educated readers. Therefore, the materials are likely to be processed in the same manner by randomly chosen college students who are assumed to have about the same background knowledge and "expertise" in these domains. This is an important assumption of subject homogeneity since different levels of background knowledge would introduce undesirable subject variability to any results.

The mental model of a narrative consists of at least three main components. First is the physical situation in which the actions occur; these provide a set of constraints on what actions are possible. Second is the cast of characters who will act in the drama. Third is a series of episodes in which the characters perform activities within the spatio-temporal framework of the model. The characters are assigned goals and problems to solve that are associated with their occupations or roles (e.g., husband, teacher, police detective). These goals motivate a series of action episodes that comprise the main path of a simple story.

B. Understanding Actions in Stories

In theorizing narrative comprehension, it is assumed that readers understand narratives about actors in the same manner as they understand actions in everyday life (Black & Bower, 1980; Bower, 1978, 1982; Schank & Abelson, 1977). They apply a "naïve commonsense psychology" to explain how and why characters in narratives act as they do. Readers perform a simple casual analysis of why things happen as the narrative describes them. This thesis, initiated by Schank and Abelson (1977) and Wilensky (1978, 1983), has been advanced most convincingly in experiments by Tom Trabasso and his collaborators (Trabasso & Sperry, 1985; Trabasso & Suh, 1993; Trabasso & van den Broek, 1985). The claim is that readers understand a story by extracting from it the goals of the characters and by relating the characters' actions to their own goals. In this way, readers are able to comprehend how and why characters execute plans, and how they overcome the myriad problems and complications those plans encounter.

By stitching together a series of such explanations, readers construct in memory a causal network of story parts, reflecting how one action enabled another action or was carried out to cause a particular outcome. The causal network so constructed is important in determining people's judgments about what is important in a story, what will be remembered, how the story will be summarized, and so on. The causal network of a story may be viewed as the gist of a story that readers extract.

Considerable research by Trabasso, his collaborators, and others has supported this view of narrative understanding and memory (see Graesser, Millis, & Zwaan, 1997). Furthermore, Langston and Trabasso (1998) and Langston, Trabasso, and Magliano (1998) have explained many of the behavioral results of narrative comprehension (e.g., memory for different narrative elements, priming within narratives, importance ratings, summaries, etc.) using a simulation model that postulates spreading activation among the mental representations of the propositions in the causal network of the narrative. In some respects, their model is the most impressive and comprehensible theoretical development in this literature (see also Kintsch, 1998).

C. Focus in Mental Models

In telling a story, narrators focus the reader's attention on a succession of characters and the flow of events as they transpire in different locations. We may think of these characters and locations as being momentarily brought into the foreground of the reader's attention and occupying "center stage" in the unfolding drama. From the viewpoint of cognitive psychology, tokens of these entities are being created (or placed) or "moved around" in the reader's short-term, working memory. As a result, information in memory about these foregrounded elements should be primed and more accessible than when they were not foregrounded.

We have performed a series of experiments examining the properties of this priming of foregrounded elements (see Bower & Morrow, 1990; Bower & Rinck, 1999); the present studies fit within that ongoing series. These experiments have followed a standard format in which college student participants first memorize a map of a building before they read some stories about events occuring within that building (see Fig. 1). We expect their memory of this building to serve as the referential field to which statements of the later stories can be connected. In order to study the effects of focal attention within a mental model, it is easiest and cleanest to examine the consequences of moving the focus from one location to another. Assuming that readers focus on the main character, the focus should move within the model when the text describes the character as moving, for example, from a starting room through an intermediate ("path") room into an ending ("current location") room.

In our experiments, after the movement sentence, we quickly tested the accessibility of previously memorized objects in rooms within this movement path as well as in rooms at varying distances from the current focus. One method of testing is to interrupt the subject's reading (after the movement sentence) with a yes/no question, either to verify an object's location, as in "Is there a VCR in the experiment room?", or to verify that

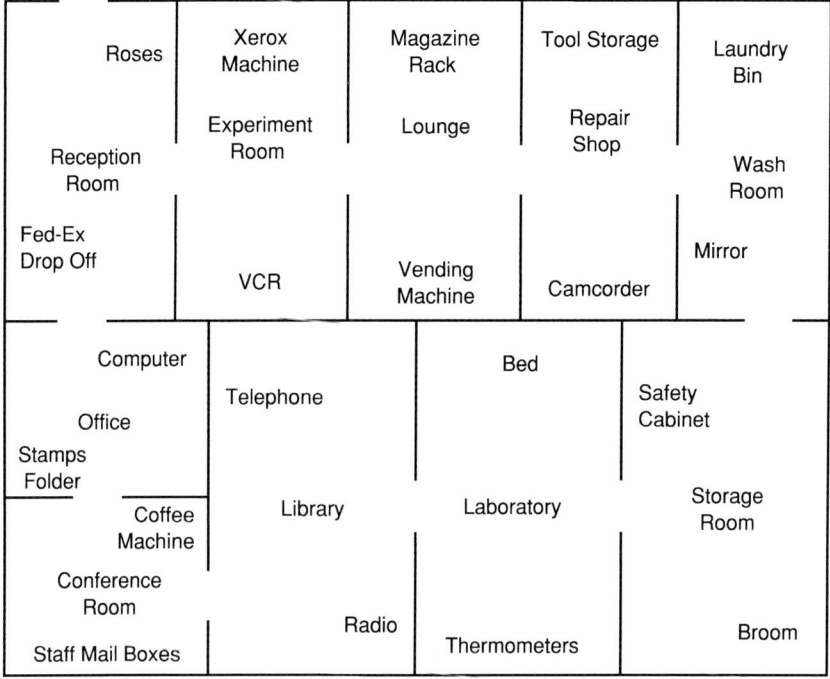

Fig. 1. Building layout studied by participants in all these experiments.

two objects are in the same location, as in "Are the VCR and Xerox machine in the same room?" (see Fig. 1).

We assume that memory elements of the model that are currently in focus will receive strong activation, so that information about them (such as their location) will be highly accessible and primed. We expect this activation would spread to other elements in a gradient according to their distance in the model from the focus. Moreover, the activation on a focused element should reveal a temporal gradient, decaying over time as it fades out of the foreground once the topic shifts.

Each of these predictions has been confirmed in several experiments in which priming was measured by the time to answer "yes" to probe questions about the location of objects in the building. The speed of answering questions about objects in the current location room was the fastest; the next fastest was answering questions about objects in the room just-left ("path"); the next fastest were answers for objects in the "source room" from which the movement began and in the room just ahead of the current room where the character will likely move next; and the slowest answers were to questions about objects even more distant from the current focus point. The absolute slowest answers were for questions asking about an object in a memorized building not involved in the current story. Moreover, if the character moved into a room in which the text described him as carrying out a prolonged activity, activation of the just-preceding path and source rooms decayed quickly towards the baseline level (see Rinck, Bower, & Wolf, 2000; Rinck, Hähnel, Bower, & Glowalla, 1997; Zwaan, 1996). This rapid decay could even be accelerated by simple time adverbials, such as: "Two minutes (versus two *hours*) later, he finished his work here."

As noted, the first several reports we published on this spatial priming in narratives used the probe reaction time measure. An objection to that procedure is that it frequently interrupts readers with test questions about locations of objects. This may cause them to read "unnaturally," attending far more to movements and locations than they normally would. Perhaps, then, the observed distance effects might reflect only participants' conscious expectations regarding the frequent tests about the location of objects.

In response to that objection, we looked for similar distance effects in anaphor resolution times during participants' normal reading (Rinck & Bower, 1995). In those experiments, as a part of line-by-line reading of a story, participants read a critical sentence that referred to an object located at varying distances from the current focus. An example would be when the character in one room remembered or thought about an object in another room, as in: "Wilbur remembered that the radio in the library needed to be repaired." These critical sentences were not marked or set off in any special manner from the participants' viewpoint. Nonetheless, the time participants required to read these critical anaphor sentences showed the same distance gradient as seen before: time to resolve the anaphor (here, the *radio*) was greater the farther back that object was in the movement sequence (Rinck & Bower, 1995). These distance effects in anaphor resolution times have been observed repeatedly since those earlier experiments (e.g., Bower & Rinck, 2001; Rinck, Bower, & Wolf, 1998).

D. EXPLAINING SPATIAL DISTANCE EFFECTS

How might we explain these distance effects in theory? A simple way to think about focus is in analogy to a spotlight shining into a dollhouse. The mental model might be thought of as an inner stage or dollhouse that readers construct in working memory. Thus, when a character is in focus, it is as though the spotlight shines on him or her, and it spreads its "illumination" in a spatial gradient around the focal point in the model. Objects located in or near the spotlight can be "seen" (accessed) more quickly that those on or beyond its fringes; items farther away take more time to verify because the spotlight must be moved to them.

This analogy is rather similar to recent proposals, such as that of Barsalou (1999; in press, a; in press, b), that knowledge should be represented as perceptual (or sensory–motor) memories. Barsalou has demonstrated how mental simulation of events, such as a character moving through a building, could be represented in working memory and how mental simulation of perceptual events would explain a number of cognitive phenomena. One minor failing of this analog representation is that our probe reaction time data indicate that distances in readers' model of our building are "chunked" into discrete "rooms" along allowable paths rather than processed as straight-line, Euclidean, metric distance (Rinck, Hännel, Bower, & Glowalla, 1997).

An alternative approach would use the concept of spreading activation in an associative network, such as the one depicted in Figure 2. In this approach, the relevant information might be represented in long-term memory as a hierarchically organized network of nodes and links (upper part of Fig. 2) that encode the spatial layout that an experimental participant would have memorized before reading the texts.

As the participant is reading, he or she is presumably entering into working memory (lower part of Fig. 2) pieces of text, such as: "Wilbur walked from the repair shop into the experiment room." Such sentences in working memory will activate the long-term memory nodes for the locations mentioned (e.g., the repair shop and experiment room). In addition, the reader will draw a few nearly automatic inferences, such as: "Wilbur is now located in the experiment room." This inference will cause more activation

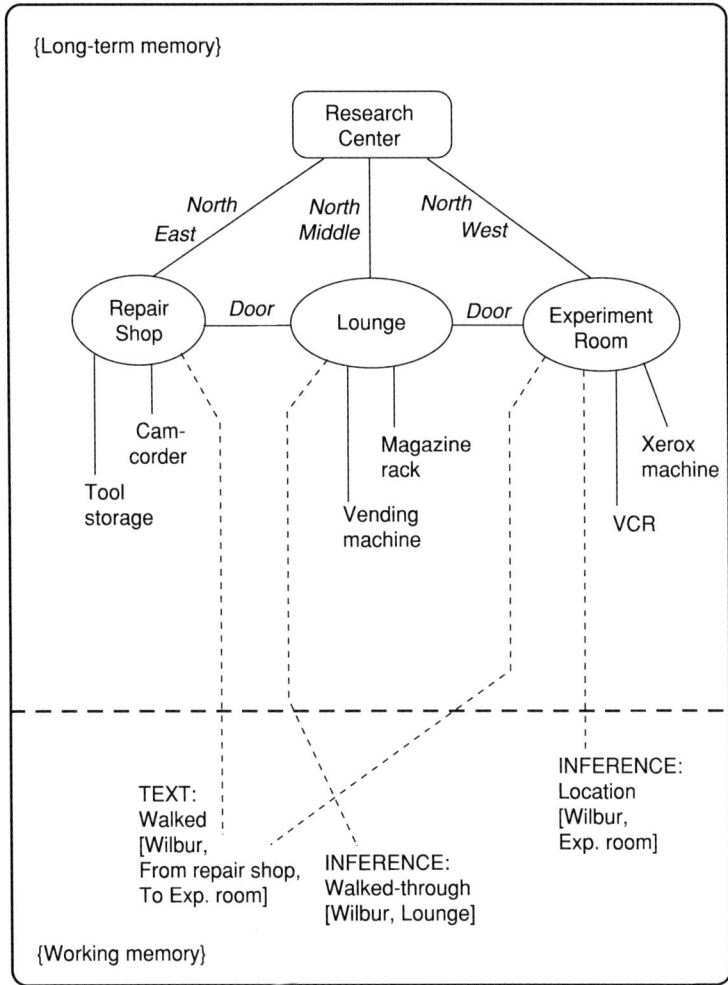

Fig. 2. An associative network that encodes knowledge of the building's spatial layout in long-term memory (above the line). Nodes denote rooms and objects, and links between nodes denote associations encoding spatial relationships and connections. Working memory (below horizontal dashed line) contains the currently active sentence and some spatial inferences from it (the Here-Now location). Vertical dashed lines indicate fleeting activation links between concepts now in working memory and their corresponding nodes in long-term memory (adapted from Bower & Rinck, 1999).

to be placed on the experiment room—where Wilbur is now—than remains on the repair shop he just left. Activation on a room node presumably spreads to memory nodes representing the associated objects in that room. Due to this spreading activation, participants are quicker to retrieve the corresponding test proposition from memory; in this way, the spread of activation facilitates verification of the probed fact (e.g., "The Xerox machine is in the experiment room"). This facilitation presumably increases with the amount of activation that has accumulated on this long-term memory proposition just before the probe question occurs.

We have investigated many variables affecting priming in this paradigm (for reviews, see Bower & Morrow, 1990; Bower & Rinck, 1999). With appropriate adjustment of parameters (e.g., decay of activation after the focus moves elsewhere), this network theory can explain our results in a general, qualitative way. So far as we can determine, this network model can provide parallel predictions to those that derive from the "spotlight" analogy or mental simulation theory. In certain respects, one's preference between the two theoretical positions is reminiscent of the preferences expressed during the former controversy regarding analog imagery versus propositional representations of knowledge (e.g., Kosslyn, 1980; Pylyshyn, 1973).

E. GOAL ACTIVATION OF OBJECTS IN MENTAL MODELS

In the experiments reviewed in the preceding text, we demonstrated differential activation of objects depending on whether they are foregrounded as something the protagonist was thinking about. This was especially prominent in our anaphor resolution studies, in which a room was mentioned as being thought about by the protagonist. Clearly, another way to get readers to appreciate what is on a character's mind is to attribute an active goal (wish, desire, plan) to that character. Thus, if the story states that the character is hungry, we can expect that items in the building associated with eating would be assigned priority in the protagonist' consciousness, and consequently in the reader's model of the protagonist. Thus, the reader's knowledge of locations of food items in the building should be activated and ready to be referred to, so long as the actor's "satisfy hunger" goal persists as part of the focus. Similarly, if the protagonist needed to make a phone call, telephones should be primed; if he needed to check his slides, the projector should be primed; and so on. The experiments to be reported test these intuitions, specifically examining the influence of the character's goals and their current status (or disposition) upon the accessibility of goal-related objects in the situation model.

F. PREVIOUS RELEVANT RESEARCH

Considerable earlier research on story understanding has examined how the protagonist's goals affect accessibility of goal-related information from the story; we will briefly review this work. As an early example, Dopkins, Klin, & Myers (1993) showed that a protagonist's goal established earlier in a text becomes active again in memory at the point in the story where that goal is being achieved. Similarly, Huitema, Dopkins, Klin, & Myers (1993) demonstrated that reading about a character's purposeful actions is likely to reactivate a corresponding goal of the character, even if the goal was stated much earlier and had been backgrounded by intervening material. One consequence of such reactivation is that readers were slower to read about an action that was inconsistent with the goal compared to a consistent action. Presumably, the inconsistent action prompted the reader's additional thought to rationalize it.

Further, several studies have compared the accessibility of goal elements depending on their current status or disposition in the protagonist's mind. Suh and Trabasso (1993) and Trabasso and Suh (1993) found that a narrative character's unsatisfied, *active goals* are more accessible in reader's memory than are that character's *completed goals*. Similarly, Lutz and Radvansky (1997) showed that failed goals (that the character still pursues) are more accessible than completed goals, and the latter in turn are more accessible than neutral information. This finding was replicated for both younger and older participants in experiments reported by Radvansky and Curiel (1998). Finally, Albrecht and Myers (1995) found that readers only noted the inconsistency of a current action with a *postponed goal* if the goal had been reinstated just before the action or if the surface distance between the goal and action was very short. Such studies demonstrate that readers generally tend to keep track of goal information that might be used to explain and predict the protagonist's actions. Most priority is accorded to the character's active, unsatisfied goals. More generally, the goals of the main character are of critical importance to the way readers create and update situation models of narrative texts.

G. CONTRIBUTION OF THE PRESENT EXPERIMENTS

The experiments reported here extend previous research on protagonist goals in several directions. First, previous studies have exclusively focused on the accessibility of goals (or goal statements) themselves, whereas we will measure the accessibility of objects relevant to achieving the goals. This is a fairly straightforward extension since previous research has shown that readers often infer the instruments that are typically used to perform described actions, such as brooms for sweeping and knives for cutting (e.g.,

Just & Carpenter, 1987; McKoon & Ratcliff, 1981). Therefore, it may be assumed that readers will also infer objects that are prototypical for *planned* actions rather than performed actions. Inferring these objects should make them highly accessible in the reader's memory, similar to the high accessibility caused by spatial proximity to the protagonist.

Since we wished to test several goal-related probes for each story, our texts were designed to introduce different momentary, minor goals (at various text locations) that were then tested with probe questions. These momentary goals interrupted the overarching goal that motivated the character throughout a given story. For example, in the story illustrated in Table I, Wilbur's overarching goal is to clean up all the rooms in the laboratory building in preparation for tomorrow's inspection by the Board of Directors. But while doing that lengthy chore, Wilbur is interrupted by the spontaneous thought that he needs to prepare copies of his handout for his speech to the lab directors the next day. Therefore, he interrupts his overarching goal (of cleaning up the building) in order to quickly pursue this interrupting goal of preparing Xerox copies of his hand-out.

Once that momentary goal is dealt with (and we have probed accessibility of some object related to that goal), the text states that Wilbur returns to his overarching goal of cleaning up the building. Then, several lines later, the character thinks of another momentarily interrupting goal, such as to telephone his wife regarding errands to do on his way home after work; once that momentary (telephoning) goal is dealt with, he returns again to the overarching goal. In this manner, we were able to introduce and test several different momentary goals within a single story, thus increasing the number of observations and statistical power of the critical conditions. So, in the following, we use the phrase "goal relevance" to refer to the relevance of the test object to the momentary, interrupting goal that has just been introduced in the storyline.

A second aim of these experiments is to examine the combined effect of varying different aspects of the situation model. By varying an object's relevance to the protagonist's momentary goal independent of its spatial proximity to him or her, it is possible to determine the relative importance of these two variables as well as their potential interactions. The latter point is of particular interest because it is possible that the effects of spatial proximity are caused to some degree by goal relevance: objects near to where the protagonist has just moved may be more accessible because, over thousands of prior experiences, readers have acquired the belief that objects near to where a person has just moved are more likely to be relevant to his or her current goal than are more distant objects. Thus, one aim of the experiments was to examine whether spatial proximity affects the accessibility of objects over and above the objects' relevance to the protagonist's goals.

TABLE I

Excerpt of Text and Test Probes Presented in Experiment 1 and Experiment 2

[Prior set up: *Wilbur, the research lab manager, has just learned that the Board of Directors will be inspecting the lab tomorrow, so he wants to clean up the lab so it will look good for the inspection.* The text continues ...] "Wilbur made a long list of things that needed to be done to make the research center decent-looking for the visiting directors."

1. Motion Sentence
  Then Wilbur walked from the repair shop into the experiment room.

2a. Goal Sentences for Relevant Object in Location Room (Xerox Machine in Experiment Room)
  Looking at his list, he noticed that he had wanted to make copies of his presentation handout for the directors. He decided to make the copies immediately before he forgot.

2b. Goal Sentences for Relevant Object in Source Room (Camcorder in Repair Shop)
  He remembered that he had wanted to practice his presentation by videotaping the talk he had to give to the directors. He decided to go and start setting that up immediately before he forgot.

2c. Control Sentence for Semantically Associated Object in Location Room (only in Exp. 2)
  Looking around, he saw copies of experimental materials lying on the floor.

2d. Control Sentence for Semantically Associated Object in Source Room (only in Exp. 2)
  Looking around, he saw instructions for making videotapes lying on the floor.

3a. Location Room Probe
  XEROX MACHINE—EXPERIMENT ROOM

3b. Source Room Probe
  CAMCORDER—REPAIR SHOP

4a. Sentence Following Location Room Goal Sentences
  After he had finished that task, he made sure that the experimenters would be busy conducting studies tomorrow so the directors would see how industrious they were.

4b. Sentence Following Source Room Goal Sentences
  After he had finished that task, he returned and made sure the experimenters would be busy conducting studies tomorrow so the directors would see how industrious they were.

4c. Sentence Following both Types of Control Sentences (only in Exp. 2)
  After that, he made sure the experimenters would be busy conducting studies tomorrow so the directors would see how industrious they were.

Note: Texts were presented without italics or underlining. Explanations are given in the text.

This question was addressed in Experiments 1 and 2 reported in the following text.

Finally, we wished to extend previous results regarding the effects of the current status or disposition of the goal. Compared to active and completed goals, the effect of *postponed goals* on accessibility has hardly been studied. In Experiments 3, 4, and 5 reported in the following text, we investigated whether objects relevant to considered-but-postponed goals become deactivated and as inaccessible as objects relevant to already completed goals. Moreover, we studied the time course (immediate versus delayed) of accessibility for active, completed, and postponed goal objects, thereby hoping to separate slower, passive decay processes from faster, active inhibition processes.

Since these experiments have not been published elsewhere, we feel it is necessary to describe the methods and procedures more fully than one typically finds in review chapters of this series. We feel this level of detail is required for anyone who wishes to replicate or extend the current experiments. To allow for easier reading, however, we have omitted the detailed statistical values in the results sections. They are available from the first author upon request. In the following, any effect or difference described as "significant" is statistically significant at least at the alpha = 0.05 level.

II. Activation Caused by Goal Relevance and Spatial Distance in Situation Models

The general goal of this experiment was to investigate how the accessibility of objects is affected by goal relevance and spatial proximity in situation models. To achieve this goal, the spatial proximity of objects to the focus of attention (e.g., to the location of the protagonist) was varied independently of the relevance of these objects to the protagonist's momentary goal. In general, all the following experiments followed the procedure introduced by Morrow and his associates (Morrow, Greenspan, & Bower, 1987; Morrow, Bower, & Greenspan, 1989) and modified by Rinck and Bower (1995). First, participants studied the layout of a research center until they were able to reproduce it perfectly. Then, they read a series of unrelated narratives taking place in the research center. While reading, the accessibility of objects located in the research center was measured with probe tests. These test objects were located either spatially close to the protagonist or spatially far from him or her. Independently, the tested objects were sometimes relevant to achieving the momentarily current goal of the protagonist or sometimes irrelevant to the current goal.

A. METHOD

Forty students of Stanford University, 27 of them students of Introductory Psychology, participated in the experiment, either to fulfill a course requirement or to receive a small monetary payment. In the first part of the experiment, participants learned the layout of the research center depicted in Figure 1. This layout was also used in the following experiments.

Participants studied the layout until they could perfectly reproduce all room and object names in their correct locations and answer questions about these locations. Subjects typically took about 25 minutes to learn the building map to criterion.

In the second part of the experiment, participants read 15 narratives (3 practice narratives, followed by 12 experimental narratives) presented one sentence at a time on the screen of a microcomputer, controlled by the "RSVP" software (Williams & Tarr, No date). Presentation of the sentences was self-paced: Participants pressed the space bar of the computer's keyboard to advance from one sentence to the next.

An excerpt of a sample experimental narrative used in Experiment 1 is given in Table I. Each narrative was approximately 20 sentences long and described the actions of a protagonist who moved through the building trying to fulfill an overall goal (e.g., to have the research center cleaned in preparation for important visitors, to look for a lost book, to look for a thief, etc.).

Distributed across the 12 experimental texts, 20 experimental "blocks" of sentences were presented. Each block started with a critical motion sentence (see Table I), describing how the protagonist moved from a source room (e.g., the repair shop) through an unmentioned path room (e.g., the lounge) into a location room (e.g., the experiment room). At the end of the motion sentence, the location room was the current location of the protagonist and presumably the focus of attention. Across stories, the 20 motion sentences were distributed equally over the 10 rooms of the building to ensure that each room served as the source room and location room with equal frequency.

As Table I illustrates, each motion sentence was followed by a pair of goal sentences. The goal sentences served to establish a momentary goal of the protagonist that would activate exactly one of the objects located in the building because it was particularly relevant to achieving the goal. The goal sentences always implied the relevant object without mentioning it explicitly. In one version of the goal sentences (see Sentence 2a in Table I), the goal-relevant object was located in the current location room, for example, "*Looking at his list, he noticed that he had wanted to make copies of his presentation hand-out for the directors. He decided to make the copies immediately before he forgot*". These sentences should activate the Xerox machine that is spatially near to the protagonist (e.g., both are now in the experiment room). Alternatively, the goal sentences could activate an object (in the "source room") that was farther from the protagonist's current location, as in Sentence 2b in Table I. "*He remembered that he had wanted to practice his presentation by videotaping the talk he had to give to the directors. He decided to go and start setting that up immediately before he forgot.*"

These sentences should activate the camcorder located in the repair shop (e.g., in the source room two rooms away from the protagonist's location). Each participant read either version 2a or 2b of the goal sentences. The control sentences 2c and 2d were not used in this experiment but in Experiment 2 to be described later.

Directly after the goal sentences, accessibility of a learned object was measured by an *object-room probe* (see Table I). As the name implies, these test probes consisted of an object name and a room name presented in capital letters, and participants had to decide as quickly as possible if the named object was located in the named room at this point in the narrative. They responded by pressing the key labeled "Yes" or the key labeled "No" on the computer's keyboard. For the 20 experimental probes following the goal sentences, the correct answer was always "yes." Noncritical false test probes were scattered throughout the texts to balance the number of "yes" with "no" answers.

The texts and probes were arranged so that the probed object could either be the one activated by the momentary goal just described or the object that would have been activated by the other goal (that remained unmentioned in this story). For instance, the goal sentences shown in Table I could be followed by either the probe "*XEROX MACHINE—EXPERIMENT ROOM*" or "*CAMCORDER—REPAIR SHOP.*" Each individual participant received only one of the two possible probes. For participants who read the two goal sentences about making copies, the first probe would test the accessibility of a close and relevant object, whereas the second probe would test a distant and irrelevant object. On the other hand, for participants who read the two goal sentences about videotaping the talk, the first probe would test the accessibility of a close but irrelevant object, and the second probe would test a distant but relevant object. This way, all four combinations of spatial proximity and goal relevance could be tested at each test point in the texts. Each participant judged five test probes in each of the four conditions. Across participants, each object was used equally often in each of the four conditions. Full combination of spatial proximity (object located in location room vs source room) and goal relevance (relevant vs irrelevant) yielded a 2 × 2 design. Both factors were varied within participants.

Two other non-experimental types of test probes were also presented to the participants. Each story contained one "protagonist probe" which consisted of the name of the protagonist and a room name. In addition, a total of 20 "filler probes" were presented and distributed over the 15 stories. These probes paired the name of a previously learned object, a recently introduced object, or a recently introduced person with a room name. Both of these probe types were included to ensure that participants would integrate information learned from the layout with updated information newly introduced into the narrative (see Wilson, Rinck, McNamara, Bower, & Morrow, 1993). Also, the majority of these 35 test probes required a "no" response, so the overall ratio of "yes" and "no" responses was balanced (30 yes vs. 25 no).

To ensure that participants read the narratives for comprehension, we had them answer three yes/no questions immediately after reading each narrative. These questions queried such details as the reason for certain actions, the location of certain activities, and the order of actions. Participants could earn a larger monetary bonus for answering increasingly more of these comprehension questions correctly. Participants were instructed to read carefully, but at their normal speed. Sentence reading times, probe reaction times, question-answer times, and correctness of the answers were all recorded by the computer. After reading all 15 narratives, participants completed a short questionnaire about their reading strategies and features of the narratives. They were then paid whatever bonus they had earned, and debriefed. Participants took about 45 minutes to read the narratives and answer the questions.

B. RESULTS AND DISCUSSION

The probe reaction times observed in Experiment 1 are displayed in Figure 3. The 2 × 2 analysis of variance (ANOVA) of the reaction times yielded a significant effect of spatial proximity, with the placement of objects in the location room being verified significantly faster than those in the source room. Goal relevance also produced a significant effect, with objects relevant to the current goal being more accessible than irrelevant objects. These two factors were additive, with no interaction between them.

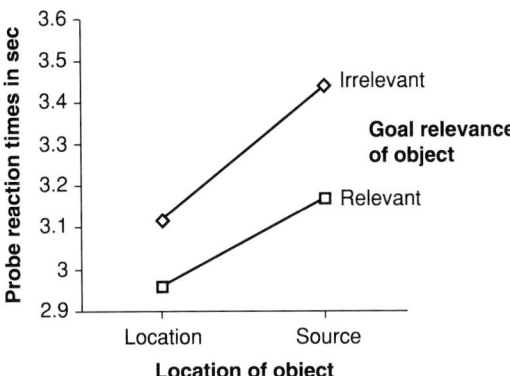

Fig. 3. Mean probe reaction times observed in Experiment 1.

To summarize, the results of the first experiment suggest that the accessibility of objects represented in the situation model depended on two independent variables: the objects' spatial proximity to the focus of attention (i.e., to the protagonist's current location), and the objects' relevance to the protagonist's momentarily current goal. Thus, both physical and mental aspects of the described situation affected the way readers focused their attention during comprehension. Interestingly, distance and goal relevance affected accessibility additively, without any hint of one variable depending on the other: relevant objects close to the protagonist were most accessible, whereas irrelevant objects far from the protagonist were least accessible, with near-irrelevant objects and far-relevant objects falling in between.

Importantly, the effect of goal relevance occurred despite the fact that relevant (instrumental) objects were never explicitly mentioned in the sentences that introduced the protagonist's momentarily interrupting goal (Table I). We avoided name repetitions by carefully choosing the wording of the goal sentences. For instance, Sentence 2a in Table I contains the verbal phrase *"wanted to make copies"* instead of *"wanted to xerox,"* thus avoiding any surface similarity to the probed item *"Xerox machine."* Similarly, in Sentence 2b, *"by videotaping the talk"* was used instead of *"by recording the talk"* to avoid any similarity with the probe item *"camcorder."* The same procedure was used with all versions of all goal sentences. Thus, the current results support the claim that readers made instrumental inferences of objects that could be used to achieve the protagonist's momentary goal.

III. Activation Caused by Goal Relevance, Spatial Distance, and Semantic Association

Unfortunately, there is an alternative explanation of the goal relevance effect in Experiment 1. The apparent accessibility of relevant objects might be due to mere semantic association between words in the text such as *copies* and *Xerox machine* (and similarly, between *videotaping* and *camcorder*). According to this semantic association hypothesis, neither a representation of the protagonist's goals nor an inference about goal-relevant objects is necessary to explain the faster access to goal-relevant objects we observed in Experiment 1. If this semantic association hypothesis was correct, then the nearby use of words such as *copies* in the story should suffice to activate the concept *Xerox machine*, even in the absence of any goal implying that the protagonist intended to use the Xerox machine located in the research center.

To test this hypothesis, we included a third type of sentence in Experiment 2. Instead of stating one or the other momentary interrupting goal (e.g., intending to make copies or videotape a talk), these control sentences simply contained the critical words (e.g., copies or videotapes) but without stating or implying a new momentary goal or intention of the protagonist. If such mere semantic associations are sufficient for the increased accessibility of goal-relevant objects, the same increase in speed should be observed following control sentences containing such words merely associated with the object as when a goal is attributed to the protagonist.

A. METHOD

Thirty-six students of Stanford University from the same sources participated in the experiment. None of them had participated in the previous experiment. The narratives were very similar to the ones of the previous experiment (see Table I), differing mostly with regard to the goal sentences. In addition to the goal sentence pairs like 2a and 2b, control sentences like 2c and 2d could be shown to the participants (see Table I). To test word association to the location room object, sentence 2c "*Looking around, he saw copies of experimental materials lying on the floor*," was presented. Likewise, sentence 2d "*Looking around, he saw instructions for making videotapes lying on the floor*," was presented to test word association to the object in the source room.

Individual participants read either 2a, 2b, 2c, or 2d, and they answered either the location room test probe or the source room test probe. Eighteen experimental test probes were presented to each participant. Therefore, each participant encountered three test probes in each of the six experimental conditions that resulted from full combination of goal relevance (relevant, irrelevant, or simply word associated) and spatial proximity (close: the location room vs. far: the source room). The six experimental conditions may be illustrated with the sample sentences in Table I: (1) goal-relevant close object: sentence 2a and location room probe; (2) irrelevant close object: sentence 2b and location room probe; (3) merely associated close object: sentence 2c and location room probe; (4) relevant far object: sentence 2b and source room probe; (5) irrelevant far object: sentence 2a and source room probe; (6) merely associated far object: sentence 2d and source room probe.

B. RESULTS AND DISCUSSION

The probe reaction times observed in Experiment 2 are displayed in Figure 4. The 2 × 3 ANOVA of these reaction times yielded a large effect of spatial proximity: objects in the location room were significantly more accessible

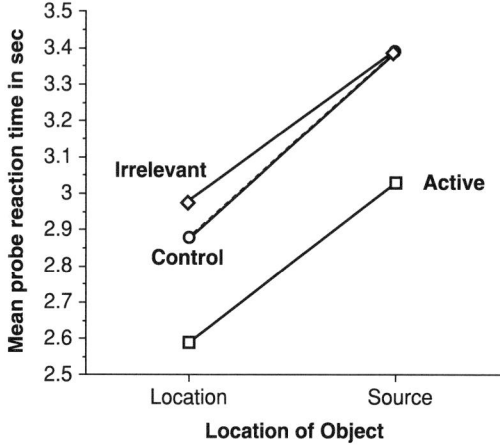

Fig. 4. Mean probe reaction times observed in Experiment 2.

than objects in the source room. The effect of goal relevance was significant as well. Planned comparisons revealed that this effect was mainly due to the high accessibility of goal-relevant objects. Relevant-object probes were responded to more quickly than both the irrelevant objects and the word-associated probes. Importantly, reaction times to irrelevant and semantically associated objects did not differ. These results, comparing reaction times to relevant and irrelevant object probes, replicate the ones observed in Experiment 1. Furthermore, for the semantically associated objects, the results suggest that the effect of mere association on accessibility is negligible.

IV. Activation Caused by Active, Completed, and Postponed Goals

Experiments 1 and 2 have shown that objects relevant to the protagonist's momentary goal are more accessible in memory than are irrelevant objects. Experiment 3, 4, and 5 were designed to investigate the accessibility of goal-relevant objects that vary in their status or disposition for the protagonist. As noted, previous research has shown that goals that have different status in the story create differences in their accessibility. For instance, Suh and Trabasso (1993), Trabasso and Suh (1993), and Lutz and Radvansky (1997) have shown that earlier statements in a text regarding *completed goals* are not as accessible in memory as are earlier statements about *active, uncompleted goals*, even if the two kinds of statements are tested at identical distances from their last explicit mention in the text. These results were taken to suggest that the protagonist's uncompleted goals are kept active in the reader's working memory, whereas completed goals are not. Completed goals lose activation, either by passive decay or by some kind of inhibition process. This deactivation would be a useful strategy because readers can usually assume that completed goals will no longer be motivating (and need to explain) the protagonist's upcoming actions. However, these earlier findings were measuring the accessibility of the goal statements themselves rather than instrumental objects associated with a goal-related plan. Therefore, one purpose of Experiment 3 was to extend these earlier findings to objects relevant to these goals.

Our second purpose was to compare active goals and completed goals to a third type of goal status, namely, goals that are introduced and considered momentarily but then *postponed*. In narratives as well as real life, a goal one considers may be postponed for several reasons. A common reason is that a top-level goal (e.g., buy a car) must be delayed until after some preconditions or sub-goals are achieved (e.g., obtain the money for the purchase). This type of postponement, of higher-level goals to pursue sub-goals, was studied by Suh and Trabasso (1993). In these cases the top-level goal remains very active in the protagonist's (and reader's) mind because it motivates the upcoming sub-goal activities. In fact, this top-level goal becomes most available at the moment that the near-final action succeeds in achieving the penultimate sub-goal (Suh & Trabasso, 1993).

A second type of postponement occurs when in the course of pursuing one goal and plan the character suddenly thinks of some unrelated goal. The character could pursue this unrelated goal but only by interrupting and diverting from his earlier goal plan. In such cases, the character may postpone pursuing the interrupting goal, delaying it until some future time after he has completed the present goal.

It is this second type of postponed goal that we wished to investigate in our experiments. We wondered what level of activation would be placed on (or persist on) a considered-but-postponed goal and its relevant objects. On the one hand, a postponed goal should not be kept highly accessible in working memory because the protagonist's near-term behavior will be guided (and explained) by completely different goals. On the other hand, the postponed goal is a wish the character still harbors, so readers should perhaps not totally dismiss it because it may well be reactivated at a later stage.

Experiment 3 was designed to investigate how the current status of a goal affects the accessibility of objects relevant to it. To this end, the texts and test probes used in the previous experiments were modified in the following way: all tested objects were goal-relevant, they were tested immediately after the momentary goal and its status had been described, and the momentary goal status was described as either active, completed, or postponed. Moreover, spatial distance of the tested object to the current location of the protagonist was varied independently of goal status, with the tested object being located in the source room or the current location room.

A. METHOD

Forty-two new students of Stanford University from the same source participated in the experiment. For this experiment, three different versions of the goal sentences were created. In the *active goal* version, the two sentences elaborated the interrupting, momentarily active goal, stressing its importance. These sentences were identical to the ones used in the previous experiments. In the *completed goal* version, the first sentence was identical, and the second one was changed to indicate that the momentarily interrupting goal had been achieved and the character was returning (or had returned) to pursuing his original, overarching goal. For this example, the second sentence read: *"He made the copies quickly and after that, went back to his task of checking the research center."* In the *postponed goal* version, the first sentence was also identical. The second sentence read: *"He decided to make the copies later because checking the research center was more important."* This indicates that the momentarily-considered goal was postponed in favor of the original overarching goal. All test probes following these goal sentences referred to objects relevant to the momentarily interrupting goal.

A total of 18 experimental blocks were included in the experimental texts. Three blocks were presented in each of the six experimental conditions, resulting from full combination of the within-subjects factors of spatial proximity (tested object in location room vs. source room) and goal status (the momentarily interrupting goal was either active, completed, or postponed). In all the participants, each block was presented equally as often in each experimental condition.

B. RESULTS AND DISCUSSION

The probe reaction times observed in this experiment are shown in Figure 5. As in the previous experiments, the 2 × 3 ANOVA of these reaction times yielded a large effect of spatial proximity: objects in the location room were significantly more accessible than objects located in the source room. The effect of goal state was significant as well, whereas the interaction was not. Planned comparisons revealed that objects relevant to postponed goals were significantly less accessible than objects relevant to active goals or objects relevant to completed goals. The active and completed goal-status

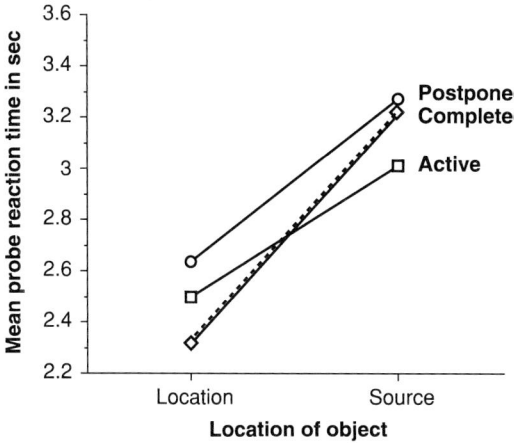

Fig. 5. Mean probe reaction times observed in Experiment 3.

conditions did not differ significantly. In general, the effect of goal status was weaker than expected, and much weaker than the strong effect of spatial distance in the situation model.

V. Delayed Effects of Active, Completed, and Postponed Goals

This experiment was designed to extend the results of the previous experiment that showed only a weak effect of goal state and yielded no significant difference between active goals and completed goals. This weak effect of goal status may be due to the fact that the accessibility of objects was tested *immediately* following the sentences describing the status of the goal. It seems likely that readers will keep the most recently read information in working memory; therefore, the goal concepts mentioned in it may be highly accessible for a brief time, independent of their goal status (see Glenberg, Meyer, & Lindem, 1987, for such a finding). Differences in accessibility may take some time to develop; if that is the case, they would be more evident when testing occurs at a brief delay after the goal sentences.

Two conclusions may be drawn from this argument. First, the fact that postponed goals yielded longer reaction times even if tested directly following the goal sentences suggests that active inhibition rather than passive decay of activation may be involved in processing postponed goals. This hypothesis was tested in Experiment 5. Second, the small and nonsignificant reaction time difference between objects relevant to active goals and those relevant to completed goals should increase if the accessibility of these objects is tested after a delay, allowing the completed goal to fade from working memory. This hypothesis was addressed in Experiment 4 by inserting one additional sentence between the goal-status sentences and the following test probe.

A. METHOD

Forty-two new students of Stanford University from the same source participated in the experiment. The texts used in Experiment 4 were identical to those of Experiment 3, except for the introduction of an intervening sentence between the sentences describing the goal status and the following test probe. For active goals, the intervening sentence elaborated the goal and stressed its importance. For completed goals, the intervening sentence elaborated the initial, overarching goal to which the character was returning. For postponed goals, the sentence described the overarching goal as more urgent than the postponed goal. For instance, after the goal sentence "Looking at his list, he noticed that he had wanted to make copies of his presentation hand-out for the directors," the complete sequence for the *active* goal then read: "He decided to make the copies immediately because otherwise he would probably forget it. He knew how important it was to have it done well before the directors arrived." For the *completed* goal, the two sentences read: "He made the copies quickly and after that, went back to his task of checking the research center. He had to make sure that everything was being checked, cleaned, and repaired." For the *postponed* goal, the sentences read: "He decided to make the copies later because checking the research center was more important. First, he had to make sure that everything was being checked, cleaned, and repaired."

B. RESULTS AND DISCUSSION

Figure 6 depicts the probe reaction times for this experiment. As before, the 2 × 3 ANOVA of these reaction times yielded a significant effect of spatial proximity: objects in the location room were significantly more accessible than objects located in the source room. The effect of goal status was significant as well. Planned comparisons revealed that, unlike the previous experiment, active goals now yielded faster accessibility overall than both completed and postponed goals. Objects relevant to completed goals did not differ in accessibility from objects relevant to postponed goals. To summarize, delaying the test of accessibility by one sentence had the expected result: the effect of goal status was stronger than in the previous

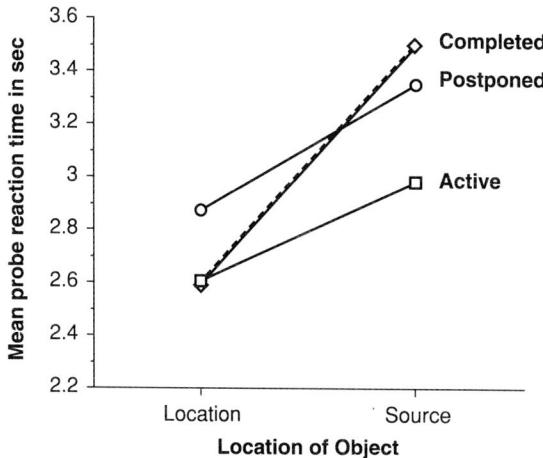

Fig. 6. Mean probe reaction times observed in Experiment 4.

experiment, and active goals yielded greater accessibility than both completed and postponed goals.

VI. The Time Course of Activation Caused by Active, Completed, and Postponed Goals

Comparing the results of Experiments 3 and 4 suggests interesting differences in the time course of activation for active, completed, and postponed goals. The accessibility of objects relevant to momentarily *active* goals did not appear to decrease over the temporal intervals (or intervening sentences) investigated here. The accessibility of objects relevant to *completed* goals decreased slowly; it was significantly lower than the accessibility of active-goal objects only after the insertion of an additional sentence. In contrast, objects relevant to *postponed* goals were less accessible than active-goal objects immediately after stating that the goal was being postponed.

These results suggest that different processes may be involved in the way readers deal with postponed versus completed goals. The decrease in accessibility of completed-goal objects may be explained by a gradual decay of activation, whereas the fast drop in accessibility of postponed-goal objects suggests that readers actively inhibit a postponed goal and their relevant objects. Inhibition, or suppression, has been suggested as an explanation for several phenomena in text processing (e.g., Gernsbacher

& Faust, 1991). For instance, Gernsbacher (1990) has suggested that individual differences in reading comprehension appear to be related to differences in people's ability to suppress irrelevant information, rather than the ability to keep relevant information active. Similarly, the poorer working memory of the elderly (compared to younger) subjects has been hypothesized to be due to their poor ability to inhibit irrelevant information (Zacks & Hasher, 1994; Zacks, Radvansky, & Hasher, 1996). This suggests, incidentally, that elderly subjects should have greater difficulty dismissing considered-but-postponed goals.

Following this line of reasoning, Experiment 5 was designed to investigate the time course of accessibility of objects that are instrumental for momentarily active, completed, and postponed goals. To increase the goal-to-probe variation of delay, either zero or three sentences were inserted between the description of the status of the momentary goal and the test probe. Because this experiment needed to collect many observations on the effects of this delay on the accessibility of objects relevant to active, completed, and postponed goals, spatial distance was not varied.

A. METHOD

Thirty-six new students of Stanford University participated in the experiment. The texts of Experiment 5 were similar to those of Experiments 3 and 4, except that the number of sentences inserted between the goal sentences and the goal-related test probe was systematically varied. For each participant, one-half of the experimental test probes were presented immediately after the goal-status sentences, as in Experiment 3. For the other one-half of the tests, three sentences were inserted between the goal sentences and the test probe. As in Experiment 4, these intervening sentences either elaborated the active goal or, in the cases of completed and postponed goals, elaborated the overarching goal. As before, a total of 18 experimental blocks were included in the experimental texts. Three blocks were presented in each of the six experimental conditions, resulting from full combination of the within-subject factors of "number of intervening sentences" (zero vs. three) and "goal status" (active, completed, or postponed goal). In all participants, each block was presented equally as often in each experimental condition.

B. RESULTS AND DISCUSSION

The probe reaction times observed in this experiment are shown in Figure 7. The 2 × 3 ANOVA of these reaction times revealed that objects were significantly more accessible if tested immediately after the goal sentences than after three intervening sentences. Goal status also yielded a significant

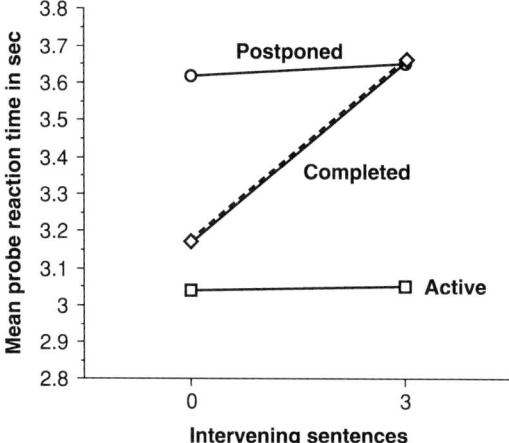
Fig. 7. Mean probe reaction times observed in Experiment 5.

effect, with objects relevant to active goals being more accessible than those relevant to postponed goals. More importantly, the interaction was also significant. Planned comparisons revealed that for active-goal objects, the number of intervening sentences had no effect: they were highly accessible even after three intervening sentences. There was also no effect of test delay for postponed-goal objects; their accessibility was low, both after zero and three intervening sentences. Finally, the accessibility of completed-goal objects decreased significantly with the number of intervening sentences: after zero intervening sentences, these objects were as accessible as active-goal objects and more accessible than postponed-goal objects. In contrast, after three intervening sentences, completed-goal objects were as inaccessible as postponed-goal objects and less accessible than active-goal objects.

This pattern of results accords with the hypothesis outlined earlier: objects relevant to active goals are kept highly accessible even over a delay of three intervening sentences, whereas objects relevant to completed goals lose accessibility over such a delay, and objects relevant to postponed goals are inhibited quickly, having low accessibility even when tested nearly immediately. Interestingly, the interaction between active and completed goals over zero versus three sentences (Fig. 7) is rather similar to that between these goals when the objects are in the location versus source room (Fig. 6). It is as though, for completed goals, the effect of the passage of time due to intervening thoughts is equivalent to that produced by the passage of time implied by movement in space.

VII. General Discussion

To summarize, the experiments reported here indicate that readers use goal information about the character in addition to spatial information to focus their attention on the most relevant parts of their situation model, that is, on the physical and mental "here and now" of the protagonist. Experiments 1 and 2 showed that spatial proximity of objects to the current location of the protagonist as well as the relevance of these objects to the protagonist's momentarily current goal increased the objects' accessibility in memory. These two factors had additive effects on accessibility, so that close, relevant objects were most accessible while distant, irrelevant objects were least accessible. Experiments 3 to 5 addressed the time course of accessibility of objects relevant to momentarily active, completed, or postponed goals. The results of these experiments suggest that objects relevant to an active goal remain highly accessible, at least over three intervening sentences; that the accessibility of objects relevant to a completed goal decays over three intervening sentences; and that objects relevant to a postponed goal are inhibited almost immediately.

This pattern of accessibility provides a clear answer to the questions raised in the preceding text. The accessibility of completed goals and objects relevant to them seems to decay passively, as the protagonist returns to pursuing the main goal. In contrast, postponed goals and the objects relevant for achieving them seem to be actively and quickly inhibited, as if not to interfere with the processing of the remaining, (active) main goal. However, it should be noted that this result was observed for momentarily interrupting goals that the protagonist postpones in order to pursue his or her overarching top-level goal. Future research will have to reveal whether similar processes are involved when the top-level goal itself must be delayed until after some subgoal has been achieved. Research by Suh and Trabasso (1993) indicates that in this case, the top-level goal remains active in the protagonist's (and reader's) mind because it motivates and explains the subgoal activities.

The present results also answer the question of whether the spatial priming of objects in the situation model is in reality just a kind of "potential goal relevance" effect in disguise. As we noted earlier, readers may direct their internal focus to places where significant events are likely to occur. Thus, when a character moves to some location, the objects in that location may be activated because readers would normally expect them to be relevant to the character's goal. This strategy is shaped and supported by the arrangement of human living spaces in which different parts of a building, say a residence, are set aside to satisfy recurrent goals, as revealed in our labeling of such rooms as the eating area, bedroom, laundry, toilet, and entertainment center.

According to this speculation, spatial priming in narratives would be a *derivative* of readers' subconscious expectations that characters go to a place in order to carry out some goal-plan with the people or objects there. This hypothesis would be in accord with the recurrent finding that relevance in narrative comprehension is largely determined by the goals and plans of the central characters.

However, several considerations argue against this "derivative hypothesis." First, one can observe graded spatial priming among objects according to their distance (even when outside a story context) when there are neither characters nor goals (McNamara, 1986; Rinck, Williams, Bower, & Becker, 1996). Merely focusing attention on one location within a map primes the availability of items at nearby locations. A second argument against the "derivative hypothesis" comes from the present results that indicate that priming by spatial proximity combines additively with priming by goal relevance. For clearly relevant objects and clearly irrelevant objects alike, spatially close objects were more accessible than distant objects. Thus, it seems that the effects of spatial proximity cannot be explained simply by assuming that spatially close objects derive their activation because they are potentially more relevant to the character's goals than are distant objects.

Given the pattern of results observed here, the obvious question is why and how spatial proximity and goal relevance affect accessibility of objects represented in the situation model. It is not clear how the spotlight model of perceptual simulation would account for these goal effects. However, an explanation is easily constructed in terms of the associative network model of Figure 2 (Bower & Rinck, 1999, 2001). Recall that the assumptions contained in this model regarding direct inferences and spreading activation suffice to explain the distance effect and the intermediate-room effect in spatial priming (that we have found repeatedly).

To account for the observed effects of goal relevance on accessibility in this network model, we begin with the plausible assumption that readers track the character's active goal stack, specifically by retaining it in working memory (see, e.g., Schank and Abelson, 1977). These goals reference plan structures that exist in long-term memory that specify inferences about instrumental objects typically used in that plan. For instance, readers know that a Xerox machine can be used for making photocopies, a camcorder for making videos, and so on. The diagram of the likely goal-related links among nodes depicted in Fig. 8 is an expanded version of the network shown in Fig. 2.

Figure 8 illustrates how the goal active in working memory sends activation to the goal-plan structure in long-term memory, which in turn transmits activation to the associated relevant instruments—such as the

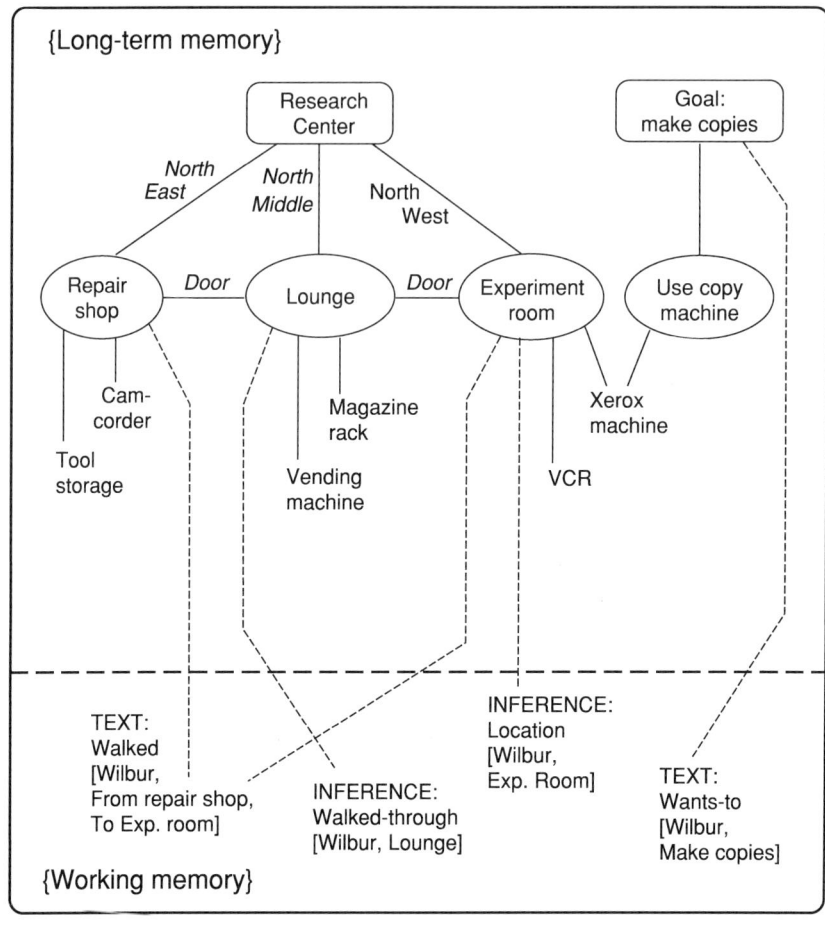

Fig. 8. An expanded version of the associated network shown in Fig. 2, incorporating goal-based activation and inferences. The recent goal statement ("Wants-To") is in working memory along with the recent movement sentence and inferences due to that movement. The goal statement activates the corresponding goal-plan structure in long-term memory and that transmits activation to nodes representing relevant instruments.

Xerox machine in this example. The activation arriving at the goal-relevant object will add to the activation coming from the room location node that has also been activated by its concept in working memory. These additive effects on reaction time are just what we found throughout the experiments reported here. Moreover, activation caused by these instrumental inferences will be maintained at high arousal so long as the current goal is active. This elevated goal-activation will decay once the goal is completed and the character moves on to another goal.

Furthermore, we must assume that the initial activation of a mentioned goal will be suppressed or inhibited almost immediately when the goal is postponed in favor of a different goal. It is as though the postponement sentence acts like a "forget" signal, causing the participant to expunge the postponed goal from working memory (cf. Bjork, 1970; Zacks & Hasher, 1994; Zacks, Rodvansky, & Hasher, 1996). As a consequence, we would expect participants to exhibit very little memory for the postponed goal sentences of the story when tested later. More research will be needed to test this hypothesis.

The effects we have observed for both spatial proximity and goal relevance clearly favor constructionist models of text comprehension (Gernsbacher, 1990; Graesser, Singer, & Trabasso, 1994; Singer, Graesser, & Trabasso, 1994). Both spatial and goal-related information are important aspects of the situation described or implied by the text compared to surface aspects of the text itself. Thus, they are represented in the reader's situation model instead of the text base or the surface representation (see Kintsch, 1988, 1998).

The experiments reported here add to the small but growing number of studies investigating different dimensions of situation models simultaneously. Among these are the studies by Bower and Rinck (2001), Rinck and Bower (2000) and Rinck, Bower, & Wolf (1998) mentioned in the preceding text as well as a study by Haenggi, Gernsbacher, & Bolliger (1994), who manipulated both emotional and spatial inconsistencies contained in short narratives. The most comprehensive, multidimensional studies of situation models were reported by Zwaan and his colleagues (Zwaan, Langston, & Graesser, 1995; Zwaan, Magliano, & Graesser, 1995; Zwaan, Radvansky, Hilliard, & Curiel, 1998). Their results supported the event-indexing model of narrative comprehension. In those studies, the authors investigated the slowing of sentence reading times produced by textual discontinuities of temporal, spatial, and causal relations as well as discontinuities related to the protagonist and his or her goals. However, by using naturalistic texts, those studies were *per force* correlational rather than experimental in nature, with sentence reading times being fit by multiple regression equations. The authors' conclusions about effective variables were then based on the relative sizes of the regression coefficients for predicting sentence reading times. But such correlational methods are inherently limited in their power to infer causal effects. We believe that in the future, more experimental studies will be needed that vary different dimensions of situation models independently of one another using carefully controlled texts, as we have done here for spatial proximity and goal relevance.

One take-home message from these investigations is that adults are remarkably flexible and adaptive in how they retrieve and use their background knowledge during narrative comprehension. They reveal substantial adaptability in selecting for use mainly the information that is highly relevant to the ongoing situation described by the text, and ignoring information which is momentarily irrelevant. Of the factors that determine relevance, so far we have identified spatial and temporal proximity as well as goal relevance. Together, these factors are skillfully tracked by readers to guide their focus of attention as they construct and update their situation models from texts.

Acknowledgments

Preparation of this paper was supported by grant Ri 600/3-3 from the German Research Foundation (DFG) to Mike Rinck, and by NIMH Grant 1R37-MH-47575 to Gordon Bower. We would like to thank Daniel Morrow for supplying primary versions of the experimental narratives. The assistance of Erin Graves in preparing and conducting Experiment 1 is gratefully acknowledged. Address correspondence to: Gordon Bower, email: gordon@psych.stanford.edu, or to Mike Rinck, TU Dresden, General Psychology, D-01062 Dresden, FR Germany, email: rinck@rcs.urz.tu-dresden.de.

References

Albrecht, J. E., & Myers, J. L. (1995). Role of context in accessing distant information during reading. *Journal of Experimental Psychology: Learning, Memory, and Cognition, 21,* 1459–1468.
Barsalou, L. W. (1999). Perceptual symbol systems. *Behavioral and Brain Sciences, 22,* 577–660.
Barsalou, L. W. (in press, a). Situated simulation in the human conceptual system. *Language and Cognitive Processes.*
Barsalou, L. W. (in press, b). Abstraction as dynamic interpretation in perceptual symbol systems. In L. Gershkoff-Stowe & D. Rakison (Eds.), *Building object categories: Carnegie Symposium Series.* Mahwah, NJ: Erlbaum.
Bjork, R. A. (1970). Positive forgetting: The noninterference of items intentionally forgotten. *Journal of Verbal Learning and Verbal Behavior, 9,* 225–268.
Black, J., & Bower, G. H. (1980). Story understanding as problem solving. *Poetics, 9,* 223–250.
Bower, G. H. (1978). Experiments on story comprehension and recall. *Discourse Processes, 1,* 211–231.
Bower, G. H. (1982). Plans and goals in understanding episodes. In A. Flammer & W. Kintsch (Eds.), *Discourse Processing.* (pp. 2–15). Amsterdam: North-Holland Publishers.
Bower, G. H., & Morrow, D. G. (1990). Mental models in narrative comprehension. *Science, 247,* 44–48.
Bower, G. H., & Rinck, M. (1999). Priming access to entities in spatial mental models. In W. Hacker & M. Rinck (Eds.), *Proceedings of the 41. Congress of the German Psychological Society.* (pp. 74–85). Berlin: Pabst Science Publishers.
Bower, G. H., & Rinck, M. (2001). Selecting one among many referents in spatial situation models. *Journal of Experimental Psychology: Learning, Memory, and Cognition, 27,* 81–98.

Dopkins, S., Klin, C., & Myers, J. L. (1993). Accessibility of information about goals during the processing of narrative text. *Journal of Experimental Psychology: Learning, Memory, and Cognition, 19*, 70–80.

Gernsbacher, M. A. (1994). *Handbook of psycholinguistics* San Diego, CA: Academic Press.

Gernsbacher, M. A. (1990). Less skilled readers have less efficient suppression mechanisms. *Psychological Science, 4*, 294–298.

Gernsbacher, M. A., & Faust, M. (1991). The mechanism of suppression: A component of general comprehension skill. *Journal of Experimental Psychology: Learning, Memory, and Cognition, 17*, 245–262.

Glenberg, A. M., & Langston, W. E. (1992). Comprehension of illustrated text: Pictures help to build mental models. *Journal of Memory and Language, 31*, 129–151.

Glenberg, A. M., Meyer, M., & Lindem, K. (1987). Mental models contribute to foregrounding during text comprehension. *Journal of Memory and Language, 26*, 69–83.

Graesser, A. C., Millis, K. K., & Zwaan, R. A. (1997). Discourse comprehension. *Annual Review of Psychology, 48*, 163–189.

Graesser, A. C., Singer, M., & Trabasso, T. (1994). Constructing inferences during narrative text comprehension. *Psychological Review, 101*, 371–395.

Haenggi, D., Gernsbacher, M. A., & Bolliger, C. A. (1994). Individual differences in situation-based inferencing during narrative text comprehension. In H. van Oostendorp & R. A. Zwaan (Eds.), *Naturalistic text comprehension*. (pp. 79–96). Norwood, NJ: Ablex.

Huitema, J. S., Dopkins, S., Klin, C., & Myers, J. L. (1993). Connecting goals and actions during reading. *Journal of Experimental Psychology: Learning, Memory, and Cognition, 19*, 1053–1060.

Johnson-Laird, P. N. (1983). *Mental models.* Cambridge, GB: Cambridge University Press.

Just, M. A., & Carpenter, P. A. (1987). *The psychology of reading and language comprehension.* Boston: Allyn and Bacon.

Kintsch, W. (1988). The role of knowledge in discourse comprehension: A construction-integration model. *Psychological Review, 95*, 163–182.

Kintsch, W. (1998). *Comprehension.* New York: Cambridge University Press.

Kosslyn, S. M. (1980). *Image and mind.* Cambridge, MA: Harvard University Press.

Langston, M. C., & Trabasso, T. (1998). Modeling causal integration and availability of information during comprehension of narrative texts. In H. van Oostendorp & S. Goldman (Eds.), *The construction of mental representations during reading.* (pp. 29–69). Mahwah, NJ: Erlbaum.

Langston, M. C., Trabasso, T., & Magliano, J. P. (1998). A connectionist model of narrative comprehension. In A. Ram & K. Moorman (Eds.), *Computational models of reading and understanding.* Cambridge, MA: MIT Press.

Lutz, M. F., & Radvansky, G. A. (1997). The fate of completed goal information in narrative comprehension. *Journal of Memory and Language, 36*, 293–310.

McKoon, G., & Ratcliff, R. A. (1981). The comprehension processes and memory structures involved in instrumental inference. *Journal of Verbal Learning and Verbal Behavior, 20*, 671–682.

McNamara, T. P. (1986). Mental representations of spatial relations. *Cognitive Psychology, 18*, 87–121.

Morrow, D. G. (1994). Spatial models created from text. In H. van Oostendorp & R. A. Zwaan (Eds.), *Naturalistic text comprehension.* (pp. 57–78). Norwood, NJ: Ablex.

Morrow, D. G., Bower, G. H., & Greenspan, S. L. (1989). Updating situation models during narrative comprehension. *Journal of Memory and Language, 28*, 292–312.

Morrow, D. G., Greenspan, S. L., & Bower, G. H. (1987). Accessibility and situation models in narrative comprehension. *Journal of Memory and Language, 26*, 165–187.

Pylyshyn, Z. W. (1973). What the mind's eye tells the mind's brain: A critique of mental imagery. *Psychological Bulletin, 80*, 1–24.

Radvansky, G. A., & Curiel, J. M. (1998). Narrative comprehension and aging: The fate of completed goal information. *Psychology and Aging, 13*, 69–79.

Rinck, M. (1994). *Treatment of outliers in reaction time data*. Unpublished manuscript. Germany: Dresden University of Technology.

Rinck, M., & Bower, G. H. (1995). Anaphora resolution and the focus of attention in situation models. *Journal of Memory and Language, 34*, 110–131.

Rinck, M., & Bower, G. H. (2000). Temporal and spatial distance in situation models. *Memory & Cognition, 28*, 1310–1320.

Rinck, M., Bower, G. H., & Wolf, K. (1998). Distance effects in surface structures and situation models. *Scientific Studies of Reading, 2*, 221–246.

Rinck, M., Bower, G. H., & Wolf, K. (2000). Temporal and spatial distance in situation models. *Memory & Cognition, 29*, 1310–1320.

Rinck, M., Hähnel, A., Bower, G. H., & Glowalla, U. (1997). The metrics of spatial situation models. *Journal of Experimental Psychology: Learning, Memory, and Cognition, 23*, 622–637.

Rinck, M., Williams, P., Bower, G. H., & Becker, E. S. (1996). Spatial situation models and narrative understanding: Some generalizations and extensions. *Discourse Processes, 21*, 23–55.

Schank, R. C., & Abelson, R. P. (1977). *Scripts, plans, goals, and understanding*. Hillsdale, NJ: Erlbaun.

Singer, M., Graesser, A. C., & Trabasso, T. (1994). Minimal or global inference during reading. *Journal of Memory and Language, 33*, 421–441.

Suh, S. Y., & Trabasso, T. (1993). Inferences during reading: Converging evidence from discourse analysis, talk-aloud protocols, and recognition priming. *Journal of Memory and Language, 32*, 279–300.

Trabasso, T., & Sperry, L. L. (1985). Causal relatedness and importance of story events. *Journal of Memory and Language, 24*, 595–611.

Trabasso, T., & Suh, S. Y. (1993). Understanding text: Achieving explanatory coherence through on-line inferences and mental operations in working memory. *Discourse Processes, 16*, 3–34.

Trabasso, T., & van den Broek, T. (1985). Causal thinking and representation of narrative events. *Journal of Memory and Language, 24*, 612–630.

van Dijk, T. A., & Kintsch, W. (1983). *Strategies of discourse comprehension*. New York: Academic Press.

Wilensky, R. (1978). Understanding goal based stories. *Research report number 140. Unpublished doctoral dissertation*. New Haven, CT: Computer Science Department, Yale University.

Wilensky, R. (1983). *Planning and understanding: A computational approach to human reasoning*. Reading, MA: Addison-Wesley.

Williams, P., & Tarr, M. J. (No date). *RSVP: Experimental control software for MacOS* [Online]. Available:http://psych.umb.edu/rsvp/[1998, October 27].

Wilson, S. G., Rinck, M., McNamara, T. P., Bower, G. H., & Morrow, D. G. (1993). Mental models and narrative comprehension: Some qualifications. *Journal of Memory and Language, 32*, 141–154.

Zacks, R. T., & Hasher, L. (1994). Directed ignoring: Inhibitory regulation of working memory. In D. Dagenbach & T. H. Carr (Eds.), *Inhibitory processes in attention, memory, and language*. (pp. 241–264). San Diego, CA: Academic Press.

Zacks, R. T., Radvansky, G., & Hasher, L. (1996). Studies of directed forgetting in older adults. *Journal of Experimental Psychology: Learning, Memory, and Cognition, 22*, 143–156.

Zwaan, R. A. (1996). Processing narrative time shifts. *Journal of Experimental Psychology: Learning, Memory, and Cognition, 22*, 1196–1207.

Zwaan, R. A., Langston, M. C., & Graesser, A. C. (1995). The construction of situation models in narrative comprehension: An event-indexing model. *Psychological Science, 6*, 292–297.

Zwaan, R. A., Magliano, J. P., & Graesser, A. C. (1995). Dimensions of situation model construction in narrative comprehension. *Journal of Experimental Psychology: Learning, Memory, and Cognition, 21*, 386–397.

Zwaan, R. A., & Radvansky, G. A. (1998). Situation models in language comprehension and memory. *Psychological Bulletin, 123*, 162–185.

Zwaan, R. A., Radvansky, G. A., Hilliard, A. E., & Curiel, J. M. (1998). Constructing multidimensional situation models during reading. *Scientific Studies of Reading, 2*, 199–220.

THE IMMERSED EXPERIENCER: TOWARD AN EMBODIED THEORY OF LANGUAGE COMPREHENSION

Rolf A. Zwaan

I. Introduction

Consider the following four sets of findings about language comprehension:

1. Words activate brain regions that are close to or overlap with brain areas that are active during perception of or actions involving the words' referents (Isenberg et al., 1999; Martin & Chao, 2001; Pulvermüller, 1999, 2002). Brain lesions in patients with selective semantic impairments affect perceptual representations (e.g., Farah & McClelland, 1991; McRae, de Sa, & Seidenberg, 1997; Miceli et al., 2001).

2. Visual representations of object shape and orientation are routinely and immediately activated during word and sentence comprehension (Dahan & Tanenhaus, 2002; Stanfield & Zwaan, 2001; Zwaan, Stanfield, & Yaxley, 2002; Zwaan & Yaxley, 2003). Visual–spatial information primes sentence processing (Boroditsky, 2000) and may interfere with comprehension (Fincher-Kiefer, 2001).

3. Information that is "in" the situation described in a text is more active in the comprehender's mind than information that is not in the situation (Glenberg, Meyer, & Lindem, 1987; Kaup & Zwaan, 2003; Morrow, Greenspan, & Bower, 1987; Horton & Rapp, 2003; Trabasso & Suh, 1993; Zwaan, Madden, & Whitten, 2000).

4. When comprehending language, people's eye and hand movements are consistent with perceiving or acting in the described situation (Glenberg & Kaschak, 2002; Klatzky, Pellegrino, McCloskey, & Doherty, 1989; Spivey, Richardson, Tyler, & Young, 2000).

These bodies of findings present a challenge to current theories of language comprehension; currently no framework exists that coherently account for these findings. The purpose of this contribution is to develop such a framework. The basic premise is that language is a set of cues to the comprehender to construct an experiential (perception plus action) simulation of the described situation. In this conceptualization, the comprehender is an immersed experiencer of the described situation, and comprehension is the vicarious experience of the described situation. Consider the following examples:

(1a) The ranger saw the eagle in the sky.

(1b) The ranger saw the eagle in the nest.

Amodal propositional representations (e.g., Kintsch & van Dijk, 1978) of these sentences would look as follows:

(2a) [[SAW[RANGER, EAGLE]], [IN[EAGLE, SKY]]]

(2b) [[SAW[RANGER, EAGLE]], [IN[EAGLE, NEST]]]

Although these representations capture the expressed relations among entities, actions, and locations, they omit critical information about the eagle: its shape. When in the sky, an eagle has its wings outstretched; when in a nest, it has its wings drawn in. The Immersed Experiencer Framework (IEF) proposed here is capable of capturing information such as this. The basic idea is that words activate experiences with their referents. For example, sentence (1a) activates visual experiences of eagles in the sky. In these visual representations, the eagle has its wings outstretched. On the other hand, (2b) activates visual experiences of seeing eagles in a nest. In these representations, the eagle has its wings drawn in. Thus, the shape of the referent results from the perceptual simulation.

The IEF distinguishes three component processes of language comprehension: (1) activation, (2) construal, and (3) integration. Activation operates at the word level, construal at the clause level, and integration at the discourse level. The IEF coherently accounts for the findings alluded to in the opening paragraph. In addition, it can account for the findings that earlier models cannot account for. As a consequence, the IEF provides a useful way of conceptualizing language comprehension, although there are significant hurdles to overcome.

II. Comparison with Other Frameworks

Fortunately, research on language comprehension is cumulative. The IEF adopts many insights from earlier theories of comprehension, specifically those developed by Kintsch and van Dijk (Ericsson & Kintsch, 1995; Kintsch, 1988; Kintsch & van Dijk, 1978; van Dijk & Kintsch, 1983), as well as the related event-indexing model (Zwaan & Radvansky, 1998). In addition, there is overlap with other well-known approaches to comprehension, such as the Structure-Building-Framework (Gernsbacher, 1990), and the constructivist framework (Graesser, Singer, & Trabasso, 1994). Along with Kintsch and van Dijk (1978), I assume that: (1) The linguistic input stream is segregated into units, which are subsequently integrated with the contents of working memory; and (2) that comprehension proceeds in an incremental fashion, whereby currently relevant information (constructed from previous input) is held in an active state so that it influences the integration of incoming information. Along with Ericsson and Kintsch (1995), I assume that parts of long-term memory are recruited for this process along with short-term working memory, thus allowing the comprehender to maintain relevant aspects of multiple construals active in working memory, thereby increasing the likelihood of overlap between the current construal and the contents of working memory.

Along with Kintsch (1988), I assume that incoming words first result in a diffuse pattern of activation, which is subsequently narrowed down by a constraint satisfaction mechanism that takes contextual information into account. However, as will become clear, I am assuming that initial activation is even more diffuse than was presumed by Kintsch. Along with many researchers (e.g., Glenberg, Meyer, & Lindem, 1987; Graesser, Singer, & Trabasso, 1994; Johnson-Laird, 1983; Sanford & Garrod, 1981; van Dijk & Kintsch 1983; Zwaan & Radvansky, 1998), I assume that the typical goal of language comprehension is the construction of a mental representation of the referential situation—a situation model. Along with Gernsbacher (1990) and Zwaan and Radvansky (1998), I assume that the online comprehension process is strongly influenced by spatio-temporal characteristics of the referential situation, in addition to characteristics of the linguistic input stream.

Although the IEF adopts assumptions and mechanisms from these earlier models, it differs from them in that it makes the explicit assumption that comprehension involves action and perceptual representations and not amodal propositions. This view is informed and inspired by theories that ground cognition in perception and action (e.g., Barsalou, 1999; Damasio, 1994, 1998; Glenberg, 1997; Lakoff, 1987; Langacker, 1987; MacWhinney, 1999; Sadoski & Paivio, 2001; Pulvermüller, 1999, 2002; Talmy, 1988). For instance, Pulvermüller (1999, 2002) has proposed a Hebbian model of semantic representation according to which the perception of a word activates "functional webs" of neurons located throughout the cortex. These functional webs are also activated when the word's referent is experienced. As such, comprehension of a word is the reconstitution of an experience with its referent. It is too rigid to assume that words will activate a single web. Which parts of the functional web will be activated depends on the semantic and task context in which the word is processed (Posner & DiGirolamo, 1999). This context-sensitivity is achieved in the IEF, as will become clear later.

In short, the basic assumption is reading or hearing a word activates experiential representations of words (lexical, grammatical, phonological, motoric, tactile) as well as associated experiential representations of their referents—motor, perceptual, and emotional representations, and often combinations of these (see also Sadoski & Paivio, 2001). These traces can be activated by verbal input and as such enable the reconstitution of experience. In this sense, comprehension is the vicarious experience of the described events through the integration and sequencing of traces from actual experience cued by the linguistic input (see Duchan, Bruder, & Hewitt, 1995, and Gerrig, 1993 for other experiential views).

III. Components of the Comprehension Process

The IEF distinguishes three general components of the comprehension process: (1) activation, (2) construal, and (3) integration. Table I lists these processes, along with the linguistic and representational units on which they

TABLE I

Components of the Comprehension Process, the Linguistic and Representational Units on Which They Operate, and the Referential Units They Denote

Process	Linguistic unit	Representational unit	Referential unit
Activation	Word/morpheme	Functional webs	Objects and actions
Construal	Clause/intonation unit	Integrated webs	Events
Integration	Connected discourse	Sequence of integrated webs	Event sequences

operate and the referential units that they denote. It is important to stress that the three component processes are not assumed to operate sequentially. Rather, it is assumed that they have a large degree of temporal overlap. However, for reasons of exposition, they will be described sequentially. Table I also shows the linguistic units that constitute the input for these processes. It is assumed that words are associated with a range of experiential traces related to their referents—functional webs. Finally, the fourth column lists the referential units, that is, the entities or events in the environment that are associated with the representational units.

IV. Activation

Incoming words *activate* functional webs that are also activated when the referent is experienced. Thus, in the case of sentences 1a and 1b, the functional webs that are also active when we see an eagle will be activated. Functional webs are widespread throughout the cortex and may involve the primary sensory areas (Pulvermüller, 2002). Given that we usually have different experiences with referents (e.g., we see objects from different viewpoints), there will initially be diffuse activation of multiple overlapping functional webs. For example, a functional web encoding experiences of seeing eagles in flight (from different perspectives) may be activated, as well as a functional web encoding visual experiences of perched eagles.

Thus, assuming there is no prior semantic context (although this is rarely the case outside the cognition lab and a game of Scrabble) and our word is the first content word of the sentence being processed, this word will diffusely activate overlapping functional webs. This web comprises the totality of our experiences with a certain entity or event. The degree of diffuseness of the representation depends on the frequency distributions, primacy, and recency of our experiences with its referent. If a certain category of experiences, for instance a specific visual perspective, is relatively frequent for that entity compared to other experiences with the same entity (e.g., we most often see hot air balloons from below, rather than from above and we most often see eagles from afar rather than from up close) then the most frequent experiential trace will be the most highly activated (see Palmer, Rosch, & Chase, 1981, on canonical viewpoints). When there are experiential categories with roughly similar frequencies, the initially activated functional web will not be strongly biased toward a specific representation. The activated representation will provide the context for the pattern of activation for the next functional web. This provides a constraint on the activation of the new web. The more specific, or "articulated," the initial representation, the stronger the constraint it exerts on the subsequent activation. The constraint–satisfaction mechanism by which a previously diffusely activated functional web is constrained to fit the mental simulation is called *articulation*, and it occurs during *construal*.

V. Construal

A. DEFINITION OF CONSTRUAL

Construal is the integration of functional webs in a mental simulation of a specific event. The grammatical unit on which construals operate is an *intonation unit*. This is grounded in the analysis of spoken language, which precedes written language both phylogenetically and ontogenetically. Chafe (1994) has observed that speech can be segmented into units, called intonation units, that are identifiable on the basis of cues such as pauses, pitch shifts, and changes in voice quality. They often, but not necessarily always, coincide with clauses. For example, a single clause sentence like (3) contains three intonation units.

(3) We will meet in my office on the fourth floor of the Longmire building.

The location of the meeting is specified in three intonation units, which convey a zooming-out from the office, to the floor it is on, to the building it is in. In terms of comprehension, intonation units can be viewed as *attentional frames* (Langacker, 2001). This notion is particularly insightful because it construes language comprehension as the language-based modulation of attention to a described state of affairs.

During construal, initially activated functional webs are integrated to yield a representation of an event. The referential unit to which construal pertains is an event. During construal, the initially diffusely activated functional webs become *articulated* by way of a constraint–satisfaction mechanism. The general principles of Kintsch's (1998) construction–integration model, not developed with perceptual symbol systems in mind, provide a way of conceptualizing this process. In the case of sentences (1a) and (1b), the constraint is provided by the prepositional phrase, which states the location of the eagle (in the sky vs. in the nest). In simpler terms, the prepositional phrase constrains the activated visual representations (functional webs), such that those consistent with the stated location (i.e., our visual representations of eagles in the sky or eagles in a nest) will receive more activation than those inconsistent with the stated location. As a result, the appropriate visual representation of the eagle in its location will be the end result of construal. The visual representation of the eagle, which initially was diffused because multiple shapes were activated is now *articulated*. Given that language comprehension normally occurs rapidly (and is incremental)—normal speech rate is about 2.5 words per second and normal reading rate is about twice as fast—and the comprehender attempts to interpret each word immediately (Chambers et al., 2001), the articulation of a functional web in a mental simulation occurs rapidly as well.

Methods with high temporal resolution (because they do not involve manual or vocal responses), such as eye tracking and event-related potentials, have provided substantial evidence that the incorporation of incoming information occurs immediately rather than at some syntactic boundary, and incorporates not only clausal information but also information from previous clauses (e.g., Chambers et al., 2001; van Berkum, Hagoort, & Brown, 1999). Thus, construal is an immediate and incremental process. In some cases, the functional web activated by one word may constrain the activation of the functional web activated by the next word (forward articulation), while the latter may at the same time constrain the former (backward articulation). This process of mutual articulation can be illustrated by the following example (see also Morrow and Clark, 1988; and Halff, Ortony, & Anderson, 1976). Consider (4a) and (4b).

(4a) The red squirrel jumped from the oak to the pine tree.

(4b) The red fire truck came swerving around the corner.

In both sentences, "red" will activate visual representations of the range of colors we call "red." The next content word helps articulate a specific instance of red, a brownish red in the case of the squirrel and a bright red in the case of the fire truck (the more prototypical red). In turn, the first word also plays a role in articulating the symbol activated by the second word. As a consequence, we now have a representation of a red squirrel—a smallish squirrel with ear tufts, common in Europe—rather one than of a gray squirrel—a slightly bigger squirrel with mouse-like ears, common in North America. Obviously, this only holds for comprehenders with the requisite visual experiences. It is important to note that many aspects of the squirrel remain unarticulated, such as the color of its eyes, the bushiness of its tail, and so on. Construals are necessarily schematic. This is so for three reasons. First, language profiles a situation in a certain way, directing attention to some aspects of the situation, but not to others (Langacker, 1987). Secondly, perception itself is limited by attentional capacity and thus the experiential traces that are used during comprehension are schematic to begin with (Barsalou, 1999; Rensink, O'Regan, & Clark, 1997; Simons & Levin, 1997). Third, comprehenders use an economy of processing (especially in the psychological laboratory), and typically do not activate more information than is necessary for comprehension (Graesser, Singer, & Trabasso, 1994).

B. COMPONENTS OF CONSTRUAL

Each construal pertains to a continuous period of time and a spatial region. Within this spatio-temporal framework (see also Zwaan & Radvansky, 1998), there is a perspective. Sometimes, the perspective is that of a protagonist, but this is not necessarily the case. In each construal there is a focal entity and a relation, which is denoted by a verb or preposition. Often, there is also a backgrounded entity. The entities may have articulated features that form part of the construal. These components are depicted in Fig. 1.

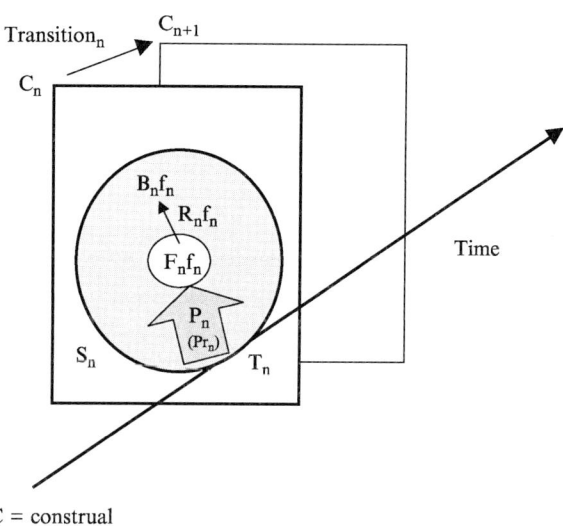

C = construal
T = time
S = spatial region (personal, action, vista)
P = perspective
F = focal entity
R = relation
B = background entity
f = feature

Fig. 1. Structure and content of an attentional frame.

1. Time Interval

Construals involve events that take place during certain time intervals. It has been shown that comprehenders keep events active in working memory through extended time intervals (in the referential world), as long as the event is ongoing (Zwaan, Madden, & Whitten, 2000). Presumably, this is because comprehenders are engaged in continuous tracking of the referent situation (Kelter, Kaup, & Claus, submitted).

2. Spatial Region

Construals pertain to situations that occur in a spatial region. A region is defined here as a section of space delimited by the human senses and effectors. Often, these will be areas with boundaries that may occlude space outside the field of vision and limit the amount of sound and odor coming from the outside space (for instance rooms). Without such obstructions, the range of the human senses provides the boundary of the region. Analysis of spatial layout perception provides an embodied tripartite classification of space (Cutting, 1997; Cutting & Vishton, 1995):

- personal space (around the observer and within arms' reach, with a 1.5-m radius)
- action space (an area around the observer in which he or she can walk quickly, talk, and throw things, with a 30-m radius)
- vista space (beyond 30 m from the observer)

A great number of studies have shown that the current location of a protagonist is more active in the comprehender's memory than other locations (e.g., Morrow, Bower, & Greenspan, 1989; Morrow, Greenspan, & Bower, 1987; Rinck & Bower, 1995).

3. Perspective

Perspective is understood here as a point within a time interval and spatial region from which the referential situation is experienced. Thus, perspective is the spatio-temporal relation between the experiencer and the situation. Sometimes, a perspective is explicitly stated, e.g., "From the mountain top, the village looked tiny," but often this is not the case. In such cases, content words may function as implicit perspective builders. For example, "The mouse approached the fence" implies not only a different distance between the focal and background entity than does "The tractor approached the fence," it also implies a different distance between the experiencer and the situation (Morrow & Clark, 1988). Given that we cannot see mice from 200 yards, but we can see tractors and fences from that distance, the mouse–fence situation is presumably construed from a different vantage point than the tractor–fence situation. In this sense, one might argue that perspective on the referent is part of a word's meaning.

Several components of perspective can be distinguished. The first one is *location*. A perspective is a location within a spatial region from which the situation is experienced. Sometimes location is implied by a verb. For example, a verb like "come" as in "He came into the room" implies that the experiencer is situated at the endpoint of the action, that is, in the room. In contrast, "go" in "He went into the room" implies that the experiencer is situated outside of the room. It has been demonstrated that comprehenders are sensitive to these verb-induced perspectival differences (Black, Turner, & Bower, 1979); in fact, this is true for young children (Rall & Harris, 2000) as well.

The second perspectival component is *distance*. This component was already addressed earlier in the example from Morrow and Clark, where experiencer-situation distance was implied by the relative sizes of the mouse and the tractor. In such cases, the human perspective is implicitly assumed. For example, "squeak" implies a different distance between the experiencer and the sound source than "blast," and the same is true in the visual domain for "mountain" and "molehill." In other words, while grammatically correct, (5) sounds odd, and therefore, may give rise to the inference that Eric is employing some listening device.

(5) Eric looked across the valley to see where the squeak came from.

Viewed this way, it may not be far-fetched to claim that perspective is part of the meaning of some words (see also Miller and Johnson-Laird, 1976, who note that the intrinsic region around an entity may be linked to perception, but is also related to social and functional constraints).

A third perspectival component is *orientation*. Again, man is the measure of all things. Our visual field is limited by the location of our eyes at the front of our heads. Although eye movements and head rotations allow us to expand our visual field without moving our bodies, the comprehender's default assumption is that something that can be seen is roughly ahead of us. Thus, the sentence about the tractor and the fence implies not only that the experiencer is a certain distance from the focal entity (the tractor) and the landmark (the fence), but also that this scene is roughly in front of him or her. Orientation is sometimes also determined vertically. For instance, "cloud" implies canonically that the experiencer is somewhere below it and "grass" implies that the experiencer is above it. Front/back is a more salient dimension for language comprehenders than is top/bottom, which is more salient than left/right (Franklin & Tversky, 1990). Borrowing terms from the anatomy literature, we can identify these dimensions as the coronal (front/back), transverse (top/bottom), and sagittal (left/right) plane. The transverse plane is more salient than the sagittal plane because our environment and our bodies are asymmetrical across the transverse plane (because of gravity), but not (so much) across the sagittal plane. It is clear that some entities have stronger implications about vantage points than others. For instance, "cloud" presumably strongly implies that it is above the experiencer, whereas "rain" does this to a lesser extent. Most obviously, this is the case with nouns denoting parts of larger entities. For example, "branch" not only denotes a part of a tree (and as such can only be understood as the attentionally focused part of tree, see Langacker, 2001, for a similar line of reasoning), it also means that the part is: (a) typically in the upper-half of the tree, and thus (b) typically above the experiencer.

A different type of perspective is *psychological perspective*. The implied experiencer may have certain emotions, goals, and knowledge that the comprehender as an immersed experiencer may adopt. A psychological perspective should have an impact on which parts of the spatial region are selected as focal entities. It is beyond the scope of this contribution to further develop this topic here, but this is an important task for future research.

4. Entities and Features

Grammatical markers (word order, case markers) signify what should be construed as the focal entity and as the background. The focal entity is often the subject of the clause (Langacker, 2001), but this may not always be the case. For example, in "We saw the castle on the hill" the object is the focal entity. Background entities are often signaled by prepositional phrases, whereas features are usually referred to by adjectives.

As noted in the preceding text, words initially and diffusely activate multiple overlapping functional webs. Empirical evidence on lexical–ambiguity resolution shows that initially multiple senses are briefly activated (Kintsch, 1998; Swinney, 1979). These findings are consistent with the IEF. However, the IEF makes finer-grained distinctions than amodal models. For example, a bird in the sky has a different shape than the same bird in its nest. Thus, in this case the shape of the focal entity depends on its location, a fact that is not captured in amodal representations. In other words, the shape is articulated during construal. The idea that a specific, but still schematic, representation of the referent is articulated during construal not only applies to referents activated by nouns, but also to those activated by verbs (Morrow & Clark, 1988) ("approach" is represented differently in "The tractor approached the fence" and "The mouse approached the fence"), prepositions ("on" means something different in "The wallpaper is on the table" than in "The wallpaper is on the wall") (Sanford & Garrod, 1998), adjectives ("fast" refers to something different in "fast runner" than in "fast car" and to something different altogether in "fast typist") (Pustejowsky, 1995).

C. SUMMARY

To summarize, during construal, articulated, but schematic, experiential representations of referents are formed. It should be noted that these representations may be dynamic (Freyd, 1987) if the corresponding experiential trace is dynamic, for example, that of seeing, hearing, and smelling a match being struck. Figure 1 summarizes the components of construal in an admittedly rather abstract format. The referential unit that a construal pertains to is an event, and an event takes place at a certain time and in a certain spatial region. Within this spatio-temporal framework (see also Zwaan & Radvansky, 1998), there is a perspective. Within this perspective are a focal entity, a relation, and a background entity. Each of these three may have features.

VI. Integration

A. DEFINITION OF INTEGRATION

Once an event representation has been (partially) construed, the comprehender proceeds to the next construal. This is indicated in Figure 1 by the arrow leading from C_n to C_{n+1}. Relevant components of the previous construal(s) will provide part of the content of working memory, along with the functional webs activated by the current word(s) and, therefore, will influence the current construal. Integration refers to the transition from one construal to the next. The assumption is that these transitions are experientially based.

B. TYPES OF TRANSITIONS

In discussing experiential transitions, it is helpful to use Langacker's (2001) notion of attentional frame because, as mentioned in the preceding text, it construes language comprehension as the language-based modulation of attention to a described state of affairs. Extensive analyses are needed to catalogue the experiential transitions that might naturally occur in discourse. Awaiting such analyses, it might be useful to review a few frequently occurring types (see Millis, King, & Kim, 2000, for a first approach).

In descriptions of static scenes, the experiencer typically modulates attention and the associated transitions are perceptual, mostly visual, in nature. Typical transitions in scene descriptions are zooming, panning, scanning, and fixating, where each construal simulates the visual experience of an object, part of an object, or an object feature. Cognitive linguists have discussed these visual operations such as scanning at the sentence level (e.g., Langacker, 2001; Talmy, 1996). Consider the following passage from Sir Arthur Conan Doyle's novel *The Hound of the Baskervilles* (p. 57), in which Watson describes Holmes' and his arrival at the house of the Baskervilles. I have segmented the text into attentional frames.

"....., [A1] and the house lay before us. [A2] .... the centre was a heavy block of building [A3] from which a porch projected. [A4] The whole front was draped in ivy [A5], with a patch clipped bare here and there [A6] where a window or a coat of arms broke through the dark veil."

A1 establishes the house as the focal unit. A2 zooms in on the central part of the house. A3 zooms in further on a section of that central part—the porch. A4 zooms further in on the front of the porch, and A5 and A6 convey scanning of and fixations on parts of the focal entity of A4. Thus, the construals prompted by these attentional frames are visual experiences of the denoted entities and the transitions between them are common visual processes. Another type of attentional change is a switch from one sensory modality to another one. Recent findings suggest that such transitions incur processing costs, both in perception and in semantic processing (Pecher, Zeelenberg, & Barsalou, 2003).

In descriptions of dynamic scenes or action sequences in which the experiencer is strictly an observer, the transitions are modulated by changes in the scene that attract attention. There is compelling evidence in the visual attention literature that changes in scenes are only detected if they are attended to and that changes more relevant to the scene are more likely to attract attention than peripheral changes (e.g., Rensink, O'Regan, & Clark, 1997; Simons & Levin, 1997). In both the description of static and dynamic scenes, it is often the case that attention shifts from the environment to an internal state of the experiencer, for instance an emotion (e.g., anger after seeing one's office broken into), a cognitive state (e.g., confusion upon seeing an abstract work of art or a memory when smelling a certain smell), or a physical state (e.g., an urge to drink when hearing someone open a beer bottle). When the experiencer—whose perspective the comprehender as an immersed experiencer is invited to take—is an agent, actively changing the environment, an internal state (e.g., a goal) might transition into an action, which may transition into a change in the environment, which may then transition into another internal state (e.g., frustration when the current state of the environment is not consistent with the goal motivating the action).

C. Factors Influencing Integration

Several classes of variables influence the ease with which a construal can be integrated with the current memory representation. First, there is concordance with human experience. Second, there is the amount of overlap between the evolving mental simulation (i.e., what Zwaan & Radvansky, 1998, called the integrated model) and the current construal. The more overlap there is among components, the easier integration should be. Third, there is predictability and, fourth, there are linguistic cues. The discussion will focus on the first two, as they are more unique to the IEF, whereas the last two are common across frameworks.

1. Concordance with Human Experience

It is perhaps not too much of a simplification to assume that the human experience involves continuity of time, space, and perspective. Confined to a single body and brain, we only experience the world from one vantage point at any moment in time. From this vantage point, we can perceive a region limited by the range of our sensory organs. If we want to change our vantage point, we need to move, thereby continuously updating our vantage point using vestibular, proprioceptive, and optic flow information. If we want to learn more about an entity, we can visually scan it in a systematic sequence of fixations and saccades, we can move closer to it, touch, manipulate, smell, or even taste it.

The *Continuity Assumption* holds that comprehenders have the default expectation (not necessarily at a conscious level) that these continuities hold when comprehending discourse. However, one of the defining features of human language is displacement, the fact that we can communicate about events and things that are not in our immediate environment, or even about things that are impossible (Hockett, 1959). Thus, language enables us to lift our communication out of our immediate environment in a way that gestures and animal communication do not. However, with this freedom come discrepancies between actual experience and experience conveyed through language. For example, in language we can abruptly shift from one time interval to a later or earlier one (e.g., by using a time adverbial such as "an hour later"). The same is true of location and vantage point. The *Continuity Assumption* proposes that this forces comprehenders to override their default expectations, which causes a momentary increase in processing activity.

Research has shown that violations of temporal continuity lead to an increase in reading times (e.g., Mandler, 1986; Zwaan, 1996) increase electrical activity in left-prefrontal areas of the brain (Munte, Schiltz, & Kutas, 1998). Similarly, abrupt changes of location and vantage point may lead to temporary processing difficulty. The operative word here is "temporary." Obviously, the utility of a communication system that leads to permanent disruptions of the comprehension process would be close to zero.

Comprehenders are adept at creating new time intervals, regions, and perspectives when instructed to do so. But why do discontinuities occur in the first place, if they lead to hiccups, however minor, of the comprehension process? This is because the goal of linguistic communication is often not to give a moment-by-moment account of some series of events. An appropriate way to phrase this idea in the context of the present framework is that language is used to modulate the comprehender's attention on a referential situation in order to convey a point of view (not in the narrow sense of perspective) on that situation. The point-of-view dictates which entities, events, and features are relevant and which ones are not. Although the omission of point-of-view irrelevant information leads to discontinuities in the referential situation, it is still necessary. Aristotle (*Poetics*, trans. 1967) was clearly aware of this when he exhorted the dramatists of this time to use plot as the organizing structure and omit events irrelevant to the plot.

2. Amount of Overlap

The second major factor influencing ease of integration is the amount of overlap between the results of successive construals. The *Overlap Assumption* generally predicts that the fewer elements that change, the easier integration of the current construal should be with the contents of (long-term) working memory. This prediction is of course not unique to the IEF. It appears in the early version of the Kintsch and van Dijk (1978) model in the form of argument overlap. Zwaan and Radvansky (1998) expanded on this notion and identified five dimensions of overlap at the level of the situation model: (1) time, (2) space, (3) causation, (4) motivation, and (5) focal entity. The IEF adopts time, space, and focal entity, and adds perspective, background entity, and features. It deals differently with causation and motivation, as will be discussed in the following text. Thus, according to the IEF, a construal can be more easily integrated with the evolving mental simulation when it has the same location, perspective, focal entity, and landmark as the previous simulation. The IEF also allows for the generation of more specific predictions. For example, it should be easier to add a feature to an entity than to add a new entity.

Taken to its extreme, the *Overlap Assumption* predicts that a construal that overlaps completely with the previous one should be the easiest to understand. However, as mentioned in the preceding text, integration involves experientially based transitions from one construal to the next. With complete redundancy between consecutive construals, there is no obvious transition (although one could be inferred) and as such, comprehension should not be facilitated. Therefore, the optimum amount of overlap is somewhat less than complete overlap.

Consider Fig. 1 again. In conjunction with the *Concordance Hypothesis*, the *Overlap Assumption* makes the general prediction that the relative processing cost incurred by a transition should in part be a function of the level of embeddedness of a construal component. Thus, feature changes should be less costly than entity or relation changes, which should be less costly than perspective changes, which should be less costly than time and region changes. However, ease of integration is also determined by predictability and the absence or presence of relevant cues. These factors are discussed in the following text.

3. Predictability

Goals and causation have been demonstrated to play an important role in narrative comprehension (e.g., Graesser, Singer, & Trabasso, 1994). Here, I simply assume that these are specific instances of the more general factor of predictability. As the history of psychology has shown time and again, if a sequence of events is experienced frequently, we tend to anticipate the second event when presented with the first. A cause–effect relation is an example of a frequently occurring sequence—an experiential trajectory. As such, it should be conceptualized as a dynamic representation in which a transformation of the focal entity occurs, for instance a change in shape, motion, direction, or color. Goal/plan structures (Schank & Abelson, 1977) are another example of experiential trajectories. These are typically longer than causal trajectories, but also facilitate integration. Subsequent construals are already anticipated (in part) before they occur.

We often experience effects before causes. We become aware of a disturbance in our environment and then look for or infer a cause. The cause is then either perceived in the case of a continuous force (e.g., the wind blowing a chair across the ice) or inferred in the case of a punctate force (e.g., the wind having snapped a branch). Also, according to the ideomotor theory of action (e.g., James, 1890; Knuf, Aschersleben, & Prinz, 2001), a mental representation of an action's intended effect is assumed to be the cause of the effect. Thus, we are accustomed to construing effects before causes. In fact, in languages such as English, the effect is foregrounded syntactically, and not the cause (Talmy, 1976). In this light, the finding of Mandler (1986) that a sequence of events reported in reversed chronological order leads to comprehension difficulty, unless the two events that are causally related make sense. Because narratives' cause–effect sequences are often familiar, syntactic cues are all that is needed for the comprehender to infer causality. However, in other cases, for example in science textbooks, a causal relation needs to be signaled explicitly in order to prevent the comprehender from interpreting the sequence simply as a temporal one. In such cases, causal connectives are used. They provide a cue to the comprehender to initiate a force–dynamic construal in the sense of Talmy (1988), rather than two successive "static" construals, as in the case of a temporal sequence.

4. Linguistic Cues

A fourth factor that influences integration is the use of linguistic cues. Syntactic cues, such as word order or case, cue the comprehender with respect to the elements of the construal. Word order and case provide cues as to what the focal and backgrounded entities are. Tense markers provide information on where the event should be placed on the timeline, whereas aspect markers indicate whether the event should be conceptualized as punctual or temporally unbounded. The indefinite article indicates that a new entity is introduced, whereas the definite article is a cue to carry the entity over from one construal to the next. For example, the indefinite article in "A blue jay landed on the bird feeder" is a cue to activate the blue jay functional web and use the relevant aspects of it (presumably visual and kinetic) in a simulation. In contrast, the definite article in "The blue jay landed on the bird feeder" is a cue to maintain activation of the blue jay representation from a previous simulation (e.g., if the previous sentence read: "A blue jay flew down from the tree") as the focal entity (Givón, 1992). Prepositions can be viewed as instructions on the placement and distribution of attention over entities in the mental simulation. For example, in one reading of "on," this preposition places one entity above the other and makes it the focal entity, whereas "under" makes the lower entity the focal one. Cognitive linguists have documented a large number of lexical and syntactic cues for integration (e.g., Langacker, 1990; Givón, 1992; Goldberg, 1998).

VII. Empirical Evidence Consistent with the IEF

There is a body of empirical findings that is consistent with the IEF—as well as with more general embodied theories of cognition (e.g., Barsalou, 1999; Glenberg, 1997)—but not with amodal models of comprehension.

A. Words Activate of Perception/Action-Related Brain Areas

Words activate brain areas that overlap with areas that are active when their referent is experienced. For instance, tool words have been shown to activate motor areas in the brain and certain animal words have been shown to activate visual areas (Büchel, Price, & Friston 1998; Martin & Chao, 2001). Similarly, threat words, such as "destroy" and "mutilate" presented as part of a modified Stroop task, activated bilateral amygdalar regions to a greater extent than do neutral control words, thus implicating subcortical structures in semantic processing (Isenberg et al., 1999). The amygdala's role in emotional processing is well documented (e.g., LeDoux, 1995). In addition, activation was found in sensory-evaluative and motor-planning areas—areas that are normally activated when the organism senses danger. This is all the more noteworthy given that the subjects ostensive task was not comprehending words, but naming the color in which they were shown. Results such as these suggest a strong link between words and experience.

B. Action Representations Are Activated During Comprehension

The role of action in language comprehension has also been demonstrated in behavioral experiments. Glenberg and Kaschak (2002, experiment 1) presented subjects with sentences such as "He closed the drawer." Subjects indicated whether or not the sentence was meaningful by pressing one of two buttons on a button box. There were three buttons, which were arranged away from the subject, rather than from left to right. At the beginning of trial, the subjects held their hand on the middle button and moved it either away from or toward themselves to respond by pressing one of the other buttons. Responses toward the participant were facilitated when the sentence described an action requiring the hand to move toward the protagonist (e.g., opening a drawer) and responses away from the participant were facilitated when the sentence described an action away from the protagonist (e.g., closing a drawer). Moreover, in a subsequent experiment, Glenberg and Kaschak (2002) obtained a similar effect for more abstract sentences dealing with the transfer of information (e.g., "I told him the story"), providing evidence for the idea that basic perceptual and motor patterns may be metaphorically extended to more abstract situations via simple syntactic patterns (Goldberg, 1998). Spivey et al. (2000) recorded eye movements while subjects imagined or recalled objects that were not present in the visual display. In both cases, observers spontaneously looked at particular blank regions of space in a systematic fashion, in an apparent effort to manipulate and organize spatial relationships between mental and/or retinal images (see also Laeng & Teodorescu, 2002). Klatzky et al. (1989) observed priming between hand shapes and semantic judgments. For example, the sensibility of "throwing a dart" was judged more quickly when subjects had their hands in the appropriate shape for throwing darts than when not. Crucially, lexical associations were ruled out as a cause of this effect.

C. Perceptual Representations Are Routinely Activated During Comprehension

Recent evidence suggests that while a word is being processed, perceptual representations of its referent are being activated. Dahan and Tanenhaus (2002) showed that the activation of perceptual information is immediate. Participants listened to words while looking at pictures. Three pictures were presented at a time. One picture matched the meaning of the word and two were semantically unrelated distractors. Crucially, one of the distractors was similar in shape to the canonical shape of the target object, while the picture denoting the target object was in a different shape. For example, if the word was snake (or "slang" in Dutch), then the three pictures would a picture of an uncoiled snake (target), a picture of a coiled rope (canonical shape distractor), and a picture of an unrelated item. Even before the participants had heard the end of the word, they were fixating more on the snake and the coiled rope. This suggests that shape information was accessed immediately. Further evidence suggests that an object's shape is articulated by a sentence context. For example, participants respond more quickly to a picture of an eagle with its wings spread out after reading "The ranger saw an eagle in the sky" than after "The ranger saw an eagle in the tree" (Zwaan, Stanfield, & Yaxley, 2002). In this case, the location of the entity constrains its shape. As a consequence, any mental simulation of the situation would include the appropriate shape. Effects have also been found for the construal of object orientation. Thus, after reading "He pounded the nail into the wall," participants responded faster to a picture of a horizontal nail than to one of a vertical nail, while the reverse was true after reading "He pounded the nail into the floor" (Stanfield & Zwaan, 2001).

Words denoting parts of objects activate visual representations of the larger object. Zwaan and Yaxley (2003) presented pairs of words in the middle of a computer screen with one word appearing below the other. On critical trials, the word pairs were of the following kind:

(6a) ATTIC
 BASEMENT

or:

(6b) BASEMENT
 ATTIC

Participants made quick judgments as to whether the two words were semantically related. The relative positions of the words either matched, as in (6a), or mismatched, as in (6b), with the relative positions of their referents in the larger object (a house in this case). Participants made faster judgments when there was a match than when there was a mismatch. This effect was not due to the order in which the words were read, because the effect disappeared when the pairs were presented horizontally. This result can be explained by assuming that the subjects engaged in a perceptual simulation to make the semantic judgments. In the context of our current argument, these results suggest that comprehenders construct integrated perceptual simulations based on just two content words, whereby the degree of overlap between the outcome of this simulation and the relative positions of linguistic symbols affected judgments. Thus, the presentation of two context words prompts a perceptual simulation in a language-processing task. Using a visual-field manipulation, Zwaan and Yaxley (2003) showed that this mismatch effect is limited to the right hemisphere.

Expecting stimuli in the wrong sensory modality (e.g., expecting a visual stimulus when receiving an auditory one) incurs processing costs in perceptual tasks (Spence, Nicholls, & Driver, 2000). The same is true in semantic priming (Pecher, Zeelenberg, & Barsalou, 2003), where subjects evaluated properties of objects (e.g., LEMON-SOUR). Property verification times were slower when participants had to switch from one modality to the next (e.g., LEMON-SOUR followed by TOMATO-RED) than when they stayed within the same modality (e.g., STRAWBERRY-SWEET), even when lexical associations were controlled for.

D. Comprehenders Respond as if "in" the Narrated Situation

If the comprehender behaves like an immersed experiencer, the contents of working memory should reflect the accessibility of objects and events in the real world given our human sensory, attentional, and action-related limitations. Therefore, working memory should be more likely to contain representations of:

- present objects than absent objects
- present features than absent features
- close objects than distant objects
- ongoing events rather than past events
- current goals than past goals and
- visible entities rather than occluded entities

Actions in the actual situation should also be constrained by what is read about the referent situation. Therefore,

- when not otherwise engaged in the actual situation, eye movements should reflect the vicarious experience of the referent situation (Laeng & Teororescu, 2002; Spivey et al., 2000)
- when not otherwise engaged, manual movements should reflect the nature of the described situation (Glenberg & Kaschak, 2002)
- when otherwise engaged, perceptual simulation of the referent situation might be interfered with (Fincher-Kiefer, 2001)

The assumption that is generally made in text comprehension research is that: (a) information that is currently in working memory is more accessible (i.e., more highly activated) than information that is not, and (b) when probed, more accessible information will yield faster responses than less accessible information. Therefore, if probe words associated with the contents of working memory are presented, responses should be facilitated. In accordance with this logic, various studies have demonstrated that the contents of working memory during comprehension reflect the nature of the described situation. Probe-word responses are faster when the probe refers to:

- a present entity rather than an absent entity (Anderson, Garrod, & Sanford, 1983; Carreiras et al., 1997)
- a present feature rather than an absent feature (Kaup & Zwaan, 2003)
- a present object rather than a distant object (Glenberg, Meyer, & Lindem, 1987; Morrow, Bower, & Greenspan, 1989; Morrow, Greenspan, & Bower, 1987; Rinck & Bower, 2000)
- an ongoing event rather than a past event (Zwaan, 1996; Zwaan, Madden, & Whitten, 2000)
- a current goal rather than an accomplished one (Trabasso & Suh, 1993)
- a visible entity rather than an occluded one (Horton & Rapp, 2002).

As mentioned in the preceding text, there is also evidence that comprehenders assume the spatial perspective of a protagonist in the story (Bower, Black, & Turner, 1979; Bryant, Tversky, & Franklin, 1992; Franklin & Tversky, 1990; Morrow & Clark, 1988; Rall & Harris, 2000).

VIII. Accounting for Propositional Findings

In arguing the case for propositional representations, a primary goal has been to distinguish them from purely verbal representations (Kintsch, 1998). The argument is that propositions have a different structure from sentences and thus that effects of propositional structure should be observable empirically. This has indeed been demonstrated. Take for instance an example discussed by Kintsch (1998): "The mausoleum that enshrined the tsar overlooked the square." This sentence contains two propositions, [OVERLOOK, MAUSOLEUM, SQUARE] and [ENSHRINE, MAUSOLEUM, TSAR]. Participants who are given the cue "overlook" are more likely to recall "mausoleum" than "tsar" (Wanner, 1975). Similarly, there is more priming between words from the same atomic proposition (e.g., mausoleum, square) than between words from different propositions (e.g., square, tsar) (Ratcliff & McKoon, 1978).

These findings certainly suggest that the mental representation generated during comprehension is structurally different from the linguistic input. However, they do not necessarily provide evidence for amodal propositions. Specifically, it seems that the IEF would make similar predictions. The sentence presents two attentional frames giving rise to two construals. The first construal takes a perspective within the mausoleum and has the tsar as the focal entity. The second construal seems to imply a perspective outside the mausoleum and has the square as the focal entity. This suggests that there may be an overlap between the information captured by amodal propositions and information captured by construals. In fact, there are theoretical arguments that predicate argument structures, such as propositions are grounded in perception and action (Hurford, in press) and that perceptual symbols can be thought of as modal propositions (Barsalou, 1999).

It is important to note that an experiential analysis is not redundant with an amodal propositional analysis. Specifically, an experiential analysis makes more subtle predictions than an amodal analysis. For example, the fact that the perspective changes from one construal to the next is not captured by an amodal analysis. For example, because of the *Continuity Assumption*, the IEF makes different predictions for "The mausoleum that enshrines the tsar overlooks the square," where the perspective changes, than for "The mausoleum that enshrines the tsar has a marble floor," where the perspective remains inside the building. For example, it should be easier to integrate the two construals in the latter case than in the former (Radvansky & Zacks, 1991). The amodal framework makes no such prediction.

Thus, it can be argued that the information captured by amodal propositions forms a subset of the information captured by a perceptual analysis. The many empirical studies discussed in previous sections show that the information not captured by amodal propositions cannot be safely ignored if we want to enhance our scientific understanding of language comprehension. In this context, it is important to reiterate the point made by Kintsch and van Dijk (1978) that (amodal) propositions are "a convenient shorthand" for representing information. Indeed, as these authors and the many researchers inspired by them have shown, impressive results can be obtained by using this shorthand, but as is shown here, it would be a mistake to elevate the shorthand to the status of longhand.

IX. Accounting for Abstract Language

A common criticism of perceptual symbol theories is that it is difficult to see how they deal with abstract information, whereas it is relatively easy to see how they deal with concrete information. In order to address this issue, Lakoff (1987) and others have advanced the notion of metaphorical extension. For instance, as infants we have learned to associate the positive physical feeling of warmth with physical proximity to our mother. By extension, we later learn to think about human relations in degrees of warmth. Similarly, it has been proposed that so-called "light" verbs, such as "put" and "take," which are acquired early in life, are associated with syntactic constructions that carry a certain concrete causal meaning which underlies the meaning of other verbs used in the same construction (Goldberg, 1998). Talmy (1988) shows how his theory of force dynamics can be metaphorically extended for the analysis of arguments. Consistent with these ideas, experiential effects on the understanding of abstract language have been demonstrated in recent research (Boroditsky & Ramscar, 2002; Glenberg & Kaschak, 2002). However, it is clear that a great deal more needs to be done in order to arrive at a full experiential account of abstract language.

X. Conclusions

The main thesis of this chapter can be summarized as follows: Language comprehension is a vicarious experience brought about by three component processes: (1) activation, (2) construal, and (3) integration. The IEF should be viewed as an engine that generates predictions about language comprehension. Like any good theory, it is falsifiable. For example, the general prediction that event sequences that are not consistent with experience are more difficult that event sequences that can be falsified. Similarly, the prediction that the contents of working memory during comprehension should reflect the contents of working memory during experience of the described situation can be falsified. These are rather general hypotheses. It should have become clear that the IEF is capable of generating far more specific hypotheses. Below is a non-exhaustive list of such predictions, segregated by the component processes of activation, construal, and integration.

Activation

- Words or morphemes activate experiential representations that have much finer shadings than word senses and may include various shapes of the referent object—a perspective on the object.

Construal

- Perspective is necessary and, therefore routinely encoded during comprehension
- Perceptible features of a referent object should be more activated than non-perceptible features.
- Transformations of focal entities that are inconsistent with human experience should be more difficult to understand than transformations that are not.
- Violations of object affordances will be more difficult to understand than non-violations (Glenberg & Kaschak, 2002).

Integration

- Temporal, spatial, and perspective shifts inconsistent with human perception and action will be more difficult to understand than consistent shifts. There already is evidence for temporal and spatial shifts (see Zwaan & Radvansky, 1998, for a review), but not yet for perspective shifts.

By putting tests of predictions such as these on the research agenda, we should be able to arrive at a better understanding of language comprehension. Although the various components of the IEF require a great deal of further specification, I hope to have demonstrated that it is a useful first approximation to an embodied theory of comprehension.

ACKNOWLEDGMENTS

This research was supported by grant MH-63972 from the National Institute of Mental Health. I thank Brian Ross, Katinka Dijkstra, Carol Madden, Rich Yaxley, Dave Therriault, and Mark Aveyard for helpful comments on previous versions. Address correspondence to: Rolf A. Zwaan, Department of Psychology, Florida State University, Tallahassee, FL 32306-1270 (email: zwaan@psy.fsu.edu).

REFERENCES

Anderson, A., Garrod, S. C., & Sanford, A. J. (1983). The accessibility of pronominal antecedents as a function of episode shifts in narrative text. *Quarterly Journal of Experimental Psychology, 35A*, 427–440.

Barsalou, L. W. (1999). Perceptual symbol systems. *Behavioral and Brain Sciences, 22*, 577–660.
Black, J. B., Turner, E., & Bower, G. H. (1979). Point of view in narrative comprehension memory. *Journal of Verbal Learning and Verbal Behavior, 18*, 187–198.
Boroditsky, L. (2000). Metaphoric structuring: Understanding time through spatial metaphors. *Cognition, 75*, 1–28.
Boroditsky, L., & Ramscar, M. (2002). The roles of body and mind in abstract thought. *Psychological Science, 13*, 185–188.
Bryant, D. J., Tversky, B., & Franklin, N. (1992). Internal and external spatial frameworks for representing described scenes. *Journal of Memory and Language, 31*, 74–98.
Büchel, C., Price, C., & Friston, K. (1998). A multimodal language region in the ventral visual pathway. *Nature, 392*, 274–277.
Carreiras, M., Carriedo, N., Alonso, M. A., & Fernandez, A. (1997). The role of verbal tense and verbal aspect in the foregrounding of information in reading. *Memory & Cognition, 23*, 438–446.
Chafe, W. (1994). *Discourse, consciousness, and time: the flow and displacement of conscious experience in speaking and writing.* Chicago, IL: University of Chicago Press.
Chambers, C. G., Tanenhaus, M. K., Eberhard, K. M., Filip, H., & Carlson, G. N. (2001). Circumscribing referential domains in real-time language comprehension. *Journal of Memory and Language, 47*, 30–49.
Cutting, J. E. (1997). How the eye measures reality and virtual reality. *Behavior Research Methods, Instrumentation, and Computers, 29*, 29–36.
Cutting, J. E., & Vishton, P. M. (1995). Perceiving layout and knowing distances: The integration, relative potency, and contextual use of different information about depth. In W. Epstein & S. Rogers (Eds.), *Handbook of perception and cognition, Vol 5: Perception of space and motion.* (pp. 69–117). San Diego, CA: Academic Press.
Dahan, D., & Tanenhaus, M. K. (2002). Activation of conceptual representations during spoken word recognition. *Abstracts of the Psychonomic Society, 7*, 14.
Damasio, A. R. (1994). *Descartes' error: Emotion, reason and the human brain.* New York: Grosset/Putnam.
Damasio, A. R. (1999). *The feeling of what happens: Body and emotion in the making of consciousness.* San Diego: Harcourt Brace & Company.
Duchan, J. F., Bruder, G. A., & Hewitt, L. E., eds. (1995). *Deixis in narrative: A cognitive Science Perspective.* Mahwah, NJ: Erlbaum.
Ericsson, K. A., & Kintsch, W. (1995). Long-term working memory. *Psychological Review, 102*, 211–245.
Farah, M. J., & McClelland, J. L. (1991). A computational model of semantic memory impairment: Modality specificity and emergent category specificity. *Journal of Experimental Psychology: General, 210*, 339–357.
Fincher-Kiefer, R. (2001). Perceptual components of situation models. *Memory & Cognition, 29*, 336–343.
Franklin, N., & Tversky, B. (1990). Searching imagined environments. *Journal of Experimental Psychology: General, 119*, 63–76.
Freyd, J. J. (1987). Dynamic mental representations. *Psychological Review, 94*, 427–438.
Gernsbacher, M. A. (1990). *Language comprehension as structure building.* Mahwah, NJ: Erlbaum.
Gerrig, R. J. (1993). *Experiencing narrative worlds.* New Haven: Yale UP.
Givón, T. (1992). The grammar of referential coherence as mental processing instructions. *Linguistics, 30*, 5–55.
Glenberg, A. M. (1997). What memory is for. *Behavioral and Brain Sciences, 20*, 1–55.

Glenberg, A. M., & Kaschak, M. P. (2002). Grounding language in action. *Psychonomic Bulletin & Review, 9*, 558–565.

Glenberg, A. M., Meyer, M., & Lindem, K. (1987). Mental models contribute to foregrounding during text comprehension. *Journal of Memory and Language, 26*, 69–83.

Goldberg, A. (1998). Patterns of experience in patterns of language. In M. Tomasello (Ed.), *The new psychology of language: Cognitive and functional approaches to language structure.* Mahwah, NY: Erlbaum.

Graesser, A. C., Millis, K. K., & Zwaan, R. A. (1997). Discourse comprehension. *Annual Review of Psychology, 48*, 163–189.

Graesser, A. C., Singer, M., & Trabasso, T. (1994). Constructing inferences during narrative text comprehension. *Psychological Review, 101*, 371–395.

Halff, H. M., Ortony, A., & Anderson, R. C. (1976). A context-sensitive representation of word meanings. *Memory & Cognition, 4*, 378–383.

Hockett, C. F. (1959). Animal 'languages' and human language. *Human Biology, 31*, 32–39.

Horton, W. S., & Rapp, D. N. (2002). Occlusion and the accessibility of information in narrative comprehension. *Psychonomic Bulletin & Review, 10*, 104–109.

Hurford, J. R. (in press). The neural basis of predicate-argument structure. *Behavioral and Brain Sciences.*

Isenberg, N., Silbersweig, D., Engelien, A., Emmerich, K., Malavade, K., Beati, B., Leon, A. C., & Stern, E. (1999). Linguistic threat activates the human amygdala. *Proceedings of the National Academy of Sciences, 96*, 10456–10459.

James, W. (1890). *Principles of psychology.* New York: Holt.

Johnson-Laird, P. N. (1983). *Mental models: Towards a cognitive science of language, inference, and consciousness.* Cambridge, MA: Harvard UP.

Kaup, B., & Zwaan, R. A. (2003). Effects of negation and situational presence on the accessibility of text information. *Journal of Experimental Psychology: Learning, Memory, and Cognition, 29*, 439–446.

Kintsch, W. (1998). *Comprehension: A paradigm for cognition.* Cambridge, UK: Cambridge University Press.

Kintsch, W., & van Dijk, T. A. (1978). Toward a model of text comprehension and production. *Psychological Review, 85*, 363–394.

Klatzky, R. L., Pellegrino, J. W., McCloskey, B. P., & Doherty, S. (1989). Can you squeeze a tomato? The role of motor representations in semantic sensibility judgments *Journal of Memory and Language, 28*, 56–77.

Knuf, L., Aschersleben, G., & Prinz, W. (2001). An analysis of ideomotor action. *Journal of Experimental Psychology: General, 130*, 779–798.

Laeng, B., & Teodorescu, D. S. (2002). Eye scanpaths during visual imagery reenact those of perception of the same visual scene. *Cognitive Science, 26*, 207–231.

Lakoff, G. (1987). *Women, fire, and dangerous things: What categories reveal about the mind.* Chicago: University of Chicago Press.

Langacker, R. W. (1987). *Foundations of cognitive grammar (Vol. 1).* Stanford, CA: Stanford University Press.

Langacker, R. W. (2001). Discourse in cognitive grammar. *Cognitive Linguistics, 12*, 143–188.

LeDoux, J. E. (1995). Emotion: Clues from the brain. *Annual Review of Psychology, 46*, 209–235.

MacWhinney, B. (1999). The emergence of language from embodiment. In B. MacWhinney (Ed.), *The Emergence of Language.* Mahwah, NJ: Erlbaum.

Mandler, J. M. (1986). On the comprehension of temporal order. *Language and Cognitive Processes, 1*, 309–320.

Martin, A., & Chao, L. L. (2001). Semantic memory and the brain: structure and processes. *Current Opinion in Neurobiology, 11*, 194–201.

McRae, K., de Sa, V. R., & Seidenberg, M. S. (1997). On the nature and scope of featural representations of word meaning. *Journal of Experimental Psychology: General, 126*, 99–130.

Miceli, G., Fouch, E., Capasso, R., Shelton, J. R., Tomaiuolo, F., & Caramazza, A. (2001). The dissociation of color from form and function knowledge. *Nature Neuroscience, 4*, 662–667.

Miller, G. A., & Johnson-Laird, P. N. (1976). *Language and perception*. Cambridge, MA: Harvard University Press.

Millis, K. K., King, A., & Kim, H. J. (2000). Updating situation models from descriptive texts: A test of the situational operator model. *Discourse Processes, 30*, 201–236.

Morrow, D. G., Bower, G. H., & Greenspan, S. L. (1989). Updating situation models during narrative comprehension. *Journal of Memory and Language, 28*, 292–312.

Morrow, D. G., & Clark, H. H. (1988). Interpreting words in spatial descriptions. *Language and Cognitive Processes, 3*, 275–291.

Morrow, D. G., Greenspan, S. L., & Bower, G. H. (1987). Accessibility and situation models in narrative comprehension. *Journal of Memory and Language, 26*, 165–187.

Munte, T. F., Schiltz, K., & Kutas, M. (1998). When temporal terms belie conceptual order. *Nature, 395*, 71–73.

Palmer, S. E., Rosch, E., & Chase, P. (1981). Canonical perspective and the perception of objects. In J. Long & A. Baddeley (Eds.), *Attention and Performance, IX*. (pp. 135–151). Hillsdale, NJ: Erlbaum.

Pecher, D., Zeelenberg, R., & Barsalou, L. W. (2003). Verifying the properties of object concepts across different modalities produces switching costs. *Psychological Science, 14*, 119–129.

Posner, M. I., & DiGirolamo, P. (1999). Flexible neural circuitry in word processing. *Behavioral and Brain Sciences, 22*, 299–300.

Pulvermüller, F. (1999). Words in the brain's language. *Behavioral and Brain Sciences, 22*, 253–270.

Pulvermüller, F. (2002). A brain perspective on language mechanisms: From discrete neuronal ensembles to serial order. *Progress in Neurobiology, 67*, 85–111.

Pustejovsky, J. (1995). *The generative lexicon*. Cambridge, MA: MIT Press.

Radvansky, G. A., & Zacks, R. T. (1991). Mental models and fact retrieval. *Journal of Experimental Psychology: Learning, Memory, and Cognition, 17*, 940–953.

Rall, J., & Harris, P. L. (2000). In Cinderella's slippers? Story comprehension from the protagonist's point of view. *Developmental Psychology, 36*, 202–208.

Rensink, R. A., O'Regan, J. K., & Clark, J. J. (1997). To see or not to see: The need for attention to perceive change in scenes. *Psychological Science, 8*, 368–373.

Rinck, M., & Bower, G. H. (1995). Anaphora resolution and the focus of attention in situation models. *Journal of Memory and Language, 34*, 110–131.

Rinck, M., & Bower, G. H. (2000). Temporal and spatial distance in situation models. *Memory & Cognition, 28*, 1310–1320.

Sadoski, M., & Paivio, A. (2001). *Imagery and text: A dual coding theory of reading and writing*. Mahwah, NJ: Erlbaum.

Sanford, A. J., & Garrod, S. C. (1981). *Understanding written language: Explorations in comprehension beyond the sentence*. Chichester, UK: John Wiley & Sons.

Sanford, A. J., & Garrod, S. C. (1998). The role of scenario mapping in text comprehension. *Discourse Processes, 26*, 159–190.

Schank, R. C., & Abelson, R. P. (1977). *Scripts, plans, goals and understanding: an inquiry into human knowledge structures*. Hillsdale, NJ: Erlbaum.

Simons, D. J., & Levin, D. T. (1997). Change blindness. *Trends in Cognitive Sciences, 1*, 261–267.
Spence, C., Nicholls, M. E. R., & Driver, J. (2000). The cost of expecting events in the wrong sensory modality. *Perception & Psychophysics, 63*, 330–336.
Spivey, M. J., Richardson, D. C., Tyler, M. J., & Young, E. E. (2000). Eye movements during comprehension of spoken scene descriptions. *Proceedings of the Twenty-Second Annual Meeting of the Cognitive Science Society*, 487–492.
Stanfield, R. A., & Zwaan, R. A. (2001). The effect of implied orientation derived from verbal context on picture recognition. *Psychological Science, 12*, 153–156.
Swinney, D. (1979). Lexical access during sentence comprehension: (Re)consideration of context effects. *Journal of Verbal Learning and Verbal Behavior, 18*, 645–660.
Talmy, L. (1976). Semantic causative types. In M. Shibatani (Ed.), *The Grammar of Causative Constructions. Syntax and Semantics, Vol. 6.* (pp. 43–116). New York: Academic Press.
Talmy, L. (1988). Force dynamics in language and cognition. *Cognitive Science, 12*, 49–100.
Talmy, L. (1996). Fictive Motion in Language and "Ception." In P. Bloom, M. Peterson, L. Nadel, & M. Garrett (Eds.), *Language and Space.* (pp. 211–276). Cambridge, MA: MIT Press.
Trabasso, T., & Suh, S. (1993). Understanding text: Achieving explanatory coherence through on-line inferences and mental operations in working memory. *Discourse Processes, 16*, 3–34.
van Berkum, J. J. A., Hagoort, P. M., & Brown, C. M. (1999). Semantic integration in sentences and discourse: Evidence from the N400. *Journal of Cognitive Neuroscience, 11*, 657–671.
van Dijk, T. A., & Kintsch, W. (1983). *Strategies of Discourse Comprehension.* New York: Academic Press.
Wanner, E. (1975). *On remembering, forgetting, and understanding sentences.* The Hague: Mouton.
Zwaan, R. A. (1996). Processing narrative time shifts. *Journal of Experimental Psychology: Learning, Memory, and Cognition, 22*, 1196–1207.
Zwaan, R. A., Madden, C. J., & Whitten, S. N. (2000). The presence of an event in the narrated situation affects its activation. *Memory & Cognition, 28*, 1022–1028.
Zwaan, R. A., & Radvansky, G. A. (1998). Situation models in language comprehension and memory. *Psychological Bulletin, 123*, 162–185.
Zwaan, R. A., Stanfield, R. A., & Yaxley, R. H. (2002). Do language comprehenders routinely represent the shapes of objects? *Psychological Science, 13*, 168–171.
Zwaan, R. A., & Yaxley, R. H. (in press, a). Spatial iconicity affects semantic-relatedness judgments. *Psychonomic Bulletin & Review.*
Zwaan, R. A., & Yaxley, R. H. (2003). Hemispheric differences in semantic-relatedness judgments. *Cognition, 87*, B79–B86.

SPEECH ERRORS AND LANGUAGE PRODUCTION: NEUROPSYCHOLOGICAL AND CONNECTIONIST PERSPECTIVES

Gary S. Dell and Jason M. Sullivan

I. Introduction

It is common to begin a discussion of how language is produced by noting that production is the neglected component of psycholinguistics. Language acquisition and comprehension are said to attract most of the attention, while production enjoys, at best, an honorary place among the major topics in the field. The classic text by Levelt (1989), for example, starts off by calling production the "stepchild of psycholinguistics."

Production would probably not be accorded even stepchild status were it not for an earlier work, Merrill Garrett's "The analysis of sentence production," which appeared here in the *Learning and Motivation* series nearly 30 years ago (1975). Garrett began his analysis by noting that production is "not easily amenable to experimental attack." To get production research off the ground, he proposed that the field first needed to develop some empirically supported working hypotheses. These hypotheses could come from examining the properties of everyday speech errors, for example, errors in which whole words or single speech sounds have exchanged places, as in (1) and (2), respectively. Armed with these hypotheses, we may then turn to the experimental laboratory.

(1) *I'm sending a brother to my email* (I'm sending an email to my brother)

(2) *teep a kape* (keep a tape)

In this article, we will evaluate the current status of two working hypotheses that Garrett derived by looking at speech errors: the *independent-levels hypothesis* and the *function-content hypothesis*. It will be shown how they continue to play a major role in present-day theory (Bock & Levelt, 1994), most notably in accounts of lexical access during speaking (e.g., Levelt, Roelofs, & Meyer, 1999). At the same time, we claim that two recent revolutions in cognitive psychology; specifically the development of connectionist models to express cognitive theory and the use of neuropsychological and neuroimaging data to test them have left their mark on Garrett's ideas. Whereas the original hypotheses outlined sharp distinctions among processing levels and between the content- and function-word categories, the modern counterparts that we support make use of connectionist principles that erode the categorical nature of the distinctions (e.g., Berg & Schade, 1992; Dell et al., 1997; Harley, 1984; Gordon & Dell, 2003; MacKay, 1987; Rapp & Goldrick, 2000; Stemberger, 1985; Vigliocco & Hartsuiker, 2002). First we will outline the two working hypotheses, and then, in turn, we will focus on each.

II. Speech Errors and Processing Levels in Production

The independent-levels and function-content hypotheses are components of a general framework for production that emerged from Garrett's 1975 paper (e.g., Bock, 1982, 1986, 1987; Dell & Reich, 1981; Garrett, 1976, 1980; Kempen & Huijbers, 1983; Lapointe & Dell, 1989; Levelt, 1989; Saffran, 1982; Schriefers, Meyer, & Levelt, 1990). In this framework, speaking has three stages: (1) *conceptualization* (deciding what to say), (2) *formulation* (deciding how to say it), and (3) *articulation* (saying it). Speech errors occur during formulation, the stage at which the speaker consults her knowledge of language to turn an intended meaning into linguistic form. Formulation consists of the generation of multiple internal representations of the utterance; Garrett's analysis emphasized two of these, the *functional* and *positional* representations, associated with processing levels bearing the same names.

The functional level constructs the underlying grammatical structure of the planned utterance. Content words such as nouns, verbs, and adjectives are retrieved on the basis of their meanings and are assigned to grammatical functions, such as main verb, subject, or direct object, without a specific commitment to their actual position in the sentence. These lexical representations are semantic and syntactic, and lack phonological information. Grammatical affixes (e.g., past tense _ed) and function words such as articles (e.g., *the*) exist in the representation as features (e.g., *past* or *definite*) rather than specific morphemes. For example, consider a planned utterance that begins, "the dogs." Its functional representation would identify the abstract lexical item **DOG** as a noun and the head of Subject NP, and might contain features such as *count, plural, definite,* and *animate*. However, there would not be a direct specification of the phrase's position in the utterance, nor any indication of how **DOG** is pronounced.

The positional representation is constructed after the functional one and differs from it in three respects: (1) the serial order of lexical items is specified; this is done through *positional frames*, which are tree structures that identify the surface phrase structure of the utterance; (2) function words and grammatical affixes are present as parts of these frames; and (3) the main content words of the utterance are specified phonologically and are inserted into categorically labeled slots in the frames. Consider the example, "the dogs," again. Its positional representation would consist of the frame fragment as illustrated in the following, with the phonological form /dag/ inserted into the frame's noun slot.

(3)

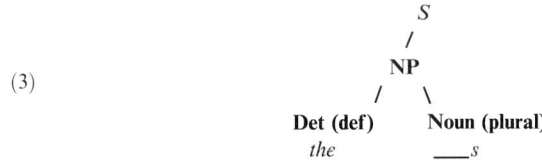

The initial evidence for the distinction between the levels came from the properties of speech errors, particularly word and sound exchanges, which are hypothesized to occur at the functional and positional levels, respectively. Consider error (1), an exchange of the words *brother* and *email*, and error (2), the exchange of the phonemes /k/ in *keep* and the /t/ in *tape*. Garrett (1975) noted that the interacting words in word exchanges have differing dimensions of similarity than those participating in sound exchanges. Exchanging words are very often in the same syntactic category—*email* and *brother* are both nouns—while the interacting words in sound exchanges exhibit no such tendency—*keep* is a verb and *tape* is a noun. In contrast, phonological similarity is relevant more for sound than for word exchanges. The exchanged sounds, /t/ and /k/, are both word-initial voiceless stops, and the syllables *keep* and *tape* are both stressed consonant-vowel-consonant syllables ending in /p/. There is typically no phonological similarity, however, between exchanging words. Hence, the processing level at which words exchange is strongly constrained by syntactic category, but not phonology, while the reverse is true for the level at which sounds exchange. In addition, the interacting elements in word exchanges are, on average, farther apart than those in sound exchanges. Typically, exchanging words come from separate phrases or even clauses; exchanging sounds come from either adjacent words or words separated by a short function word as in error (2).

The contrasting dimensions of similarity of the interacting elements and the differences in their distance for word and sound exchanges accord well with their assignment to the functional and positional levels, respectively. The functional level is a level at which words' syntactic properties, not their phonological ones, are important. Moreover, it is a level at which the utterance elements are not ordered, and hence distant interactions are possible. The exchange of *brother* and *email* occurs when the abstract lexical units for these words are incorrectly assigned to noun phrases. Because both are nouns, the exchange is possible. Another example of a functional-level error is a semantic substitution; a word is replaced by a semantically related word (e.g., 4, below). Semantic substitutions are assumed to occur when conceptual-semantic information is mapped onto lexical items, and an item with a similar mapping is chosen for a particular functional role instead of the correct one. In keeping with their association with the functional level, semantic substitutions are nearly always in the same syntactic category as the target word (Garrett, 1975).

(4) *on my knee* (on my elbow)

The positional level, in contrast, is an appropriate home for phonological errors such as sound exchanges. It is this level where phonological form is first specified. Exchanges of phonological material can be identified with erroneous insertion of that material into slots in the positional frames. Garrett (1975) noted that nearly every sound exchange in his error corpus involved content words, which are assumed to require insertion of their phonology. Function words, by hypothesis, are part of the frame and therefore do not need to be inserted.

We are now in a position to state the independent-levels and function-content hypotheses. The independent-levels hypothesis asserts that the functional and positional levels are *informationally distinct* and *strictly ordered*. Each level has access to its own type of information and is blind to the type of information used at the other level. The functional level has access to the semantic and syntactic properties of lexical items and their grammatical function in the utterance, but not their phonological and positional properties. The positional level has access to the phonologically specified morphemes of the utterance and their positions, but is unaware of the grammatical function of the phonological strings that it manipulates. The strict ordering of the levels means that information flows from the functional to the positional representation, and not the other way.

The function-content hypothesis asserts a fundamental distinction between content words (nouns, verbs, and adjectives) and function items (including grammatical affixes, such as -*ed* or -*ing*, and function words, such as articles, conjunctions, auxiliary verbs, and prepositions). The difference is manifest in the positional representation where the phonological forms of content items are actively inserted into positional frame slots, while function items are part of the frames themselves. This notion of being "part of the frame" fits well with the fact that function morphemes almost never participate in sound exchanges. For example, no one has ever reported an error such as "luh thine" instead of "the line," while errors such as "lite whine" for "white line" are common. Furthermore, Garrett (1975) noted that function morphemes participate in errors by shifting rather than exchanging. For example, the grammatical affix *s* in (5) and the function word *out* in (6) shifted positions leaving everything else undisturbed. On the assumption that exchanging is an error of slot insertion, while shifting is one of frame construction, the association between content words and sound exchanges, and between function morphemes and shifts supports the distinction between the vocabulary types.

(5) *he get its done* (he gets it done)

(6) *if you can't figure what that out is* (figure out what that is)

Both the independent-levels and the function-content hypotheses assert hard and fast distinctions within the production system, and both receive considerable support from Garrett's speech error analysis. It is our contention, however, that connectionist processing and learning principles, when applied to production, change how we view these distinctions. The next section focuses on the extent to which functional- and positional-level decisions are subject to extra-level influences, and specifically examines the role of interactive feedback from phonological to lexical representations.

III. Spreading Activation and Lexical-Phonological Feedback

A. Two-Step Theories of Lexical Access

The hypothesized independence of the functional and positional levels has consequences for lexical access, the process of retrieving words while speaking. In Garrett's analysis, there are two distinct steps in lexical access, one associated with each level. The first step is the retrieval of a word as an abstract entity specifying its syntactic properties. This abstract representation has become known as the *lemma*, a term coined by Kempen and Huijbers (1983). The lemma is associated with the grammatical structure of the sentence and would be assigned to the functional level in Garrett's framework. The second step is the retrieval of the word's phonological form. Form retrieval is a prerequisite for insertion of that form into the slots in the positional representation of the utterance.

The two-step nature of lexical access has been formalized in two recent computational models: the *discrete model* (Levelt, Roelofs, & Meyer, 1999; Roelofs, 1992, 1997) and the *interactive two-step model* (Dell et al., 1997; Dell & O'Seaghdha, 1991; Foygel & Dell, 2000). Both models distinguish between lemma access and phonological access, and agree that lemma access comes first. In addition, both are connectionist models in the sense that computation is carried out by spreading activation through a network of units representing lexical knowledge. Figure 1 illustrates the network implemented by Dell et al. (1997), which has a conceptual/semantic layer of units, a word (or lemma) layer, and a layer of phonological units. There are also links from the word units to their syntactic properties and from phonological units to

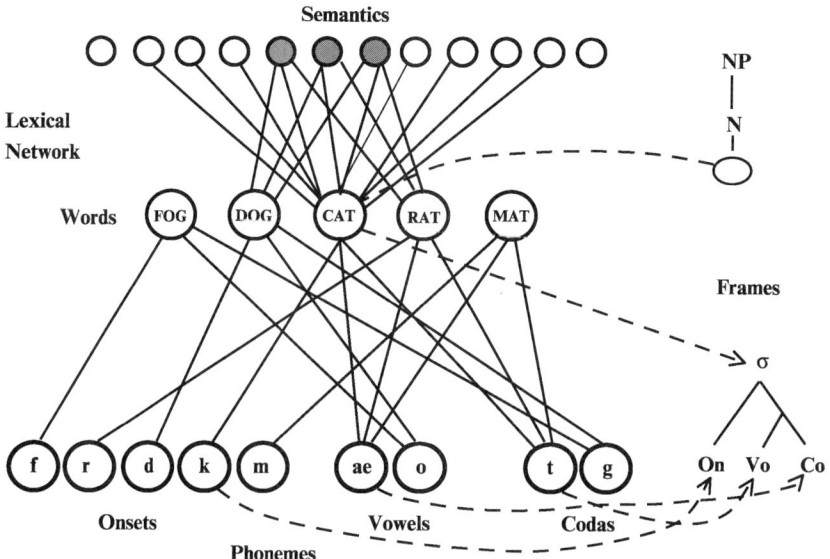

Fig. 1. A lexical network consisting of semantic, word (lemma), and phonological units. From Dell et al. (1997) and Foygel and Dell (2000).

phonological patterns that they can participate in. The model by Levelt et al. is broader and more complex, particularly with regard to its representations of word form, but this figure can stand in for both models for the purpose of explaining the key difference between them, which is the separateness of the lemma and phonological access steps.

Of the two lexical-access models, the discrete model best reflects Garrett's independent-levels hypothesis. It proposes that lemma access is unaffected by the phonological properties of words, whereas retrieval of word form is unaffected by semantic properties. Furthermore, in this model the two steps do not overlap in time; lemma access is finished before phonological access begins. In other words, the discrete model makes the steps informationally and temporally distinct. The interactive model, in contrast, makes the steps less distinct in both respects.

To appreciate the similarities and differences between the models, consider the access of the word *cat*. In both models, lemma access begins with the activation of the conceptual/semantic units corresponding to *cat*.[1] (In the Levelt *et al.* discrete model, this is a single unit; in the Dell et al. model, it is a set of units.) Activation spreads to potential word/lemma units, including *semantic competitor* units (e.g., **DOG**) as well as the target unit. Eventually, lemma access concludes with the selection of a word/lemma unit (e.g., **CAT**, the correct unit, or **DOG**, a semantic error). Phonological access entails the further spread of activation from the selected word/lemma unit to phonological units. It ends with the selection of an ordered set of these units (e.g., / k/, /ae/, and /t/) and the arrangement of them into syllables (e.g., a single CVC syllable for *cat*). The differences between the models concern whether the spread of activation is *cascaded*—activation flows to phonological units before lemma access is finished—and whether it includes *phonological-lexical feedback*—activation spreads from the phonological to word units. The interactive two-step model allows for cascading and phonological-lexical feedback, while the discrete model does not. Thus, the interactive model would permit activation to spread from word/lemma units to phonological units and in the reverse direction during both lemma and phonological access. As a result, the phonological units of semantic competitors may become active (e.g., the unit /d/ could receive activation from the active semantic competitor **DOG**). In addition, phonological units (e.g., /ae/ and /t/) activated by the target could send activation to phonologically similar word units (*formal competitors*, such as **MAT**). In a purely discrete model, neither formal competitors (**MAT**) nor the phonological units of semantic competitors (/d/ in **DOG**) can receive activation.

---

[1] We will use *cat* to identify a lexical item generally, **CAT** for the abstract word unit or lemma, and /kaet/ for the item's phonological form.

B. Motivations for Interaction

The question of the discreteness of lexical access is an instance of the long-standing debate about the modularity of processing in hierarchical systems (Fodor, 1983). Interactive, top-down, or constraint-satisfaction models of word recognition (e.g., McClelland & Rumelhart, 1981) and sentence processing (e.g., MacDonald, Pearlmutter & Seidenberg, 1994) are opposed by noninteractive, bottom-up, or modular approaches (e.g., Norris, McQueen, & Cutler, 2000; Frazier & Clifton, 1996). Whether the task is one of input or output, the issue is whether processing at a particular level (e.g., What word should I say? What letter am I looking at?) is affected by information from later levels (e.g., What phonological properties does this word have? Will that letter form a word in this context?). Interactive models use feedback from later levels to provide such influence. Noninteractive models deny the existence of such feedback.

Arguments for and against interactive feedback appeal to functional, biological, and behavioral facts. We briefly consider the first two of these and then present a longer review of the behavioral evidence.

What is the purpose of interactive feedback? Simply put, feedback provides additional information that may be relevant to a processing decision. When we perceive a string of letters, knowing that **THE** is a word, but **TAE** is not, can help us decide whether we are looking at an **H** or **A**. During the processing of letter input, feedback from an activated word unit for **THE** biases the perception of an ambiguous **H/A** toward **H**. The downside of such feedback is that it changes the activation at the earlier level so that the system then lacks an unbiased record of the input to an earlier level. In an extreme case, one can imagine a system that would be unable to process unexpected events, such as an **A** flanked by **T** and **E**. Thus, the benefit of using later-level knowledge to inform earlier processing must be weighed against the cost of altering the record.

With regard to lexical access in production, the kind of interaction that we are concerned with is feedback from the later phonological units to the earlier word units. Here one can identify two potential functions of such feedback. The first is that the feedback may be a byproduct of a system in which recognition and production use the same lexical and phonological representations (e.g., Dell, 1988; MacKay, 1987; Plaut & Kello, 1999). Mapping from phonological to lexical units is essential for recognition, and the connections that do so continue to operate during production simply because the same units are used for production. Thus, the primary function of phonological-lexical feedback is found in recognition, not production. We believe that there is some merit to this proposal. However, it rests on the assumption that phonological representations are wholly or partly shared between comprehension and production, an assumption that may be incompatible with neuropsychological data (e.g., Martin, Lesch & Bartha, 1999). Even the assumption of shared lexical representations has been questioned on the basis of such data (e.g., Caramazza, 1997).

The second potential function of phonological-lexical feedback is to avoid retrieval failures during production (Dell et al., 1997). If the lemma access step of retrieval is not informed by activation from the phonological level, it could choose a word whose phonological form is not easily retrievable, leading to a "tip-of-the-tongue" state. In fact, given the common assumption that word frequency affects phonological, but not lemma access (e.g., Griffin & Bock, 1998; Levelt, Roelofs, & Meyer, 1999), the absence of phonological feedback means that the system will select a known, but rare, word (e.g., *prevaricator*) as often as a common one (e.g., *liar*), assuming that both are equally appropriate. Phonological feedback eliminates this problem. A word/lemma unit whose phonology is easily accessible gains more activation during lemma access than one whose word form is less accessible, thus increasing the chances of selecting a word that can be easily pronounced at that moment.

Neurophysiological and neuroanatomical evidence for interaction is largely confined to studies of visual processing by animals. For example, neurons in the early visual area V1 are sensitive to higher-order information such as an expectation of a particularly shaped object (Lee, 2002). Feedback connections from later visual areas to V1 may provide a mechanism for such sensitivity. These kinds of studies have been deemed as evidence that the brain is a hierarchical interactive processor (e.g., O'Reilly & Munakata, 2000). However, their implications for human language processing and for the particular question of lexical-phonological feedback in production are unclear, given the many differences between, say, a monkey's perception of visual objects and a person producing a word.

We can summarize the functional arguments and the biological evidence on the issue of feedback in production very simply: they do not compel one to accept either the discrete or the interactive positions. However, they do lend some plausibility to the interactive approach, which, at least on the surface, is more complex than a purely discrete one and therefore requires justification for that added complexity. With this in mind, we now turn to the most pertinent evidence, empirical studies of the production process. We begin, as Garrett did, with speech errors, and examine evidence for feedback from speech errors. Then we discuss experimental studies of the time course of lexical access in production, studies that are informative about when semantic and phonological information are active. We conclude this section by presenting simulations of the interactive two-step model designed to explain the influence of formal competitors (e.g. *mat* or *cap* for the target *cat*) on retrieval.

C. THE LEXICAL BIAS EFFECT

Interactive theories of perception have long been associated with the *word superiority effect*, the tendency for letters to be more accurately perceived if they belong to a word-like letter string (e.g., McClelland & Rumelhart, 1981). There is an analogous effect in production: phonological speech errors are more likely if they create words than if they create nonwords. This *lexical bias effect* was initially demonstrated by Baars, Motley, and MacKay (1975), who used an experimental method to create initial consonant exchanges. Word pairs whose error outcomes were words (e.g., "long rice" spoken as "wrong lice") were associated with more than twice as many errors as those whose outcomes were nonwords (e.g., "log ripe" spoken as "rog lipe"). The lexical bias effect has been demonstrated several times in both experimental and error-corpus studies (e.g., Dell, 1986, 1990; Dell & Reich, 1981; Humphreys, 2002; Nooteboom, 2003, in press).

Baars, Motley, & MacKay (1975) interpreted the lexical bias effect as the product of an internal lexical editor, an optional process that prevents nonwords from being spoken. We know that speakers edit their own speech; they monitor it and correct it if they detect an error, for example, "It's the blue...I mean, the *red* one." The internal lexical editor, however, is hypothesized to work on planned speech rather than on material that has already been uttered. That some kind of internal monitoring occurs is generally accepted. Speakers can stop themselves quite early ("It's the b...I mean, the *red* one,") showing that the error must have been detected internally (e.g., Levelt, 1983; Hartsuiker & Kolk, 2001). However, whether internal monitoring is sensitive to lexical status in a manner that can produce the lexical bias effect is uncertain (Humphreys, 2002; Nooteboom, in press; Roelofs, in press).

Phonological-lexical interaction provides an alternative account of lexical bias (Dell & Reich, 1981). Consider the potential error "wrong" for "long." In an interactive model with the architecture shown in Fig. 1, the substitution of /r/ for /l/ would be promoted by feedback from /r/, /aw/, and /ng/ units because the feedback would activate the lexical unit **WRONG**, which would, in turn, further strengthen the erroneous unit /r/. When the potential substitution creates a nonword ("rog" for "log"), there is no lexical unit fully activated from the feedback and the /r/ for /l/ substitution is not promoted.

Some properties of the lexical bias effect are consistent with the feedback account. First, the effect appears to go away when speech is fast. Dell (1986, 1990) gave subjects a deadline for completing their utterance of each critical word pair (e.g., "long rice") and found no lexical bias when the deadline was

500 or 600 ms, but a robust effect at 700, 800, or 1,000 ms. The dependence of the effect on time was simulated by a model with phonological-lexical feedback (Dell, 1986). Since it takes time for feedback to contact the erroneous lexical unit and then influence the activation of phonological units, lexical bias tends to increase over time. The time dependence of the effect suggests that the bias is not inherent to the phonological units themselves, but instead comes from elsewhere (e.g., from the lexical units in the feedback account). A second noteworthy property of lexical bias is that it operates largely on the first outcome string of an exchange. Humphreys (2002) compared target word pairs such as "long ripe" in which the first error outcome is a word ("wrong") and the second is not ("lipe") to pairs such as "log rice" in which the first outcome is a nonword ("rog") and the second is a word ("lice"). Exchange errors were much more likely with the word-nonword outcomes (51 errors) than the nonword-word outcomes (20 errors). On the assumption that the true cause of an exchange is the first substitution (e.g., "long ripe" → "wrong...") with the completion of the exchange (→...lipe") occurring by default (e.g., Dell, 1986; Shattuck-Hufnagel, 1979), this asymmetric lexical bias suggests that a lexical outcome increases the chance of an error directly, which is consistent with the feedback account.

Although the positional asymmetry in lexical bias and the dependence of the effect on time are consistent with the interactive feedback account, both findings can also be explained by the editorial account. It should take time to monitor for lexical status. If little time is available, the editorial process is either cancelled or operates ineffectively. Similarly, one can hypothesize that the attention of the editor is directed more at the first word of a pair than the second, thus increasing the chance that nonword-word outcomes are edited and omitted more than word-nonword outcomes. Thus, these two findings do not definitively discriminate between feedback and editorial explanations of lexical bias.

A key difference between the feedback and lexical-editor accounts of lexical bias concerns the extent to which the effect is under strategic control. A lexical editor can be disengaged under circumstances under which it is not useful, while interactive spreading activation is assumed to be automatic. Baars, Motley, & MacKay (1975) tested whether lexical bias can be turned off by using nonword target pairs that created either word or nonword outcomes. Crucially, some subjects experienced those targets in lists of other nonword targets (nonword-context condition), while some experienced them in lists of mostly word targets (word-context condition). Under the former condition, all experimental targets were nonwords and, consequently, the lexical editor should be disengaged and lexical bias not observed. If lexical bias is due to phonological-lexical feedback, it should be unaffected by context.

The findings of Baars et al. were somewhat equivocal but consistent with the editorial account. In the word-context condition, initial consonant exchanges showed a strong lexical bias effect. For the nonword-context condition, the difference between word and nonword outcomes was reduced and was no longer significant. Thus, these data suggest that lexical bias is subject to strategic control and therefore is the product of an editor rather than interactive feedback.

But how strong is the evidence for strategic control? Humphreys (2002) noted that the difference in lexical bias between the word–and nonword context conditions in the Baars et al. (1975) study was not compelling or supported by a statistical interaction. In their word-context condition, word-outcome exchanges outnumbered nonword outcomes by 19 to 5. In the nonword-context condition, these numbers were 19 to 13. To provide a stronger test, Humphreys replicated the study under conditions that led to a sufficient number of errors to examine whether context interacts with lexical bias. The result was a clear null effect of context. Lexical bias was as apparent in the nonword-context condition (43 to 26 exchanges) as in the word-context condition (40 to 24 exchanges). Considering both studies together, there is little evidence that lexical bias disappears when targets are nonwords and, consequently, no support for the editorial account over the interactive one from studies of strategic control of the effect.

In summary, the interactive feedback account of lexical bias provides a motivated account of the general effect, its dependence on speech rate, its stronger presence on the first part of an exchange, and its indifference to lexical context. The editorial account naturally explains the rate dependence, and could possibly be configured to explain the other two effects. However, the latter two explanations would be post hoc. Indeed, the general idea of editing may be an overly powerful theoretical tool (Rapp & Goldrick, in press). The stipulation that word outcomes are less subject to editorial veto than nonword outcomes is itself post hoc. One can easily imagine an editor that is more likely to detect erroneous word outcomes than erroneous nonwords. After all, erroneous words possess deviant lexical-semantic as well as phonological representations; erroneous nonwords only deviate phonologically. Thus, with respect to the lexical bias effect generally, phonological–lexical feedback offers the best explanation.

D. Malapropisms and the Mixed-Error Effect

We have already introduced semantic substitution errors such as *knee* replacing *elbow*, or *dog* replacing *cat*. By all accounts, these errors happen during the lemma access step of lexical access and result because the conceptual/semantic representation of the target word sends activation to semantically related words. We also briefly introduced the possibility that formally related words (e.g., *mat* for *cat*) may be active and, in extreme cases, erroneously selected. Although formal substitutions were not discussed in Garrett's original paper, such errors are not uncommon, for example, (7) and (8) from Fromkin (1980). Fay and Cutler (1977) called these errors *malapropisms*, and distinguished them from sound errors (despite the obvious influence of phonology) by pointing out that malapropisms are, most likely, substitutions of words rather than speech sounds. The replacing word is very often in the same syntactic category as the target (e.g., nouns in 7, and adjectives in 8) suggesting a lexical origin of the error.

(7) *a verbal outfit* (a verbal output)

(8) *sufficiently ambitious* (sufficiently ambiguous)

At what level do malapropisms occur? It is not immediately obvious. The influence of phonology suggests that they occur during the second step of lexical access, the retrieval of phonological form. However, the fact that these errors are sensitive to syntactic categories implicates the first step, lemma access, which is the level where grammatical information is available. The discrete and interactive models account for these errors differently. The interactive model assigns them to the lemma access step, explaining the influence of phonology by appealing to phonological-lexical feedback. Thus, **MAT** becomes active through feedback when **CAT** is the target. Because it is also a noun, it may be selected instead of **CAT** during lemma access. Discrete models associate malapropisms with a step later than lemma access. In some discrete models (e.g., Fay & Cutler, 1977; Fromkin, 1971), there is a later step in lexical access in which word-form units are selected from a store that is organized by syntactic class and by phonological similarity. Words such as *ambitious* and *ambiguous* are close in this store and, hence, are confusable. In the discrete model of Levelt et al. (1999), malapropisms occur when incomplete phonological strings are morphed into grammatically appropriate words by an editorial process, somewhat like the lexical editor (Roelofs, in press). We will call these three accounts of malapropisms, the interactive, discrete-store, and editorial accounts.

Occasionally, an error appears to be both a semantic substitution and a malapropism at the same time (e.g., 9, below). These *mixed errors* simultaneously exhibit semantic and phonological similarity, and can be used to discriminate between the discrete-store account of malapropisms on the one hand, and the interactive and editorial accounts on the other. According to the discrete-store account, an error such as *start* replaced by *stop* is either a semantic substitution that just happened to be phonologically similar, or a malapropism that happened to be semantically similar. It cannot be both at the same time.[2]

(9) *Let's not stop* (Let's not start)

The interactive account, in contrast, emphasizes that semantic and phonological similarity work together to promote errors. Consider Figure 1: A unit corresponding to a mixed error such as **RAT**, when the target is **CAT**, gains activation from both shared semantic units and, through interactive feedback, shared phonological units. As a result, mixed errors are especially likely. More precisely, there should be a *mixed-error effect*: mixed errors should be more likely than what would be expected if such errors were either caused by semantic similarity or by phonological similarity but not both. The editorial account also allows for a mixed-error effect. A semantic error that happens also to be phonologically related to the target will be more likely missed by an editor that is knowledgeable about the target's phonology.

The evidence for a mixed-error effect is strong. The simplest demonstrations of the effect select semantic errors from particular sources, such as natural error corpora (e.g., Dell & Reich, 1981; Harley, 1984), or errors from a picture-naming experiment (Martin et al., 1996). It is then shown that the error words are more phonologically similar to their targets than what would be expected by chance. In every study of this sort involving normal speakers, a mixed-error effect has been obtained, that is, the semantic errors also exhibit phonological effects. For example, Dell and Reich (1981) found that semantic word substitutions share their initial phoneme about 20% of the time. By chance, one expects fewer than 8% matches. The mixed-error effect has also been observed in the errors of aphasic patients, but interestingly, some patients and patient groups show the effect and some do not (Dell et al., 1997; Rapp & Goldrick, 2000), an observation that we will return to later.

In summary, the existence of errors that are sensitive to both phonology and syntactic category (malapropisms) and errors that reflect both phonology and semantics (the mixed-error effect) is easily explained by models that allow for phonological-lexical feedback. Discrete models that attribute malapropisms to a step in lexical access that follows the step at which semantic errors occurs cannot explain the mixed-error effect. The discrete

---

[2] A semantic error that occurred during lemma access followed by a misselection from the phonologically-related word store would not result in a mixed error. It would, instead, create what we can call a mediated error, something like saying *house* instead of *unicorn*. A lemma-access error results in **HORSE**, which is itself subject to a malapropism, "house." These mediated errors are never reported for normal speakers; they can, however, occur in some aphasic patients. (This example is from the Martin et al., 1994 study of patient NC.)

model of Levelt et al. (1999), however, can account for both the existence of malapropisms and the mixed-error effect through the action of an editorial process.

E. STUDIES OF THE TIME-COURSE OF LEXICAL ACCESS

The claim that lexical access involves separate lemma and phonological steps has been tested in controlled experiments, as well as by analyses of speech errors. What the experimental studies have to offer is that they determine *when* particular kinds of information are active during lexical access, specifically semantic, syntactic, and phonological information. Most of the studies measure response times in behavioral tasks, although some recent studies use brain-imaging techniques. We begin with the behavioral studies. Rather than review all of them, we will give one extended example and then draw general conclusions from the set of studies.

1. Behavioral Studies

Peterson and Savoy (1998) asked subjects to produce the names of pictured objects as quickly as possible, and used a probe response time paradigm to assess the activation of semantic and phonological information during access of the names. On a fraction of the trials, a probe word appeared after the picture, but before subjects had named the picture (stimulus-onset-asynchrony [SOA] of 50 to 600 ms). If a probe word appeared, the subject had to read it aloud before naming the picture. The crucial independent variables were the relation of the probe word to the picture name and the picture-probe SOA. For a picture of, for example, a COUCH, the probe could be semantically related (BED), phonologically related (COUNT), or unrelated (HORSE). Across several experiments, Peterson and Savoy found that semantically related probes were named faster than unrelated ones when the SOA's ranged from 50 to 300 ms, thus demonstrating the expected early access of semantic information. Furthermore, they found that phonologically related probes were named faster than unrelated ones, but at SOAs from 150 to 600 ms (Fig. 2). This study along with several others (e.g., Cutting & Ferreira, 1999; Levelt et al., 1991; Schriefers, Meyer, & Levelt, 1990; van Turennout, Hagoort, & Brown, 1997) allows us to conclude that semantic information is activated before phonological information, consistent with two-step models of lexical access. There may also be a period of time in which both kinds of information are simultaneously active (e.g., in the 150 to 300 ms SOA range in the Peterson & Savoy study), which would be contrary to a discrete two-step model. However, the activation of both semantic and phonological information at a particular SOA does not, by itself, challenge discreteness. If there is variability in duration of the

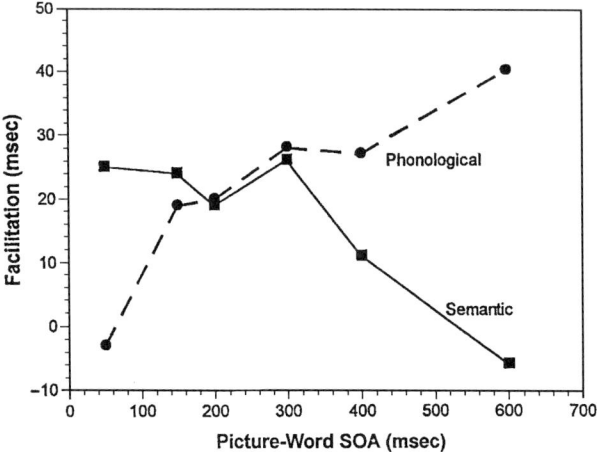

Fig. 2. Unrelated minus related response times for semantic and phonologically related probes as a function of picture-word stimulus-onset-asynchrony (SOA). From Peterson and Savoy (1998).

semantically sensitive stage, averaging over trials gives the illusion of simultaneous semantic and phonological activation (Levelt et al., 1991).

There is a better way to use these experimental methods to determine whether semantic and phonological properties of a lexical access target are simultaneously active. Levelt et al. (1991) suggested that if lexical access is nondiscrete, specifically if it is cascaded, then the phonological properties of semantic competitors should be accessed. For example, assuming that **COUCH** is the target picture, the unit for /b/ (from semantic competitor **BED**) would be active. They went on to show that a mediated semantic-phonological probe (e.g., **BET**) was not responded to any differently than an unrelated probe (e.g., **HORSE**) using a response-time method somewhat similar to that of Peterson and Savoy (1998). Therefore, the Levelt et al. study provided no evidence that phonological properties of semantic competitors are active, thus supporting the discrete model. Peterson and Savoy replicated the Levelt et al. finding that mediated probes such as **BET** (when the target is **COUCH**) are functionally unrelated. However, Peterson and Savoy suggested that mediated probes might be detectably facilitated only if the mediating semantic competitor (here, **BED**) is itself strongly activated (Dell & O'Seaghdha, 1991). So, they tested for probes that were phonologically related to a strong semantic competitor, for example, **SOFA** for a picture of a **COUCH**. Specifically, they compared phonologically related probes, such as **COUNT** (related to the target **COUCH**) and **SODA** (related to the strong competitor **SOFA**) at varying SOAs. The results showed clear facilitation for both at 150 and 300 ms, relative to an unrelated probe. Importantly, the facilitation was maintained at 600 ms for **COUNT**, the probe phonologically related to actual name that speakers chose, but was absent at this SOA for **SODA**. These results show that strong semantic competitors do lead to activation of their phonological form. More generally, they suggest that there is some cascading or nondiscreteness in the lexical access process (Costa, Caramazza, & Sebastian-Galles, 2000; Ferreira & Griffin, 2003; Jescheniak & Schriefers, 1998).

The behavioral studies of the time course of lexical access support the claim that lexical access moves from word meaning to word form. Semantic processing begins before phonological processing begins, and is finished before phonological processing concludes. However, under some circumstances semantic and phonological information are jointly active, that is, there is some cascading in the system. Although we have not considered studies that show where syntactic information fits into this time course, it seems that syntactic information such as grammatical gender or major syntactic category is, like semantic information, initially accessed before phonological information (Pechmann & Zerbst, 2003; van Turennout, Hagoort, & Brown, 1998). The temporal dynamics of processing grammatical gender, however, are far from certain and may vary across languages (e.g., Caramazza & Miozzo, 1997; Costa, Sebastian-Galles, Miozzo, & Caramazza, 1999). Overall, the behavioral results are consistent with a two-step approach to lexical access, and while they suggest that the steps are largely discrete, the results also favor some cascading, that is, some phonological activation before the lemma access step is concluded.

None of these experimental studies of the time-course of lexical access, however, tested for phonological-lexical feedback and, consequently, our claims for interaction based on the speech-error data receive no direct support from these studies. Nonetheless, it must be recognized that cascading, which does receive experimental support, goes hand in hand with interactive feedback. The interactive account of malapropisms and the mixed-error effect requires the cascaded flow of activation to phonological units during lemma access. The feedback then delivers this phonological activation back to formally related word units.

2. Neuroimaging Studies

Studies of lexical access using measures derived from neuronal events (event-related brain potentials: ERP; magneto-encephalography: MEG) or the brain's hemodynamic responses (functional magnetic resonance imaging: fMRI; positron emission tomography: PET) generally support the behavioral findings that we have just reviewed, insofar as they identify differences in time-course between semantic and phonological aspects of lexical access. For instance, ERP components related to response activation and preparation (N200, lateralized readiness potentials) have shorter latencies in response to semantic manipulations than phonological manipulations (van Turennout, Hagoort, & Brown, 1997; Schmitt, Munte, & Kutas, 2000). This is true in the absence of an overt response, or in conditions where more than one response is activated, lending support to behavioral measures. Similarly, an ERP component related to priming (N400) has also been shown to be sensitive to the expected semantic-before-phonological time course of available information in picture naming (Jescheniak, Schriefers, Garrett, & Friederici, 2002; Jescheniak, Hahne, & Schriefers, 2003).

Levelt and colleagues have attempted to obtain more direct evidence for both the temporal and neural separability of the different stages in production. MEG studies of picture naming (Levelt et al., 1998; Maess et al., 2002) have identified left temporal lobe areas that have activation consistent with the time course of lemma access and regions in the vicinity of Wernicke's area that have activation consistent with the time course of phonological retrieval. These sites are consistent with Indefrey and Levelt's (2000) meta-analysis of neurophysiological studies of speech production. After reviewing 58 studies using varying tasks and methodologies (fMRI, PET, MEG, cortical stimulation), they concluded that separate areas in the temporal lobe were active during lemma and phonological form retrieval, while areas of the frontal lobe were more active during later stages of phonological and phonetic processing.

While the analysis of the MEG data required an assumption of discrete, non-interactive processing stages, the results neither confirm nor depend on such an assumption. For instance, in an fMRI study by de Zubicaray, Wilson, McMahon, and Muthiah (2001) utilizing a picture-word interference paradigm, localized activation consistent with the MEG data was observed. The activation patterns, however, were inconsistent with discrete serial models, in that increased activation was observed in both semantic and phonological processing regions in response to semantic interference. If lemma access is completed before phonological processing begins, one would not expect to find such a pattern. To date, the neuroimaging data support the notion of multiple stages in production, but have not yet provided convincing support for either discrete two-step or interactive models.

F. APPLYING THE INTERACTIVE TWO-STEP MODEL TO APHASIA

Theories of production that account for speech errors have a natural application to aphasia (e.g., Saffran, Schwartz, & Marin, 1980; Garrett, 1980). Here, we examine the ability of the interactive two-step model to explain aphasic production errors, by testing a prediction of one such model (Foygel & Dell, 2000), a prediction that follows directly from the interactive property of the model.

Foygel and Dell's (2000) model is a later version of one by Dell et al. (1997). Both models make the same assumptions about normal lexical access, but differ in their accounts of aphasic deficits. These models maintain the distinction between lemma and phonological access that is central to the discrete model, but each of the steps is associated with an interactive flow of activation.

Fig. 1 illustrates the lexical network of the models. All of the connections are bi-directional, allowing for activation to spread in a feedforward and feedback manner. Normal lemma access begins with a jolt of activation to the semantic features of the target (e.g., *cat*). This activation then spreads according to a noisy, linear spreading activation rule:

(10) $A_{j,t} = A_{j,t-1}(1 - q) + \Sigma w_{ij} A_{i,t-1} + noise$

where $A_{j,t}$ is the activation of unit j at time t, q is the decay rate, and w_{ij} is the connection weight from unit i to j. The *noise* term indicates that, during each time step, each unit's activation is perturbed by a normally distributed random value with a zero mean and a standard deviation that is a linear function of the current activation, with a non-zero intercept. This noise function makes the model's decisions follow a generalized Weber's Law: error in determining which of two units is most active reflects the ratio of their activations rather than their difference, except when activation levels are very small (e.g., Killeen & Weiss, 1987).

During lemma access, the target lemma **CAT**, potential semantic substitutions (e.g., **DOG**), malapropisms (e.g., **MAT**), and mixed errors (e.g., **RAT**) all gain activation, with the activation of the latter two error types being enhanced by phonological-lexical feedback. Normally the target possesses the most activation, but due to noise, others may supplant it. After a fixed period of time, the most activated word unit of the proper syntactic category is *selected* and linked to a slot in a syntactic frame, somewhat like the positional or functional frames in Garrett's framework. For example, when the task involves naming objects, such as a picture of a cat, nouns are the proper category.

The second step, phonological access, begins with a jolt of activation to the selected word unit. Once again, activation spreads through the network and, this time, is concluded by the selection of the most activated phoneme units instead of a word unit. The implemented model only encoded CVC words, such as *cat*. The possible phonemes were organized into sets of onsets, vowels, and codas, and the most active of each set was selected and linked to slots in a phonological frame, a data structure that indicates the hierarchical and serial structure of the word's form. Errors that occur during phonological access involved the substitution of one or more phonemes, most likely creating nonwords or formally related words. Because of phonological-lexical feedback, the lexical bias effect occurs in the model, thus creating some tendency for phoneme substitutions to result in words over nonwords (see Rapp & Goldrick, 2000, for an analysis of lexical bias in a similar interactive two-step model).

The model was initially set up to simulate the picture-naming errors of normal speakers. This required specification of the lexical network[3] and values for the connection weights and decay rate. The data came from 60 normal controls who had been given the 175-item Philadelphia Naming Test (Dell et al., 1997). The naming responses were coded as either correct (e.g., "cat"), semantic ("dog"), formal ("mat," "cap"), mixed ("rat"), unrelated ("log"), or nonword ("cog," "dag"). Table I shows the obtained proportions for the categories, the proportions generated by the model, and the model's parameter values. The key parameters are the strength of the bi-directional semantic-lexical connections, which are assigned to parameter s, and that of the lexical-phonological connections, associated with parameter p. These values are strong enough to allow activation to spread sufficiently to overcome noise and decay, leading to accurate lexical access. The errors in the control subjects and the model are few and are largely confined to the semantic and mixed categories.

Applying the model to aphasic lexical access requires a theory of how the model can be "lesioned," that is, how its characteristics can vary to simulate brain damage. Dell et al. (1997) proposed that patient error patterns reflect quantitative variation between the normal error pattern and a pattern of random responses. They called this the *continuity thesis*, and realized this idea by assuming that brain damage globally lowers the connection weights, causing deficits in the transmission of activation. Damage may, as well, raise the decay rate, causing representations to degrade quickly over time. Lowered weights or increased decay leads to more errors by reducing activation to such an extent that noise overwhelms the signal. Extreme lesions promote error patterns that are essentially random. Foygel and Dell (2000) modified this proposal by associating damage just with lowered connection weights, but allowed for the semantic-lexical connections (parameter s) and the lexical-phonological connections (parameter p) to be independently

---

[3] The words in the model's lexical network were chosen to keep the model simple while at the same time preserving something of the characteristics of the English lexicon with respect to the density of words in phonological space and the phonological and semantic neighborhoods of the target words. See Dell et al. (1997) for details.

TABLE I

Obtained Response Proportions in a Picture-Naming Test and Fitted Model Proportions (Foygel & Dell, 2000; and Dell et al., in press) for 60 Control Subjects (Dell et al., 1997), and 9 Aphasic Subjects (Gagnon et al., 1997)

Source	Correct	Semantic	Formal	Mixed	Unrelated	Nonword	s	p	RMSD	χ^2
60 controls	0.97	0.01	0.00	0.01	0.00	0.00				
model	0.98	0.01	0.00	0.01	0.00	0.00	0.049	0.057	0.002	—
$s > p$ Patients										
LB	0.82	0.04	0.02	0.01	0.01	0.09				
Model	0.83	0.04	0.02	0.01	0.00	0.08	0.029	0.022	0.008	1.54
HB	0.61	0.06	0.13	0.02	0.01	0.18				
Model	0.59	0.08	0.08	0.02	0.04	0.19	0.020	0.018	0.028	11.13
NC	0.80	0.03	0.07	0.01	0.00	0.09				
Model	0.76	0.06	0.04	0.02	0.01	0.11	0.026	0.020	0.024	8.33
JG	0.59	0.06	0.09	0.04	0.03	0.20				
Model	0.56	0.08	0.08	0.02	0.05	0.21	0.019	0.017	0.018	4.80
LH	0.71	0.03	0.07	0.01	0.02	0.15				
Model	0.71	0.06	0.05	0.02	0.02	0.15	0.024	0.019	0.015	4.53
$p > s$ Patients										
GB	0.57	0.10	0.13	0.02	0.04	0.12				
Model	0.58	0.09	0.09	0.02	0.06	0.14	0.017	0.021	0.022	3.40
VP	0.39	0.10	0.15	0.07	0.24	0.06				
Model	0.39	0.15	0.19	0.03	0.19	0.05	0.008	0.028	0.036	10.07
GL	0.29	0.04	0.22	0.03	0.10	0.32				
Model	0.29	0.10	0.14	0.02	0.13	0.31	0.010	0.016	0.043	15.15
WR	0.08	0.06	0.16	0.05	0.35	0.30				
Model	0.14	0.12	0.21	0.03	0.23	0.27	0.001	0.017	0.065	25.95

Based on 175-item Philadelphia Naming Test, with proportions normalized to add to 1.0. Other parameters: decay = 0.6; 8 time steps for lemma and for phonological access; intrinsic noise SD = 0.01; activation-dependent noise SD = 0.16 $A_{j,t}$; jolt to semantic feature = 10; jolt to selected word unit = 100. s = semantic; p = phonological.

lesioned. On this proposal, each patient's error pattern is characterized by the assigned values for s and p. The values are determined by comparing the patient's proportions for correct responses, semantic substitutions, and so on, with those generated by the model as a function of s and p. Those values that make the model proportions closest to those for the patient are then assigned to the patient.

The application of the model to aphasia is evaluated by examining the fit between the model and patient-error patterns. For naming-error patterns, the model has had considerable success, but there are a few patients whose patterns cannot be closely matched (Cuetos, Aguado, & Caramazza, 2000; Dell, Lawler, Harris, & Gordon, in press; Foygel & Dell, 2000; Rapp & Goldrick, 2000; Ruml, Caramazza, Shelton, & Chialant, 2000). What these exceptional patients have in common is that they make a large number of semantic errors without making other lexical errors, suggesting perhaps that the assumption of unimpaired jolts of activation to the semantic features is incorrect. Another important model evaluation method is to use the assigned parameters to make predictions about previously unexamined aspects of the patient behavior. For example, Hanley, Dell, Kay, and Baron (in press) used the model to predict performance on a word repetition task, based on parameters derived from a picture-naming task. In the following analysis, we use this predictive method, specifically testing a prediction that arises from the model's interactive nature.

1. Syntactic Category Effects in Malapropisms

Earlier, we reported that formally related word substitutions, or malapropisms, have a strong tendency to respect syntactic categories; nouns replace nouns, verbs replace verbs, and so on. According to the interactive two-step model, these errors can arise from two mechanisms. They can occur at lemma access—the unit for **MAT** is chosen instead of the unit **CAT**—or they can arise during phonological access—the unit for /m/ is chosen instead of /k/. It is only the former kind of error, however, that should respect syntactic categories, according to the model. Phonological substitutions that create words during phonological access could replace nouns with verbs ("sat" for "cat") just as readily as with nouns ("mat" for "cat").

Since malapropisms that occur during lemma access, in this model, are caused by phonological-lexical feedback, it follows that form-related word substitutions should respect syntactic categories only if two conditions are present: (1) the phonological-lexical feedback connections are strong enough to send appreciable activation to potential malapropisms, and (2) the lexical-semantic connections are weak enough to allow these to compete with the target. Thus, when applying this model to aphasia, one can actually predict which patients should exhibit the syntactic category effect and which should not, based on an independent determination of the strength of the model's weights—the s and p parameters.

To test this prediction, we first need to know which model parameters actually lead to a genuine tendency to produce malapropisms during lemma access. Consequently, we varied the model's s and p parameters, while keeping all other parameters constant at their normal values, and compared the probability that the model would select potential malapropisms such as **MAT** for **CAT** with that of unrelated items such as **LOG**. If there is no functional phonological-lexical feedback, there will be little difference in the number of times comparable formal and unrelated items are selected during lemma access. Figure 3 shows a contour map of this difference, with the darker color associated with a stronger tendency for malapropisms and white specifically indicating no tendency at all. The figure shows that, as expected, malapropisms require relatively strong phonological weights, and relatively weak semantic weights. As a rule of thumb, we can say that if $p > s$, that is, when the lesion is more semantic than phonological, the model has

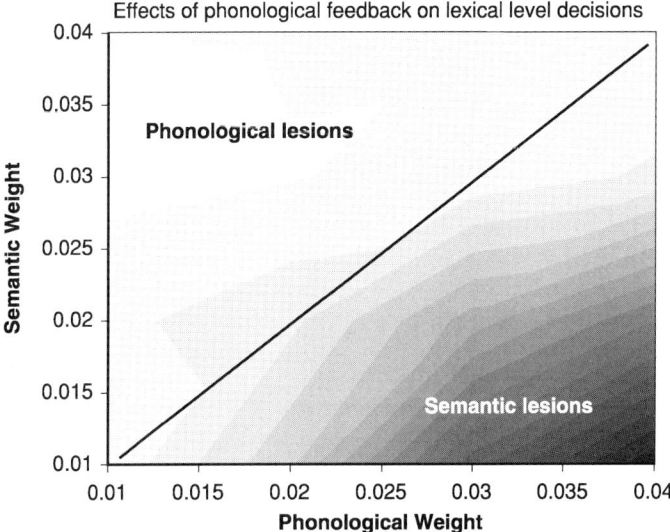

Fig. 3. The tendency to produce malapropisms as a function of semantic (s) and phonological (p) weights in the model of Foygel and Dell (2000). White indicates the absence of such a tendency, with increasing darkness showing increasing tendencies. When there is no tendency, unrelated words are as likely to be selected during lemma access as formally related words (malapropisms).

a true tendency to produce malapropisms. Moreover, the greater the difference ($p - s$), the greater the tendency.

The next step in testing the prediction is to identify patients who make a sufficient number of formally related word errors. To the extent that these patients are assigned lesions that are relatively more semantic ($p > s$), their formal errors should tend to be nouns; nouns are the target syntactic category in the naming tests being used. Gagnon et al. (1997) identified nine patients from the picture-naming study of Dell et al. (1997), for whom at least 10% of the errors were formal errors. These errors were labeled as nouns or non-nouns based on whether the most common meaning of the response was a noun or not. They also determined the chance that a random vocabulary item would be a noun for English to be 64%. We then calculated "noun scores" for each patient, the number of noun formal errors in excess of chance expectation. The prediction is that the noun scores should tend to be positive (in excess of chance) for patients for whom p is greater than s, and near zero for those patients where s is greater than p.

The naming-error patterns of the nine patients were fit to the model using methods described in Dell, Lawler, Harris, and Gordon (in press), and the obtained and modeled proportions for each category and the resulting parameters are shown in Table I. Four of the patients were assigned $p > s$ lesions, and five were assigned $s > p$ lesions. Figure 4 shows the individual

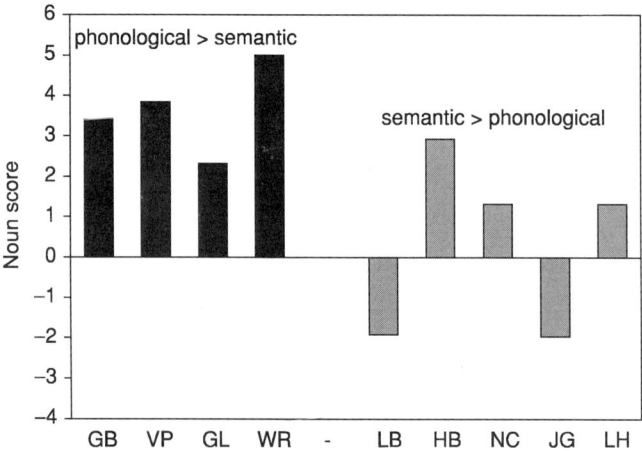

Fig. 4. Noun scores for the formally related word errors from nine patients from Gagnon et al. (1997). The dark bars indicate patients whose lesions are predominately semantic and the grey bars identify the scores for patients whose lesions are more phonological (as determined from the parameters assigned in Table I).

noun scores for the patients grouped in this way. As predicted, the noun scores for the group with relatively larger semantic lesions were greater than 0, (t (3) = 6.6) and significantly greater than chance (one-tailed) for patients GB (13 nouns; 2 non-nouns), VP (16 3), and WR (21 4). Moreover, noun scores for the group with relatively larger phonological lesions did not differ from zero, and the group mean was significantly less than that of the other group using a one-tailed test (t (7) = 2.3). If one ignores the assignment of patients to these two groups and simply correlates noun scores with $s - p$, the result is reliable and in the predicted direction (r (7) = -0.74, Fig. 5).

These data allow us to conclude that the extent to which a patient's formal errors obey syntactic category constraints is consistent with the model's characterization of the strength of the lexical-semantic and lexical-phonological weights for that patient. Importantly, the assessment of model parameters is independent of the extent to which formal errors are nouns. That is, the syntactic category of the formal errors is not considered during the parameter fitting. Hence, the relationship between syntactic category and model characterization is a true prediction. More generally, the success of the prediction is supportive of the assumption of interactive feedback from the phonological to the lexical level, because it is only through this mechanism that the model produces malapropisms, formally related errors that obey the syntactic category constraint. Such errors are only likely when

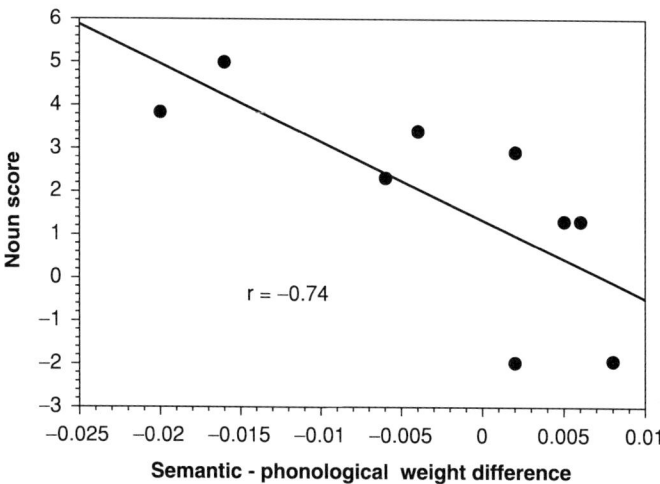

Fig. 5. Scatterplot showing a negative relation between noun scores and the extent to which lesions are phonological as opposed to semantic, specifically the value $s - p$, for the nine patients from Gagnon et al. (1997).

lexical-phonological weights are large enough to deliver bottom-up activation to potential malapropisms, and lexical-semantic weights are small enough that these word units compete successfully with the target.

One can make similar predictions about the extent to which aphasic individuals show the mixed-error effect, the tendency for semantic substitutions to show contamination from phonological factors (e.g., *rat* for *cat*). The same regions of parameter space that promote malapropisms also should promote mixed errors. We have not systematically examined this prediction for the model of Foygel and Dell (2000) because patient mixed-error percentages are used to assign parameters and hence the resulting parameters are not independent of any obtained mixed-error effect. However, Rapp and Goldrick (2000) and Dell et al. (1997) have showed that the mixed-error effect is present in some patients and demonstrably absent in others. More importantly, whether there is such an effect or not is predictable from other aspects of the patients' errors and from the assumption that mixed errors are promoted by phonological-lexical feedback

G. THE EFFECT OF PHONOLOGICAL NEIGHBORHOODS ON LEXICAL ACCESS

Malapropisms involve the replacement of a target word with a phonological neighbor, another word that is phonologically similar to it. This raises the question: is there any relationship between ease of production for a word and the number of potential malapropisms that exist in the lexicon? The number of words that are phonologically very similar to a given word defines that word's *phonological neighborhood density*. Neighborhood density, and related measures that also take into account the frequency of the neighbors, have a powerful effect on word recognition. Words are more difficult to recognize in dense than in sparse neighborhoods, presumably because the neighbors are active and compete with the target in some manner (e.g., Luce & Pisoni, 1998; Vitevitch & Luce, 1999). But what happens during production?

It turns out that neighborhood density has the opposite effect on production. Words in dense neighborhoods are easier (Gordon, 2002; Harley & Bown, 1998; Vitevitch, 2002). For example, Vitevitch (2002) elicited phonological speech errors using two different experimental techniques. For both techniques, targets in dense neighborhoods were more immune to error. He also compared picture-naming latencies for words from sparse and dense neighborhoods matched for frequency, familiarity ratings, and the phonotactic probability of the phoneme combinations. Again, targets from dense neighborhoods were easier, and in this case, more rapidly named.

How is it that neighbors harm recognition but benefit production? The two-step interactive model may have an explanation. Neighbors gain activation during lexical access in production because of the interactive flow of activation. During both lemma and phonological access, activation flows from the target's phonemes (e.g., /k/, /ae/, and /t/) to word units for neighbors (e.g., **MAT, CAP**). These activated neighbors have both good and bad consequences for lexical access. They are bad insofar as they may be chosen instead of the target, or perhaps delay target selection if their activation level is close to the target. However, they are good because they, in turn, send activation to the target following the reverse of the pathways that caused them to be active in the first place. In this way, having many neighbors increases the activation of the target.

The balance between the competitive and supportive role of neighbors depends on what the principal competitors to the target are. In word recognition, a form-driven task, the principal competitors are the phonological neighbors themselves. When hearing "cat," one is hard pressed to distinguish it from "cap." Consequently, the greater the neighborhood density, the more difficult the task. Word production, in contrast, is a semantically-driven task. The speaker gets more competition from "dog" than from "cap" when trying to say "cat." Note, for example, in Table I, that errors by the control subjects are semantic, rather than purely formal. Given this state of affairs, if neighbors receive activation from targets, as they do in a model with lexical-phonological feedback, one expects that dense neighborhoods should promote accurate lexical access. Table II demonstrates that this is the case, using the Foygel and Dell (2000) model with normal parameters. The table shows the outcome of 100,000 lexical access trials, when the target has zero, one, or two neighbors. (A neighbor in this case shares two out of three phonemes). Because normal parameters are used, the model is extremely accurate. Yet, one can clearly see that greater density leads to greater accuracy and it does so primarily by reducing the chance of a semantic error.

TABLE II

RESPONSE FREQUENCIES FROM THE INTERACTIVE TWO-STEP MODEL OF LEXICAL ACCESS AS A FUNCTION OF TARGET NEIGHBORHOOD DENSITY

Neighborhood (Number of Neighbors)	Correct	Semantic	Formal	Nonwords
Empty (0)	98,413	1566	0	21
Sparse (1)	98,556	1434	2	8
Dense (2)	98,604	1383	8	5

Based on 100,000 attempts for each density condition. Model parameters are from the fitted model for the control data in Table I.

Although formal errors increase with density, they are sufficiently rare that the cost of making more formal errors is more than offset by the reduction of other error types.

The effects of neighborhood density are only beginning to be researched with regard to production. For now, we can conclude that, for unimpaired speakers (and possibly aphasic speakers, Gordon, 2002; Gordon & Dell, 2001), neighbors have a facilitative effect, the opposite of what happens in word recognition. Most importantly for our purposes, these effects can be explained by interactive feedback. During production, neighbors are activated through this feedback and these in turn strengthen the activation of the target relative to its principal semantic competitors.

H. Conclusions: Interaction and Lexical Access

Garrett's (1975) independent-levels hypothesis is, 30 years later, reflected in the modular discrete-stage accounts of lexical access in production (e.g., Levelt, 1989; Levelt et al., 1999; Roelofs, in press). Discrete-stage models have the advantage of simplicity, and accord well with much of the data concerned with the time course of lexical access and with the qualitative properties regarding speech errors pointed to by Garrett. However, we claim that some form of interaction between the processing steps best explains the totality of the data. Interaction provides a motivated account of several facts about lexical bias, the existence of malapropisms and the mixed error effect, the variability of these effects in aphasia, and the facilitative influence of dense neighborhoods on production. While there are alternative accounts of many of these effects that do not require interaction, the case for interaction is strong by virtue of the fact that these diverse phenomena arise from a single hypothesized cause—lexical-phonological feedback.

While we argue for interaction, we acknowledge that the time course of lexical access (e.g., Levelt et al., 1991; Peterson & Savoy, 1998) and studies of aphasia (e.g., Garrett, 1982; Rapp & Goldrick, 2000) point to considerable discreteness in the system. According to Rapp and Goldrick, interaction is restricted to phonological-lexical feedback and is fairly weak. Similarly, Dell and O'Seaghdha (1991) called the lexical access system, "globally modular but locally interactive," meaning that the growth of activation caused by interactive feedback is small in comparison to the jolts of activation that initiate each step. Hence, the steps are separate for the most part and it is primarily in the errors that one sees evidence for a lack of discreteness. In the implemented model presented here, such is the case. The jolts that initiate lemma and phonological access dominate the activation created by interaction, leading to activation patterns that move from (mostly) word meaning during lemma access to (mostly) word form during phonological access. The two steps associated with Garrett's independent-levels hypothesis are clearly present, but are somewhat blurry at the edges.

IV. The Function-Content Distinction and Connectionist Learning Theory

A. NEUROPSYCHOLOGICAL AND NEUROIMAGING EVIDENCE

Like the independent-levels hypothesis, Garrett's function-content hypothesis asserts a sharp distinction in the production process. In Garrett's framework, content words such as *cat* are retrieved in two steps: their abstract forms are inserted into slots in the functional representation and their phonological forms are placed into slots in positional frames. Function morphemes, such as *the* or plural *s*, are not inserted into frame slots; they are part of the structural representations themselves (Garrett, 1975; Bock & Levelt, 1994; Lapointe & Dell, 1989). That is why the function items are not typically involved in substitution or exchange errors.[4]

The function-content hypothesis is closely related to the widely held view that function and content items come from different linguistic components: function items from the syntax, and content items from the lexicon (e.g., Gleason, 1961). On this view, function and content items are categorically distinct, and thus should be represented and processed quite differently. A great deal of evidence supports this position (for reviews see, Bock, 1989; Dell, 1990; Garrett, 1980). We have already mentioned the differences in speech-error patterns. Another major source of evidence for a function-content distinction is aphasia. Function and content items are differentially affected in patient speech. The standard claim centers on the distinction between anomic and agrammatic speech patterns. Agrammatic aphasics have more trouble with function than content items, whereas anomic aphasics exhibit the opposite pattern (Goodglass & Kaplan, 1983).

Agrammatic speech is characterized by the frequent omission of function morphemes (in languages such as English), along with a reduction of syntactic complexity and utterance length (e.g., Kolk & Heeschen, 1992; Saffran, Berndt, & Schwartz, 1989). The dialogue (11) from Goodglass (1993) is a good example:

---

[4] Pronouns and some prepositions are assumed to be actively inserted into slots at the functional level and, consistent with this claim, these items do participate in exchange errors.

(11) Examiner: Can you tell me about why you came back to the hospital?

Patient: *Yes....eh...Monday...eh...dad...Peter Hogan and dad...hospital*

These properties can be quantified through four indices developed by Saffran et al., the proportion of words that appear in sentences (minimally NP V), the ratio of nouns to verbs,[5] the proportion of words that are function words, and score that indicates the complexity of auxiliary verbs that are used. Patient SS, from Breedin, Saffran, and Schwartz (1998) is agrammatic by all four indices with only 15% of words in sentences (compared to nearly 100% with control subjects), 6.4 noun/verb ratio (1.2 for controls), 15% function words (56% for controls), and an auxiliary complexity score of 0.13 (1.43 for controls). Moreover, the SS's speech is quite slow and labored (17 words per minute) compared to the controls' rate (132 words per minute).

Anomic aphasia is quite different. Anomia generally means impaired access to one's vocabulary. Anomic aphasia, however, refers to a deficit in which speech is fluent for the most part, but with impaired access mostly to the content word categories. Anomic speakers often experience blockages when retrieving substantive words (12), or they may replace these with other words or nonwords (13) (examples from Goodglass, 1993).

(12) *I gave him a...Oh God! I know it! I can't...Why can't I say it?*

(13) *I had a vord...a lord...* (I had a valve)

Importantly, the speech of anomic aphasics is mostly grammatical, as the examples above indicate. Anomic patient VP from Breedin et al. (1998), for example, falls within the normal range on the Saffran et al. (1989) indices of agrammatism (94% of words in sentences; 1.2 noun/verb ratio; 62% function words; 1.47 auxiliary complexity).

The contrast between agrammatic patients such as SS and anomic ones such as VP supports the function-content distinction by presenting a double dissociation, a situation in which one patient's disability corresponds to another's ability, and vice-versa. Moreover, the association between the loss of function morphemes and a general loss of fluent grammatical speech in

---

[5] Greater difficulty with verbs than nouns is, to some extent, associated with agrammatism (Miceli, Silveri, Villa, & Caramazza, 1984; Zingeser & Berndt, 1990). To the extent that this is true, it is consistent with the fact that verbs are more associated with particular sentence structures than nouns. However, not all patients with selective deficits in verb production are agrammatic (e.g., Caramazza & Hillis, 1991).

agrammatism further supports the association of the function vocabulary with grammatical processes.[6]

How sharp is the distinction between function and content items? In Garrett's original hypothesis, the function items are part of the structural frames, and the content items are not. There is no middle ground. However, as Garrett (1975) and Levelt (1989) have noted, function morphemes are not all equally void of content. Consider the differences between *to* in *I want to go*, which seems to have little content, and *above* in *It's above the rack*, which has more. If the production system does make a processing distinction between items that are part of frames and those inserted into frame slots, it may be the case that only some function items are part of the frame, while others are inserted just as content words. For example, Bock (1989) argued that dative prepositions *to* and *for* (*gave the money to/for the foundation*) are not part of the frame because structural priming in production is indifferent to whether or not prime and target dative sentences have the same or different prepositions.

The variability within the function items with respect to how function-like they are also occurs with the content items. Consider the difference between the verbs *go* and *fly*. *Go* is a semantically primitive verb of motion. It is less complex than *fly*, which includes the notion of going, but adds to it that the motion is through the air (e.g., Bierwisch & Schreuder, 1992). Simple verbs such as *go* are sometimes called "light" (e.g., also *be, have, make, do*) and are contrasted with complex or "heavy" verbs, such as *fly*.

We claim that the difference between light and heavy verbs is akin to that between function and content items. It turns out that the agrammatic/anomic double dissociation for function/content extends to light and heavy verbs. Breedin et al. (1998) tested eight patients with verb retrieval deficits and found that the agrammatic patients were better able to retrieve heavy than light verbs. For example, only 9% of SS's verbs in narrative speech were light. Moreover, in a sentence completion task targeting particular verbs, SS tended to substitute heavy for light verbs, for example, saying "build...build boats" for the target "Carl makes boats" (17 heavy-for-light substitutions compared to 5 light-for-heavy replacements). Anomic aphasics such as VP produced the opposite pattern. For VP's narrative speech, 85% of the verbs were light, and in his sentence completion errors there were only 5 heavy-for-light substitutions compared to 29 light-for-heavy errors. Figure 6 shows that SS (agrammatic by 4 indices) and VP (agrammatic by 0 indices) are extreme cases. Patients who are intermediate on the

---

[6] Although loss of function morphemes usually co-occurs with a loss of sentence complexity, sentence-structure and function-morpheme difficulties can dissociate (see Martin, 2003, for a review).

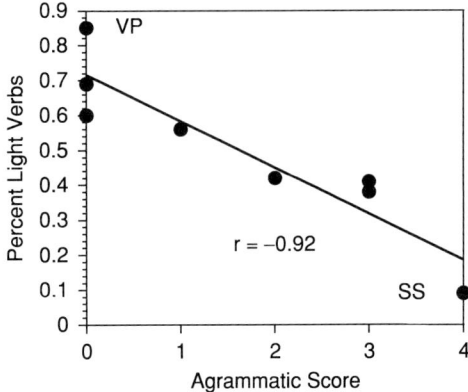

Fig. 6. Percentage of light verbs in the narrative speech of eight patients from Breedin et al. (1998) as a function of how many agrammatic indices the patients exhibit. The more agrammatic the patient is, the smaller the percentage of light verbs.

agrammatism indices had no particular preference for light or heavy verbs in their narration. The correlation between the proportion of light verbs and number of agrammatic indices is reliable ($r = -0.92$).

We interpret the finding of Breedin et al. (1998) of a double dissociation between light and heavy verb retrieval involving agrammatic and anomic aphasia as evidence that the function-content distinction is a continuum, with light verbs more like function items, and heavy verbs more like content items. If this is true, the dichotomous processing distinction corresponding to "part of the frame" versus "inserted into frame slots" must be modified. Before we present such a modification, however, we briefly review recent evidence from neuroimaging studies regarding the function-content distinction.

Attempts to find neurophysiological correlates of the function/content distinction in healthy subjects have followed a course similar to that of investigations of production errors by aphasics. Neville, Mills, and Lawson (1992) reported an early ERP component that distinguished function words from content words in comprehension. While other researchers had found some differences in the patterns of ERPs in response to content and function words (e.g., Garnsey, 1985), this was taken as the first real evidence supporting separate processing streams in lexical access for the two word classes.

Subsequent studies, however, have cast doubt on this interpretation of the findings. Function words as a group tend not only to be less semantically rich than content words, but also shorter, more frequent, and less likely to carry stress. When these factors are controlled for (or used as predictors in a regression model), the early word class difference in the ERP waveform tends to disappear (Osterhout, Allen, & McLaughlin, 2002; Munte et al., 2001; King & Kutas, 1998; Pulvermuller, Lutzenburger, & Birbaumer 1995; Osterhout, Bersick, & McKinnon, 1997).

In an fMRI study comparing the processing of function and content words, Friederici, Opitz, and von Cramon (2000) had participants perform either syntactic or semantic judgments on content words and function words, both of which were subdivided into abstract and concrete items. While they found several interactions between word class and task, as well as word class and concreteness, there was little evidence supporting a main effect of word class on patterns of brain activation.

A recent MEG study (Halgren et al., 2002) did find distinct patterns of brain activation that honored the function/content distinction. This study, however, did not attempt to control for the factors that tend to co-vary with the function/content distinction.

Overall, while there is still debate as to whether neurophysiological distinctions can be made between function word access and content word access (see Brown, Hagoort, & Terkeurs, 1999 for a review of evidence favoring such a distinction), the consensus is that there is no definitive qualitative neural signature of the function/content word distinction. In general, the neurophysiological data provide support for a continuum with abstract, short, high-frequency function words at one end and concrete content words at the other.

B. A LEARNING-BASED MODEL OF LEXICAL ACCESS IN SENTENCE PRODUCTION

Here we review the model of Gordon and Dell (2003), which applies connectionist learning principles to lexical access in sentence production. Our claim is that this model successfully turns the function-content distinction into a continuum by treating semantic units representing the sentence's meaning, or message, and units representing *syntactic-sequential states* as weighted cues for particular lexical items. The weights on these cues are learned in the course of learning to speak, with the result that different kinds of words become differentially dependent on semantic and syntactic cues. The greater the dependence on semantic cues, the more content-like the lexical item; the greater the dependence on syntactic-sequential states, the more function-like the item. However, each word depends, to some extent, on both kinds of cues. In this way, the function-content distinction becomes a continuum. To demonstrate this point, Gordon and Dell created "anomic" and "agrammatic" lesions in the model by reducing either the semantic-lexical or the syntactic-lexical weights. The lesioned models exhibited the double dissociation between light and heavy verbs found by Breedin et al. (1998), as well as the double dissociation between function and content items.

Unlike the other models that we have reviewed thus far, the sentence-production model of Gordon and Dell (2003) uses a learning algorithm to set its connection weights. Figure 7 illustrates the network. There are two kinds of inputs to the model: the semantic features of the message and syntactic-sequential states. Suppose that the target sentence is something like "The bird flies." Its message would consist of the activated features for the *bird* concept (*winged, animal*) and the *flying* concept (*motion, through_air*). The model makes what we call the *static-message assumption*: The features of the message—or at least a simple message like this one—are in place prior to sentence formulation, and remain in place throughout formulation (see Griffin & Bock, 2000, for evidence that messages are present before lexical access begins).

Because the message is static, it is up to the other input units, the syntactic-sequential state units, to keep track of where the formulation process is. Hence, the activation pattern across the syntactic-sequential state units is

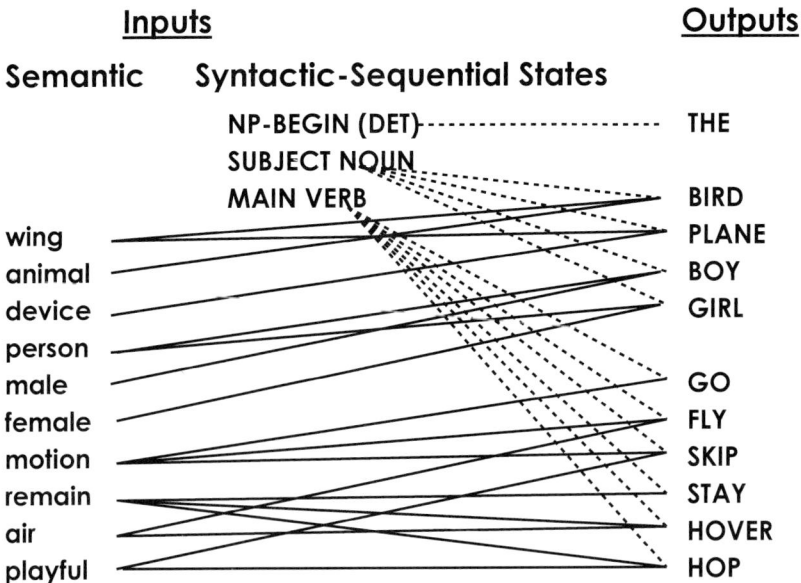

Fig. 7. The inputs and outputs from the model of Gordon and Dell (2003). The lines identify the target mappings, rather than actual connection weights. For example, the output *bird* is the target associated with the semantic units *wing* and *animal* and the syntactic-sequential state for *subject-noun*.

dynamic; it changes throughout the course of the sentence. In Gordon and Dell's implementation, the sentences all followed the pattern *The* **NOUN VERBs**. Consequently, there were only three state units: one for the initial *the* (*DET*, for determiner), one for the noun (*N*), and one for the verb (*V*). At the beginning of the formulation process, *DET* alone is activated, signaling the beginning of the subject noun phrase. After the determiner has been encoded, *DET* turns off, and *N* becomes active, and so on until the end of the sentence. Thus, the syntactic-sequential units form a small state-transition network. In a more realistic implementation, there would, of course, be many states. Moreover, the states need not correspond to single units. Distributed states such as those arising from sequential recurrent networks could be used as well (e.g., Chang, 2002; Elman, 1990; Tabor & Tanenhaus, 1999).

The model outputted lexical items, one at a time, as the syntactic-sequential states changed. For each word, activation from the static message converged with that from the current syntactic unit on a particular lexical item (e.g., *the*). As the syntactic-sequential state changed, the activation was redirected to the remaining items in sequence (e.g., *bird*, then *flies*).

The connection weights were set by the *delta rule*, a connectionist learning rule in which the change in weight between an input unit i and an output j is proportional to the product

(13) $a_i(t_j - a_j)$

where *a* represents the activation of a unit and *t* is the target or desired value of this activation. The delta rule is the simplest version of a class of learning rules that change weights in response to error (e.g., Rescorla & Wagner, 1972; Widrow & Hoff, 1988). Error-based learning creates *cue competition*, the tendency for inputs to compete with one another to control output. For example, if two input units are both associated with a single output, the weights from those inputs to the output will compete. If one weight happens to become strong, the other will be weak. When one input bears much of the responsibility for activating the output, the other's weight cannot grow even though it is predictive of the output. This is because learning stops as output activation a_j approaches the desired value t_j.

In Gordon and Dell's model, competition between semantic and syntactic cues leads to a continuum among different kinds of words with respect to the strengths of the cues. For a content word such as *bird*, semantic features such as *animal* are strongly predictive and, consequently, semantic-to-lexical weights strongly control the access of the word. Specifically, the weight from *animal* to *bird* became large and excitatory because *bird* was the only animal in their implemented model. Because the semantic weights for content words become strong, the relevant syntactic-sequential weights from the

N syntactic-sequential state to *bird* cannot grow to be excessively large, even though the N state is a prerequisite for accessing the noun *bird* at the proper time. The strong semantic weights preclude larger syntactic ones. For a function word such as *the*, the semantic cues are quite weak (in Gordon & Dell's implementation, nonexistent) and, consequently, the syntactic-sequential cues must bear the responsibility for access. For example, the weight from the syntactic-sequential state for *DET* to *the* was a large +3.44. In contrast, the weight from N to *bird* was only +1.33. Thus, in the model, function words are more associated to the syntax than are content words.

The semantic-syntactic competition that leads to differences between function and content words in the model also creates differences between light and heavy verbs. Light verbs are assumed to be semantically primitive. For example, the semantic representation of *go* is a single feature, *motion*. The representations of heavy verbs are more complex. *Fly*, for example, has the features *motion* and *through_air*. In addition, the model's experience with light and heavy verbs differed. In the sentences that the model was trained on, each light verb could take many different subjects. *Boys, girls, birds*, and *planes* can all *go*. Heavy verbs, by virtue of their more specific meanings, are more restricted. For example, in the model's experience, *birds* and *planes*, but not *boys* and *girls*, can *fly*. Thus, heavy verbs have more predictive semantic cues—more intrinsic features and more specific features from co-occurring nouns—than light verbs.

Because of the differing strength of the semantic cues for light and heavy verbs, the cue competition that arises from the model's learning rule created corresponding differences between these verb types in the strengths of their syntactic associations. The result was that the primary responsibility for accessing heavy verbs was borne by the semantic-lexical connections, and, for the light verbs, the syntactic-lexical connections were more important. Table III shows the connection weights to the light verb *go* and the heavy verb *fly* from the syntactic-sequential state for verbs, V, the semantic features, *motion* and *through_air*, and a feature associated with the nouns *boy* and *girl*, labeled *person*. First, note that *go* has a much larger weight from V than does *fly*. Because of the relatively impoverished semantics of *go*, the relevant syntactic sequential-state acquires a stronger weight to this item. Second, *fly* has a large positive weight from its strongly predictive semantic feature *through_air*. Light verbs, by virtue of their primitive nature, do not have features that are uniquely associated with them. Finally, one can see from the weights reported in the table how a verb's distribution matters. The *person* feature is naturally negatively associated with verbs, because it is most strongly predictive of the production of the nouns, *boy* and *girl*. However, because *boys* and *girls* cannot *fly*, but they can *go*, the inhibitory weight to *go* is not as negative as it is to *fly*.

TABLE III

CONNECTION WEIGHTS FROM SELECTED INPUT UNITS TO THE LIGHT VERB GO AND THE HEAVY VERB FLY

	Input units			
	Syntactic	Semantic (Verb)		Semantic (Noun)
	Verb	Through_Air	Motion	Person
Lexical item				
GO	+1.27	−1.73	+0.50	−0.70
FLY	+0.43	+1.22	−0.37	−1.41

Adapted from Gordon and Dell (2003).

TABLE IV

PRODUCTION ACCURACY PERCENTAGES FOR VARIOUS KINDS OF WORDS AS A FUNCTION OF LESION TYPE FOR THE LEARNING MODEL OF GORDON AND DELL (2003)

	Type of lexical item			
	Determiner (The)	Noun	Light verb	Heavy verb
Type of lesion				
Agrammatic	11	54	18	34
Anomic	100	25	38	6

Based on the most extreme lesion of each type (relevant weights = 0).

The contrasting weight configurations for function and content items and for light and heavy verbs have consequences for the model's behavior when it is lesioned. Gordon and Dell simulated agrammatic and anomic deficits by reducing the syntactic-sequential and the semantic weights, respectively. Table IV shows the effects of these lesions for accessing different kinds of lexical items. As expected, the agrammatic lesion is associated with a loss of function words and affects light verbs more than heavy verbs; the anomic lesion shows the reverse pattern. Thus, the model is in accord with the aphasic data, illustrating its potential for explaining dissociations between function and content items and how this distinction may be more of a continuum than a categorical one. More generally, the model demonstrates how connectionist learning principles may be applied to Garrett's ideas about structural frames and the insertion of lexical items into frame slots.

In the model, the dynamic syntactic-sequential representations implement the frame, and the convergence of activation from syntactic-sequential and semantic-feature units achieves lexical insertion.

This model has another property that is worth noting insofar as it is also consistent with aphasic data. It can be set up to simulate single-word retrieval tasks, such as picture-naming, as well as sentence production, simply by limiting the message to the semantic features of the target word (e.g., *animal* and *winged* for *bird*) and setting the syntactic-sequential state to one that is appropriate for naming a single object (a bare noun). This enables one to compare the model's accuracy, when lesioned, for words produced in sentences and words produced in isolation. The aphasic literature has identified patients for whom lexical retrieval in sentences is worse than retrieval of words in isolation, that is, they have a "naming-in-context" deficit (e.g., Schwartz & Hodgson, 2002; Williams & Canter, 1982). These individuals tend to be agrammatic rather than anomic in their speech patterns.

The model of Gordon and Dell exhibits a naming-in-context deficit with agrammatic lesions. For example, nouns, light verbs, and heavy verbs are associated with 54%, 18%, and 34% accuracy, respectively, when they are produced in sentences. If these words are produced in isolation, however, accuracy jumps to 92%, 64%, and 86%, respectively. The model's naming-in-context deficit does not occur with anomic lesions; it only occurs with agrammatic lesions, in agreement with the patient data. The deficit occurs because the model's dynamic syntactic-sequential states act like a "traffic cop." They let words of particular syntactic categories through at one point in time, and words of another category through at another time. Thus, they keep the semantic features associated with the nouns and verbs of a sentence from interfering with one another during sentence production. When an agrammatic lesion is present, one that reduces the input from syntactic sequential states, the sentence's words "crash" without the directive function of the syntactic traffic cop. When words are produced in isolation by an agrammatic model, there is no crash because the features of the message correspond to a single word.

This syntactic traffic cop is the part of Gordon and Dell's model that is responsible for the syntactic category constraint on word substitution errors. It is the mechanism that allows nouns to replace other nouns and verbs to replace other verbs. Such a mechanism was assumed to operate in the interactive two-step model of lexical access, when it was stipulated that the most active word of proper syntactic category is selected. In Gordon and Dell's model, however, this stipulation is realized and motivated through learned connections. Moreover, when those learned connections are disabled, as in the agrammatic lesion, the syntactic category constraint can be violated. In contrast, the anomic lesion should lead to errors that uphold the category constraint. This prediction appears to be supported by aphasic data. In the

Berndt, Mitchum, Haendiges, and Sandson (1997) study of noun and verb picture-naming from a variety of patients, the four agrammatic patients' semantic errors respected the target's syntactic category only 61% of the time. Verbs were often replaced by nouns, and occasionally, nouns were replaced by verbs. In contrast, the semantic substitutions made by three anomic patients respected the target syntactic category at a much higher rate, 89% of the time.

In summary, the connectionist learning model of Gordon and Dell touches on two points that were originally emphasized in Garrett's study of speech errors: the function-content distinction including the association of function morphemes with structural frames, and the syntactic category constraint on word substitution errors. The model explains how these arise. The association between function items and syntactic states emerges from cue competition in learning. These learning assumptions also create a continuum rather than a sharp distinction between function and content items, ultimately enabling the model to explain the differences between the production of light and heavy verbs as well as that between function and content items. The syntactic category constraint on speech errors is a product of the traffic cop function of the syntactic-sequential states, which ultimately arises from the model's conception of the task of sentence production, to turn a static message into a sequence of words by means of a changing set of syntactic-sequential states.

V. Summary and Conclusions

We examined two working hypotheses arising from Garrett's (1975) analysis of speech errors: the independent-levels and the function-content hypotheses. Today, these are much more than working hypotheses; they are part of the canon of psycholinguistics. The functional and positional levels have been spelled out in theories of sentence and word production (Bock, 1982; Dell, 1986; Hartsuiker, 2002; Kempen & Hoenkamp, 1987; Levelt, 1989; Stemberger, 1985), particularly in discrete two-step theories of lexical access (Levelt et al., 1999; Roelofs, 1997). Similarly, the function-content distinction and the related distinction between content items and inflectional affixes are present in modern theories of production and production deficits (e.g., Alario & Caramazza, 2002; Bock & Levelt, 1994; Ferreira & Humphreys, 2001; Segalowitz & Lane, 2000).

The thrust of this article, however, is that recent connectionist models of production blur Garrett's sharp distinctions. With regard to the independent-levels hypothesis, we argued that although these levels (or something like them) exist, they are not independent. Lemma selection is influenced by phonological information; such information is normally part of a later step in the process. This influence can be modeled by interactive or feedback connections from phonological to word units. The interactive two-step model, in particular, offers an account of a variety of phenomena that may arise from interaction, while retaining the staged character of lexical access emphasized in discrete approaches.

The function-content distinction also becomes blurred through the application of connectionist principles (Gordon & Dell, 2003). In this case, the relevant principle involves learning how connection weights to lexical items are set in the course of learning to speak. The function-content distinction is present in the relative strengths of semantic and syntactic-sequential inputs. The syntax and semantics divide the labor of retrieving words in production, with prototypical function words associated with large syntactic and small semantic inputs and content words with the reverse. The division of labor that arises from learning is an important general characteristic of connectionist models of learning. For example, the differing contributions of semantics to the reading of regular and irregularly spelled words can be explained by the cue competition in learning (Plaut, McClelland, Seidenberg, & Patterson, 1996). In the Plaut et al. reading model, the regular-irregular distinction becomes a continuum as different representations make quantitatively varying contributions to the processing. We are asserting the same for the function-content distinction.

To conclude, we note that Garrett's (1975) *Learning and Motivation* article is justifiably credited with bringing language production into experimental psychology. Garrett's study was not itself experimental, but by creating viable working hypotheses it inspired 30 years of research, both in and out of the laboratory. If production started out as Levelt's (1989) "stepchild of psycholinguistics," it has grown up to make its family proud.

Acknowledgments

This research was supported by NIH DC-00191. The authors thank Brian Ross, Jean Gordon, Myrna Schwartz, Nadine Martin, Eleanor Saffran, Susan Garnsey, Kay Bock, and Kara Federmeier for valuable comments, and Judy Allen for work on the manuscript. Address correspondence to: Gary S. Dell, Beckman Institute, University of Illinois, 405 North Mathews avenue, Urbana, IL 61801 (email: gdell@s.psych.uiuc.edu).

References

Alario, F.-X., & Caramazza, A. (2002). The production of determiners: Evidence from French. *Cognition, 82*, 179–223.

Baars, B. J., Motley, M. T., & MacKay, D. G. (1975). Output editing for lexical status in artificially elicited slips of the tongue. *Journal of Verbal Learning and Verbal Behavior, 14*, 382–391.

Berg, T., & Schade, U. (1992). The role of inhibition in a spreading activation model of language production: I. The psycholinguistic perspective. *Journal of Psycholinguistic Research, 22*, 405–434.

Berndt, R. S., Mitchum, C. C., Haendiges, A. H., & Sandson, J. (1997). Verb retrieval in aphasia. *Brain and Language, 56*, 68–106.

Bierwisch, M., & Schreuder, R. (1992). From concepts to lexical items. *Cognition, 42*, 23–60.

Bock, J. K. (1982). Towards a cognitive psychology of syntax: Information processing contributions to sentence formulation. *Psychological Review, 89*, 1–47.

Bock, J. K. (1986). Meaning, sound, and syntax: Lexical priming in sentence production. *Journal of Experimental Psychology: Learning, Memory and Cognition, 12*, 575–586.

Bock, J. K. (1987). An effect of accessibility of word forms on sentence structures. *Journal of Memory and Language, 26*, 119–137.

Bock, J. K. (1989). Closed-class immanence in sentence production. *Cognition, 31*, 163–186.

Bock, J. K., & Levelt, W. J. M. (1994). Language production: Grammatical encoding. In M. Gernsbacher (Ed.), *Handbook of psycholinguistics*. (pp. 945–984). San Diego, CA: Academic Press.

Breedin, S. D., Saffran, E. M., & Schwartz, M. F. (1998). Semantic factors in verb retrieval: An effect of complexity. *Brain and Language, 63*, 1–35.

Brown, C. M., Hagoort, P., & ter Keurs, M. (1999). Electrophysiological signatures of visual lexical processing: Open- and closed-class words. *Journal of Cognitive Neuroscience, 11*, 261–281.

Caramazza, A. (1997). How many levels of processing are there in lexical access? *Cognitive Neuropsychology, 14*, 177–208.

Caramazza, A., & Hillis, A. (1991). Lexical organization of nouns and verbs in the brain. *Nature, 349*, 788–790.

Caramazza, A., & Miozzo, M. (1997). The relation between syntactic and phonological knowledge in lexical access: Evidence from the 'tip-of-the-tongue' phenomenon. *Cognition, 64*, 309–343.

Chang, F. (2002). Symbolically speaking: A connectionist model of sentence production. *Cognitive Science, 26*, 609–651.

Costa, A., Caramazza, A., & Sebastian-Galles, N. (2000). The cognate facilitation effect: Implications for models of lexical access. *Journal of Experimental Psychology: Learning, Memory, and Cognition, 26*, 1283–1296.

Costa, A., Sebastian-Galles, N., Miozzo, M., & Caramazza, A. (1999). The gender congruity effect: Evidence from Spanish and Catalan. *Language and Cognitive Processes, 14*, 381–391.

Cuetos, F., Aguado, G., & Caramazza, A. (2000). Dissociation of semantic and phonological errors in naming. *Brain and Language, 75*, 451–460.

Cutting, J. C., & Ferreira, V. S. (1999). Semantic and phonological information flow in the production lexicon. *Journal of Experimental Psychology: Learning, Memory, and Cognition, 25*, 318–344.

Dell, G. S. (1986). A spreading activation theory of retrieval in language production. *Psychological Review, 93*, 283–321.

Dell, G. S. (1988). The retrieval of phonological forms in production: Tests of predictions from a connectionist model. *Journal of Memory and Language, 27*, 124–142.

Dell, G. S. (1990). Effects of frequency and vocabulary type on phonological speech errors. *Language and Cognitive Processes, 5*, 313–349.

Dell, G. S., Lawler, E. N., Harris, H. D., & Gordon, J. K. (in press). Models of errors of omission in aphasic naming. *Cognitive Neuropsychology*.

Dell, G. S., & O'Seaghdha, P. G. (1991). Mediated vs. convergent lexical priming in language production: Comment on Levelt et al. *Psychological Review, 98*, 604–614.

Dell, G. S., & Reich, P. A. (1981). Stages in sentence production: An analysis of speech error data. *Journal of Verbal Learning and Verbal Behavior, 20*, 611–629.

Dell, G. S., Schwartz, M. F., Martin, N., Saffran, E. M., & Gagnon, D. A. (1997). Lexical access in aphasic and nonaphasic speakers. *Psychological Review, 104*, 801–838.

de Zubicaray, G. I., Wilson, S. J., McMahon, K. L., & Muthiah, S. (2001). The semantic interference effect in the picture-word paradigm: An event-related fMRI study employing overt responses. *Human Brain Mapping, 14*, 218–227.

Elman, J. L. (1990). Finding structure in time. *Cognitive Science, 14*, 179–211.

Fay, D., & Cutler, A. (1977). Malapropisms and the structure of the mental lexicon. *Linguistic Inquiry, 8*, 505–520.

Ferreira, V. S., & Griffin, Z. M. (2003). Phonological influence on lexical (mis)selection. *Psychological Science, 14*, 86–90.

Ferreira, V. S., & Humphreys, K. R. (2001). Syntactic influences on lexical and morphological processing in language production. *Journal of Memory and Language, 44*, 52–80.

Fodor, J. A. (1983). *The modularity of mind*. Cambridge, MA: MIT Press.

Foygel, D., & Dell, G. S. (2000). Models of impaired lexical access in speech production. *Journal of Memory and Language, 43*, 182–216.

Frazier, L., & Clifton, C. E., Jr. (1996). *Construal*. Cambridge, MA: MIT Press.

Friederici, A. D., Opitz, B., & von Cramon, D. Y. (2000). Segregating semantic and syntactic aspects of processing in the human brain: An fMRI investigation of different word types. *Cerebral Cortex, 10*, 698–705.

Fromkin, V. A. (1971). The non-anomalous nature of anomalous utterances. *Language, 47*, 27–52.

Fromkin, V. A. (1980). *Errors in linguistic performance: Slips of the tongue, ear, pen, and hand*. New York: Academic Press.

Gagnon, D. A., Schwartz, M. F., Martin, N., Dell, G. S., & Saffran, E. M. (1997). The origins of formal paraphasias in aphasics' picture naming. *Brain and Language, 59*, 450–472.

Garnsey, S. M. (1985). Function words and content words: Reaction time and evoked potential measures of word recognition. Ph.D. dissertation, University of Rochester.

Garrett, M. F. (1975). The analysis of sentence production. In G. H. Bower (Ed.), *The psychology of learning and motivation*. (pp. 133–175). San Diego, CA: Academic Press.

Garrett, M. F. (1976). Syntactic processes in sentence production. In R. J. Wales & E. C. T. Walker (Eds.), *New approaches to language mechanisms*. (pp. 231–255). Amsterdam: North-Holland.

Garrett, M. F. (1980). Levels of processing in sentence production. In B. Butterworth (Ed.), *Language production, Volume 1*. (pp. 177–210). London: Academic Press.

Garrett, M. F. (1982). Production of speech: Observations from normal and pathological language use. In A. W. Ellis (Ed.), *Normality and pathology in cognitive functions*. (pp. 19–76). London: Academic Press.

Gleason, H. A. (1961). *An introduction to descriptive linguistics*. New York: Holt, Rinehart, and Winston.

Goodglass, H. (1993). *Understanding Aphasia*. pp. 1–7. San Diego: Academic Press, Inc.

Goodglass, H., & Kaplan, E. (1983). *The assessment of aphasia and related disorders*. 2nd ed. Philadelphia: Lea & Febiger.

Gordon, J. K. (2002). Phonological neighborhood effects in aphasic speech errors: Spontaneous and structured contexts. *Brain and Language, 82*, 113–145.

Gordon, J. K., & Dell, G. S. (2001). Phonological neighborhood effects: Evidence from aphasia and connectionist modeling. *Brain and Language, 79*, 21–23.

Gordon, J. K., & Dell, G. S. (2003). Learning to divide the labor: An account of deficits in light and heavy verb production. *Cognitive Science, 27*, 1–40.

Griffin, Z. M., & Bock, J. K. (1998). Constraint, word frequency, and the relationship between lexical processing levels in spoken word production. *Journal of Memory and Language, 38*, 313–338.

Griffin, Z. M., & Bock, J. K. (2000). What the eyes say about speaking. *Psychological Science, 11*, 274–279.

Halgren, E., Dhond, R. P., Christensen, N., Van Petten, C., Marinkovic, K., Lewine, J. D., & Dale, A. M. (2002). N400-like magnetoencephalography responses modulated by semantic context, word frequency, and lexical class in sentences. *Neuroimage, 17*, 1101–1116.

Hanley, J. R., Dell, G. S., Kay, J., & Baron, R. (in press). Evidence for the involvement of a nonlexical route in the repetition of familiar words: A comparison of single and dual-route models of auditory repetition. *Cognitive Neuropsychology*.

Harley, T. A. (1984). A critique of top-down independent levels models of speech production: Evidence from non-plan-internal speech errors. *Cognitive Science, 8*, 191–219.

Harley, T. A., & Bown, H. E. (1998). What causes a tip-of-the-tongue state? Evidence for lexical neighbourhood effects in speech production *British Journal of Psychology, 89*, 151–174.

Hartsuiker, R. J. (2002). The addition bias in Dutch and Spanish phonological speech errors: The role of structural context. *Language and Cognitive Processes, 17*, 61–96.

Hartsuiker, R. J., & Kolk, H. H. J. (2001). Error monitoring in speech production: A computational test of the perceptual loop theory. *Cognitive Psychology, 42*, 113–157.

Humphreys, K. R. (2002). *Lexical bias in speech errors*. Ph.D. dissertation. University of Illinois at Urbana-Champaign.

Indefrey, P., & Levelt, W. J. M. (2000). The neural correlates of language production. In M. Gazzaniga (Ed.), *The new cognitive neurosciences*. (pp. 845–865). Cambridge, MA: MIT Press.

Jescheniak, J. D., & Schriefers, H. (1998). Discrete serial versus cascaded processing in lexical access in speech production. Further evidence from the coactivation of near-synonyms. *Journal of Experimental Psychology: Learning, Memory, and Cognition, 24*, 1256–1274.

Jescheniak, J. D., Schriefers, H., Garrett, M. F., & Friederici, A. D. (2002). Exploring the activation of semantic and phonological codes during speech planning with event-related brain potentials. *Journal of Cognitive Neuroscience, 14*, 951–964.

Jescheniak, J. D., Hahne, A., & Schriefers, H. (2003). Information flow in the mental lexicon during speech planning: evidence from event-related brain potentials. *Cognitive Brain Research, 15*, 261–276.

Kempen, G., & Hoenkamp, E. (1987). An incremental procedural grammar for sentence production. *Cognitive Science, 11*, 201–258.

Kempen, G., & Huijbers, P. (1983). The lexicalization process in sentence production and naming: Indirect election of words. *Cognition, 14*, 185–209.

Killeen, P. R., & Weiss, N. A. (1987). Optimal timing and the Weber function. *Psychological Review, 94*, 455–468.

King, J. W., & Kutas, M. (1998). Neural plasticity in the dynamics of human visual word recognition. *Neuroscience Letters, 244*, 61–64.

Kolk, H., & Heeschen, C. (1992). Agrammatism, paragrammatism, and the management of language. *Language and Cognitive Processes, 7*, 89–129.

Lapointe, S., & Dell, G. S. (1989). A synthesis of some recent work in sentence production. In G. Carlson & M. K. Tanenhaus (Eds.), *Linguistic structure in language processing*. (pp. 107–156). Dordrecht: Kluwer.

Lee, T. S. (2002). Top-down influence in early visual processing: A Bayesian perspective. *Physiology & Behavior, 77*, 645–650.

Levelt, W. J. M. (1983). Monitoring and self-repair in speech. *Cognition, 14*, 41–104.

Levelt, W. J. M. (1989). *Speaking: From intention to articulation*. Cambridge, MA: MIT Press.
Levelt, W. J., Praamstra, P., Meyer, A. S., Helenius, P., & Salmelin, R. (1998). An MEG study of picture naming. *Journal of Cognitive Neuroscience, 10*, 553–567.
Levelt, W. J. M., Roelofs, A., & Meyer, A. S. (1999). A theory of lexical access in speech production. *Behavioral and Brain Science, 21*, 1–38.
Levelt, W. J. M., Schriefers, H., Vorberg, D., Meyer, A. S., Pechmann, T., & Havinga, J. (1991). The time course of lexical access in speech production: A study of picture naming. *Psychological Review, 98*, 122–142.
Luce, P. A., & Pisoni, D. B. (1998). Recognizing spoken words: The neighborhood activation model. *Ear & Hearing, 1*, 1–36.
MacDonald, M. C., Pearlmutter, N. J., & Seidenberg, M. S. (1994). The lexical nature of syntactic ambiguity resolution. *Psychological Review, 101*, 676–703.
MacKay, D. G. (1987). *The organization of perception and action: A theory for language and other cognitive skills*. New York: Springer-Verlag.
Maess, B., Friederici, A. D., Damian, M., Meyer, A. S., & Levelt, W. J. (2002). Semantic category interference in overt picture naming: Sharpening current density localization by PCA. *Journal of Cognitive Neuroscience, 14*, 455–462.
Martin, N., Dell, G. S., Saffran, E., & Schwartz, M. F. (1994). Origins of Paraphasias in deep dysphasia: Testing the consequence of a decay impairment of an interactive spreading activation model of lexical retrieval. *Brain and Language, 47*, 609–660.
Martin, N., Gagnon, D. A., Schwartz, M. F., Dell, G. S., & Saffran, E. M. (1996). Phonological facilitation of semantic errors in normal aphasic speakers. *Language and Cognitive Processes, 11*, 257–282.
Martin, R. C. (2003). Language processing: Functional organization and neuroanatomical basis. *Annual Review of Psychology, 54*, 55–89.
Martin, R. C., Lesch, M. F., & Bartha, M. C. (1999). Independence of input and output phonology in word processing and short-term memory. *Journal of Memory and Language, 41*, 3–29.
McClelland, J. L., & Rumelhart, D. E. (1981). An interactive activation model of context effects in letter perception: Part 1. An account of basic findings. *Psychological Review, 88*, 375–407.
Miceli, G., Silveri, M. C., Villa, G., & Caramazza, A. (1984). On the basis for the agrammatic's difficulty in producing main verbs. *Cortex, 20*, 207–220.
Munte, T. F., Wieringa, B. M., Weyerts, H., Szentkuti, A., Matzke, M., & Johannes, S. (2001). Differences in brain potentials to open and closed class words: Class and frequency effects. *Neuropsychologia, 39*, 91–102.
Neville, H. J., Mills, D. L., & Lawson, D. S. (1992). Fractionating language: Different neural subsystems with different sensitive periods. *Cerebral Cortex, 2*(3), 244–258.
Nooteboom, S. (2003). Does perceiving your own inner speech cause phoneme-to-word feedback in speech production? Manuscript.
Nooteboom, S. (in press). Listening to oneself: Monitoring speech production. In: R. J. Hartsuiker et al. (Eds.), *Phonological encoding and monitoring in normal and pathological speech*. Hove, UK: Psychology Press.
Norris, D., McQueen, J. M., & Cutler, A. (2000). Merging information in speech recognition: Feedback is never necessary. *Behavioral and Brain Sciences, 23*, 299–370.
O'Reilly, R. C., & Munakata, Y. (2000). *Computational explorations in cognitive neuroscience: Understanding the mind by simulating the brain*. Cambridge, MA: MIT Press.
Osterhout, L., Allen, M., & McLaughlin, J. (2002). Words in the brain: Lexical determinants of word-induced brain activity. *Journal of Neurolinguistics, 15*, 171–187.

Osterhout, L., Bersick, M., & McKinnon, R. (1997). Brain potentials elicited by words: Word length and frequency predict the latency of an early negativity. *Biological Psychology, 46*, 143–168.

Pechmann, T., & Zerbst, D. (2003). The activation of syntactic, semantic, and phonological features of words during lexical access in speech production. Manuscript.

Peterson, R. R., & Savoy, P. (1998). Lexical selection and phonological encoding during language production: Evidence for cascaded processing. *Journal of Experimental Psychology: Learning, Memory, & Cognition, 24*, 539–557.

Plaut, D. C., & Kello, C. T. (1999). The emergence of phonology from the interplay of speech comprehension and production: A distributed connectionist approach. In B. MacWhinney (Ed.), *The emergence of language*. Mahwah, NJ: Erlbaum.

Plaut, D. C., McClelland, J. L., Seidenberg, M. S., & Patterson, K. (1996). Understanding normal and impaired word reading: Computational principles in quasi-regular domains. *Psychological Review, 103*, 56–115.

Pulvermuller, F., Lutzenberger, W., & Birbaumer, N. (1995). Electrocortical distinction of vocabulary types. *Electroencephalography and Clinical Neurophysiology, 94*, 357–370.

Rapp, B., & Goldrick, M. (2000). Discreteness and interactivity in spoken word production. *Psychological Review, 107*, 460–499.

Rapp, B., & Goldrick, M. (in press). Feedback by any other name is still interactivity: A reply to Roelofs' comment on Rapp & Goldrick (2000). *Psychological Review*.

Rescorla, R. A., & Wagner, A. R. (1972). A theory of Pavlovian conditioning: Variations in the effectiveness of reinforcement and non-reinforcement. In A. H. Black & W. F. Prokasy (Eds.), *Classical conditioning. II. Current research and theory*. (pp. 64–99). New York: Appleton.

Roelofs, A. (1992). A spreading-activation theory of lemma retrieval in speaking. *Cognition, 42*, 107–142.

Roelofs, A. (1997). The WEAVER model of word-form encoding in speech production. *Cognition, 64*, 249–284.

Roelofs, A. (in press). Error biases in spoken word planning and monitoring by aphasic and nonaphasic speakers: Comment on Rapp and Goldrick (2000). *Psychological Review*.

Ruml, W., Caramazza, A., Shelton, J. R., & Chialant, D (2000). Testing assumptions in computational theories of aphasia. *Journal of Memory and Language, 43*, 217–248.

Saffran, E. M. (1982). Neuropsychological approaches to the study of language. *British Journal of Psychology, 73*, 317–337.

Saffran, E. M., Berndt, R. S., & Schwartz, M. F. (1989). The quantitative analysis of agrammatic production: Procedure and data. *Brain and Language, 37*, 440–479.

Saffran, E. M., Schwartz, M. F., & Marin, O. S. M. (1980). The word order problem in agrammatism, II, Production. *Brain and Language, 10*, 263–280.

Schmitt, B. M., Munte, T. F., & Kutas, M. (2000). Electrophysiological estimates of the time course of semantic and phonological encoding during implicit picture naming. *Psychophysiology, 37*, 473–484.

Schriefers, H., Meyer, A. S., & Levelt, W. J. M. (1990). Exploring the time-course of lexical access in production: Picture-word interference studies. *Journal of Memory and Language, 29*, 86–102.

Schwartz, M. F., & Hodgson, C. (2002). A new multiword naming deficit: Evidence and interpretation. *Cognitive Neuropsychology, 19*, 263–288.

Segalowitz, S. J., & Lane, K. C. (2000). Lexical access of function versus content words. *Brain and Language, 75*, 376–389.

Shattuck-Hufnagel, S. (1979). Speech errors as evidence for a serial order mechanism in sentence production. In W. E. Cooper & E. C. T. Walker (Eds.), *Sentence processing: Psycholinguistic studies presented to Merrill Garrett.* (pp. 295–342). Hillsdale NJ: Erlbaum.

Stemberger, J. P. (1985). An interactive activation model of language production. In A. W. Ellis (Ed.), *Progress in the psychology of language, Vol. 1.* (pp. 143–186). Hillsdale, NJ: Erlbaum.

Tabor, W., & Tanenhaus, M. D. (1999). Dynamical theories of sentence processing. *Cognitive Science, 23*, 491–515.

van Turennout, M., Hagoort, P., & Brown, C. M. (1997). Electrophysiological evidence on the time course of semantic and phonological processes in speech production. *Journal of Experimental Psychology: Learning, Memory, and Cognition, 23*, 787–806.

van Turennout, M., Hagoort, P., & Brown, C. M. (1998). Brain activity during speaking: From syntax to phonology in 40 milliseconds. *Science, 280*, 572–574.

Vigliocco, G., & Hartsuiker, R. J. (2002). The interplay of meaning, sound & syntax in language production. *Psychological Bulletin, 128*, 442–472.

Vitevitch, M. S., & Luce, P. A. (1999). Probabilistic phonotactics and neighborhood activation in spoken word recognition. *Journal of Memory and Language, 40*, 374–408.

Vitevitch, M. S. (2002). The influence of phonological similarity neighborhoods on speech production. *Journal of Experimental Psychology: Learning, Memory, and Cognition, 28*, 735–747.

Widrow, B., & Hoff, M. E. (1988). Adaptive switching circuits. In J. A. Anderson & E. Rosenfeld (Eds.), *Neurocomputing: Foundation of research.* (pp. 126–134). Cambridge, MA: MIT Press.

Williams, S. E., & Canter, G. J. (1982). The influence of situational context on naming performance in aphasic syndromes. *Brain and Language, 17*, 92–106.

Zingeser, L. B., & Berndt, R. (1990). Retrieval of nouns and verbs in agrammatism and anomia. *Brain and Language, 39*, 14–32.

PSYCHOLINGUISTICALLY SPEAKING: SOME MATTERS OF MEANING, MARKING, AND MORPHING

Kathryn Bock

I. Introduction

Meaning, marking, and morphing are topics in the psycholinguistics of grammatical agreement. Anyone who is still reading this may not realize that, for most literate speakers of English, agreement has all the charm of a lone nocturnal mosquito and considerably less importance. In the eyes of the "language police" (Pinker, 1994) and English teachers of yore, agreement is a recondite trap of language, a place where speakers and writers go wrong when attention flags, logic fails, or training falters. What could possibly make it a worthwhile topic of psycholinguistic investigation?

One thing is the actual rate at which choices between singular and plural forms must be made. Speakers tend to become aware of agreement only on the rare occasions when they no longer remember the number of the subject. This experience contributes to the sense of agreement as an incidental part of language. Objectively, however, agreement is one of the most common things we do when speaking. Every sentence has a verb, and verbs agree in number, overtly or covertly, with their subjects. Personal pronouns, which rank among the most frequently used words in the language, agree in number with their antecedents. The combined frequencies of personal pronouns and the six most common verb forms in English imply that English speakers and writers implement number agreement more than once in every 16 words, more than once every 5 seconds in running speech.

Errors occur, of course, but less often than the reputation of agreement as a troublemaker suggests. Four-year-olds get it right 94% of the time in spontaneous speech (Keeney & Wolfe, 1972). Although normally developing three-year-olds successfully use the most explicit and most demanding agreement marker in English, the third-person singular verb form, only 54% of the time when it is called for (Rice & Oetting, 1993), adults do much better. And they do much better even in situations specifically contrived to trip them up (Bock, Eberhard, & Cutting, 2001).

One indicator of the stability of agreement in everyday speech comes from the effects of violations on language comprehension. Although agreement may seem subtle, the impact of mistakes on an audience suggests otherwise. Native English listeners and readers readily detect violations of normal agreement relations (e.g., *The teachers is nice* or *My grandfather like ice cream*), which create disruptions in the movements of the eyes during reading (Pearlmutter, Garnsey, & Bock, 1999) and event-related changes in the electrical activity of the brain (Osterhout & Mobley, 1995, Experiment 3).

So, far from being a fragile linguistic ornament, rarely displayed, and easily broken, agreement belongs to the nuts and bolts of language. That is its psycholinguistic relevance. The goal of this chapter is to examine what we know and, more commonly, do not know about how speakers manage the psycholinguistic challenges of producing grammatical agreement. These challenges involve the topics of meaning, marking, and morphing, which I introduce in the next section.

A. MEANING, MARKING, AND MORPHING IN AGREEMENT

Meaning, marking, and morphing represent three core facets of agreement. *Meaning* shapes communicative intentions. For purposes of number agreement, meaning can provide the notions that motivate number distinctions. *Marking* channels number meaning into the forms of sentences. *Morphing* adapts number morphology to the changing contexts of connected speech, yielding covariations among the forms associated with number agreement. Like the adhesive products of a familiar American three-M company, the three Ms of meaning, marking, and morphing help to glue the separate words of utterances together. Let's look at how they might do this.

1. Meaning in Agreement

The roots of meaning in number agreement, presumably, are the number categorizations that speakers make, whether something is one or more than one. If some object of perception or conception is categorized as "more than one," we might predict that the corresponding referring expression will be plural. Though the exceptions to this simple relationship are legion and the source of knotty problems in formal semantics, the presumed correlation between number categorizations and number in language may play at least three important parts in language. One involves learning, another involves reference, and a third involves syntax in normal language use.

Take learning. The relationship between nonlinguistic number meaning on the one hand and the linguistic marking and morphing associated with number on the other offers a bootstrap, a scaffolding, for learning the language. Differences in the numerosity of objects in the world are perceptible to infants (Starkey, Spelke, & Gelman, 1990). If these perceptible differences are reliably correlated with distinctions between singular and plural in the input language, children may have an easier time learning one basis for the distinction. Especially helpful is the fact that the number differences that languages care about are within human limits on the more-or-less direct apprehension of numerosity, without counting (*subitization*; Dehaene, 1997). Languages like English draw the line between one and more than one. Other languages include a dual, and a few languages contrast one, two, three, and "small but unspecified numbers" against more items (Corbett, 2000). The learnability of such systems should increase to the extent that the perceptual or conceptual information on which they depend is available to infants. Though there is ongoing debate about the ontogeny of number knowledge, from the standpoint of its contribution to language learning it matters little whether it is innate or an early and unavoidable product of experience (Newcombe, 2002). What does matter is that it be universally accessible, preparing infants to deal with any language that makes use of number in its grammar.

A second set of potential benefits from accessible number information is in ordinary communication. Because all of us are able to count small numbers, at least tacitly and whether or not we have been taught to, and because virtually anything can be counted, specifications of the numerosity of things can almost always be employed as a reference device, an attribute of things that can separate them from other things. This makes number a tool that can be used over a wide range of situations. If I point to a picture of two girls and say *she*, you will infer that I am referring to just one of the girls. If I say *they*, you will infer that I am referring to both.

Finally, piggybacking on its putative usefulness as a referential device, number specifications and covariations in number specification (i.e., agreement in number) can signal what things belong together in connected speech. That is, covariations can signal what things modify one another or are coreferential across separate elements within utterances. The covariations in form constitute the signals of the relationship. Such signals are useful because language is rife with discontinuous dependencies. Agreeing elements are not always contiguous (e.g., ***All of the telephones** in the house **are*** *ringing*). Note that number need not be material to the content. In ***Every single telephone** in the house **is** ringing*, agreement is singular despite the number of ringing phones, but the idea behind the utterance remains the same. Agreement fills the bill of tying things together.

So, in addition to having a handy connection to meaning for purposes of reference, number may also give the grammar a general-purpose tool. It can be used in a motivated way, when there is genuinely valuable information about numerosity to be conveyed (*look out, there **are** two of them*). But it can also be effective, in a different way, when it is purely arbitrary, when there is no real conceptual motivation for singular or plural, as long as it is used consistently in a system of covariations. Consistent covariations in agreement features are enforced by the agreement devices of marking and morphing.

2. From Meaning to Marking

Although the singular and plural subjects with which verbs agree appear to have a clear difference in meaning, just as singular and plural pronouns do, the same does not seem to hold for verbs. Whereas *she* and *they* carry different number meanings, *does* and *do* do not. *Does* is not one doing, and *do* is not many doings, nor is *does* transparently a doing by one person or *do* a doing by many (Keeney & Wolfe, 1972). When we describe an event that is the product of a single joint action of a group of people, the number of the verb depends not on the fact that the action is singular and joint, but on how we refer to the people: a legislature *passes* a bill, but legislators *pass* a bill. Likewise, the number of a verb that implies multiple actions (e.g., *drum*) does not depend on whether a specific event actually involves multiple acts, but on how the subject is expressed: a drummer *drums* and so does a drum corps, while drummers *drum*. (Compare the verb forms!) A *drum corps* (singular) comprises *drummers* (plural), but the corps nonetheless *drums* (singular); drummers compose a drum corps, but the drummers *drum* (plural). The difference between the verbs *drums* and *drum* is not the same as the difference between the nouns *drum* and *drums*.

It is hard to escape the conclusion that variations in verb number do not convey number in the way that variations in noun number do. The event-related potentials elicited by agreement violations in language comprehension are relevant here. The changes in brain activity that accompany agreement anomalies differ in timing, in form, and in scalp distribution from those that accompany semantic anomalies (Hagoort, Brown, & Groothusen, 1993; Kutas & Hillyard, 1983). This is consistent with the intuition that disruptions to comprehension from disagreement need not arise from a misunderstanding of meaning. Verb number is numb to number meaning; noun number is sensitive to number meaning.

The relationship between number meaning and verb number is mediated by the subjects of sentences, the part of utterances with which verbs normally agree. This reflects the abstract *marking* of subjects for number, some flag of number to which verbs respond without partaking of any number meaning proper.

3. From Marking to Morphing

Covariations among agreeing elements constitute the overt signals of agreement, and these are the province of *morphing*. Some of these covariations are hard to explain in terms of meaning, pure and simple, which is why something like morphing is needed to adjust words to their grammatical contexts. Most things that can objectively be seen as "more than one" of something, a perceptual plural, can also constitute a conceptual singular, forming a set of some kind (e.g., an orchestra or some furniture). Linguistically, these things may be conveyed either as singulars or as plurals (that is, as singular collectives like *orchestra* or plurals like *musicians*; as singular mass nouns like *furniture* or as plurals like *furnishings*). Something might be conceived and perceived as a singleton, but be conventionally referred to with a plural word (e.g., *underpants*). One thing perceived as a singleton might be referred to as a singleton (e.g., a *bean*) while a very similar thing perceived as a singleton will not work in the same way (e.g., a grain of corn is not a *corn*). Moreover, number categorizations can be wholly irrelevant to what the speaker wants to say. For example, I could have written "number categorization can be wholly irrelevant," with little or no change in your understanding of what I mean.

To make matters worse, some of the covariations involved in agreement are subtle and, inspected closely, paradoxical. You may have noticed by now that the morpheme that specifies plural number on nouns is perfectly homophonous with the morpheme that specifies *singular* number on third-person present-tense regular verbs. The noun *drums* refers to *multiple* instruments while the verb *drums* is used when a *singular* entity performs the drumming. Moreover, verb inflections vary not only for number but for other properties, such as person. *You* may be either singular or plural, but *are* and *do*, both superficially plural verbs, go with *you* regardless.

All of this raises suspicions that English may be the culprit in the numbness of verb number and other oddities of grammar, although the arbitrariness within agreement systems in languages around the world is a perennial linguistic conundrum. It is an interesting question whether the transparency of number morphology makes a difference to the number sense of verbs, but the point here is merely that verb forms cannot be unerringly predicted from number meaning. Instead, the form follows from features of the grammatical context, specifically from the number of the subject (technically, and too generally, from the number of the head noun of the subject noun phrase). Because of this, agreement morphology cannot be directly selected from meanings or directly triggered by the marking that flags meaning. The specific forms used depend on the specific *words* chosen to serve as the subject.

As this suggests, the number distinctions that support agreement systems, which repeatedly come into play in language use, can be next to irrelevant to communication. Many languages manage perfectly well without grammatical contrasts between singulars and plurals, as speakers of Japanese will attest (Li, 1998; Nicol, 1998), and the seemingly spotty realization of number in English tempts the conclusion that it does not matter a lot to us either. Yet we create it almost slavishly. What are we doing?

II. Reaching Agreement

To explain how agreement works in language production, psycholinguistic studies of the mechanisms of agreement have focused on the conceptual and linguistic factors responsible for variations in the use of agreement targets. The method used in most of these studies was first employed by Bock and Miller (1991), and is called sentence-fragment completion. In it, speakers hear a *preamble* consisting of a simple or complex subject noun-phrase. The preamble incorporates variations in number of various kinds. A common kind of variation is illustrated in the set

The baby on the blanket

The baby on the blankets

The babies on the blanket

The babies on the blankets.

The head noun (*baby, babies*) is either singular or plural, and it matches or mismatches the number of a local noun (*blanket, blankets*). The subject noun-phrase is the agreement controller. Speakers repeat and complete the preambles to create full sentences. The completions naturally contain verb forms that can agree or disagree with the subject in number, allowing the effect of the number variations in the agreement controllers to be assessed on the agreement targets.

Variants of the method have been used to examine different kinds of agreement (e.g., verb agreement, pronoun agreement), different features used in agreement (e.g., number agreement, gender agreement), and different languages (Dutch, British and American English, French, German, Italian, and Spanish). There are beginning efforts to explore whether different kinds and features of agreement fulfill similar functions in similar ways, in the form of a few systematic, controlled comparisons of verb and pronoun agreement (Bock, Nicol, & Cutting, 1999; Bock, Eberhard, & Cutting, 2001; Bock, Humphreys, Butterfield, Eberhard, & Cutler, 2003) and of number and gender agreement (van Berkum, Brown, & Hagoort, 1999; Vigliocco, Butterworth, & Semenza, 1995). There are a few cross-language comparisons as well, between Dutch and English (Bock, Eberhard, Cutting, Meyer, & Schriefers, 2001), Dutch and French (Vigliocco, Hartsuiker, Jarema, & Kolk, 1996), Dutch and German (Hartsuiker, Schriefers, Bock, & Kikstra, in press), English and Spanish (Bock, Carreiras, Meseguer, & Octigan, 2003; Vigliocco, Butterworth, & Garrett, 1996), and French and Italian (Vigliocco & Franck, 1999, 2001).

In the remainder of the chapter I sketch the empirical case for whether and how meaning, marking, and morphing matter in agreement. Where possible and where relevant I draw on the comparative studies just cited involving different agreement types, agreement features, and languages. Of necessity, the main emphasis is on findings from work concerned with single types of agreement (primarily verb or adjective agreement), single sets of agreement features (number or gender), and single languages. That is what most of the research is about.

A. MEANING

The role of meaning in agreement is controversial because a stereotypic view in linguistics is that agreement is purely grammatical. That view is suspect on both observational and logical grounds. Morgan (1972) detailed a range of examples in which agreement conveys semantic information. For example, if a waiter tells the short-order cook that "The ham-and-eggs at table 5 *is* getting impatient," the *is* reflects the singular number of the referent, the patron, and not the plural number of *ham and eggs*. Logically, speakers begin with meaning in the messages they intend to convey, and those meanings appear to include agreement-relevant information. It would be odd for one to have nothing to do with the other.

What they have to do with each other, and how, is less easy to explain. One interpretation was proposed by Vigliocco and Hartsuiker (2002), who argued that the computation of agreement uses all of the relevant information available, including information about nonlinguistic meaning. They called this the *maximal input* hypothesis, and contrasted it with what they dubbed *minimal input*. The minimal input hypothesis, a version of which was proposed by Bock, Eberhard, Cutting, Meyer, and Schriefers (2001) argues that the computation of agreement has to start with meaning, but that the mechanism that implements agreement can proceed without direct semantic influence, under control of syntactic formulation. The idea is that what the mechanism does (create singular or plural agreement) is determined by meaning, but how it does it is not. Bock, Eberhard, and Cutting (2001) called this the marking-and-morphing (M&M) approach.

To assess whether and how meaning drives the production of agreement, psycholinguistic research has concentrated on three major issues. One is whether variations in notional number (number in the speaker's referent model) influence subject-verb number agreement in ways that would not be predicted from the syntactic or grammatical properties of the agreeing elements. The semantic properties that have received the most attention are *distributivity* and *semantic integration*. The second question is whether different dimensions of agreement (number, gender) reflect the involvement or noninvolvement of meaning in comparable ways. Here, a distinction between *intrinsic* and *extrinsic* features of agreement becomes important. The third is whether meaning matters differently to different types of agreement *targets* (verbs, pronouns).

1. Distributivity and Semantic Integration in Agreement

Distributivity. The property of distributivity is illustrated in Figure 1. Grammatically singular phrases such as *the picture on the postcards* can denote multiple entities (the postcards) that share a property (namely, the same picture). The consequence is that the abstract referent of the phrase (the picture-type) ranges over multiple concrete tokens (postcards), creating multiple instances in the mental model. Other grammatically singular phrases such as *the key for the doors* are more likely to be construed as referring to a single concrete entity (a key) that fits multiple doors. In terms of the mental models behind the phrases, *the picture on the postcards* will have multiple tokens of the same type (pictures), whereas *the key for the doors* will have but one token of the relevant type (a key). Despite this underlying difference, the expected agreement pattern is a singular verb, since the head of the subject noun-phrase is singular.

A preliminary assessment of the effects of distributivity on verb-number agreement in English was reported by Bock and Miller (1991), who found no differences in number for verbs produced with subjects like *the key for the doors* compared with *the picture on the postcards*. They suggested that subtle notional variations (like distributivity) may have little impact on agreement when the grammatical number of the subject noun-phrase remains the same.

Later work challenged this result. Eberhard (1999) found that distributivity did create more plural agreement when the referent of the subject

Distributive, notional plural referent
the picture on the postcards

Nondistributive, notional singular referent
the key for the doors

Fig. 1. Illustration of distributive and nondistributive situations.

noun-phrase was made more concrete or imageable. Humphreys and Bock (in press) found a significant 8% increase in plural verb agreement with distributive subjects, even when the lexical differences associated with distributive and nondistributive contexts were minimized. These results are more consistent with maximal than minimal input.

Distributivity effects on number agreement have also been observed in other languages. Because some of these languages have different and in many ways more challenging agreement requirements than English, an intriguing question is whether the speakers of such languages are more alert to variations in notional number than English speakers. Vigliocco, Butterworth, and Semenza (1995) proposed that languages in which sentence subjects are often unexpressed (such as Spanish and Italian) may reveal more sensitivity to notional number than languages in which subjects are normally expressed (such as Dutch and English). The idea is that if the subject is not mentioned, speakers may have to retrieve the number information needed for agreement from the conceptual representation.

Several experiments have tested this hypothesis in Italian, Spanish, Dutch, and French, with mixed results. Though Italian and Spanish revealed stronger notional effects than English (Vigliocco, Butterworth, & Garrett, 1996), so did Dutch and French (Vigliocco, Hartsuiker, Jarema, & Kolk, 1996), where subjects are normally expressed. This contradicts the unexpressed-subject proposal.

An alternative suggestion is that languages with richer morphology and greater freedom of constituent order depend more on number meaning than languages with sparse morphology and rigid order (Vigliocco & Hartsuiker, 2002). Here, the argument is that the number information associated with the subject may often have to be retrieved *before* the subject is lexicalized in order to implement agreement. To test this, Bock, Carreiras, Meseguer, and Octigan (2003) compared subject-verb number agreement in English and Spanish. English requires the expression of subjects, has sparse agreement morphology, and rigid word order; Spanish allows subjects to be unexpressed, has rich agreement morphology, and more flexible word order. Accordingly, Spanish speakers should be more sensitive to number meanings than English speakers.

Bock, Carreiras, Meseguer, and Octigan (2003) used the sentence-fragment completion task with native speakers of English and Spanish, employing translation-equivalent preambles. (Most other language comparisons have used different materials in each language, weakening the test.) The speakers saw preambles that they repeated and completed extemporaneously, with whatever came to mind, and in doing so they almost always produced a verb form. The critical manipulation involved distributivity. Half the experimental preambles had distributive construals, meaning that the speaker's referent model would contain multiple tokens of the subject noun-phrase (e.g., *the picture on the postcards*). The other half were nondistributive, biasing a construal with a single-token referent (e.g., *the key for the doors*). Bock et al. examined the incidence of plural verb-agreement in the completions, assessed relative to a control condition with singular local nouns (e.g., *postcard, door*). Notice that in both cases the expected verb number is singular.

The results were straightforward, with nearly identical agreement patterns in English and Spanish. Speakers of both languages were sensitive to variations in distributivity, and to the same degree. Spanish speakers produced 16% plural verbs after distributive subjects and 7% after nondistributive. English speakers produced 16% plural verbs after distributive and 6% after nondistributive subjects.

The findings discourage the view that languages with different morphological demands create different sensitivities to number meaning in their speakers. Instead, they argue that *despite* the different morphological demands of Spanish and English, their speakers use number meaning in the same ways. Equally important is the evidence that speakers do use number meaning in agreement. Plural meaning increased plural agreement by a little less than 10% even when the grammatical number of the subject was singular.

Semantic integration. There is a second notional number property whose effects on agreement have been clearly and carefully established by Solomon and Pearlmutter (in press). *Semantic integration* refers to how conceptually unified or cohesive the elements of a subject noun-phrase are. For example, a *bracelet of gold nuggets* is a single integrated object; a *bracelet with gold nuggets* might be a single object, but one in which there is something more than gold nuggets in the bracelet. That is, the bracelet and the gold nuggets are not co-extensive.

Semantic integrity in some ways seems like the opposite of distributivity, inasmuch as it has to do with how well the properties of an object cohere. If integrity and distributivity are conceptual opposites, they could be treated as different ends of the same dimension. Consistent with this, Humphreys and Bock (in press) collected semantic integration ratings for phrases that varied in distributivity, and found that distributive phrases tended to be rated as less semantically integrated than nondistributive phrases. Solomon and Pearlmutter, however, found that more integrated phrases *increased* the use of plural agreement, whereas Humphreys and Bock found that distributive (and less integrated) phrases were more likely to elicit plural agreement than nondistributive (and more integrated) phrases. This suggests that semantic integrity and distributivity may represent separate sources of notional number valuation.

2. *Intrinsic and Extrinsic Agreement Control*

The role of meaning in agreement may depend on what kind of agreement is involved. For number, the semantic correlates are slippery but undeniable. Gender in English is similar to number in having a fairly clear semantic correlate, in the form of biological sex. In other respects, the gender system is much more restricted than the number system. In most cases, variations in gender for purposes of reference and agreement occur only among pronouns. The frequency of pronoun use gives this variation considerable communicative value nevertheless, offering benefits for learning and using the gender system, and serving both referential and linking functions.

In other languages, gender systems can be more elaborate and extend to inanimate as well as animate objects. This has the interesting consequence that, except for most biologically gendered things, learning the gender system must proceed with the help of linguistic cues to gender class. Phonological differences in the words sometimes seem to help (see Kelly, 1992, for review). So do category consistencies in gender membership. For instance, the names for metals in Dutch belong to just one gender. However, the most consistent cue may be the grammatical covariations that accompany words from different gender categories. These covariations can be a more reliable way to discover whatever meaning consistencies there are to be found, instead of the other way around (Maratsos & Chalkley, 1981).

Disparities between grammatical gender and grammatical number in their sources of semantic support normally make gender an intrinsically governed agreement feature and number an extrinsically governed feature (Corbett, 1998). Intrinsic features are bound to particular words rather than to conceptual distinctions; extrinsic features reflect conceptual distinctions. For instance, nothing about the concept of *bicycle* in Dutch determines whether it is one gender or the other (and in fact, there are two synonymous nouns meaning *bicycle* that differ in gender). However, there is an obvious conceptual distinction between one bicycle and more than one bicycle that is realized as a singular/plural distinction, and its realization is the same for both *bicycle* words.

Correlated with extrinsic features (for which number is the prototype) is the property of *variability*. Most words can be either singular or plural, so they accept both values of the number feature. However, as the word *intrinsic* implies, gender feature values for most individual words are invariable. If the word for *house* happens to be neuter, there will be no sensible way to make it masculine or feminine that does not make it something other than a house.

Though grammatical number and grammatical gender are the prototypes, respectively, of extrinsic and intrinsic feature categories, there are exceptions to extrinsicality in number and intrinsicality in gender. In English, although the majority of nouns can be either singular or plural, there are nouns that are rarely or never plural (e.g., invariant singulars such as *silverware* and *news*) and nouns that are rarely or never singular (e.g., invariant plurals such as *suds, pliers,* and *people*). In languages with grammatical gender, there can be word stems whose gender varies depending on the biological gender of the referent, making their gender extrinsic. In French, for example, there is a ready feminine version for biologically masculine nouns ending in /n/: *Lionne, gamine, championne, chienne, patronne,* and so on are feminine lions, urchins, champions, dogs, and patrons.

This creates a cross-cutting distinction that may affect how number and gender operate with respect to reference and agreement. For both number and gender, there are words that vary in form depending on conceptual, sometimes even perceptible, properties of their referents. For both number and gender, there are words that do not vary in predictable ways depending on conceptual or perceptual features. With respect to this distinction, the main difference between number and gender is that number is more often extrinsic than intrinsic, whereas gender in grammatical-gender languages has more opportunities to be intrinsic.

Linguistically, number and gender morphology and agreement work differently within the languages that have them, particularly in terms of the covariations in which they participate. The covariations involve, on one hand, what controls the number or gender features (agreement controllers) and, on the other hand, what takes on the number or gender features as a consequence (agreement targets). For example, in English, Dutch, and German, number is specified on and controlled by subject nouns; verbs are the main number agreement targets. In Dutch and German, nouns also carry gender information, but their agreement targets are different than the targets for number. Gender controls the forms of determiners and adjectives and pronouns but not verbs.

Accordingly, gender and number agreement are entwined in two different grammatical systems. However, the cross-cutting distinction in semantic motivation behind intrinsic and extrinsic features could have similar consequences for how agreement works psycholinguistically. That is, intrinsic features may work differently from extrinsic features, and do so regardless of the agreement system, whether number or gender. If so, it would suggest a cognitively motivated link between the semantic referential functions of number and gender and the grammatical agreement functions of number and gender (Bock, Eberhard, Cutting, Meyer, & Schriefers, 2001; Bock, Eberhard, & Cutting, 2001).

Extrinsic gender and number have been found to control agreement more reliably than intrinsic gender and number. Vigliocco and Franck (1999, 2001) showed that, in French and Italian, adjective agreement with human nouns was more reliable than with inanimate nouns, but only when the referent's sex was congruent with the noun's gender. To examine the analogous question for number, Middleton and Bock (2003) compared the presumably extrinsic singulars and plurals of count nouns to more arbitrary, less semantically motivated singulars (mass nouns) and invariant plurals. Mass nouns were decidedly more error-prone than their singular count counterparts.

This points again to a role for notional information in agreement. However, variations in the effects indicate that the role is not simple. In Middleton and Bock's data (2003), there were no consistent differences between the invariant and count plurals. Vigliocco and Franck (1999, Experiment 2) found variations in the magnitude of conceptual effects for different head-noun genders in French. Unlike Italian, where masculines and feminines displayed similar conceptual effects, in French the effect tended to be weaker for masculine than for feminine head nouns. It remains to be determined when and why such variations occur, but their existence makes it clear that there is more to the story than variations in conceptual input.

3. Meaning and the Targets of Agreement

A complementary approach to the psycholinguistic workings of agreement is to compare different kinds of agreement targets, including verbs and pronouns. Subject-verb number agreement and pronoun-antecedent number agreement share roots in linguistic history (Givón, 1976) to which some of the similarities in their agreement behavior can be traced. Semantically, both turn on a distinction between "one thing" and "more than one thing." For verbs and pronouns alike, what carries and superficially controls the number distinction is a nominal, which has been attributed by some to the referential function of agreement (Lehmann, 1988). For verbs, the nominal is almost always a subject noun-phrase; for pronouns, it is typically a subject noun-phrase (Garnham, 2001). Verbs and pronouns are both members of the so-called *closed class*, which tend to behave differently from open-class elements in language performance (Garrett, 1982; Herron & Bates, 1997; Stemberger, 1984), language acquisition (Gleitman & Wanner, 1982), and language breakdown (Bates & Wulfeck, 1989). Some linguists argue that there are no good reasons for distinguishing verb and pronoun agreement (Barlow, 1991; Lehmann, 1988) and in one influential grammatical theory, the basic mechanisms of verb and pronoun agreement are the same (Pollard & Sag, 1994, Chapter 2).

For all of these reasons, verbs and pronouns might be expected to carry the same one-or-more-than-one information under the same circumstances. However, they do not. Verb number can differ from pronoun number even when they have the same controllers (Bock, Nicol, & Cutting, 1999; Bock, Eberhard, & Cutting, 2001) and even, brooking unacceptability, in the same utterances. In "We can live with the errors that classification software *make* when *its* output is subsequently reviewed by hand" (Nunberg, 2003) the verb that agrees with *software* is plural while the pronoun is singular, and in "One day your child *turns* 16 and you let *them* borrow the keys to the wagon" (cited by Safire, 1994) the verb that agrees with *child* is singular and the pronoun is plural. Most important, pronouns seem to be more sensitive than verbs to extrinsic number meanings in both American and British English (Bock, Eberhard, & Cutting, 2001; Bock, Nicol, & Cutting, 1999; Bock, Humphreys, Butterfield, Eberhard, & Cutler, 2003), consistent with the numb-number nature of verbs. The implication is that different processes may be at work. This finds further support in results which show that verb agreement has different cognitive demands than pronoun agreement (Almor, MacDonald, Kempler, Andersen, & Tyler, 2001; Bock, 2003).

One reason why verbs and pronouns might differ is the natural distributional differences between them. Verbs tend to immediately follow their controllers; pronouns do not. Verbs are controlled by elements in the same clause; pronouns can be controlled by elements in different clauses. These distributional properties create different temporal and structural distances between controllers and targets in verb and pronoun agreement. However, holding these properties constant does not eliminate the agreement variations (Bock, Nicol, & Cutting, 1999; Bock, Humphreys, Butterfield, Eberhard, & Cutler, 2003). In short, verb number agreement and pronoun number agreement can differ even when the verbs and pronouns have the same controllers.

To summarize, meaning does matter in agreement. However, there are variations in the realization of number meaning in agreement, both in the differences associated with extrinsic and intrinsic agreement features and in the differences between verb and pronoun agreement. These variations make it necessary to look at mechanisms that might modulate the realization of agreement. One of these is *marking*.

B. MARKING

Although there is considerable evidence that number meaning matters to agreement, the evidence falls short of saying that meaning is *all* that matters in agreement. In particular, the differences between verb and pronoun agreement imply that there is more notional number information available than verbs actually use. The workings of intrinsic and extrinsic agreement features imply that agreement can occur in the absence of semantic support, sometimes without substantial differences from semantically supported agreement.

There is a third phenomenon of agreement that argues for something other than meaning at work, and illuminates what that something may be. In *attraction*, the number of an agreement target reflects the number of a noun other than the normal controller. For instance, in *The use of cellular phones and pagers are prohibited,* the verb *are* is plural, whereas the subject *use,* is singular. The plural verb seems to have fallen under the influence of the neighboring plurals, which I call the *local* nouns.

Is this influence the same as agreement? That is, will anything that separates the "real" subject from its verb take over control of agreement? The answer to this question is clearly no. Bock and Miller (1991) and other studies of attraction since have shown that plurals are much more likely to attract agreement than singulars. Further, the plural meanings behind local nouns are much less important to attraction than they are to agreement. For instance, singular collectives and even mass nouns tend to elicit plural-agreeing verbs (Bock et al., 1999), but as local nouns they create no more attraction than corresponding singulars (Bock & Eberhard, 1993; Bock, Eberhard, & Cutting, 2001).

Gender attraction also occurs (Meyer & Bock, 1999) but it, too, is less susceptible to the semantic than the grammatical features of the attractor. Franck and Bock (2003) compared the attractiveness of animate local nouns that bore consistent grammatical and biological gender to animate local nouns that bore uninformative grammatical gender, and found no differences between them. This, too, contrasts with the difference found for agreement: grammatical gender on its own is a less reliable agreement controller than the combination of grammatical with biological gender (Vigliocco & Franck, 1999, 2001).

Surprisingly, these same patterns occur when pronouns are attracted to their neighbors. Recall that pronouns are more sensitive to the meanings of their controllers in agreement. But in attraction, pronouns behave like verbs. Plural matters more than singular, but it is not semantic plurality that matters so much as grammatical plurality (Bock, Eberhard, & Cutting, 2001). In attraction, then, we see that the control of verb and pronoun number is very similar, but the nature of the control seems to differ from what goes on in agreement.

So, what does agreement have that attraction lacks (or vice versa)? The M&M proposal is that agreement is set into motion by the notional or conceptual information behind an utterance, whereas attraction occurs at a time when this information is less accessible or unavailable (for present purposes, it does not matter which). The function of the marking mechanism is to ensure that notional number is linguistically preserved on the elements that control agreement. The mechanism does this by marking the relevant linguistic territory with a number value. The relevant territory is the plan for the subject noun phrase. This marking is distinct (but obviously not independent) from the processes that cause words to be plural: Lexical retrieval processes are also sensitive to notional number, but they implement word-finding. To oversimplify, marking is a syntactic mechanism. Because marking and lexical retrieval are different, a plural-marked subject is likely to have a plural head noun, but it need not; a singular-marked subject is likely to have a singular head noun, but it need not.

How does marking capture the differences between agreement and attraction? Recall that there are two crucial distinctions. First, agreement is sensitive to the notional properties of agreement controllers; attraction is insensitive to the notional properties of attractors. Second, pronouns are more sensitive than verbs to the notional properties of agreement controllers, but just as insensitive as verbs to the notional properties of attractors.

The explanation for the first difference is in terms of how notional information is grammatically preserved. Structural marking is hypothesized to maintain notional number in a form that makes the number value accessible to agreement targets. The plan or scheme for a subject-as-a-whole bears the number marking. Its individual components do not, barring embedding and other complexities. Consequently, the plan for an entire subject phrase such as *the team in the commercials* will carry a singular or plural marking that reflects the underlying notional-number representation, but the modifying phrase *the commercials* will not normally be marked independently. Though *the commercials* is plural, it lacks an external agreement target (it is merely a supporting actor, reinforcing or defining the role played by the subject as a whole) and so it lacks marking.

Because the apparent controllers of attraction are local nouns, only their lexical specifications (as singulars or plurals) are available to influence verb number. If the lexical specification differs from the notional number (as it can when the local noun is a member of a class of number-peculiars, such as invariant plurals), the attracted number need not correspond to the relevant notional number.

A finding that might be seen as a challenge to the marking hypothesis comes from the results of an experiment by Hartsuiker, Antón-Méndez, and van Zee (2001). Hartsuiker et al. showed that a grammatically plural object noun-phrase (which preceded the verb, as objects readily do in Dutch) produced attraction. This is an important finding. Attraction normally comes from phrases embedded within subjects, but Hartsuiker et al.'s results suggest that being associated with the subject is not necessary for attraction to occur. However, marking is not the mechanism of attraction; it is the mechanism by which notional plurality is conveyed into the syntax. Hartsuiker et al. were concerned only with attraction from grammatical plurality, and marking is not necessary for a grammatically plural noun-phrase to serve as an attractor: the attractor simply has to get its number to the verb, which is the province of morphing. Damage to the marking hypothesis would, however, come from evidence for attraction to the notional value of a phrase that lacked an independent agreement target.

The explanation for the different behaviors of pronouns and verbs with respect to agreement has to do with how pronouns and verbs get number in the first place. Verbs have numb number, acquiring it indirectly via agreement. Pronouns have "live" number, getting it in the first instance directly from the notional number of the pronoun's referent in the message. The implication is that pronouns have two sources of number, one of them the number in the message, which, as words, they acquire naturally during lexicalization, and a second the grammatical number of their linguistic controller in the clause. This makes pronouns more sensitive to notional

TABLE I

NOUN PHRASES ILLUSTRATING DIFFERENCES OF NOTIONAL NUMBER AND GRAMMATICAL NUMBER IN SUBJECTS AND LOCAL NOUNS

Subject number differences	Local-noun number differences
1. Notionally plural, grammatically singular subject: *The army with the incompetent commander* 2. Notionally singular, grammatically singular subject: *The soldier with the incompetent commander*	3. Notionally plural, grammatically singular local noun: *The strength of the army* 4. Notionally singular, grammatically singular local noun: *The strength of the soldier* 5. Notionally singular, grammatically plural local noun: *The view through the binoculars* 6. Notionally plural, grammatically plural local noun: *The view through the telescopes*

variations than verbs (by virtue of getting number directly) and equally sensitive to attraction, where the source of number is a spurious controller, the local noun.

Evidence for the marking hypothesis was found in a series of experiments by Bock, Eberhard, and Cutting (2001). They compared verb and pronoun number agreement across a range of notional and grammatical variations, illustrated in Table I. The notional number variations included manipulations of the number meaning of the head noun, the entire subject noun phrase, and the local noun. The grammatical number variations involved the head and local noun. Four predictions from the marking hypothesis were tested, two for agreement (number control of the agreement target by the subject noun-phrase) and two for attraction (number control of the agreement target by the local noun):

(a) In agreement, when notional-number variations occur in the referent of the subject noun-phrase, the notional number will affect both verb and pronoun number. So, the notionally plural, grammatically singular subjects illustrated in examples 1 and 2 in Table I should elicit more plural verbs and more plural pronouns than the notionally singular, grammatically singular subjects.

(b) In agreement, notional effects on pronouns will be greater than on verbs. So, the notionally plural, grammatically singular subjects illustrated in Table I should elicit more plural pronouns than plural verbs.

(c) In attraction, if a notional variation involves only the local noun, only the grammatical number of the local noun will affect verb and pronoun number. So, only grammatical plural local nouns (examples 5 and 6 in Table I) should elicit attraction, relative to the grammatical singulars (examples 3 and 4), and the difference between 3 and 6 should be the same as the difference between 4 and 5.

(d) In attraction, the effect of grammatical number will be the same for verbs and pronouns. So, the predictions in (c) hold equally for verbs and pronouns.

Figure 2 summarizes the results from six experiments that tested these predictions. The top panel of the figure shows the impact on agreement and attraction of adding grammatical plurality to the heads and local nouns of

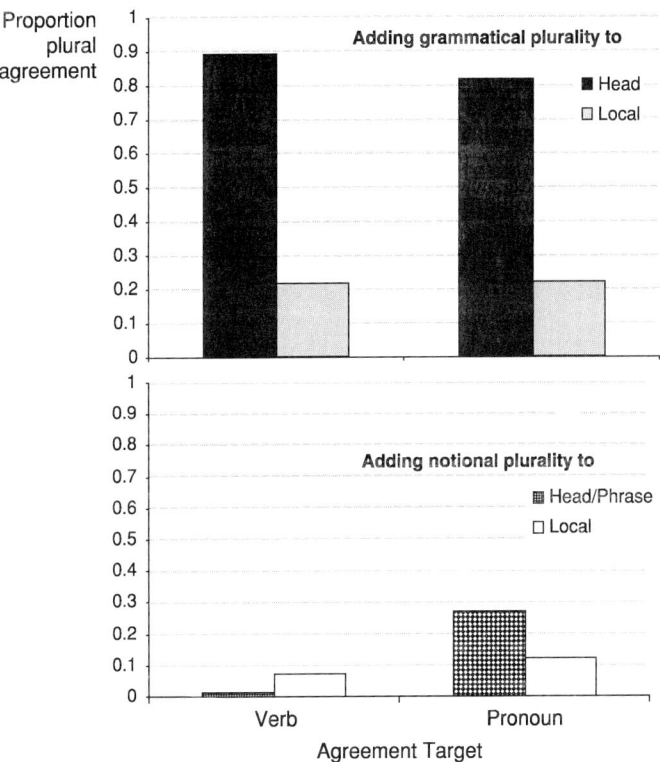

Fig. 2. Effects of grammatical and notional plurality on plural agreement in verbs and pronouns. Upper panel shows average effect on plural agreement of adding grammatical plurality to grammatically singular heads and local nouns of an agreement controller; lower panel shows average effect on plural agreement of adding notional plurality to notionally singular phrases and heads or local nouns of an agreement controller (from Bock, Eberhard, & Cutting, 2001).

subject noun phrases. It shows similar effects for verbs and pronouns. Grammatical plurality normally combines notional and grammatical number, of course, and the bottom panel of the figure displays the effect of notional plurality on its own. Here, the effect is similar for verbs and pronouns when the local noun was notionally plural, and the effect is vanishingly small. When the subject as a whole was notionally plural, pronouns are more likely than verbs to reflect it.

This is strong support for the marking hypothesis, and big trouble for a maximalist view of agreement. The difference between pronouns and verbs in notional number sensitivity, and the difference between subject noun phrases and local noun phrases in notional impact suggest that there is number meaning available that could affect agreement, and should, according to the maximalist hypothesis. But something moderates the effect of number meaning.

Thornton and MacDonald (2003) contested this claim with data from a clever experiment showing that the plausibility of local nouns affects attraction. Speakers performed a task in which they had to create passive sentences using specific verb forms. For example, speakers saw the verb form *played* displayed on the screen and then heard the phrase *The album by the classical composers*. Other speakers saw the word *praised* and heard the same phrase. Notice that *played* is a highly plausible thing to be done to an album; it is not a highly plausible thing to be done to a composer. However, *praising* can be done to either. If these predictability relationships (Keil, 1979) matter to attraction, there should be more attraction from the local noun when the verb is *praised* than when it is *played*. That was what happened: speakers were more likely to say *The album by the classical composers were praised* than *The album by the classical composers were played*.

This is an interesting and informative result, but it does not address the central M&M point, which has to do with where the *number* that is used in agreement comes from and what kind of number it is. In both conditions, the spurious number came from the grammatical plural of the local noun, which is completely consistent with the M&M prediction. What would be inconsistent with M&M is a demonstration that the notional number of a plausible local noun creates attraction.

Still, the difference between the conditions in Thornton and MacDonald's work shows nicely that something more than grammatical number can modulate attraction, and the plausibility of predication looks like one of them. The mechanism of modulation remains to be established. One question is whether it reflects plausibility per se or a correlated surface property of plausibility. For instance, plausible subjects and predicates tend to occur, creating collocational, associative relationships that may perturb agreement operations.

The marking hypothesis has not been as thoroughly evaluated for gender as for number, but there are indications that it works there, too. As already noted, Vigliocco and Franck (1999, 2001) showed that consistency in the biological and grammatical gender of head nouns affects agreement; Franck and Bock (2003) found that the same consistency does not modulate attraction.

So far, what has gone into this story about agreement are a couple sources of agreement features (notional and grammatical), a couple vehicles of notional features (syntactic marking and lexical retrieval), a couple ways in which features can take control of targets (agreement and attraction), and a couple of targets of control (verbs and pronouns). What is still missing is how a target succumbs to a controller, or *morphs*.

C. MORPHING

The mechanism that actually implements grammatical agreement is called *morphing* in the M&M framework. Its function is to specify number or gender on an agreement target. It determines whether the verb target of a particular number controller will be *is* or *are*, *drums* or *drum*, or *played*. It determines whether the pronoun target of a number controller will be *it* or *them*, *she* or *they*, *I* or *we*, or *you*.

There are two fundamentally different ways in which separate elements of an utterance can come to bear the same agreement features. Only one of them involves morphing. Morphing is required when the feature value of one element in an utterance must be duplicated on another element, so that an agreement controller (a linguistic antecedent) and an agreement target within the utterance are involved. Subject-verb agreement is a clear instance of this kind of relationship: the number of the subject determines the number of the verb. A second mechanism can yield the same result in a different way: the feature values of two constituents of an utterance can be jointly specified by the same message element. To distinguish this from morphing, I call it *concord*. In M&M the similar features of antecedents and pronouns are rooted in concord, because both refer to a common message element. Similarly, in a sentence such as *she is my niece,* *she* and *my niece* share features because they co-refer, though they do not agree in a grammatical sense. However, when antecedents and pronouns stand in a structural relationship (i.e., when a pronoun and its antecedent occur in the same sentence), morphing comes into play. That is how attraction happens.

Verbs and pronouns can both undergo morphing under the influence of a controller. Pronouns, in addition, reflect concord. Concord comes about simply enough, when different words are retrieved at different times to refer to the same thing and share features by virtue of doing so. Morphing is harder to explain. Three empirical questions have been asked about how a controller comes to impose its features on its agreement targets, or how it *morphs* them. The questions have to do with the *representation* of control features, their *transmission* (how features get from the controller to the target), and the *scope* of morphing (how far it extends or what its domain is).

1. The Representation of Agreement Features

The first issue has to do with how the agreement features of words or morphemes are stored and represented. What makes *people* plural and *news* (for example) singular? This question intersects with an ongoing debate in psycholinguistics about the nature of lexical representation and grammatical rules. The debate is over the cognitive underpinnings of rule-like behavior in language, and whether the explanation of such behavior requires the mental representation of rules that operate on abstract linguistic variables (Marcus, 1998; Pinker, 1999). A leading alternative to mental rules for language is a rich, distributed lexical memory in which regular and irregular, inflected and uninflected words are stored in a uniform way and retrieved when needed under the control of meaning, with no need for inflectional rules (Plaut, McClelland, Seidenberg, & Patterson, 1996; Seidenberg & McClelland, 1989).

One way to address this question is to ask whether the morphological features of words, the features that control agreement, can do so separately (or separably) from the words in which they occur. To the degree that they do, it suggests that features such as grammatical number values can operate as variables in linguistic rules. Attraction is a useful way of examining this question, because the features involved are positioned noncanonically with respect to one another. If the occurrence of attraction depends heavily on the specific words or word forms involved, it would suggest that the role of agreement rules might at least be secondary to lexical associations. Alternatively, if attraction reflects changes in abstract number properties that come and go irrespective of specific word forms, something more rule-like and general may be involved.

To address this, Bock and Eberhard (1993) used the sentence-fragment-completion task to test a series of hypotheses about the roles of lexical phonology and regular and irregular morphology in attraction. If number is directly associated with word forms, singulars that sound plural (such as *hose* and *tax*) might be expected to create more attraction than singulars that do not sound plural (such as *hoe*). Bock and Eberhard's results suggested that 'sounding plural' was, on its own, insufficient to attract verb agreement: words like *hose* and *tax* created not a single incidence of plural attraction. In addition, regular and irregular plurals (e.g., *rats* compared to *mice*) both created attraction, to nearly equal degrees (there was one more instance of regular than irregular attraction). This argues for plural features being to a considerable extent abstract.

Haskell and MacDonald (2003) carried out two similar experiments in which they examined attraction to regular and irregular local nouns. Like Bock and Eberhard (1993, Experiment 3), in their second experiment they found no significant differences between regulars and irregulars, although the magnitude of the difference was larger than Bock and Eberhard's. In their third experiment, however, they obtained a significant difference by using collective head nouns in the subject noun-phrases (e.g., *the family of mice*).

Haskell and MacDonald (2003) concluded that the form of the word that carries the plural does indeed matter to number, but there are weaknesses in their experiments that make this conclusion suspect. There were no singular controls for the regular and irregular plurals, so the baseline differences in plural verb production are unknown. With collective head nouns, distributive meanings come into play (see section "Distributivity and Semantic Integration in Agreement"). It is probable that irregular plurals are less powerful at eliciting distributive construals than regular plurals, due to the nature of their typical referents (Tiersma, 1982), creating a difference in number meaning between the conditions. Finally, one of the eight irregular plurals used in Haskell and MacDonald's experiment was *people*, which differs from the other irregulars in having no singular form (and was the only irregular that differed from the irregulars used by Bock and Eberhard). *People* is an invariant or intrinsic plural, and intrinsic agreement features (as we have seen) can be weaker than extrinsic features in all agreement and attraction relationships.

Bock, Eberhard, Cutting, Meyer, and Schriefer (2001) demonstrated the impact of plural invariance in experiments that assessed the effects of number-meaning differences. In English, invariant plurals like *binoculars* are less attractive than the regular plural *telescopes* (which has a singular counterpart) and the invariant *suds* is less attractive than *bubbles*. That this has little to do with the meaning of *binoculars* and its invariant counterparts was shown in a companion experiment in Dutch. In Dutch, the plural word for *binoculars* is regular and has a normal singular alternative (*verrekijker* is a single pair of binoculars and *verrekijkers* are two or more pairs of binoculars). In Dutch, unlike English, plural *verrekijkers* behaved just like plural telescopes (*telescopen*). This suggests that there is, indeed, something different about irregular plurals, but it is not in their morphological irregularity. Rather, it is their intrinsic plurality that matters, which implicates the irregularity of their semantics (having no normal singular sense) as much as the irregularity of their morphology.

The most basic question about the representation of agreement features has to do with the nature of grammatical number. When we say that *scissors* is syntactically plural but notionally singular, that *hair* in its scalp-covering sense is syntactically singular but notionally plural (unlike French, for example, where *hair* [*chevaux*] is syntactically as well as semantically plural), where does the grammatical number come from? It cannot be marking, if marking is rooted in meaning. Bock et al. (2003) addressed this in a comparison of American and British English. British English speakers are much more likely than American speakers to treat collective nouns as plurals with respect to verb agreement, saying, for example, *the team were beaten in the last seconds of the match* and *the government are inviting a crisis of confidence*.

Bock et al. explored various explanations for this difference, including whether American and British speakers differ in sensitivity to notional number in general and whether British speakers are more likely to discriminate between the alternative number senses of collectives (as referring to a single set or to a group). Neither of these hypotheses was supported. Instead, the results of experiments and corpus comparisons of British and American collective agreement converged on the conclusion that British speakers are more likely than Americans to treat collectives as invariant plurals, similar to the noun *people*. Not all collectives are treated this way, nor do all speakers treat the same sets of collectives as plurals. But it is the words themselves that seem to be specified as plurals. In short, the lexical entries for words, at least for intrinsically featured words, may indicate their grammatical or conventional agreement value. This feature of the lexical entry is a number *specification*.

One of the unequivocal findings in the psycholinguistics of agreement production is that, in English, singular and plural grammatical number are not created equal. Bock and Miller (1991) showed that attraction to plural local nouns is very much more likely than attraction to singulars (relative to controls), a result that has been replicated dozens of times and is known as the *singular-plural asymmetry*.

Bock and Eberhard (1993) and Eberhard (1997) explained this asymmetry in terms of how singular and plural number are specified. Plural nouns have a specification. They get their specification either intrinsically, as part of their lexical entry, or more often, from a plural inflection (which can be realized either regularly or irregularly). Singular nouns lack a specification, unless they are intrinsically singular (like mass nouns or other invariant singulars). That is, unless they are semantically irregular, lacking a singular/plural linguistic alternation, singulars may be unspecified for number. Eberhard (1997) tested and confirmed this hypothesis in a series of fragment completion experiments. Eberhard found a reduction in the singular-plural asymmetry when singular local nouns were overtly specified as singulars (e.g., with a quantifier such as *one*), but no increase in plural attraction when plural local nouns were similarly flagged (e.g., with *many*). The inference is that plural local nouns have something that singulars lack, and that something is a number specification.

Results for pronoun agreement lead to the same conclusions about the representation of grammatical number. Pronouns behave just like verbs with respect to the number specifications of local nouns, revealing the same singular/plural asymmetry and the same differences between intrinsic and extrinsic number in English (Bock, Eberhard, & Cutting, 2001).

Dutch and German display patterns of attraction much like those in English (Hartsuiker, Schriefers, Bock, & Kikstra, in press), consistent with the three languages' similarities in number morphology and agreement control. Other languages might be expected to differ depending on their morphological systems, and they do. In Italian, Vigliocco, Butterworth, and Semenza (1995) found scarce evidence for a singular/plural asymmetry in attraction. Unlike English, the stems of many nouns in Italian have to be inflected for both singular and plural number, as a consequence of the gender system. For instance, the basic-level nouns meaning *child* or *friend* must be inflected for both singular and plural number and masculine and feminine gender, so that children come as boy-child, girl-child, boy-children, and girl-children (for example).

What about the representation of grammatical gender features? In work on gender attraction, it appears that gender features, like number features, vary in whether or how they are specified. This leads to asymmetries in the strength of attraction to masculine and feminine (for instance) features on local nouns, with the size and direction of the asymmetries varying depending on the languages involved (see Franck & Bock, 2003 and Vigliocco & Franck, 1999 for French, and Meyer & Bock, 1999 for Dutch).

An important question that is not yet settled in this work is whether the morphological specifications of grammatical gender are abstract in the way that number specifications are, and do not vary simply because their morphological forms are more or less transparent. This is the crux of a controversy in word-production research over how grammatical gender is represented (see Janssen & Caramazza, 2003, for one installment in an ongoing debate). Like number morphology, the representation of gender morphology is relevant to an explanation of how linguistic regularities come to be.

If gender, too, is an abstract lexical or morphological specification, its ability to attract agreement targets should not depend on its surface realization. Evidence for this can be found in Meyer and Bock (1999). They showed that covert grammatical gender-specification in Dutch yielded agreement and attraction patterns very similar to those of overt specification, though the effects of covert specification tended to be less pronounced.

2. The Transmission of Agreement Features

The metaphor of transmission implies a broadcaster and a receiver. If agreement features are in any sense transmitted from a controller to a target, it means that the features originate with the controller and end up with something that previously lacked them, the agreement target. In agreement (but note carefully, not in concord) the controller is the marking of the subject noun-phrase. Number marking carries a value that represents number meaning, but it transmits only the value, and not the meaning, to the verb. Recall that (a) verbs do not appear to carry number consistently, in the ways that most nouns do; and (b) even when they have number specifications, they lack number meaning. This account differs from others in the literature (Vigliocco, Butterworth, & Garrett, 1996) which argue for a joint marking of number on the subject and verb.

Three questions are raised by this approach. The most important one is how agreement between subjects and verbs comes about when the number that actually materializes on the verb is not rooted in number meaning or, worse, contradicts the apparent notional number. Here, linguistic approaches to semantically bereft grammatical agreement begin to provide an answer. Something called *percolation* in linguistics describes how features move around in a structural tree. Percolation moves number specifications from words (head nouns of subjects, for example) to phrases as wholes, from which they spread to verbs. Vigliocco and colleagues in several publications have described how this works to create attraction and other phenomena of agreement (see especially Vigliocco & Nicol, 1998).

The effects of number marking can be readily incorporated into this picture, in a manner proposed by Eberhard (1997) and elaborated in Bock, Eberhard, and Cutting (2001). Lexical specifications must be merged, reconciled, or unified (Kay, 1985) with the marking in force. Lexical specifications carry relatively more weight than marking in this process in part because, in production, they come into play later than marking does, and closer in time to the point at which verb number is specified in agreement. In most circumstances, then, the number that the verb agrees with will be the lexical specification. Fortunately, lexical specifications reflect the relevant number meaning most of the time; only for number peculiars, words with intrinsic number, is the specified number likely to differ. For grammatical gender, however, the only relevant information comes from the lexical specification, at least when gender is intrinsic. This makes contrasts of intrinsic number and gender agreement with extrinsic number and gender agreement especially important for our understanding of how transmission proceeds.

A second question is the mechanism of transmission. In Bock, Eberhard, and Cutting (2001, following Eberhard, 1997) the "movement" or spread of morphological features is modeled in terms of activation within a temporary structural network or dynamic workspace. As morphemes are temporally bound to terminal positions in the utterance structure, their agreement features begin to send activation through the network, searching for targets.

Finally, there are interlocking questions about the strength or rate of transmission. Some of the results already mentioned carry implications for the answers to these questions. If singular specifications exist, the results from research on attraction indicate that plurals must be stronger. Extrinsic features seem to be stronger than intrinsic features, either because they are redundantly represented (in both marking and lexical specification) or because of how marking has its effect (e.g., through inflection). If marking and lexical specification are graded in strength, rather than being dichotomies of presence and absence or plural and singular, variations in the stability, reliability, and fluency of agreement should follow (Bock, Eberhard, & Cutting, 2001).

3. The Scope of Agreement

Related to the problem of transmission is the problem of scope. For verb agreement, the prescriptive linguistic view of scope is very simple: Verbs do not agree with subjects outside of the clause in which they both occur, except by mistake. But how often do such mistakes occur? The phenomenon of attraction, being a mistake, makes it possible to determine whether the influence of agreement features can extend beyond a current clause. Bock and Cutting (1992) tested this and found that clause boundaries significantly reduced, but did not eliminate, verb attraction across clauses, relative to attraction across phrases, holding linear distance constant. So, speakers were more likely to fall prey to attraction of the verbs they used to complete *The editor of the history books* (where the local noun *books* is phrase bounded) than verbs used to complete *The editor who rejected the books* (where *books* is clause bounded). Solomon and Pearlmutter (in press) obtained similar results, showing in addition that clause effects occur over and above the impact of semantic integration.

Further support for clausal scope comes from another of Bock and Cutting's experiments (1992, Experiment 3). They varied the surface distance in words and syllables between the subject controller and the verb target, both within and between clauses. Speakers in this experiment responded to preambles such as

The report of the destructive (forest) fires

The report that they controlled the (forest) fires,

where the parenthesized adjective was included only in the long-distance conditions. The longer interruptions increased attraction (i.e., decreased the reliability of agreement), but significantly more for within-clause, phrasal interruptions than for clause-crossing interruptions. Longer clauses had no larger an effect than shorter ones. This implies that, for verbs, clauses do function as partially separable agreement domains, but they are not fully insulated from one another.

Vigliocco and Nicol (1998) generalized Bock and Cutting's results to show that structural proximity affects the scope of attraction effects. Within a sentence or clause structure, material in a constituent phrase is "higher" or structurally closer to the verb than material in a clause. Vigliocco and Nicol manipulated structural proximity within single clauses, and showed that structurally close local nouns created more attraction than structurally distant ones. They suggested that structural distance could replace clausal membership as a determinant of transmission scope. However, Solomon and Pearlmutter (in press, Experiment 5) show that the viability of this simplification depends on unresolved details of the mental representation of sentence structures.

Although verbs have a relatively well-defined agreement scope in grammatical terms, pronouns do not. That is, pronouns can successfully agree in gender and number with antecedents from preceding clauses, sentences, paragraphs, and even unmentioned antecedents in the context. This makes it implausible to suppose that pronouns and verbs would reflect the same scope of feature transmission. Suppositions to the contrary notwithstanding, Bock (2003) found the same pattern of results for pronoun attraction that Bock and Cutting did for verb attraction: there was less attraction when the local noun occurred in an embedded clause than when it did not. So, speakers were more likely to use the expected singular pronoun in sentences like *The report that they controlled the fires aired, didn't it?* than in sentences like *The report of the destructive fires aired, didn't it?* In the latter, responses along the lines of *The report of the destructive fires aired, didn't they?* increased in frequency.

The location of a pronoun *target*, unlike a verb target, can also be varied. In this situation, the attractor stays in the same structural location and the target occurs either with it in the same clause or in a different clause. Data from Bock, Nicol, and Cutting (1999) showed a small increase in attraction when a pronoun was in the same clause as the attracting local noun relative to when the pronoun was in a different clause, although the increase was not significant. Generally, however, these findings are compatible with the M&M contention that the mechanisms of pronoun attraction are the same as those of verb attraction; where they differ is in agreement control and concord.

Gender has not been explored with the question of transmission scope in mind, but there is at least one relevant result to report. In their study of grammatical gender agreement, Meyer and Bock (1999) looked at the gender realizations of Dutch pronouns whose controllers were in the same or a different sentence. Errors in grammatical gender were significantly more likely across sentence boundaries than within them. This is consistent with traditional wisdom (Drosdowski, 1984) that grammatical gender agreement on pronouns is more reliable within than across sentences, and reminiscent of findings about the comprehension of grammatically gendered pronouns in French, Italian, and Spanish. Garnham, Oakhill, Ehrlich, and Carreiras (1995) and Cacciari, Carreiras, and Cionini (1997) found that readers initially access the surface gender properties of a pronoun antecedent but soon begin to make use of the antecedent's conceptual properties. So, in comprehension, the surface morphology of agreement features is a first step toward understanding the connection between a pronoun and its antecedent.

In production, the creation of surface agreement morphology—morphing—is a last step toward reaching agreement. It is the mechanism by which a grammatical agreement controller or an attractor affects the form of an agreement target. Concord, in contrast, occurs when a message element jointly specifies the features of separate parts of an utterance. The difference between concord and morphing highlights the essence of morphing: concord conveys meaning, and morphing conveys form.

III. Conclusions

You now know more than you ever wanted (and may ever need) to know about the psycholinguistics of meaning, marking, and morphing. In the face of the intricate workings of grammatical agreement, it is worth returning to the question of what they are good for. Some of the intricacies, particularly those involving number and gender peculiarity, rightly raise skepticism about What Agreement Does (or could do) for You and Me. Despite compelling reasons to believe that number features—to take just one example—could function to support language learning and language use, there is little direct evidence that they do. What evidence there is falls far short of explaining why some languages burden their speakers with *always* having to evaluate numerosity.

And there may not be a good explanation. Perhaps number and gender and the agreement systems in which they participate are historical accidents or byproducts, spandrels of language architecture. Perhaps they are vestiges of something that once played a more transparent role in conveying meaning. Considering the widespread difficulty of agreement morphology for second-language learners (Klein & Perdue, 1992), it is even possible that agreement systems are elaborate shibboleths, ways of distinguishing the good guys (the native speakers) from the bad guys (everyone else). In other words, number and number agreement may do nothing or next to nothing for language acquisition and performance.

The absence of functional value would not erase the scientific challenge of figuring out how speakers and listeners handle agreement or where the raw materials for agreement come from. It would also leave the mystery of why agreement systems are found in so many languages around the world. And it would certainly take some of the fun out of the scientific enterprise.

In an effort to put the fun back in, at least to hint at where the fun will be, I close with a frankly speculative view of where the psycholinguistic fun and function of agreement may be. The speculation takes the form of a long example that illustrates meaning, marking, and morphing in action.

Suppose I want to tell my pal Greg that someone in a photograph is my niece. I say "She is my niece." The *meaning* I wish to communicate, roughly, is that the teenager depicted is a daughter of my brother. The grammar of English places many restrictions on how I can do this. The restrictions come both from the lexicon and the syntax. The English lexicon requires a distinction between male and female children of siblings but does not distinguish between children of brothers or sisters, or between siblings by birth and siblings by marriage. The consequence is that in some ways I convey more information than I need or want to, and in other ways less. *Niece* provides the correct gender (redundantly, given the picture), but it fails to distinguish between my own siblings and my husband's. It does, however, communicate informative generational information. Nieces and nephews are the children of siblings, unlike cousins (for instance), who are the children of aunts and uncles. In comparison, the Dutch word for *niece* (*nichtje*) means female cousin, too. So Dutch, like English, obliges one to indicate gender, but it neglects generation. Conversely, English *cousin* indicates generation but neglects gender, forcing awkward locutions like "boy cousin" and "girl cousin."

Operating within such restrictions requires that I *dis-integrate* what is, in my mind, part of a rich and tightly woven tapestry of personal memories. The memories involve my family, one of my two brothers, his family, my two nieces, and our shared lives. Dis-integration makes it possible to use language to convey rudiments of personal experience and thought into another mind. It is the opposite of what is sometimes called embodiment in language understanding (Glenberg & Robertson, 2000),[1] serving to digitize and filter an embodied memory record for purposes of communication. Dis-integration in this technical sense shares connotations with the ordinary

---

[1] Dis-integration, or the difficulty of it, is to blame for a common problem among academics: The hardest things to give introductory lectures about are the things we know best.

sense of disintegration: things fall apart. This creates a conundrum. What puts the pieces back together? In order for communication of meaning to succeed, the manifestly separate words in an utterance with their at-best-sketchy senses must be re-woven by the reader or listener into some semblance of the tapestry in the speaker's mind.

Language supports this reweaving or reconstruction in various ways. An obvious source of support comes from the related senses of individual words. For instance, *she* and *niece* are both feminine in English and typically human, so they have a natural association. These natural associations and other lexical co-occurrences can be a powerful force in language (Landauer & Dumais, 1997). But beyond the senses of individual words, syntax codes some things explicitly, *marking* basic information for preservation. This provides a safety net for dis-integration. The safety net maintains a few basic types of information that are essential to the relational job of syntax. This relational information, in turn, serves to support the listener's (Greg's) reconstruction of my communicative intention.

The safety net is woven something like this. Except for imperatives (*Stop!*), the syntax of English almost always forces speakers to select a subject for the sentences they utter. The subject in English establishes a perspective against which the rest of the information in an utterance can be arranged, and a tether to which other information can be tied. The tethering has observable linguistic consequences. One consequence is that if the subject is expressed as a pronoun, the pronoun takes a different form (*she*) than it would if it were the object (*her*), for example. Another consequence is verb agreement: English verbs agree with their subjects in number.

Agreement has its own ramifications, which make the net tighter. English speakers must choose between singular and plural forms: Unlike Japanese (and other languages, which have different kinds of requirements), English demands that a speaker decide whether the referent of a phrase is one thing or more than one thing. Recall my niece. She is one and not more than one (so, a *she* and not a *they*). Simple though this may seem, it is not. Look at a skeleton partially assembled by a paleontologist. Is it singular or plural? A skeleton or some bones? Obviously, it depends. On what it depends is less obvious, but it is clearly a tricky problem of perception and categorization (McCawley, 1975; Middleton, Wisniewski, & Trindel, 2002; Wisniewski, Imai, & Casey, 1996; Wisniewski, Lamb, & Middleton, in press). When pronouns are involved, further problems about animacy and gender present themselves.

The twin demands of identifying something to serve as the subject and deciding on its number (and other features) yield a *number marked* subject relation or subject function. In the intended sense of marking, meanings that matter to the syntax of a language are flagged for special treatment during a speaker's formulation of an utterance.

To stitch an actual utterance together from linguistic pieces, forms must be retrieved from memory and assembled. Ultimately, they will be turned into articulatory gestures that create changes in air pressure that wash over listeners like Greg. In writing, the transformation is into manual gestures for drawing symbols that make changes in light for readers like you. Just as for the words chosen, the forms retrieved depend both on things the speaker wants to convey and things that must be conveyed because the grammar of the language requires them. In English, the determiners used with certain nouns can have little or no direct motivation in the meanings of phrases or sentences. We say *a niece* or *the niece* depending on whether the referent is nonspecific or specific, whether it is any old niece (Jessica, Rachel, whoever) or *my* niece, but we must say *the mud* and do not say *a mud* for reasons that are opaque to virtually all speakers of English, and have very little to do with meaning: the distinction that we sense between *a niece* and *the niece* is decidedly not the distinction that makes *the mud* fine and *a mud* odd. If specificity or individuality were involved, we would expect *the mud* to be the odd one.

The variations in form that accompany variations in the grammatical context of an utterance, that select among articles, inflections, and the like, whether they are rooted in meaning or something else, are accomplished by *morphing*. Morphing flies linguistic flags that can help listeners figure out what goes with what, and because the language requires it, it works regardless of whether speakers are trying to help their listeners understand. Since speakers can be highly unreliable about such services to listeners (Ferreira & Dell, 2000), the legislation of morphing by the language can be seen as a general service to communication.

This story about What Agreement Does for You and Me sketches the transformation from thought to speech for one simple utterance. At the moment, it is science fiction. What is on the way to becoming science fact is our understanding of how agreement works in normal language production. There is good evidence that verb and pronoun agreement are in important respects similar, that agreement in number and gender are, likewise, in important respects similar, and even that agreement in typologically different languages is in its basic workings remarkably similar. If these conclusions remain intact after expansion of the woefully small sample of languages, agreement types, and agreement features that have been examined so far, we will be well on our way to a psycholinguistic explanation of one of the most basic and most universal features of language, the unlovable but unavoidable phenomena of grammatical agreement.

Acknowledgments

Preparation of this chapter was supported in part by grants from the National Science Foundation (BCS-0214270) and the National Institute of Mental Health (R01-MH66089). Address correspondence to Kathryn Bock, Beckman Institute, University of Illinois at Urbana-Champaign, 405 North Matthews Avenue, Urbana, IL 61801.

References

Almor, A., MacDonald, M. C., Kempler, D., Andersen, E. S., & Tyler, L. K. (2001). Comprehension of long distance number agreement in probable Alzheimer's disease. *Language and Cognitive Processes, 16*, 35–63.
Barlow, M. (1991). The agreement hierarchy and grammatical theory. In L. A. Sutton & C. Johnson (Eds.), *Proceedings of the Seventeenth Annual Meeting of the Berkeley Linguistics Society.* (pp. 30–40). Berkeley, CA: Berkeley Linguistics Society.
Bates, E., & Wulfeck, B. (1989). Crosslinguistic studies of aphasia. In B. MacWhinney & E. Bates (Eds.), *The crosslinguistic study of sentence processing.* (pp. 328–371). Cambridge, England: Cambridge University Press.
Bock, J. K., Carreiras, M., Meseguer, E., & Octigan, E. (2003). *Subject-verb agreement in Spanish and English: Similarities in the role of conceptual constraints.* Manuscript in preparation.
Bock, J. K., & Cutting, J. C. (1992). Regulating mental energy: Performance units in language production. *Journal of Memory and Language, 31*, 99–127.
Bock, J. K., & Eberhard, K. M. (1993). Meaning, sound, and syntax in English number agreement. *Language and Cognitive Processes, 8*, 57–99.
Bock, J. K., Eberhard, K. M., & Cutting, J. C. (2001). *Making syntax of sense: Number agreement in sentence production.* Manuscript submitted for publication.
Bock, J. K., Eberhard, K. M., & Cutting, J. C. (2003, November). *Making syntax of sense.* Paper presented at the meeting of the Psychonomic Society, Vancouver, British Columbia.
Bock, J. K., Eberhard, K. M., Cutting, J. C., Meyer, A. S., & Schriefers, H. (2001). Some attractions of verb agreement. *Cognitive Psychology, 43*, 83–128.
Bock, J. K., Humphreys, K. R., Butterfield, S., Eberhard, K. M., & Cutler, A. (2003). *Collective agreement in British and American English.* Manuscript in preparation.
Bock, J. K., & Miller, C. A. (1991). Broken agreement. *Cognitive Psychology, 23*, 45–93.
Bock, K., Nicol, J., & Cutting, J. C. (1999). The ties that bind: Creating number agreement in speech. *Journal of Memory and Language, 40*, 330–346.
Bock, J. K. (2003). *Gender attraction in English.* Manuscript in preparation.
Cacciari, C., Carreiras, M., & Cionini, C. B. (1997). When words have two genders: Anaphor resolution for Italian functionally ambiguous words. *Journal of Memory and Language, 37*, 517–532.
Corbett, G. (1998). Morphology and agreement. In A. Spencer & A. M. Zwicky (Eds.), *The handbook of morphology.* (pp. 191–205). Oxford, England: Blackwell.
Corbett, G. S. (2000). *Number.* Cambridge, England: Cambridge University Press.
Dehaene, S. (1997). *The number sense: How the mind creates mathematics.* New York: Oxford University Press.
Drosdowski, G. (1984). *Duden Grammatik der deutschen Gegenwartssprache* (Vol. 4). Mannheim: Dudenverlag.
Eberhard, K. M. (1997). The marked effect of number on subject-verb agreement. *Journal of Memory and Language, 36*, 147–164.

Eberhard, K. M. (1999). The accessibility of conceptual number to the processes of subject-verb agreement in English. *Journal of Memory and Language, 41*, 560–578.

Ferreira, V., & Dell, G. (2000). Effect of ambiguity and lexical availability on syntactic and lexical production. *Cognitive Psychology, 40*, 296–340.

Franck, J., & Bock, J. K. (2003, March). *Do conceptual and morphological features influence attraction in gender agreement?* Poster presented at the 6th Simposio de Psicolingüística, Barcelona, Spain.

Garnham, A. (2001). *Mental models and the interpretation of anaphora.* Hove, England: Psychology Press.

Garnham, A., Oakhill, J., Ehrlich, M.-F., & Carreiras, M. (1995). Representations and processes in the interpretation of pronouns: New evidence from Spanish and French. *Journal of Memory and Language, 34*, 41–62.

Garrett, M. F. (1982). Production of speech: Observations from normal and pathological language use. In A. Ellis (Ed.), *Normality and pathology in cognitive functions.* London: Academic Press.

Givón, T. (1976). Topic, pronoun, and grammatical agreement. In C. N. Li (Ed.), *Subject and topic.* (pp. 149–188). New York: Academic Press.

Gleitman, L. R., & Wanner, E. (1982). Language acquisition: The state of the state of the art. In E. Wanner & L. R. Gleitman (Eds.), *Language acquisition: The state of the art.* (pp. 3–48). Cambridge, England: Cambridge University Press.

Glenberg, A. M., & Robertson, D. A. (2000). Symbol grounding and meaning: A comparison of high-dimensional and embodied theories of meaning. *Journal of Memory and Language, 43*, 379–401.

Hagoort, P., Brown, C., & Groothusen, J. (1993). The syntactic positive shift (SPS) as an ERP measure of syntactic processing. *Language and Cognitive Processes, 8*, 439–483.

Hartsuiker, R. J., Antón-Méndez, I., & van Zee, M. (2001). Object attraction in subject-verb agreement construction. *Journal of Memory and Language, 45*, 546–573.

Hartsuiker, R. J., Schriefers, H. J., Bock, J. K., & Kikstra, G. M. (in press). Morphophonological influences on the construction of subject-verb agreement. *Memory & Cognition.*

Haskell, T. R., & MacDonald, M. C. (2003). Conflicting cues and competition in subject-verb agreement. *Journal of Memory and Language, 48*, 760–778.

Herron, D. T., & Bates, E. A. (1997). Sentential and acoustic factors in the recognition of open- and closed-class words. *Journal of Memory and Language, 37*, 217–239.

Humphreys, K. R., & Bock, J. K. (in press). Notional number agreement in English. *Psychonomic Bulletin & Review.*

Janssen, N., & Caramazza, A. (2003). The selection of closed-class words in noun phrase production: The case of Dutch determiners. *Journal of Memory and Language, 48*, 635–652.

Kay, M. (1985). Parsing in functional unification grammar. In D. R. Dowty, L. Karttunen, & A. M. Zwicky (Eds.), *Natural language parsing: Psychological, computational, and theoretical perspectives.* (pp. 251–278). Cambridge: Cambridge University Press.

Keeney, T. J., & Wolfe, J. (1972). The acquisition of agreement in English. *Journal of Verbal Learning and Verbal Behavior, 11*, 698–705.

Keil, F. C. (1979). *Semantic and conceptual development.* Cambridge, MA: Harvard University Press.

Kelly, M. H. (1992). Using sound to solve syntactic problems: The role of phonology in grammatical category assignments. *Psychological Review, 99*, 349–364.

Klein, W., & Perdue, C. (1992). *Utterance structure: Developing grammars again.* Amsterdam: Benjamins.

Kutas, M., & Hillyard, S. A. (1983). Event-related brain potentials to grammatical errors and semantic anomalies. *Memory & Cognition, 11*, 539–550.

Landauer, T. K., & Dumais, S. T. (1997). A solution to Plato's problem: The latent semantic analysis theory of acquisition, induction and representation of knowledge. *Psychological Bulletin, 104,* 211–240.

Lehmann, C. (1988). On the function of agreement. In M. Barlow & C. A. Ferguson (Eds.), *Agreement in natural language: Approaches, theories, descriptions.* (pp. 55–65). Stanford, CA: Center for the Study of Language and Information.

Li, P. (1998). Crosslinguistic variation and sentence processing: The case of Chinese. In D. Hillert (Ed.), *Syntax and semantics (Vol. 31): A crosslinguistic perspective.* (pp. 33–53). San Diego: Academic Press.

Maratsos, M., & Chalkley, M. A. (1981). The internal language of children's syntax: The ontogenesis and representation of syntactic categories. In K. Nelson (Ed.), *Children's language (Vol. II).* New York: Gardner Press.

Marcus, G. F. (1998). Rethinking eliminative connectionism. *Cognitive Psychology, 37,* 243–282.

McCawley, J. D. (1975). Lexicography and the count-mass distinction. In C. Cogan, H. Thompson, G. Thurgood, K. Whistler, & J. Wright (Eds.), *Proceedings of the First Annual Meeting of the Berkeley Linguistics Society.* (pp. 314–321). Berkeley, CA: Berkeley Linguistics Society.

Meyer, A. S., & Bock, J. K. (1999). Representations and processes in the production of pronouns: Some perspectives from Dutch. *Journal of Memory and Language, 41,* 281–301.

Middleton, E., & Bock, J. K. (2003). *Peculiar plurals and senseless singulars.* Research in progress.

Middleton, E. L., Wisniewski, E. J., & Trindel, K. A. (2002). *Separating the chaff from the oats: Evidence for a conceptual distinction between count noun and mass noun aggregates.* Manuscript submitted for publication.

Morgan, J. L. (1972). Verb agreement as a rule of English. In P. M. Peranteau, J. N. Levi, & G. C. Phares (Eds.), *Papers from the Eighth Regional Meeting, Chicago Linguistic Society.* (pp. 278–286). Chicago, IL: Chicago Linguistic Society.

Newcombe, N. (2002). The nativist-empiricist controversy in the context of recent research on spatial and quantitative development. *Psychological Science, 13,* 395–401.

Nicol, J. L. (1998). The production of agreement in English and Japanese: Animacy effects (or lack thereof). In D. Hillert (Ed.), *Syntax and semantics (Vol. 31): A crosslinguistic perspective.* (pp. 113–129). San Diego: Academic Press.

Nunberg, G. (2003, March 9). *Machines make moral judgements, selectivity.* The New York Times.

Osterhout, L., & Mobley, L. A. (1995). Event-related brain potentials elicited by failure to agree. *Journal of Memory and Language, 34,* 739–773.

Pearlmutter, N. J., Garnsey, S. M., & Bock, J. K. (1999). Agreement processes in sentence comprehension. *Journal of Memory and Language, 41,* 427–456.

Pinker, S. (1994). *The language instinct.* New York: Morrow.

Pinker, S. (1999). *Words and rules.* New York: Basic Books.

Plaut, D. C., McClelland, J. L., Seidenberg, M. S., & Patterson, K. (1996). Understanding normal and impaired word reading: Computational principles in quasi-regular domains. *Psychological Review, 103,* 56–115.

Pollard, C., & Sag, I. A. (1994). *Head-driven phrase structure grammer.* Chicago: University of Chicago Press.

Rice, M. L., & Oetting, J. B. (1993). Morphological deficits of children with SLI: Evaluation of number marking and agreement. *Journal of Speech & Hearing Research, 36,* 1249–1257.

Safire, W. (1994, May 29). The coveted Bloopie Awards. The New York Times Magazine, 12, 14.

Seidenberg, M. S., & McClelland, J. L. (1989). A distributed, developmental model of word recognition and naming. *Psychological Review, 96*, 523–568.

Solomon, E. S., & Pearlmutter, N. J. (in press). Semantic integration and syntactic planning in language production. *Cognitive Psychology*.

Starkey, P., Spelke, E. S., & Gelman, R. (1990). Numerical abstraction by human infants. *Cognition, 36*, 97–127.

Stemberger, J. P. (1984). Structural errors in normal and agrammatic speech. *Cognitive Neuropsychology, 1*, 281–313.

Thornton, R., & MacDonald, M. C. (2003). Plausibility and grammatical agreement. *Journal of Memory and Language, 48*, 740–759.

Tiersma, P. M. (1982). Local and general markedness. *Language, 58*, 832–849.

van Berkum, J. J. A., Brown, C. M., & Hagoort, P. (1999). When does gender constrain parsing? Evidence from ERPs. *Journal of Psycholinguistic Research, 28*, 555–571.

Vigliocco, G., Butterworth, B., & Garrett, M. F. (1996). Subject-verb agreement in Spanish and English: Differences in the role of conceptual constraints. *Cognition, 61*, 261–298.

Vigliocco, G., Butterworth, B., & Semenza, C. (1995). Constructing subject-verb agreement in speech: The role of semantic and morphological factors. *Journal of Memory and Language, 34*, 186–215.

Vigliocco, G., & Franck, J. (1999). When sex and syntax go hand in hand: Gender agreement in language production. *Journal of Memory and Language, 40*, 455–478.

Vigliocco, G., & Franck, J. (2001). When sex affects syntax: Contextual influences in sentence production. *Journal of Memory and Language, 45*, 368–390.

Vigliocco, G., & Hartsuiker, R. J. (2002). The interplay of meaning, sound, and syntax in language production. *Psychological Bulletin, 128*, 442–472.

Vigliocco, G., Hartsuiker, R. J., Jarema, G., & Kolk, H. H. J. (1996). One or more labels on the bottles? Notional concord in Dutch and French. *Language and Cognitive Processes, 11*, 407–442.

Vigliocco, G., & Nicol, J. (1998). Separating hierarchical relations and word order in language production: Is proximity concord syntactic or linear? *Cognition, 68*, 13–29.

Wisniewski, E. J., Imai, M., & Casey, L. (1996). On the equivalence of superordinate concepts. *Cognition, 60*, 269–298.

Wisniewski, E. J., Lamb, C. A., & Middleton, E. L. (in press). On the conceptual basis for the count and mass noun distinction. *Journal of Memory and Language*.

EXECUTIVE ATTENTION, WORKING MEMORY CAPACITY, AND A TWO-FACTOR THEORY OF COGNITIVE CONTROL

Randall W. Engle and Michael J. Kane

I. Introduction

This paper is about the nature of working memory capacity (WMC), and it will address the nature of WMC limitations, their effects on higher order cognitive tasks, their relationship to attention control and general fluid intelligence, and their neurological substrates. Much of our work has explored these issues in the context of individual differences in WMC and the cause of those individual differences. However, our ultimate goal is to understand WMC in its most general sense. We have used individual differences much in the way suggested by classic papers by Underwood (1975), who urged that individual differences be used as a crucible in which to test theory (see also Kosslyn et al., 2002), and Cronbach (1957) who argued that the two schools of psychology based on experimental and psychometric methods could be synergistic of one another.

We report the status of a nearly two-decade pursuit of the nature and cause of the relationship between "span" measures of WMC and complex cognition. One of the most robust and, we believe, interesting, important findings in research on working memory is that WMC span measures strongly predict a very broad range of higher-order cognitive capabilities, including language comprehension, reasoning, and even general intelligence.

In due course, we describe our current thinking about the nature of these relationships and the ramifications for theories of working memory, executive attention, intelligence, and the brain mechanisms underlying those constructs.

Let us first try to place WMC in a context of general theories of immediate memory. In the 1970s and 1980s, after 20 years of work on short-term memory (STM) from the information-processing perspective, many theorists questioned the value of that work, the methods used, and the importance of the findings. Crowder (1982), in a paper pointedly entitled "The demise of short-term memory," argued against the idea that we needed two sets of principles to explain the results of tasks measuring immediate memory and tasks clearly reflecting long-term memory (LTM). He concluded, much as his mentor Arthur Melton did in 1963, that there was insufficient evidence to support the notion of multiple memories. Evidence for a long-term recency effect similar to that found with immediate recall seemed to nullify the relationship between the recency portion of the serial position curve and STM (e.g., Baddeley & Hitch, 1974; Roediger & Crowder, 1976). Studies from the levels-of-processing perspective (e.g., Craik & Watkins, 1973; Hyde & Jenkins, 1973) demonstrated that length of time in storage had little or no impact on delayed recall, contrary to quite specific predictions of the Atkinson and Shiffrin (1968) model. These studies suggested that memory was the residual of perceptual processing of an event and that orienting tasks that drove different perceptions of the event would lead to different types of codes and, in turn, differential recall. Crowder (1982) also called attention to the fact that individual differences studies had shown an inconsistent relationship between simple STM measures and such complex tasks as reading (Perfetti & Lesgold, 1977). If STM exists and is as important to higher-order cognition as early models suggested—that is, if STM is the bottleneck of the processing system—then one would expect measures of STM to correlate with performance in complex tasks such as reading comprehension.

Baddeley and Hitch (1974) questioned the simple notion of STM on these very grounds, but rather than abandon the notion of an immediate memory that is separate from LTM, they proposed a "working memory" model to supplant STM. Unlike the modal model of STM, working memory theory stressed the functional importance of an immediate-memory system that could briefly store a limited amount of information in the service of ongoing mental activity. It is quite unlikely that immediate memory evolved for the purpose of allowing an organism to store or rehearse information (such as a phone number) while doing nothing else. Instead, an adaptive immediate-memory system would allow the organism to keep task-relevant information active and accessible during the execution of complex cognitive and behavioral tasks. The "work" of immediate memory is to serve an organism's goals for action. Therefore, Baddeley and Hitch were more concerned about the interplay of storage and processing of information than about short-term storage alone. Empirically, they demonstrated that requiring concurrent memory for one or two items had virtually no impact on reasoning, sentence comprehension, and learning. Even when the concurrent memory load approached span length, performance was not devastated as should have been the case if STM was crucial to performance in these tasks. This finding led Baddeley and Hitch to propose separate components of the working memory system that traded off resources in order to handle competing storage and processing functions.

As developed by Baddeley (1986, 1996, 2000), the working memory model now arguably emphasizes structure over function. It consists of both speech-based and visual/spatial-based temporary storage systems (the phonological loop and visuo-spatial sketchpad), with associated rehearsal buffers, as well as an "episodic buffer" thought to maintain episodic information using integrated, multi-modal codes. Finally, a central executive component, analogous to Norman and Shallice's (1986) supervisory attention system, regulates the flow of thought and is responsible for implementing task goals. Much of the experimental and neuroscience research on working memory has been directed at the nature of the phonological loop and visual-spatial sketchpad (Baddeley, 1986; Jonides & Smith, 1997), and although these "slave systems" are easily demonstrated by a variety of lab-based experimental paradigms, their importance to real-world cognition appears to be rather limited in scope (but see Baddeley, Gathercole, & Papagno, 1998).

We take a functional approach to the study of immediate memory, which is more akin to the original Baddeley and Hitch (1974) work than to Baddeley's more recent proposals (1986, 1996, 2000; Baddeley & Logie, 1999). Specifically, we emphasize the interaction of attentional and memorial processes in the working memory system, and we argue that this interaction between attention and memory is an elementary determinant of broad cognitive ability. Moreover, we endorse Cowan's (1995, 1999) proposal that the coding, rehearsal, and maintenance processes of immediate memory work upon activated LTM traces, rather than retaining separate representations in domain-specific storage structures. As illustrated in our measurement model depicted in Figure 1, STM is represented as activated LTM, and this activation may be maintained or made accessible via a number of strategies or skills (e.g., chunking, phonological rehearsal) that may differ across various stimulus and/or response domains. Attentional or "executive" processes may also contribute to maintaining access to memory traces if routine rehearsal strategies, such as inner speech, are unavailable, unpracticed, or otherwise unhelpful for the task at hand, or if potent distractors are present in the environment. Our idea is that immediate memory, and

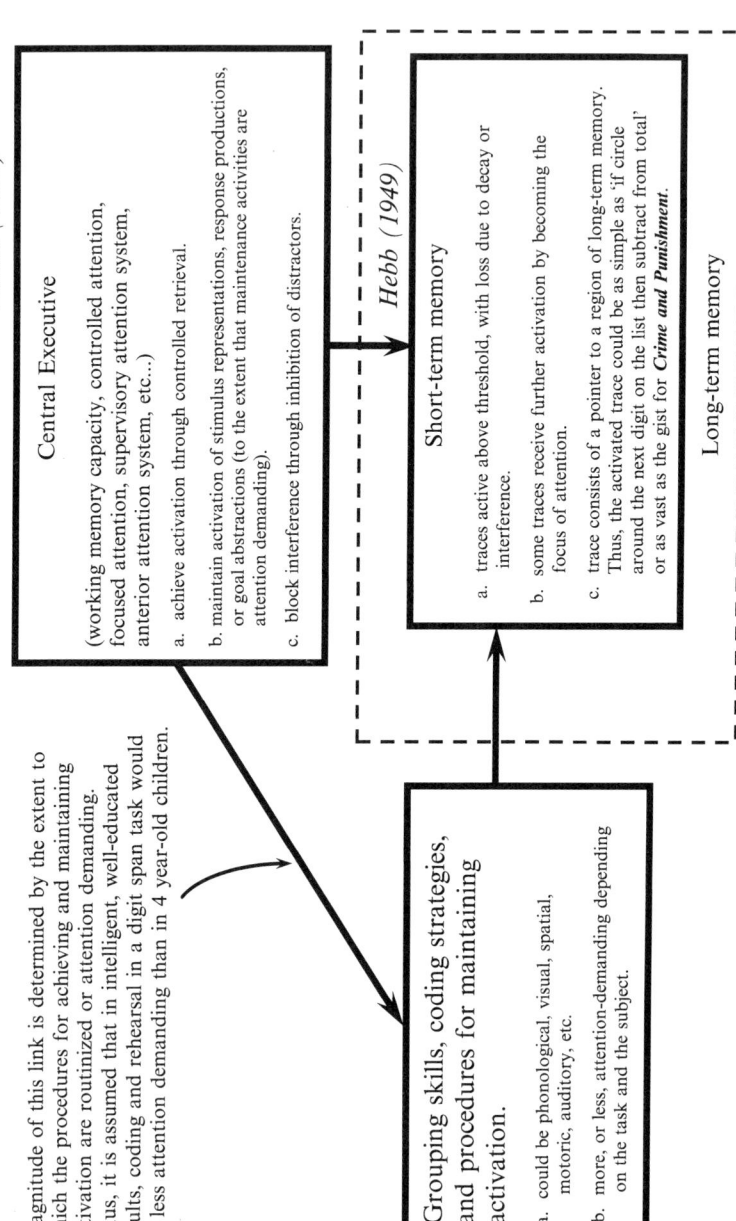

Fig. 1. Measurement model of the working memory system (modified from Fig.1, Engle et al., 1999). The labels for James and Hebb refer to our observation that those two different perspectives led to the two different views of primary/STM as noted in Engle and Oransky (1999). Copyright © 1999 by the American Psychological Association. Adapted with permission.

executive attention in particular, is especially important for maintaining access to stimulus, context, and goal information in the face of interference or other sources of conflict.

By our view, then, working memory is a system of: (a) short-term "stores," consisting of LTM traces in a variety of representational formats active above a threshold; (b) rehearsal processes and strategies for achieving and maintaining that activation; and (c) executive attention. However, when we refer to individual differences in WMC, we really mean the capability of just one element of the system: executive-attention. Thus, we assume that individual differences in WMC are not really about memory storage per se, but about executive control in maintaining goal-relevant information in a highly active, accessible state under conditions of interference or competition. In other words, we believe that WMC is critical for dealing with the effects of interference and in avoiding the effects of distraction that would capture attention away from maintenance of stimulus representations, novel productions, or less habitual response tendencies. We also believe that WMC is a domain general construct, important to complex cognitive function across all stimulus and processing domains.

To better illustrate our view, let us place WMC in a context of general cognition. We believe that much of what we need to know to function, even in the modern world, can be derived from retrieval of LTM—retrieval that is largely automatic and cue-driven in nature. Under those circumstances, WMC is not very important. Even in some putatively complex tasks such as reading, WMC is not required in all circumstances (Caplan & Waters, 1999; Engle & Conway, 1998). However, as we see in the following example, proactive interference can lead to problems from automatic retrieval. When the present context leads to the automatic retrieval of information, which in turn leads to an incorrect or inappropriate response in a task currently being performed, a conflict occurs between the automatically retrieved response tendency and the response tendency necessary for the current task. That conflict must often be resolved rather quickly, and so we need to have some way to keep new, novel, and important task-relevant information easily accessible.

Take a simple example obvious to every American walking the streets of London for the first time. While driving in a country such as England can lead to potentially dangerous effects of proactive interference, there are numerous cues such as the location of the steering wheel, the cars on your side of the road, etc., prompting the maintenance of the proper task goals. However, in walking the streets of England, the cues are much like those present when walking the streets of any large American city and the temptation—shall we say prepotent behavior—is to look to the left when crossing the street. This can be disastrous. So much so that London places a warning, written on the sidewalk itself, on many busy crosswalks used by tourists. This is a situation in which the highly-learned production, "if crossing street then look left," must be countered by a new production system leading to looking to the right when crossing streets. This task seems particularly problematic when operating under a load such as reading a map or maintaining a conversation. For individuals that travel back and forth between England and America, they must keep the relevant production in active memory to avoid disaster.

II. The Measurement of WMC

The construct, WMC, is tied to a sizable number of complex span tasks that we will detail in the following text. We will describe these in some detail because measures of WMC and STM, like all other measures used by psychologists, reflect multiple constructs or influences. Simple span measures of STM (such as word, letter, and digit span) require subjects to recall short sequences of stimuli immediately after their presentation. We believe that these tasks tell us primarily about domain-specific rehearsal processes, such as inner speech, and domain-specific knowledge, for example, pertaining to word meanings or the recognition of salient digit patterns. Therefore, at least among healthy adults, these simple STM tasks tell us relatively little about executive attention (although we assume that attentional processes play some role even here). In contrast, performance of complex WMC span tasks (such as the operation span, reading span, and counting span), while also relying on speech-based or visual-spatial-based coding, also reflect an individual's capability for executive attention above and beyond domain-specific STM. This is because these tasks require subjects to maintain stimulus lists, in the face of proactive interference from prior lists, while also performing a demanding secondary task. Here, then, stimulus information must remain accessible across attention shifts to and from the processing-task stimuli, thus taxing executive control.

Complex span tasks of WMC were first developed by Daneman and Carpenter (1980), in the context of prior research that failed to find a relation between measures of immediate memory and measures of complex cognition. Daneman and Carpenter reported results from a task that measured memory for short lists of recently presented items and that also showed substantial correlations with a variety of reading comprehension measures. Their reading span task required subjects to read sets of sentences and to recall the last word of each sentence. They defined reading span as the largest set of sentence-final words recalled perfectly. The assumption behind the task was that reading requires a variety of procedures and processes and that those procedures will be more efficient and automated in good readers. Hence, good readers will perform them more efficiently than will poor readers. This, in turn, leaves additional resources available for good readers to store the intermediate products of the comprehension process and for other processes. Thus, in the reading span task, simply reading the sentences aloud and comprehending them would result in differential resources available for storage across subjects. Good readers would have more resources available for storage-related processes such as encoding and rehearsal and consequently would recall more sentence-final words. To reiterate, the assumption is that better recall of the words results from better reading-specific skills used to read and comprehend the sentence portion of the task. A simple word span task involving a quite similar demand to the storage portion of the reading span and with similar words should not show a correlation with comprehension measures because the task did not invoke reading-specific processing.

Daneman and Carpenter had subjects perform the reading span task, a simple word span task, and a reading comprehension task consisting of silent reading of 12 passages, averaging 140 words each, with each passage followed by questions about facts or pronominal referents from the passage. In addition, subjects self reported their Verbal Scholastic Aptitude Test (VSAT) score. The word span task showed modest but nonsignificant correlations with reading comprehension (average 0.35). However, the reading span correlated 0.59 with VSAT, 0.72 with answers to fact questions from the passages, and 0.90 with answers to questions about the noun in the passage to which a pronoun referred. Further, the relationship between correct pronominal reference and reading span increased as a direct function of the distance between the pronoun and the noun to which it referred. This supported Daneman and Carpenter's contention that people who scored high on the reading span task kept more information active in memory and/or for a longer period of time than those who scored low on the task.

Daneman and Carpenter (1980, 1983) argued that the substantial correlation between recall on the reading span and measures of comprehension occurs because of individual differences in performing reading-specific procedures during reading. That is, differences on the reading span are caused by differences in residual capacity, in turn, caused by differences in skill at performing reading-specific procedures. If the correlation between the reading span score and reading comprehension occurs because of reading-specific skills and knowledge common to both tasks as Daneman and Carpenter argued, then a complex span task that requires a very different set of skills than reading should not correlate with measures of reading comprehension. By their logic, people have a large reading span score because they are good readers.

Turner and Engle (1989) suggested an alternative view, namely, that people are good readers because they have large WMCs independent of the task they are currently performing. They tested a large sample of subjects on four different complex span tasks and two simple span tasks. Two tasks were modeled after the reading span. The sentence-word task was identical to reading span except half the sentences were nonsense and subjects had to decide whether each sentence made sense and recall the sentence-final words. In the sentence-digit task, subjects read and made decisions about sentences but instead of remembering the last word, they recalled a digit that occurred after each sentence. In the operation spans, subjects saw and read aloud an operation string such as, "Is $(9/3) - 2 = 1$?" They were to say yes or no as to whether the equation was correct. In the operation-digit span task, they were to recall the digit to the right of the equal sign for each operation in the set. In the operation-word span task, they were to recall a word that appeared to the right of the question mark. Thus, half the tasks involved reading sentences and half involved solving arithmetic strings; half involved recalling words and half involved recalling digits. In addition, subjects received a simple word span and simple digit span task. As measures of comprehension, Turner and Engle tested subjects on the Nelson-Denny Reading Comprehension Test and obtained their Scholastic Aptitude Test (SAT) scores from university records. The Daneman and Carpenter view predicts that only those tasks requiring reading would correlate with the comprehension measures. On the other hand, if WMC is an abiding characteristic of the person, relatively independent of the particular task, then the complex span tasks might correlate with comprehension regardless of whether they involved reading sentences or performing arithmetic.

The results showed that all four of the complex span tasks predicted reading comprehension and the correlations involving the operation spans were actually a bit higher than those tasks requiring reading sentences. Neither of the simple span tasks correlated with comprehension. The complex span tasks clearly reflect some construct important to comprehension that is not reflected in the simple span tasks. However, whether the tasks involve reading sentences or solving arithmetic does not appear to be important. Another analysis performed by Turner and Engle is notable. One possible explanation for the results is that they reflect a spurious correlation between verbal and quantitative skills. That is, people who are good readers may also be good at solving arithmetic and this could provide the results obtained by Turner and Engle but for reasons commensurate with the Daneman and Carpenter argument. However, when the quantitative SAT was partialled out of the correlation between the span tasks and comprehension, the operation-word span remained a significant predictor of comprehension and, indeed, the operation-word span contributed significant variation in comprehension even after the effects due to the sentence-word span were eliminated. These findings led Turner and Engle to conclude that "Working memory may be a unitary individual characteristic, independent of the nature of the task in which the individual makes use of it" (p. 150).

A. VALIDITY OF THE RELATIONSHIP

If the measures of WMC are valid measures of a construct with wide ranging importance, then the measures should correlate with a wide range of other cognitive measures, and that is indeed the case. In the following, we provide a partial and evolving list of tasks that correlate with measures of WMC. This list is particularly impressive given the notable lack of such relationships with simple span measures of temporary memory (Dempster, 1981).

We view WMC as an abiding trait of the individual, resulting from differences in the functioning of normal brain circuits and neurotransmitters. We see WMC as a cause of inter-individual differences in performance of a huge array of cognitive tasks where the control of attention is important. However, intra-individual reductions in capability for attention control can also be a *result* of many different conditions from drunkenness to fatigue, from damage to the frontal lobe to psychopathology. It is becoming clear that conditions such as depression (Arnett et al., 1999), post-traumatic stress disorder (Clark et al., 2003), and schizophrenia (Barch et al., 2003), lead to reductions in WMC even when measures of STM show no decrement. Thus, studies of the results of individual differences in WMC should enlighten us about cognition in these other conditions as well.

Scores on WMC tasks have been shown to predict a wide range of higher-order cognitive functions, including: reading and listening comprehension (Daneman & Carpenter, 1983), language comprehension (King & Just, 1991), following directions (Engle, Carullo, & Collins, 1991), vocabulary learning (Daneman & Green, 1986), note-taking (Kiewra & Benton, 1988), writing (Benton, Kraft, Glover, & Plake, 1984), reasoning (Barrouillet, 1996; Kyllonen & Christal, 1990), bridge-playing (Clarkson-Smith & Hartley, 1990), and computer-language learning (Kyllonen & Stephens, 1990; Shute, 1991). Recent studies have begun to demonstrate the importance of WMC in the domains of social/emotional psychology and in psychopathology, either through individual differences studies or studies using a working memory load during the performance of a task (Feldman-Barrett et al., in press). For example, high-WMC subjects are better at suppressing thoughts about a designated event (Brewin & Beaton, 2002). Likewise, low WMC individuals are less good at suppressing counterfactual thoughts, that is, those thoughts irrelevant to, or counter to, reality. We have also made the argument (Engle, Kane, & Tuholski, 1999) that attentional-load studies are a valuable technique to study intra-individual differences in WMC since a secondary attentional load would reduce WMC. For example, Goldinger et al. (2003) found that low WMC subjects showed more counterfactual thinking than high WMC subjects, but only under conditions of a secondary load.[1] In the absence of a load, there was no difference between high and low WMC subjects since both groups could presumably control their counterfactual thoughts.

Richeson & Shelton (2003) have argued that WMC comes into play in the regulation of automatically activated prejudicial attitudes. White subjects were given a test of implicit attitudes, and then interacted with a white or black "partner" before performing the Stroop task. The argument was that individuals whose implicit attitude showed them to be more prejudicial against blacks would have to use more of their WMC to block their attitudes while interacting with a black partner than with a white partner and should do worse on the subsequent Stroop task. That is what Richeson and Shelton (2003) found. Whites who scored high on prejudice on the attitude test did worse on the Stroop task after interacting with a black partner than when they interacted with a white partner. (See also Schmader & Johns, 2003.)

WMC has also been used in explanations of various psychopathologies. For example, Finn (2002) proposed a cognitive-motivational theory of vulnerability to alcoholism and one of the key factors is WMC. He argues that greater WMC allows an individual to better monitor, manipulate, and control behavioral tendencies resulting from personality characteristics, and that this directly affects the ability to resist a prepotent behavior such as taking a drink in spite of being aware that such behavior is ultimately maladaptive.

Measures of WMC also appear to have some utility as diagnostic measures in neuropsychology. Rosen et al. (2002) tested two groups of middle-aged individuals, one of whom consisted of individuals who were carriers of the e4 allele associated with early onset Alzheimer's disease, and the other consisting of non-carriers of the allele. Even though the carriers showed no symptoms of Alzheimer's disease and very few other cognitive measures to distinguish between the two groups, the e4 carriers performed significantly worse on the operation span task than controls. This suggests that operation span, and likely other WMC measures as well, reflect a construct that is unusually sensitive to early changes associated with Alzheimer's.

---

[1] This finding is one of the few studies contradictory to our earlier conclusion that low WMC individuals show little effect of secondary load. We expect that the nature of the load is important in whether low spans make use of attention control with and without load.

The wide range of tasks and conditions associated with performance on WMC measures suggests that tasks, such as operation and reading span, are valid measures of a construct that is an important component of complex cognition reflective of neurological function, thus showing good construct validity. However, as we will see in the following text, WMC is not important to all cognitive tasks; the measures also reflect good and lawful discriminant validity. When discussing our studies using structural equation modeling, we will argue that this suggests WMC to be a single construct reflecting a domain-free ability for maintaining information in a highly active, easily retrievable state, particularly under conditions of endogenous or exogenous interference.

B. Reliability of the Measures of WMC

Another important characteristic of tasks used to study individual differences is reliability. Experimental psychologists often think of reliability as the likelihood that a phenomenon will replicate from one study to the next as opposed to being due to random fluctuation. Psychometricians think of reliability in terms of whether individuals will show a similar pattern of performance on a given measure from one time to the next. Since our studies often use extreme-groups designs, we are concerned about whether a difference or non-difference found between high and low WMC subjects will replicate across studies. However, we are also concerned about whether performance on a given WMC task shows strong test-retest correlations with identical or similar forms of the task, as well as whether WMC span tasks are multiply determined.

Reliability is affected by several variables. One that is particularly problematic is the range of the measure. As we will see in the following, WMC at the construct level is strongly related to general fluid intelligence. Thus, studies using a sample from a highly selected university population will likely have a very restricted range of true-score WMC and the reliability of the measures will be reduced substantially under those conditions. Likewise, extreme-groups designs that use a median split to define high and low WMC subjects are likely to be insensitive to true-score differences in the groups and would need quite large samples to replicate findings from extreme-groups studies using upper and lower quartiles to define the groups.

Reliability of WMC measures has been measured in several ways. One is the internal consistency of the measures, normally done with split-half correlations known as coefficient alphas. Alphas for WMC measures are rarely as low as 0.7 and are often in the 0.8 to 0.9 range. In other words, half the test will correlate with the other half the test in that range (Engle et al., 1999; Turner & Engle, 1989). The other way reliability has been assessed is to calculate the correlation between scores on the task from two or more administrations. Klein and Fiss (1999) tested a sample of subjects on the operation span task, and then tested them again after three weeks on an equivalent form of the task, then tested them again six to seven weeks later. They found a corrected reliability estimate of 0.88 across the three administrations. They also found the rankings of individuals from all three test times to be quite similar. Thus, the operation span task appears to be highly reliable and quite stable across time. Such extensive analyses has not been performed for the reliability of other WMC measures, but we would expect them also to be quite high if the sample of subjects is not highly restricted on general ability measures.

III. Alternative Explanations of the WMC × Higher-Order Cognition Correlation

Measures of WMC are reliable and valid, but what are the psychological mechanisms responsible for the fact that they correlate with such a wide array of higher-level cognitive tasks? First, we need to make a methodological point here that is probably obvious but needs to be stated. We need to constantly remind ourselves about the difficulty of attributing cause-effect relationships in psychology. Further, all readers will certainly understand the difficulty of attribution about cause and effect when describing a correlation between two variables. Daneman and Carpenter reported, at base, a correlation between a span measure and one or more measures of comprehension. Turner and Engle showed that the explanation for the correlation given by Daneman and Carpenter was inadequate. However, the question as to what causes a correlation is a tricky one to answer and just about everything else we describe in this paper was done in pursuit of an answer to that question. The difficulty, of course, is that some third variable, bearing little direct relationship to either of the two measures, might drive the putative relationship between the two observed variables. Our strategy for understanding the nature of this correlation takes a two-pronged approach greatly following Cronbach's (1957) advice about the two schools of psychology, one experimental and the other psychometric. One approach, referred to as *microanalytic* (Hambrick, Kane, & Engle, in press), has been to treat the correlation as a dependent variable and to perform experimental manipulations testing various hypotheses to see whether the correlation between WMC measures and higher-order cognition is affected. The presumption is that if we can make the correlation appear and disappear with a given manipulation, some aspect of the manipulation controls the correlation. A typical experiment uses an extreme-groups design with subjects from the upper and lower quartiles on one or more WMC measures, with the test being whether high and low WMC subjects perform differently on some cognitive task. For example, a study showing that high and low WMC subjects differ on a version of a task under conditions of proactive interference but do not differ on a version of the task absent the interference is suggestive that interference might play a role in the nature of the correlation.

The other approach, referred to as *macroanalytic* (Hambrick et al., in press), is to test a large number of subjects on a large number of tasks representing various constructs and perform structural equation modeling to determine the relationship among various constructs. The first approach is cheaper and quicker to determine whether individual differences in WMC are important to a task and the variables that interact with WMC in that task. It allows subtle manipulations in tasks that would be prohibitive using the second approach. However, one cost is that it overestimates the degree of relationship between the two variables. The second approach is more expensive in time and labor but gives a much cleaner and clearer picture of WMC at the construct level and the degree of relationship of other constructs with WMC.

The following alternative explanations have been suggested, but as will be seen, have not been supported by the evidence.

A. WORD KNOWLEDGE

We have used both approaches, sometimes in the same study, to investigate potential explanations for the correlation. For example, Engle, Nations, and Cantor (1990) tested the idea that the correlation between the span and comprehension measures occurs because of individual differences in word knowledge. Complex span measures requiring recall of words typically are more predictive of comprehension than those requiring recall of digits (Daneman & Merickle, 1996; Turner & Engle, 1989), thus, the correlation could be a spurious one involving word knowledge. People who know more words and more about words will be more familiar with the words in span tasks and in text passages and will score higher on both types of tasks. If that explanation were correct, then the span-comprehension correlation should be high when the span task requires retention of low frequency words, because word knowledge would be more variable across subjects, but low when very high frequency words are used since word knowledge should not differ that much across subjects. Engle et al. (1990) tested 90 subjects representing a rectilinear distribution of the Verbal SAT range on simple and operation span tasks using low and high frequency words. The question was whether comprehension, as represented by the VSAT, would correlate with span measures with both high and low frequency words. The answer was yes for the complex span measures, both low and high frequency words equally predicted VSAT. Thus, the idea that variation in word knowledge is the third variable responsible for the correlation between complex span and comprehension is not supported.

Engle, Cantor, and Carullo (1992) reported a test of other alternative explanations of the WMC correlation with higher-order cognitive tasks. We first describe the methodology, then the various explanations, and then describe the results pertinent to each of the possible explanations. In one experiment, subjects performed a self-paced version of the operation span task and, in a second experiment, the reading span task. Both used a moving-window procedure to present each element of the operation or sentence and the to-be-remembered word. Key-press times were used as an estimate of processing efficiency for the processing portion of the task and for the amount of time subjects spent studying the to-be-remembered word following either the operation or the sentence. For example, to show the operation-word string "(6/2) − 1 = _____ knife," the first key-press would present an open parenthesis and a single digit { (6 }, the second key-press would turn off the first display and present either a multiplication or division sign { / }, the third would present a single digit and a close parenthesis { 2) }, the next press would present an addition or subtraction sign { − }, next a single digit { 1 }, next an equal sign and underscore line { =___ }, the subject then typed in the single digit answer, and the word { knife } was shown until a key press started the next string.

Subjects first performed a series of the operations without recalling the word and in the other experiment, with reading span, simply read the sentences. The time between key presses was measured as an index of the processing efficiency for the elements of the processing portion of the task. Subjects then performed the operation span task with sets of two to six items and recall of the words from that set afterward. Again, processing times were recorded for the elements of the display including the time that subjects spent looking at the words to be recalled. Reading comprehension was measured by the VSAT.

B. Task-Specific Hypothesis

This view, the original explanation advanced by Daneman and Carptenter (1980), is that the correlation between a measure of higher-order cognition and a measure of WMC will only occur if the processing portion of the WMC task requires the same skills and procedures as the higher-order task. If that explanation is correct, we should see a correlation between the time to view the sentence words of the reading span task, words recalled in the reading span task, and VSAT. Note that these relationships should hold for the processing task *without recall* as well as the reading span task *with* recall, since it is based on skill at performing the processing portion of the task. However, the relationship should not hold for the operation span task because the processes required to solve the equations are unlikely to be similar to those used in reading the passages for the VSAT.

C. GENERAL PROCESSING HYPOTHESIS

This view, representing the thinking of Case (1985), argues that individual differences in WMC occur because some people do *all* mental operations faster and more efficiently than others. Thus, reading and arithmetic operations both would be done faster and more efficiently, leading to greater residual resources for storage of the to-be-remembered words. If this hypothesis is correct, then the correlation between number of words recalled in both the reading span and operation span and VSAT should be significant. However, it also predicts a correlation between the viewing times for the elements of the arithmetic and reading portions of the task and the number of items recalled in the span task. Further, this relationship between element viewing times and recalled items should hold even for viewing the elements in a task *without* recall. In addition, if we partialled out the variance attributable to viewing the elements, from either the tasks with or without recall, from the span/VSAT correlation, that correlation should be eliminated or at least significantly reduced.

D. STRATEGIC ALLOCATION HYPOTHESIS

This view is an extension of the ideas reported in Carpenter and Just (1988). They suggested that high spans better allocate their resources between the processing and storage portions of the task than low spans. That is, as load increases, high spans redirect resources away from the processing portion to the increasing storage element. Low spans do not adjust their resource allocation strategy as load increases. If this explanation accounts for the greater recall in complex span tasks by high-span subjects, then we should see that high spans spend less and less time viewing the elements of the processing portion of the task as load increases. Further, there should be a negative correlation between processing time and number of span words recalled. Additionally, if we partialled processing times out of the span/VSAT relationship, the correlation should be eliminated or reduced. These predictions should hold for both operation span and reading span.

E. REHEARSAL DIFFERENCES HYPOTHESIS

The idea behind this hypothesis is that the correlation between WMC scores and higher-order cognition occurs because some high WMC individuals are more likely to rehearse in the span tasks and also to be more strategic in other tasks as well. According to this hypothesis, there should be a positive correlation between time spent viewing the to-be-remembered words in both operation and reading span and the number of words recalled. More importantly, however, partialling out the time spent studying the to-be-remembered words from the span/VSAT relationship should eliminate or reduce the correlation.

The Engle et al. (1992) results were quite clear in eliminating all of these hypotheses. First, replicating Turner and Engle (1989), the number of words recalled in both operation span and reading span significantly correlated with VSAT and at the same level. Second, processing times on the storage-free versions of the task did not distinguish between high and low WMC individuals. Time spent viewing the elements did not consistently correlate with the span score. Third, when the processing times for the elements of operation and reading spans, both with and without recall, were partialled out of the span/VSAT correlation, the correlation was not diminished. In fact, there was a slight trend for the correlation between operation span and VSAT to increase. Fourth, there was a significant correlation between viewing time of the to-be-remembered words and the span score, with high spans spending more time viewing the words than low spans. However, when those times were partialled out from the span/VSAT correlation, the correlation was unchanged.

This suggested to us that individual differences in rehearsal time did affect the number of words recalled in this task, but that this is a *nuisance variable* unrelated to the construct responsible for the relationship between WMC and reading comprehension. This issue merits further discussion since it is apparently misunderstood in the literature. For example, McNamara and Scott (2001) demonstrated that strategy training led to an increase in scores on a WMC span task. From that, they concluded that the correlation between span and higher-order cognition was a result of differences in strategy use with high WMC subjects more likely to use strategies than low spans. We have repeatedly made the point (Engle et al., 1999) that the complex span score, like all cognitive measures, is a result of a multitude of constructs and that manipulations may affect some contributors to the score while having no impact on the construct mediating the score and the vast array of higher-order cognitive tasks. As Engle et al. (1992) showed, subjects who studied the to-be-remembered words longer on the operation span and reading span had higher span scores. However, study time did not contribute to the relationship between span and VSAT. Many different variables would lead to better or worse performance on WMC tasks, such as operation span and reading span. However, the critical question is whether those same variables eliminate or reduce the correlation between the span score and measures of higher-order cognition such as reading comprehension or spatial reasoning. That is the only way to determine whether the variable is important to an explanation of the correlation. Thus, although McNamara and Scott demonstrated that training a particular strategy may increase span scores overall, they did not demonstrate that strategies are at all related to the processes that link WMC to complex cognition. In fact, one may infer that their strategy training actually *increased* individual differences in complex span, rather than reduced them, as the standard deviations in span were slightly larger after training than before, especially for subjects who were less strategic originally. Thus, these findings leave open the possibility that strategy training benefits some individuals more than others, with the degree of this benefit tied to WMC, therefore, reversing the causal inference made by McNamara and Scott.

A more direct test of the rehearsal or strategy differences hypothesis was made by Turley-Ames and Whitfield (2003). Their study measured a large number of subjects (n = 360) on the operation span task who were then assigned to either a no-training control group, rote rehearsal group, imagery strategy group, or semantic association group similar to McNamara and Scott's chaining condition. All subjects were retested on the operation span and then the Nelson-Denney Reading Comprehension test. If the correlation between operation span and comprehension results from differences in rehearsal, then training should eliminate or reduce the correlation between the second operation span and Nelson-Denny. However, if Engle et al. (1992) were correct in arguing that rehearsal differences do occur and are important to span score, *but* they are a nuisance variable with no causal influence, then procedures designed to encourage subjects to behave more similarly with respect to rehearsal strategy should not reduce the span/comprehension correlation. In fact, such procedures should *increase* the correlation by reducing error variance resulting from the nuisance variable. Turley-Ames and Whitfield (2003) found that strategy training was effective in increasing the operation span scores, compared to the control group. However, the correlation between the operation span and Nelson-Denny was *higher* after strategy training (rote rehearsal [r = 0.56], imagery [r = 0.32], and semantic association [r = 0.47] than in the control condition (r = 0.30). Thus, differential rehearsal and strategy-use do not account for the correlation and, in fact, appear to serve as a suppressor variable for the true relationship between the span score and higher-order cognition.

Complicating the picture of the relationship between rehearsal and WMC is that greater WMC apparently leads to a greater benefit from rehearsal and encoding strategy use, as we foreshadowed previously. Pressley, Cariglia-Bull, Deane, and Schneider (1987) tested children who heard concrete sentences they were to learn. Half the children received instruction in how to construct images representing the sentences. In addition to the sentence-learning task, children also completed a battery of STM tasks including simple word span. Pressley et al. found that, while STM capacity was not related to performance in the control condition, it did predict sentence learning quite highly in the strategy learning group, even with age held constant. These results suggest that children with greater WMC may be better able to learn and/or use strategies for learning and retrieval of information. (Note, again, that the causal path implied here is from greater WMC to greater strategy effectiveness and not from greater strategy use to greater WMC.)

F. Speed Hypothesis

Another explanation for the covariation of WMC tasks and other cognitive tasks is that both reflect individual differences in speed of processing. This is a variant of a hypothesis popular in explaining the effects of aging on cognition called "age-related slowing" (Kail & Salthouse, 1994; Salthouse, 1996); it is also similar to views advocated by some theorists of intelligence (Jensen, 1982, 1998). The idea behind age-related slowing is that elemental cognitive processes become slower as we age and this slowing has a ubiquitous, deleterious effect on higher-order cognitive functioning. Thus, the argument remains, low WMC individuals are simply slower to process all information, and this leads to lower scores on complex WMC measures (perhaps because slowing allows for greater trace decay) and lower scores on other cognitive measures as well.

Many studies in the literature do, in fact, report reasonably strong correlations between processing-speed and WMC constructs (Ackerman, Beier, & Boyle, 2002; Kyllonen, 1993; Kyllonen & Christal, 1990; Oberauer, Süß, Schulze, Wilhelm, & Wittmann, 2000; Park, Lautenschlager, Hedden, Davidson, Smith, & Smith, 2002; Salthouse & Meinz, 1995). The question is what to make of these correlations. We believe many of them to be artifactual. For example, some studies tested an age range from young adults to elderly adults (Park et al., 2002; Salthouse & Meinz, 1995), and speed need not have the same relation to WMC within an age group, such as young adults, as it does across age groups (Salthouse, 1995). More worrisome, however, is the fact that in some studies the WMC tasks were presented under time pressure at either study or test (Ackerman et al., 2000; Oberauer et al., 2000). Obviously, presenting subjects with a speeded WMC test will artificially inflate correlations between WMC and "processing speed" measures. In some studies, moreover, the "speed" tasks were quite complex, for example requiring task-set switching, mathematical operations, or the association of arbitrary codes to individual items (Ackerman et al., 2000; Kyllonen, 1993; Kyllonen & Christal, 1991; Oberauer et al., 2000). Although such complexity is desirable because it increases variability and allows correlations to occur, a task analysis of these complex speed tasks strongly suggests that they tax executive attention, immediate memory, and/or LTM retrieval processes (Conway, Cowan, Bunting, Therriault, & Minkoff, 2002; Conway, Kane, & Engle, 1999). Given our view that WMC measures fundamentally tap an attention-control capability, causal inferences regarding correlations between WMC and complex speed measures are highly ambiguous—it is just as likely that WMC differences lead to speed differences as is the reverse.

On the logic that WMC and speed measures should be as unconfounded as possible, Conway et al. (2002) tested their subjects in complex span tasks that were untimed, as well as in relatively simple processing-speed tasks. The speed tasks involved making same-different judgments about individual pairs of verbal and non-verbal stimuli, or copying visual lists of digits or letters. Despite their simplicity, these speed tasks yielded substantial variability in the sample. However, Conway et al. found very weak correlations between WMC and speed measures, and furthermore, only the WMC tasks correlated significantly with fluid intelligence. Speed measures did not. A structural equation model clearly demonstrated that processing speed did not account for the relationship between WMC and general cognitive ability.

In our own laboratories, we recently began testing high and low WMC span subjects in attention-control tasks (for a full discussion see the following). Important for present purposes is that we typically fail to find response time (RT) differences between span groups in the baseline conditions that assess relatively automatic processes (Kane, Bleckley, Conway & Engle, 2001; Kane & Engle, 2003b). If low-level processing-speed mechanisms were responsible for WMC differences, then span differences in baseline speed would be expected. Indeed, we have also failed to find span differences in RTs in some fairly complex and difficult tasks such as visual search, even with large arrays of distractors that share perceptual features with the target. As we will discuss in the following, findings of independence between WMC and "controlled" visual search appear to present boundary conditions on the relationship between WMC and attention control, but here they serve to reinforce the idea that WMC differences cannot be explained merely by variation in "processing speed."

G. MENTAL EFFORT/MOTIVATION

Another alternative to the explanation we offer here is that differences in motivation mediate the WMC × higher-order cognition relationship. That is, some individuals are simply more motivated than others to do well on tasks of all types, including complex working-memory tasks and tasks of higher-order cognition. There are four lines of logic against this argument. First, quite lawfully, we find differences between high and low WMC individuals on tasks that require the control of attention but do not see differences in tasks that can be thought of as automatic. As we will describe in the following, span does not predict performance in the prosaccade task, which depends on a relatively low-level attention capture. We do observe differences, however, on the antisaccade task, which requires that the attentional capture by an exogenous cue be resisted in order to make the correct response of looking to a different region of space (Kane et al., 2001; Unsworth, Schrock, and Engle, 2003). WMC differences are not observed in speed to count objects where the number is within the subitizing range of 1 to 3, but substantial differences are observed when counting a larger number of objects (Tuholski, Engle, & Baylis, 2001).

Second, we see WMC differences on memory tasks involving a high level of proactive or retroactive interference but not on the same tasks in the absence of interference. For example, high- and low-span subjects do not differ on the fan task unless there is overlap among the propositions (Bunting et al., 2003; Cantor & Engle, 1993; Conway & Engle, 1994). Further, Rosen & Engle (1998) and Kane & Engle (2000) found that low-span subjects are much more vulnerable than high-span subjects to the effects of interference. However, in the absence of interference conditions, high- and low-span subjects do not differ, despite the fact that their performance was not close to perfect (i.e., avoiding ceiling effects) and well above chance (i.e., avoiding floor effects). We will describe these studies in more detail in the following, but for now the WMC equivalence in demanding but low-interference memory contexts is difficult to reconcile with motivation explanations for WMC effects.

Third, a motivation explanation must argue that differences between high and low WMC subjects on other tasks should increase as the task becomes more difficult or complex (i.e., as it becomes more effortful). We have observed two strong counterexamples of this prediction, however, in studies not originally directed at the motivation explanation. In one, discussed in the preceding text in regards to processing speed, we have studied visual search in three different experiments with high- and low-span subjects (Kane, Poole, Tuholski, & Engle, 2003). In all of these studies, subjects searched for a target letter F. Stimulus arrays consisted of few (0 to 3), several (8 to 9), or many (15 to 18) distractors, and these distractors were either dissimilar or similar to the target ("O"s vs. "E"s, respectively). As clearly seen in

Figure 2, high and low WMC subjects performed identically in both the more "automatic" and the more "controlled" search conditions, despite massive RT increases from small to large stimulus arrays across studies.

We have found similar results in studies of WMC and task-set switching (Kane & Engle, 2003a). Three experiments used a numerical Stroop task (Allport, Styles & Hseih, 1994), in which subjects were cued unpredictably to either switch between counting arrays of digits and reporting the digits'

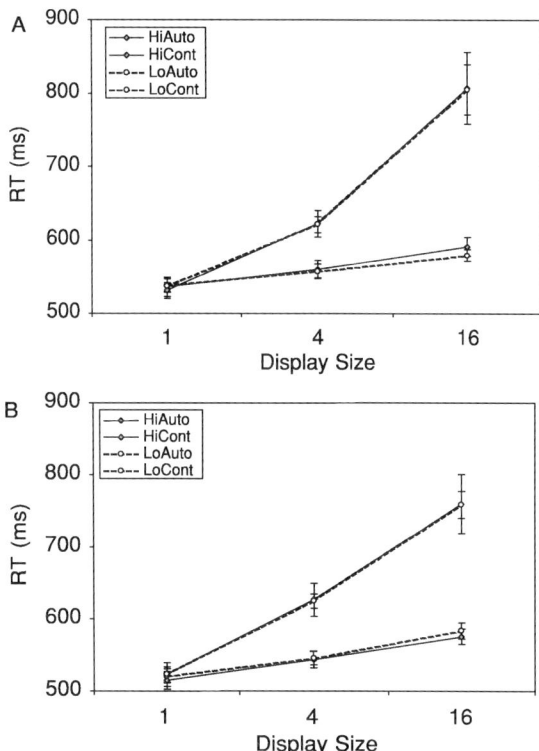

Fig. 2. (A) Mean visual-search latencies on target-present trials for high and low WMC span subjects in regularly arranged, 4 × 4 search arrays. (B) Mean visual-search latencies on target-present trials for high- and low-span subjects for spatially irregular search arrays. For both panels, the less steep lines reflect latencies under relatively "automatic" search conditions and the upper two lines reflect latencies under relatively "controlled" search conditions. Display set size refers to the number of targets plus distractors in the arrays. Error bars depict standard errors of the means. HiAuto = high spans under automatic search conditions; HiCont = high spans under controlled search conditions; LoAuto = low spans under automatic search conditions; LoCont = low spans under controlled search condition; RT = response time.

identity, or repeat the same task with consecutive arrays. A fourth experiment, with four between-subject conditions, used a letter/digit judgment task (Rogers & Monsell, 1995) in which subjects predictably repeat and switch tasks in an AABB task sequence. We found the typical switch cost, that is, the RT difference between task-switch and task-repeat trials, in all experiments. However, in no experiment did we find any span difference in switch costs despite the fact that overall switch costs were robust. Clearly, a motivation explanation cannot account for the absence of span differences in demanding search and switching tasks. Indeed, in one of our Stroop switching experiments, subjects were allowed to study the task cues for the upcoming trial pair (e.g., "DIGIT → COUNT") for as long as they wanted, and low spans actually studied the cues for significantly more time than high spans; this span difference was especially pronounced on switch trials. Such extra effort on the most difficult trials is certainly not expected from an unmotivated sample.

Fourth and finally, a series of studies by Heitz et al. (2003) used pupil dilation as a measure of mental effort to directly address the contribution of motivation to WMC effects. Pupil dilation has proven to be a sensitive and reliable index of the mental effort allocated to cognitive tasks, with pupil size tending to increase as a task becomes more and more difficult (Kahneman & Beatty, 1966). The motivation explanation argues that performance differences between high-and low-span subjects results from low spans being poorly motivated relative to high spans. Hence, a manipulation that increases motivation should lead to low spans performing more like high spans. On the other hand, if high and low WMC subjects are similar in their motivational level, the motivation-enhancing manipulation should lead to similar performance increases for both groups.

Heitz et al. (2003) had subjects who had been selected as high and low span, on the basis of the operation span task, subsequently perform the reading span task under conditions designed to manipulate motivation. In addition to measuring performance on the reading span task, we measured pupil size. In one study, high- and low-span subjects were provided a financial incentive for performance on the reading span task. They could make up to $20 depending on their recall of letters that followed the to-be-read sentences and on their ability to answer questions about the sentences. The incentive manipulation led to an equivalent increase in reading-span performance for high- and low-span subjects; that is, both high- and low-span subjects improved their observed "span" with incentives, but the difference between the two WMC groups remained unchanged. In addition, the incentive manipulation increased baseline pupil size taken before the beginning of each trial. However, again, the increase was the same for high- and low-span subjects. Pupil size clearly reflected level of mental effort in the task because pupil size closely mirrored memory load in the reading span task. For example, as a 5-item set progressed from item 1 to 5, pupil size increased for both groups. However, the increase in pupil size was, again, identical for high- and low-span subjects. It is clear that Heitz et al. successfully manipulated motivation and it is equally clear that the lack of differential incentive effects between high- and low-span subjects means that performance differences related to WMC do not result from generic motivation differences.

IV. Macroanalytic Studies of WMC: Its Generality and Relation to Other Constructs

Our large-scale, latent-variable studies have addressed questions about WMC at the construct level. Specifically, these studies have assessed the relationship between WMC and other constructs such as STM and general fluid intelligence, and they have also tested whether WMC should be thought of as a unitary, domain-general construct or whether separate verbal and visuo-spatial WMC constructs are necessary.

Before discussing this research in more detail, however, let us briefly note the advantages of latent-variable approaches to the study of WMC. Latent-variable procedures require that each hypothetical construct be measured by multiple tasks (such as using operation span, reading span, and counting span to measure WMC) and they statistically remove the task-specific error variance associated with the individual, multiply determined tasks. What remains, then, is only the variance that is shared among all the tasks, which putatively represents the latent construct of interest, free of measurement error. These statistical methods are valuable because no single task is a pure measure of any one single construct. Operation span, for example, measures not only the latent construct of WMC, but also some degree of math skill, word knowledge, and encoding and rehearsal strategies. Therefore, construct measurement that is based on multiple tasks that differ in their surface characteristics will be more valid than that based on single tasks, which can never be process pure. Latent-variable techniques used with correlational data, therefore, are analogous to the converging-operations approach in experimental research, in which constructs are validated through multiple and diverse experimental conditions that eliminate alternative hypotheses (Garner, Hake, & Eriksen, 1956; Salthouse, 2001).

Recall that we have portrayed working memory as a system consisting of domain-specific memory stores with associated rehearsal procedures and domain-general executive attention. Engle et al. (1999) tested that idea using an approach by which we identified latent variables through structural equation modeling and determined the relationship among those latent variables. We reasoned that all span tasks are mediated by multiple latent variables. For instance, simple STM tasks such as word, letter, and digit span are verbal tasks, and so they reflect variance due to differences in verbal knowledge and experience with the particular item types. In addition, performance on these tasks is affected by individual differences in pattern recognition (in the case of digit strings) and the frequency and type of rehearsal strategies used. To the extent that such strategies are less well practiced or routinized, one would also expect some contribution of attention control to successful performance.

Complex WMC tasks, such as reading span, operation span, and counting span, also require retention and recall of words, letters, and digits, and so they also reflect variance attributable to these variables. However, we also reasoned that WMC tasks principally reflect individual differences in ability to control attention, due to the demand to maintain items in the face of attention shifts to and from the "processing-task" stimuli. If that were true, then the two types of tasks (WMC and STM) should reflect different—but correlated—latent variables. Moreover, when we extract the variance common to the two constructs, the residual, unique variance from WMC should reflect individual differences in the ability to control attention. We also tested the idea, proposed by Kyllonen & Christal (1990), that WMC is strongly associated with general fluid intelligence (gF). If that were true, then the WMC construct should be strongly associated with gF, but the STM construct should not. Further, the residual variance from WMC that remains after extraction of a "common" variable from WMC and STM, representing executive attention, should be strongly associated with gF.

We used three measures of WMC: (1) reading span, (2) operation span, and (3) counting span; three measures of STM: (1) forward word span with dissimilar sounding words, (2) forward word span with similar sounding words, and (3) backward word span; and two measures of gF: (1) Ravens Progressive Matrices (Raven, Raven, & Court, 1998) and (2) Cattell Culture Fair Test (Institute for Personality Testing, 1973). Figure 3 shows that a model with separate factors for WMC and STM fit the data quite well and better than a single factor representing all six span tasks. Clearly, the two factors are as strongly associated (0.68) as we expected, but two factors provided the best fit of the data. You also see from Figs. 3 and 4 that, while the link between WMC and gF is quite strong, once the association between WMC and STM is accounted for there is no significant association between STM and gF. In other words, any association that STM tasks, such as digit and word span, have with fluid abilities occurs because of the strong association STM has with WMC.

Figure 4 shows what happens when the variance common to the two memory constructs is extracted to the latent variable labeled as "common."

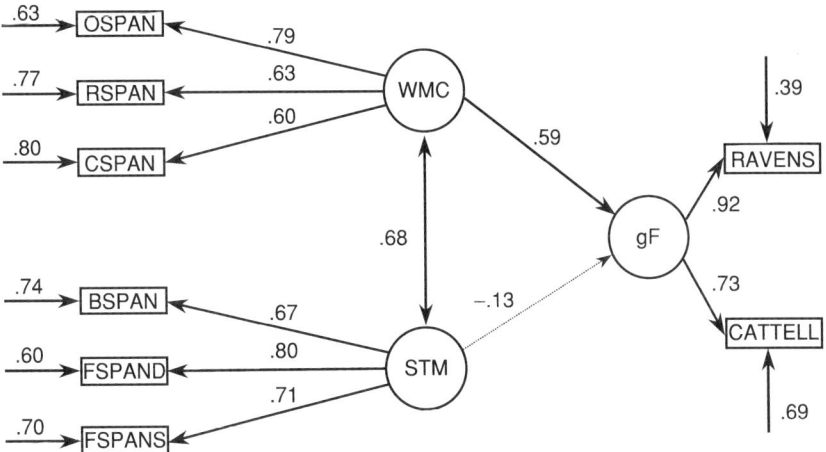

Fig. 3. Path model for confirmatory factor analysis from Figure 3, Engle et al. (1999) showing the significant link between WMC and gF but the non-significant link between STM and gF. OSPAN = operation span; RSPAN = reading span; CSPAN = counting span; BSPAN = backward word span; FSPAND = forward word span with dissimilar sounding words; FSPANS = forword word span with similar sounding words. Copyright © 1999 by the American Psychological Association. Reprinted by permission.

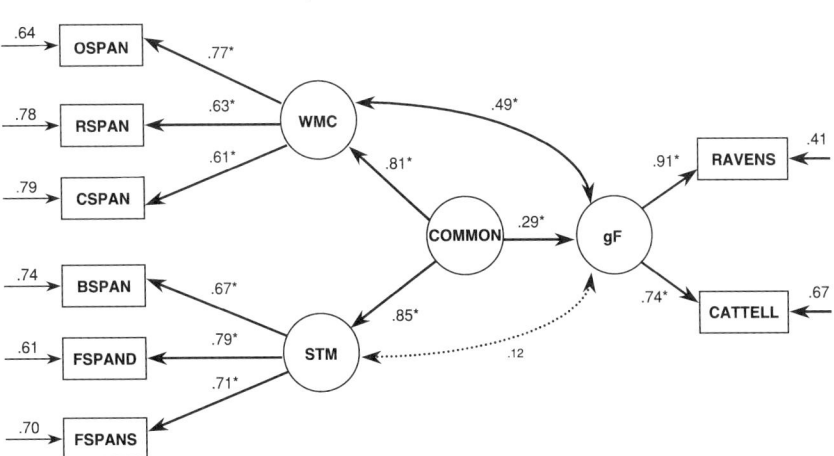

Fig. 4. Path model for confirmatory factor analysis from Figure 4, Engle et al. (1999) showing that, after variance common to the STM tasks and the WMC tasks was removed as "common," the correlation between the residual or left-over variance in WMC and gF was highly significant. Copyright © 1999 by the American Psychological Association. Reprinted by permission.

The curved lines represent the correlation between the residuals for WMC and STM and gF, that is, the correlation between each construct and gF after extracting the variance that was shared between WMC and STM tasks. The correlation between gF and the residual variance remaining in WMC after "common" was extracted was high and significant (0.49). However, the similar correlation between gF and the residual for STM was not significant. This supports the notion that some aspect of WMC other than STM is important to fluid intelligence and presumably to other aspects of higher-order cognition as well. We argue that that critical aspect of WMC tasks is the ability to control attention. This follows from the logic that, if the working memory system consists of STM processes plus executive attention, then after "common" is extracted, this should leave executive attention as residual. Of course, there was no direct evidence for this inference by Engle et al. (1999) but, in the following text, we will provide ample evidence to support that conclusion.

In a more recent large-scale study (Kane et al., 2003), we have also addressed the question of how much shared variance exists between verbal and visuo-spatial WMC—that is, is it necessary to posit separate latent variables for verbal and spatial complex span tasks, or instead should WMC be considered an entirely domain-general construct? The latter, domain-general hypothesis most easily follows from our view that individual differences in WMC correspond to individual differences in general attentional capabilities. Although there is little doubt that verbal and visual/spatial information are coded differently and by apparently different structures in the brain (Jonides & Smith, 1997; Logie, 1995), a separate question is whether what we have referred to as executive attention must also be fractionated for verbal and visual/spatial formats. Our belief is that executive attention is general across representation formats and is common to both verbal and spatial tasks requiring the control of attention. However, Engle et al. (1999) used only verbal tasks, which did not allow us to address this issue.

In conflict with our view, several correlational studies have suggested, in fact, that verbal and visuo-spatial WMC may not only be separable, but also virtually independent (Daneman & Tardif, 1987; Friedman & Miyake, 2000; Handley, Capon, Copp, & Harper, 2002; Morrell & Park, 1993; Shah & Miyake, 1996). All of these studies presented university students with one complex span task using verbal materials and one complex span task using visuo-spatial materials, and these WMC tasks were used to predict some higher-order verbal and visuo-spatial task (or task composite). In short, the verbal and visuo-spatial span tasks were poorly to modestly correlated with one another, and each correlated more strongly with complex cognition in its matching domain than in the mismatching domain:

verbal span predicted verbal ability better than spatial ability, and spatial span predicted spatial ability better than verbal ability. Indeed, the correlations for mismatching span and ability tasks were typically non-significant and often near zero.

Nonetheless, we had good reason to doubt that WMC was primarily or entirely domain-specific. First, the breadth of predictive utility demonstrated by verbal WMC tasks, including their strong correlations with non-verbal tests of fluid intelligence (Conway et al., 2002; Engle et al., 1999) and their relation to rather low-level attention tasks (to be discussed in the following; Conway, Cowan, & Bunting, 2001; Kane et al., 2001; Kane & Engle, 2003b; Long & Prat, 2002) indicates that verbal WMC tasks tap something important beyond just verbal ability.

Second, the studies that indicated domain specificity had methodological problems that could have systematically led to an underestimation of WMC's generality. Most obviously, some of the verbal and visuo-spatial tasks differed markedly in their difficulty, making their discrepant patterns of correlations impossible to interpret (Daneman & Tardif, 1987; Morrell & Park, 1993). Moreover, several studies used the same exact verbal and visuo-spatial task, and these two tasks correlated very inconsistently with one another across subject samples, with rs between 0.04 and 0.42 (Friedman & Miyake, 2000; Handley et al., 2002; Shah & Miyake, 1996). Such unreliable correlations obfuscate whatever the true association may be between these verbal and spatial tasks. A more subtle, but perhaps more serious, problem is that the domain-specific studies tested subject samples from a restricted range of general intellectual ability. Data were primarily collected from university students, and some from relatively prestigious universities at that. The problem with such a strategy from a psychometric perspective is that restricting the range of general ability in a sample must also restrict the contribution that general ability can make to any correlations that are observed. That is, without variation in general ability across subjects, any variability that is detected in WMC span must be due to domain-specific skills or strategies. If these same studies were conducted with more diverse subject samples, we believe that they would have yielded stronger correlations between verbal and spatial WMC measures, as well as between domain-mismatching WMC and complex-ability tests.

Our third and final reason to believe that WMC is largely domain general, derived from a collection of recent studies using factor-analytic and latent-variable techniques with verbal and visuo-spatial span tasks. As a group, these studies find that latent variables comprised of verbal and visuo-spatial WMC tasks either are indistinguishable from one another, or, if separable, are very strongly correlated with one another (Ackerman, Beier, & Perdue, 2002; Kyllonen, 1993; Law, Morrin, & Pellegrino, 1995; Oberauer, 2000;

Oberauer, Süß, Wilhelm, & Wittmann, 2003; Park, 2002; Salthouse, 1995; Süß, 2002; Swanson, 1996; Wilson & Swanson, 2001). Typically, when separate verbal and visuo-spatial factors are indicated, the two share more than 65% of their variance. This is, of course, consistent with our view that both domain-general and domain-specific mechanisms are important to performance on complex span tasks of WMC, but that the lion's share of variance picked up by these tasks is quite general.

Kane et al. (2003) tested 236 subjects, from both university and community populations, in verbal and visuo-spatial tests of WMC. In contrast to many of the extant latent-variable studies of verbal versus spatial WMC, we additionally tested subjects in verbal and spatial STM tasks. These differed from the WMC tasks only in their lack of a secondary processing demand between the presentation of each memorandum. Specifically, the verbal tasks we used were word, letter, and digit span for STM, and operation-word, reading-letter, and counting-digit span for WMC (operation-word required word memory against a equation-verification task; reading-letter required letter memory against a sentence-judgment task; counting-digit span required digit memory against an object-counting task). For the spatial domain, each STM task required subjects to reproduce sequences of visuo-spatial stimuli, such as different-sized arrows pointing in different directions, squares occupying different positions within a 4 × 4 matrix, and balls moving from one side of the screen to another across one of 16 paths. Each spatial WMC task presented the target memory items in alternation with a spatial processing task. The rotation-arrow task (RotaSpan) required subjects to mentally rotate letters and decide whether they were normal or mirror-reversed, and then to recall the sequence of arrows. The symmetry-matrix task (SymmSpan) required subjects to judge whether a pattern was symmetrical along its vertical axis and then recall the matrix locations. The navigation-ball task (NavSpan) presented subjects with a version of the Brooks (1967) task, in which they saw a block letter with a star in one corner and an arrow pointing along one edge, and had to mentally navigate along the corners of the letter to report whether each corner was at the extreme top or bottom of the letter. Subjects then recalled the sequence of ball paths.

In addition to the span tasks, subjects completed a variety of standardized tasks reflecting verbal reasoning (e.g., analogies, reading comprehension, remote associates), spatial visualization (e.g., mental paper folding, mental rotation, shape assembly), and decontextualized inductive reasoning (e.g., matrix-completion tasks with novel figural stimuli, such as the Ravens Advanced Matrices). The goal was to determine whether verbal and visuo-spatial WMC differentially predicted gF, as well as reasoning in matching versus mismatching domains.

Our key predictions for the study were that: (1) verbal and visuo-spatial WMC tasks would reflect, if not a single domain-general construct, then two very strongly correlated constructs; and (2) a latent variable derived from the domain-general WMC variance would be a strong predictor of a gF latent variable defined by the common variance among all of our reasoning tasks. Both predictions were strongly confirmed, as we detail in the following. We additionally explored the relation between STM, WMC, and reasoning in verbal versus visuospatial domains. While there is clear and consistent evidence that verbal STM and WMC are distinguishable, and that WMC is the stronger predictor of general cognitive abilities (Conway et al., 2002; Engle et al., 1999; for a review, see Daneman & Merickle, 1996), the data from spatial tasks suggest a less clear distinction between constructs. For example, Shah and Miyake (1996) found that a spatial STM task was as good a predictor of complex spatial ability as was a spatial WMC task, and Miyake et al. (2001) found that spatial STM and WMC could not be distinguished at the latent variable level in a confirmatory factor analysis. Here we sought to replicate these findings and begin to explore the question of why spatial STM might behave so differently from verbal STM, that is, why spatial span tasks without secondary processing demands seem to capture executive processes in ways that verbal tasks do not.

With respect to our primary question about the generality of WMC, an exploratory factor analysis conducted on all of the memory and reasoning tasks indicated that WMC reflected a single factor (comprised of the three verbal and the three spatial tasks), whereas STM was best represented by two domain-specific factors. As more rigorous tests of generality, we then conducted two series of confirmatory factor analyses on the WMC span tasks. In each series, we statistically contrasted the fit of a single-factor unitary model with the fit of a two-factor model comprised of separate verbal and spatial WMC. In the first series of analyses we allowed task-specific error to correlate when it statistically improved the fit of the model. Correlated errors reflect shared variance among pairs of tasks that is independent of the shared variance among all the tasks comprising the latent variable (recall that latent variables reflect the variance that is shared among all its indicator tasks). Among our verbal WMC tasks, operation span and reading span shared variance that they did not both share with counting span, perhaps because they both included word stimuli and counting span did not. Likewise, operation span and counting span shared variance that they did not share with reading span, perhaps because they both dealt with numbers. As illustrated in Figure 5 (Panel A), this first series of confirmatory factor analyses indicated that the six WMC tasks reflected a single, unitary construct rather than two WMC tasks. An analysis that forced the verbal and spatial WMC tasks to load onto separate factors not only failed to

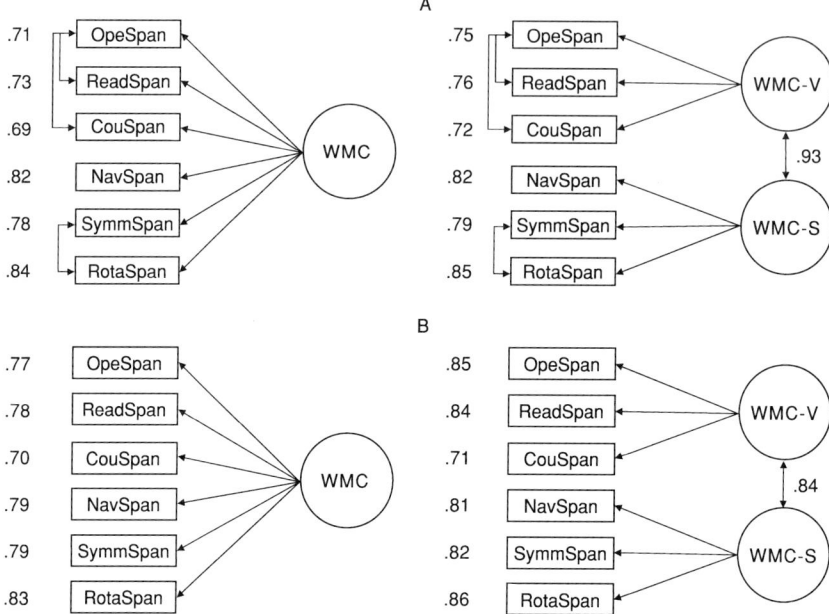

Fig. 5. (A) Path model for confirmatory factor analysis consisting of a single WMC factor versus two domain-specific factors. Paths connecting manifest variables (boxes) to each other represent correlated error terms added to the model. (B) Path model for confirmatory factor analyses contrasting one- versus two-factor models, but with no correlated errors. In both panels, paths connecting latent variables (circles) to each other represent the correlations between the constructs, and numbers to the left of each manifest variable represent the loadings for each task onto the latent variable. WMC-V = working memory capacity-verbal; WMC-S = working memory capacity-spatial. OpeSpan = operation span; CouSpan = Counting span. Copyright Randall W. Engle.

improve model fit, but it also yielded a correlation between the factors of 0.93!

In our second series of confirmatory analyses, shown in Figure 5 (Panel B), we took a more conservative approach and did not allow errors to correlate. Because the correlated errors in our model were not predicted (although they were explainable post-hoc), and because the correlated errors could be interpreted as reflecting domain-specific variance (i.e., the use of words and numbers as stimuli), the inclusion of correlated errors may have biased our analyses against finding domain-specificity to improve model fit. In fact, the two-factor model did improve fit over the one-factor model here, indicating some domain-specificity in the WMC construct. However, the correlation between the two factors was 0.84, indicating that verbal and spatial WMC shared 70% of their variance. Clearly, WMC, as measured by complex span tasks, is largely general across verbal and spatial domains.

Depending on the specifics of the analyses, they may even be indistinguishable from one another.

Our second prediction was that the shared variance among WMC tasks would correlate strongly with fluid reasoning ability. This was tested in several ways. Here we did not use the two-factor WMC model that we previously found to fit the data well. This is because in structural equation modeling one cannot build interpretable models when the predictor variables are highly correlated among themselves—referred to as the multicollinearity problem. In the two-factor model, recall that verbal and spatial WMC were correlated at 0.84. So, our first solution to this problem was to use the domain-general WMC factor that was comprised of all six complex-span tasks (including correlated errors) to predict the gF factor derived from all of the standardized tests. This model is illustrated in Figure 6. WMC accounted for approximately 30% of the variance in gF, as in prior work (Conway et al., 2002; Engle et al., 1999). In addition to loading all the reasoning tasks onto a gF factor, we simultaneously loaded all the verbal tasks onto a residual, domain-specific verbal reasoning factor, representing the variance shared by the verbal tasks that was not shared by the other tasks. Similarly, we loaded all the spatial tasks onto a residual, domain-specific spatial reasoning factor, representing the variance shared by the spatial tasks that was not shared by the other tasks. Here, domain-general WMC correlated significantly with these domain-specific verbal and spatial reasoning factors (sharing ≈8% of the variance), albeit more weakly than it did with gF. We suggest that these correlations result from the contribution of WMC to learning across various domains (e.g., Daneman & Green, 1986; Hambrick & Engle, 2002; Kyllonen & Stephens, 1990).

In a subsequent test for the relations among all our memory constructs and reasoning, both WMC and STM, our solution to the multicollinearity problem was to capture the considerable shared variance among our memory tasks in a similar manner to the way we modeled our reasoning-task data, by using a nested, or "bifactor," structure. Nested models allow tasks to simultaneously load onto more than one factor, and so variance attributable to different underlying constructs can be extracted independently from each task. The logic of our analysis was that no WMC or STM task provides a pure measure of either domain-general executive attention or domain-specific storage and rehearsal; all memory-span tasks will reflect storage, rehearsal, and executive attention to some degree (indeed, all cognitive tasks may reflect executive attention to some degree). By our view, WMC tasks capture executive attention primarily but also domain-specific rehearsal and storage, whereas STM tasks capture domain-specific storage primarily but also executive attention. As illustrated in Figure 7, our nested model thus consisted of an "Exec-Attn" factor, with loadings from *all* memory variables, reflecting the domain-general "executive" variance shared by all the STM

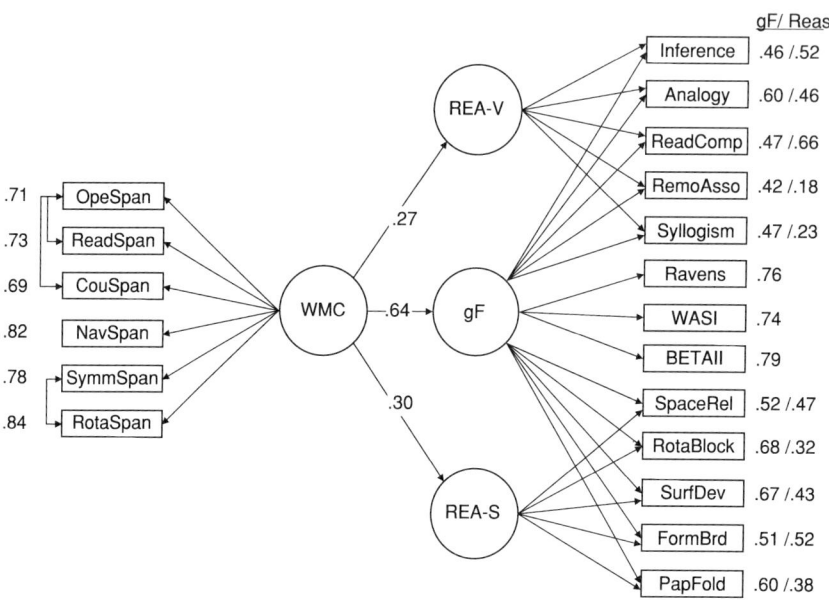

Fig. 6. Path model for structural equation analysis of the relation between working memory capacity and reasoning factors. All paths are statistically significant at p <.05. Numbers appearing next to each manifest working-memory variable represent the loadings for each task onto the latent variable. The numbers under the Gf column on the right represent the factor loadings for each reasoning task onto the Gf factor; the numbers under the REA column represent the simultaneous factor loadings for each reasoning task onto either the REA-V or REA-S factor, with the verbal tasks loading onto REA-V and the spatial tasks loading onto REA-S (matrix reasoning tasks were loaded only onto the Gf factor). *Note:* WMC = working memory capacity; Gf = general fluid intelligence; REA-V = reasoning-verbal; REA-S = reasoning-spatial; OpeSpan = Operation Span; ReadSpan = Reading Span; CouSpan = Counting Span; NavSpan = Navigation Span; SymmSpan = Symmetry Span; RotaSpan = Rotation Span; Inference = ETS Inferences; Analogy = AFOQT Analogies; ReadComp = AFOQT Reading Comprehension; RemoAsso = Remote Associates; Syllogism = ETS Nonsense Syllogisms; SpaceRel = DAT Space Relations; RotaBlock = AFOQT Rotated Blocks; SurfDev = ETS Surface Development; FormBrd = ETS Form Board; PapFold = ETS Paper Folding; Ravens = Ravens Advanced Progressive Matrices; WASI = Weschsler Abbreviated Scale of Intelligence, Matrix Test; BETAIII = Beta III Matrix Test. Copyright Randall W. Engle.

and WMC tasks. The model also consisted of domain-specific storage/rehearsal factors, with loadings from the six verbal span tasks on the "Storage-V" factor and loadings from the six spatial span tasks on the "Storage-S" factor. Thus, from each task we extracted variance hypothesized to reflect domain-general executive-attention *and* variance hypothesized to reflect storage, rehearsal, or coding processes that were specific to either verbal or

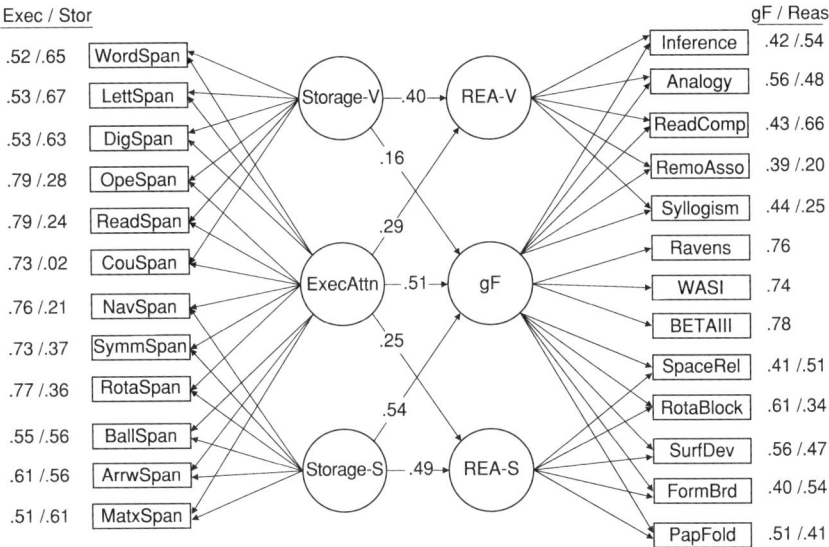

Fig. 7. Path model for structural equation analysis of the relation between memory span and reasoning factors. All paths are statistically significant at p <.05. The numbers under the Exec column on the left represent the factor loadings for each memory span task onto the ExecAttn factor; the numbers under the Stor column represent the simultaneous factor loadings for each memory span task onto either the Storage-V or Storage-S factor, with the verbal span tasks loading onto Storage-V and the spatial span tasks loading onto Storage-S. The numbers under the Gf column on the right represent the factor loadings for each reasoning task onto the Gf factor; the numbers under the REA column represent the simultaneous factor loadings for each reasoning task onto either the REA-V or REA-S factor, with the verbal tasks loading onto REA-V and the spatial tasks loading onto REA-S (matrix reasoning tasks were loaded only onto the Gf factor). ExecAttn = Executive Attention; Storage-V = storage-verbal; Storage-S = storage-spatial; Gf = general fluid intelligence; REA-V = reasoning-verbal; REA-S = reasoning-spatial; OpeSpan = Operation Span; ReadSpan = Reading Span; CouSpan = Counting Span; NavSpan = Navigation Span; SymmSpan = Symmetry Span; RotaSpan = Rotation Span; WordSpan = Word Span; LettSpan = Letter Span; DigSpan = Digit Span; BallSpan = Ball Span; ArrwSpan = Arrow Span; MatxSpan = Matrix Span; Inference = ETS Inferences; Analogy = AFOQT Analogies; ReadComp = AFOQT Reading Comprehension; RemoAsso = Remote Associates; Syllogism = ETS Nonsense Syllogisms; SpaceRel = DAT Space Relations; RotaBlock = AFOQT Rotated Blocks; SurfDev = ETS Surface Development; FormBrd = ETS Form Board; PapFold = ETS Paper Folding; Ravens = Ravens Advanced Progressive Matrices; WASI = Weschsler Abbreviated Scale of Intelligence, Matrix Test; BETAIII = Beta III Matrix Test. Copyright Randall W. Engle.

spatial stimuli. The Exec-Attn factor yielded high factor loadings from verbal and spatial WMC tasks and low loadings from verbal and spatial STM tasks, indicating empirically that it represented primarily domain-general attention control. In contrast, the domain-specific storage factors each elicited high loadings from their respective STM tasks and lower loadings from their WMC tasks, indicating that they reflected primarily domain-specific storage and rehearsal processes.

As illustrated in Figure 7, the executive factor correlated substantially with gF ($\approx$30% shared variance) and significantly, but more weakly, with domain-specific reasoning ($\approx$8% shared variance). Thus, this executive-attention factor behaved very similarly to our unitary WMC factor from our previous analysis. These two models together clearly indicate that the domain-general executive processes shared among WMC tasks, and not the domain-specific storage and rehearsal processes they also measure, are what drives the correlation between WMC and gF.

Another interesting feature of this structural model is that the verbal and spatial storage factors showed quite divergent patterns of correlations with reasoning. Verbal storage predicted unique variance in verbal reasoning beyond that accounted for by WMC, but it did not significantly predict unique variance in gF. Both findings are consistent with our prior work (Cantor, Engle, & Hamilton, 1991; Engle et al., 1990; Engle et al., 1999). In contrast, spatial storage not only predicted unique variance in spatial reasoning, it also accounted for as much unique variance in gF as did executive attention. The variance associated with spatial storage appears to be quite general in its predictive power, correlating with both domain-specific and domain-general aspects of complex reasoning (see also Miyake et al., 2001; Oberauer, 1993; Shah & Miyake, 1996).

How can we account for the apparent generality of spatial storage? Why do these "simple" span tasks work so well in predicting complex cognition? Shah and Miyake (1996) argued that subjects who do well on spatial STM tasks may be more strategic than those who do poorly, perhaps employing spatial chunking or some other beneficial coding processes, and this strategic superiority also improves performance in complex ability tasks. Another possibility is that spatial STM measures are purer measures of executive attention than are verbal STM measures. That is, spatial STM tasks with abstract, novel stimuli do not benefit from either the well-learned rehearsal strategies that are available to verbal materials (such as inner speech, associative chaining, etc.), nor do they afford the use of semantic or lexical knowledge to help encode or retrieve list items. Therefore, spatial tasks may rely more on "brute force" executive-fueled maintenance than on specialized rehearsal routines. By this view, spatial STM is really an executive task similar to WMC tasks. We find this to be an attractive view, and one that is consistent with the spatial WMC/STM findings of Miyake et al. (2001). The difficulty with it, however, is that in our data, as in Shah and Miyake (1996), spatial storage accounts for different variance in gF than executive attention/WMC. If spatial storage was simply another executive-attention measure, then it should account for much of the same gF variance that WMC tasks do.

A very different solution to these questions about spatial STM, at least for our data, is that our gF factor may have been more biased to the spatial domain than to the verbal domain. If true, then what looked like "general" reasoning ability being predicted by spatial storage was, instead, largely spatial reasoning. Although our gF factor consisted of five putatively-verbal and five putatively-spatial reasoning tasks, one of the verbal tasks (syllogisms) loaded with the spatial tasks in our exploratory factor analysis. Plus, the three matrix-reasoning tasks that loaded onto gF also consisted of some items that involved visuo-spatial processing (this was especially true of the Ravens test). Therefore, we used our nested model of memory span, consisting of executive attention, spatial storage, and verbal storage, to predict gF factors derived from different combinations of reasoning tasks.

In the first model, the gF latent variable was extracted from the three matrix reasoning tasks, which are "gold standard" gF tasks that nonetheless may have some spatial component. Here, the correlations of gF with executive attention, spatial storage, and verbal storage were 0.55, 0.54, and 0.17, respectively; spatial storage accounted for as much unique variance in gF as did executive attention. In the second model, however, we balanced the verbal/spatial contribution to gF by extracting it from three verbal and visuo-spatial measures; no matrix tasks were used. Here, the resulting correlations with memory factors were 0.57, 0.47, and 0.24, respectively. Although spatial storage still accounted for substantial variance in this more balanced gF factor, its contribution was reduced relative to Model 1 and relative to the executive-attention contribution. Note that the executive-attention contribution did not change between analyses. In a third and final model, we defined gF using the three verbal tasks from Model 2, in addition to the remote associates task, a putatively "verbal" task that nonetheless measured domain-general inductive reasoning according to our exploratory factor analysis. The correlations with this more verbal gF factor were 0.51, 0.29, and 0.36, respectively. Clearly, spatial storage still does share variance with fluid verbal abilities, but it accounts for less and less gF variance as gF became more verbal (with correlations of 0.54, 0.47, and 0.29). In contrast, the executive attention factor shared 25% to 30% of the variance in gF (with correlations of 0.55, 0.57, and 0.51) no matter how gF was defined. These analyses suggest that spatial storage may be a bit more general in its predictive power than is verbal storage, but it is not as general as the executive-attention contribution to memory span.

Altogether then, the Kane et al. (2003) data strongly indicate that verbal and visuo-spatial WMC tasks share a core, domain-general set of processes that represent more than simple STM storage and rehearsal. We would argue that the shared variance among WMC tasks represents domain-general executive attention, which is an important determinant of gF and reasoning ability. Although the contributions of verbal and spatial storage to memory span also predict variance to reasoning ability, these correlations are stronger with reasoning in the matching stimulus domain than with domain-general thinking abilities. Spatial storage appears at first to be somewhat "special" in its relation to general ability, but our final set of analyses indicates spatial storage to be less general in predicting complex cognition than is the executive-attention contribution to memory span.

V. Microanalytic Studies of WMC: Its Relation to Executive Attentional Control

We have argued, based on our large-scale macroanalytic studies, that the critical element of complex WMC span tasks for higher-order cognition and general fluid abilities, whether spatial or verbal, is the domain-general ability to control attention. That conclusion was inferential at the time we proposed it (Engle, Kane, & Tuholski, 1999; Engle et al., 1999), but we had no direct evidence for support. There is now considerable data to support that thesis and we will describe it here.

A. WMC AND RETRIEVAL INTERFERENCE

As we discussed at length in our introduction to this chapter, it is now clear that WMC is an important factor in the degree to which an individual's recall performance will be diminished by proactive interference. One line of research supporting this conclusion is based on "fan effect" manipulations (Anderson, 1983), whereby cues that are associated with many items or events allow slower recognition than cues associated with few items or events. Bunting et al. (2003) and Cantor and Engle (1993) both found that low WMC subjects show a much steeper fan effect than high-span subjects for propositional information if there is overlap among the fan items in set membership. However, if all the items are unique to a given fan, thereby eliminating response competition between sets, then high and low spans do not differ.

Conway and Engle (1994) demonstrated the importance of competition, or conflict, to eliciting WMC differences in fan effects by having subjects learn to associate letters with a digit cue representing the number of items in a set. Thus, C and S might be associated with the digit 2, associated with the letters W, G, H, and X with 4, and so on. After an extensive learning phase, subjects saw a digit (e.g., 2) and a letter (e.g., C) and they were to press a key indicating whether or not the letter was in the set represented by the digit. When there was no overlap among the set items (i.e., a letter was unique to a given set), the set size function for high- and low-WMC subjects did not differ. Moreover, the performance of high-span subjects was not further disrupted in a condition with conflict, in which each item was a member of two different sets. However, the set size function for low spans was substantially steeper in the response competition condition—they showed greater interference than high spans, and they showed greater interference than they did under no competition. In other words, high- and low-span subjects showed similar search rates of active memory in the absence of interference, but low spans were differentially slowed under conditions of interference, or what we might think of as response competition. Conway and Engle argued that high spans were able to attentionally inhibit the conflict from competing sets in the overlap condition, but low spans were not, and so low spans were more vulnerable to blocking and/or confusion among competing sets.

Kane and Engle (2000) provided a more direct demonstration of the role of attention control in the interaction between WMC and interference vulnerability. Our subjects read a 10-word list from a category such as "animals," then performed a 15-s rehearsal-preventative task, and then were cued to recall the 10 words. They received a series of such lists, all drawn from the same category, thereby inducing proactive interference across lists. On the very first such list, both high- and low-span subjects recalled approximately 6 words—not different from one another and not near ceiling or floor. On subsequent lists, the recall by low spans fell off at a faster rate than that of high spans. In other words, low spans showed a steeper interference function than high spans.

Some of our subjects additionally performed an attention-demanding secondary task either during the encoding or retrieval phase of the memory task. The interference function (i.e., the change from trial 1 to trial 2 to trial 3), did not change for low spans under attentional load compared to low spans under no load. However, the load manipulation caused the interference function for the high spans to become considerably steeper and virtually identical to that of the low spans. Thus, under standard conditions low spans were more vulnerable to interference than high spans, but under load, the span groups were equivalently vulnerable. Our interpretation of these findings was that, in the absence of an attention-demanding secondary task, high WMC individuals were capable of controlling their attention in such a manner that they encoded new list items as distinct from earlier list items and, during retrieval, blocked intrusions from the interfering lists. However, under load, high spans were incapable of using control in these ways. We further argued that low-span subjects were less capable of engaging attentional processes to resist interference, and so by failing to use controlled processing under normal conditions, they were not able to be hurt further by the load of the secondary task. Interestingly, low spans showed a larger dual-task decrement than high spans on list 1 of the task, before interference had built up. This suggests that low spans may have been exhausting their attention-control capabilities simply to encode and retrieve a single list of associated items, even in the absence of interference, and so they essentially had nothing left to give to combat the added effects of interference on subsequent lists.

The Kane and Engle (2000) finding that low spans have more difficulty than high spans in blocking the effects of prior-list information is consistent with previous findings reported in two papers by Rosen and Engle. In the first (1997), they conducted a series of studies using a fluency retrieval task. Subjects were to recall as many different exemplars of the category "animals" as possible in 10 min, with instructions to not repeat any items. In three experiments, high-span subjects retrieved many more animals than low-span subjects. In a fourth experiment, subjects were instructed that, while we were interested in how many different animals they could name, if an already recalled item came to mind, they should say it anyway "to clear their minds." High spans made relatively few re-retrievals but low spans repeated nearly one-half of their retrieved items. Again, we reasoned that high spans had sufficient attentional resources to monitor for previously retrieved items and to suppress their activation. However, low spans did not have sufficient attentional resources to both monitor whether a retrieved item had been previously retrieved and also to suppress activation of those items. This series of studies also found that, while a secondary-load task greatly reduced the number of exemplars retrieved by high spans, it had little effect on retrieval by low spans. This suggested, as in the Kane and Engle (2000) study, that high spans were using their ability to focus and maintain attention for controlled strategic retrieval as well as for suppression of previously retrieved items. Low spans were not using such attention control to strategic retrieval or suppression during the regular version of the task, and so their performance was not impaired further by divided attention.

Traditional paired-associates tasks also support the conclusion that low-span subjects are impaired in the attentional blocking of competition during memory retrieval. Rosen and Engle (1998) had subjects learn three lists of paired associates using an A-B, A-C, A-B design with answers given orally in response to the cue word and, in the first experiment, a response deadline of 1,300 ms. List 1 was composed of items with high pre-experimental associations, for example, "*bird-bath*" and "*knee-bend.*" High- and low-span subjects did not differ in the trials to learn this first list. The second list consisted of the cue words from list one associated with new words that were weak associates, for example, "*bird-dawn*" and "*knee-bone.*" The interference from list 1 caused both groups to take longer to learn list 2, but low spans took substantially longer to learn the list than high spans, indicating a relation between WMC and negative transfer (or proactive interference at learning). Further, low spans made many more intrusions from list 1 during the learning of list 2 than high spans. The third list consisted of re-learning the items from list one (*bird-bath, knee-bend*). Even though both groups had previously learned this list and in an equivalent number of trials, low spans now required more trials to re-learn the list and, in so doing, made more intrusions than high spans.

B. WMC AND INHIBITION/SUPPRESSION

The notion of inhibition or deactivation of a representation remains a controversial topic in cognitive research (MacLeod, in press). For example, in learning the second list of the Rosen and Engle (1998) study described in the preceding text, high spans could make few intrusions of "*bath*" to "*bird*" because they have dampened that connection (Postman, Stark, & Frasier, 1968). Or, they could make few intrusions, instead, because they quickly strengthen the "*bird-dawn*" connection to a higher level. Most techniques for studying so-called inhibition do not allow a distinction between a mechanism based on true inhibition and one based on an increase in excitation. We have taken the position that both mechanisms require the control of attention and, therefore, will depend on WMC.

We have shown that the negative priming effect, in which a distractor letter to be ignored on trial n is the target letter to be named on trial $n + 1$, is resource-dependent (Engle, Conway, Tuholski, & Shister, 1995); that is, the effect disappears under a secondary load task. Further, whether subjects show the negative priming effect depends on their WMC, with high-span subjects showing larger effects than low span subjects (Conway et al., 1999). Perhaps the strongest evidence for what appear to be true inhibition differences is the second study of the Rosen and Engle (1998) paper. We used an identical A-B, A-C, A-B procedure to that described in the preceding text, except that instead of forcing the subjects to respond quickly so that we could focus on intrusions, we emphasized accuracy of response so that we could measure time to retrieve the item. If high spans suppress activation of the "*bird-bath*" connection from list 1 during the learning of "*bird-dawn*" in list 2, then when we test them on list 3, which is the re-learning of list 1, they should be slower than a control group of high spans learning the "*bird-bath*" connection for the first time. They may even be slower to respond than they themselves had been on the first recall phase of list 1. In contrast, if low WMC individuals have less capability to suppress the list 1 items during the learning of list 2, then they might show less of an increase in the time to retrieve list 1 items in the first recall phase of list 3 learning. That is exactly what Rosen and Engle found. Low spans in the interference condition were actually faster than in the non-interference condition to retrieve *"bath"* as a response to *"bird"* on list 3. However, high spans in the interference condition were significantly slower to retrieve list 3 responses during the first recall phase than the non-interference group. In addition, high spans in the interference condition were slower to retrieve *"bath"* to *"bird"* during the first recall phase of list 3 learning than they were themselves during the first recall phase of learning the same items on list 1. This strikes us as strong evidence that high spans suppressed the list 1 (*"bird-bath"*) connections during the learning of list 2 and that low spans learned the A-C list with relatively little evidence of suppression of the A-B connection.

C. WMC AND RESISTANCE TO PREPOTENT RESPONSES

If our thesis that performance on complex WMC tasks, such as operation span and reading span, reflect primarily an ability to control attention irrespective of mode of representation, then we should find that high and low spans perform differently on tasks that require responses counter to strongly established stimulus-response connections. That is, WMC differences should be measurable in "attention control" tasks that are further removed from a memory context. We will describe our work using the antisaccade task and the Stroop task to support this contention.

The antisaccade task is perhaps the best possible task with which to test this idea. Millions of years of evolution have prepared us to attend to any stimulus that cues movement. After all, moving objects might be predator or prey, and so survival depends on attending to them. The task is as follows: you are seated in front of a computer monitor and asked to look at a fixation point. At some time, there is a flickering cue, 11° to one side or the other, randomly. Your natural tendency is to shift your attention and to move your eyes to the flickering cue. However, your task is instead to immediately move your eyes to the *opposite* side of the screen, thus disobeying Mother Nature's instructions. The antisaccade task typically has two conditions: (1) the prosaccade condition, in which you are to move your eyes to the flickering cue, and (2) the antisaccade condition, in which you are to shift your attention and eye gaze to the opposite side of the screen.

If WMC reflects individual differences in ability to control attention, then people who score high on a complex WMC span task should perform better on the antisaccade task than those who score low in complex span. At the same time, high and low spans should not differ on the prosaccade task, because here attention can be drawn or captured by the exogenous event, resulting in the automatic fixation at the location of the target. Kane et al.

(2001) used a procedure in which one of three visually similar letters—B, P, or R—was presented either at the location of the previous flickering cue (prosaccade condition) or at the equivalent location on the opposite side of the screen (antisaccade condition). The letter occurred very briefly and was pattern-masked, so if the subject shifted attention toward the exogenous cue even briefly while in the antisaccade condition, they would likely misidentify the letter or at least have a slowed response. We found that the two groups were not different in the prosaccade condition, either in number of errors or in time to initiate correct responses. However, in the antisaccade condition, low spans made more identification errors and were slower on correct trials than high spans. Nearly an hour of antisaccade practice still showed that high spans made fewer reflexive saccades to the flickering cue than low spans. And, even on trials in which both high and low spans made an accurate antisaccade, high spans did so significantly more quickly than low spans.

One potential problem with the Kane et al. (2001) procedure is the possibility that low spans had more difficulty than high spans with the letter-identification task. Roberts, Hager, and Heron (1994) demonstrated that subjects under a secondary, attention-demanding load made more antisaccade errors than subjects under normal conditions. Therefore, if the letter task was more demanding for the low spans than for the high spans, this could have resulted in low spans making more antisaccade errors. To correct for this potential problem, Unsworth, Schrock, and Engle (2003) developed a task in which subjects simply had to move their eyes to a box located 11° left or right of fixation. In the prosaccade condition, subjects were to move their fixation as quickly as possible to the box that flickered. In the antisaccade condition, subjects were to move their gaze to the box on the opposite side of the screen from the box that flickered. Figure 8 shows the percentage of errors on the first saccade. Consistent with our prior work, high and low spans did not differ in the prosaccade condition. They were equivalent in the accuracy of direction of the first saccade and in the time to initiate that first saccade. In addition, even if the first saccade was in the correct direction, low spans were slower to initiate that saccade. These findings are consistent with those of Kane et al. (2001), and suggest that the span differences we originally found were not an artifact of the embedded letter-identification task.

VI. A Two-Factor Theory of Executive Control

Our antisaccade findings support a two-factor model of the executive control of behavior, which also seems to explain the Stroop results we will describe in the following. We propose one factor of control to be the maintenance of

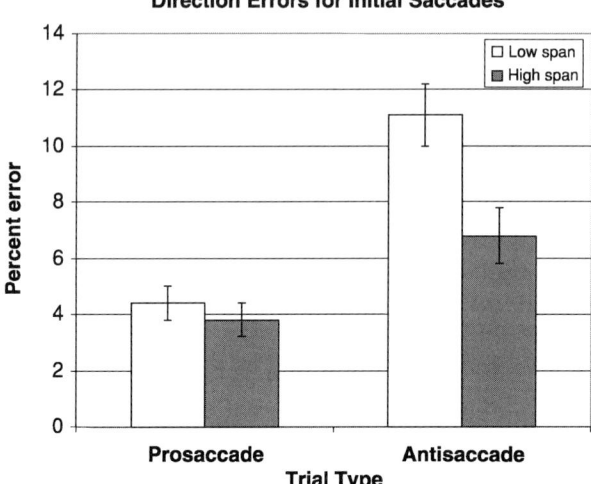

Fig. 8. Percent error for high and low WMC subjects in prosaccade and antisaccade conditions. Error bars depict the standard errors of the means.

the task goals in active memory, and that low-span subjects are simply less able to maintain the novel production necessary to do the task ("*Look away from the flash*") in active memory. All subjects clearly knew what they were supposed to do in the task, and they could easily tell you what they were to do, presumably based on retrieval of the goal from LTM. However, in the context of doing the antisaccade task, trial after trial, low spans failed on some trials to do the mental work necessary to maintain the production in active memory such that it could control behavior. Under these circumstances low-span subjects were more likely to make a saccade to the cue, in error, than high spans. Our view is that maintenance is a resource-demanding endeavor and that high WMC individuals are better able to expend that resource on a continuing basis. We believe that the prefrontal cortex is important in successful maintenance of the task goals in active memory as we will discuss further in the following.

The second factor in the executive control of behavior is the resolution of response competition or conflict, particularly when prepotent or habitual behaviors conflict with behaviors appropriate to the current task goal. We argue that, even when the production necessary to perform the antisaccade task is in active memory, there is conflict between the natural, prepotent response tendency to attend to and look toward the flickering exogenous cue and the response tendency resulting from the task goal provided by the experimental context. Low spans have greater difficulty resolving that conflict as demonstrated by the fact that even when they made the correct initial saccade, indicating effective goal maintenance, they were slower to initiate the saccade than high spans.

Our studies with the Stroop (1935) paradigm show a striking parallel to our studies using the antisaccade task, and in fact they were explicitly designed to test our dual-process idea. Kane and Engle (2003b) tested high- and low-span subjects in different versions of the Stroop color-word task, in which subjects name the colors in which words are presented (e.g., *RED* presented in the color blue). These studies were motivated, in part, by failures in the psychometric and neuropsychological literatures to demonstrate a consistent relationship between Stroop performance and either intelligence or prefrontal cortex damage. These failures were interesting to us—and initially surprising—because both intelligence and prefrontal cortex have been strongly implicated in WMC and attention-control functions (for a review, see Kane & Engle, 2002). However, our reading of the relevant literatures suggested to us that studies where relation between Stroop performance and intelligence or prefrontal function was found, tended to use versions of the Stroop task in which all (or almost all) of the words and colors were in conflict. We thought that this was significant because, by our view, part of the challenge in the Stroop task is to actively maintain a novel goal ("*name the color*") in the face of a powerful opposing habit (i.e., to read the word). Therefore, a task context in which all the stimuli reinforced the task goal by presenting only incongruent stimuli would minimize the need for active goal maintenance. When trial after trial forces subjects to ignore the word, ignore the word, and again, ignore the word, the task goal may become overlearned and thus run off without active, controlled maintenance.

Consider, in contrast, a task context in which a majority of trials are *congruent*, with the word and color matching each other (e.g., *BLUE* presented in blue). Here a subject could respond accurately on most trials even if they completely failed to act according to the goal, and instead slipped into reading the words rather than naming the colors. When that subject encountered one of the rare incongruent stimuli, it is unlikely that he or she could respond both quickly and accurately. For a subject to respond quickly and accurately to an infrequent incongruent stimulus in a high-congruency task, he or she must actively maintain accessibility to the goal of the task. Otherwise, the habitual and incorrect response will be elicited. Therefore, we predicted that, as in the antisaccade task, low-span subjects would show evidence of failed goal maintenance in the Stroop task, but perhaps only in a high-congruency context. We expected that when most Stroop trials were congruent, low spans would make many more errors on incongruent trials than high spans. Moreover, by the dual-process view of executive control, even in contexts in which goal maintenance was less critical, for example in a low-congruency context, a span difference in resolving response conflict might be evident in response-time interference.

In fact, this is exactly what Kane and Engle (2003b) observed. In task contexts where 75% or 80% of the trials were congruent, low spans showed significantly greater interference, as measured by errors, than high spans. The results from four such conditions (each with different groups of subjects) are presented in Fig. 9. Moreover, in one experiment we had a large enough subject sample to examine the latencies of errors in the 80%-congruent condition, with the expectation that errors resulting from goal neglect (and subsequent word reading) should be relatively fast compared to other kinds of errors. Therefore, we expected that when subjects' errors represented unambiguous, "clean" responses of reading the word on incongruent trials, they would be faster than other errors such as stuttering, slurring two words together, or naming a word that was not presented. We also predicted that low spans would show more of these "clean" errors than high spans. To test this idea, we examined error latencies for subjects who made at least a 16% error rate on incongruent trials. Twenty-two high spans and 47 low spans met this criterion, and on average, 68% of low-span subjects' errors, but only 58% of high spans' errors, were "clean," or indicative of goal-maintenance failure. Irrespective of WMC, clean errors were committed over 1000 ms faster than

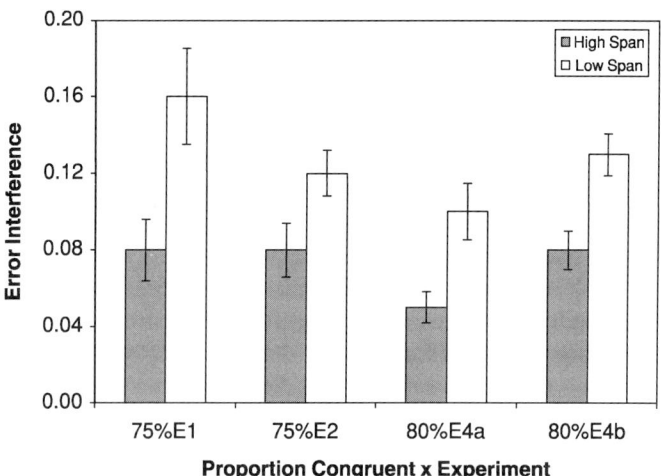

Fig. 9. Mean error-rate interference effects for high and low WMC span participants in high-congruency contexts (75% or 80%) across four experimental groups from Kane and Engle (2003). Interference effects were calculated by subtracting participants' mean baseline error rate from incongruent-trial error rate. Error bars depict standard errors of the means. E1 = Experiment 1; E2 = Experiment 2; E4a = Experiment 4a; E4b = Experiment 4b.

were other errors, and with latencies very similar to correct responses on congruent trials, strongly suggesting that these errors represented rapid word reading due to failed access to the goal state.

As a final source of evidence for failed goal maintenance, low spans also demonstrated greater response-time facilitation than high spans in the high-congruency conditions. That is, low spans showed a differential latency benefit on congruent trials, where word and color match, compared to neutral trials. What does facilitation have to do with goal maintenance? MacLeod (1998; MacLeod & MacDonald, 2000) has argued that facilitation in the Stroop task reflects the fact that subjects sometimes read the word on congruent trials rather than naming the color, and because word reading is faster than color naming, these undetectable reading responses reduce the mean latency for congruent trials. Put into our words, the word reading responsible for facilitation effects is a result of periodic failure of goal maintenance. Low spans, therefore, should show greater facilitation than high spans; this is just what we found. Moreover, collapsed across span groups, we found significant correlations between error interference and response-time facilitation in our high-congruency conditions (rs between 0.35 and 0.45), the two measures we hypothesized to reflect word reading due to failures of goal maintenance.

We also found evidence for span differences in resolving response competition under conditions where goal-maintenance failures were unlikely, supporting our idea that WMC is related to two aspects of executive control. In Stroop contexts that reinforced the task goal by presenting 0% congruent trials, we found modest span differences in response-time interference. These differences were on the order of only 20 to 30 ms, and they required much larger samples to be statistically significant than the error effects we discussed previously. Our idea is that these low-congruency contexts did not put a premium on actively maintaining access to the task goals, and so the latency differences we observed between high and low spans reflect low spans' deficiency in resolving response competition (as in our antisaccade and memory-interference studies). Further support for this idea came from two experiments in which a 75% congruent context was presented to subjects after they had extensively practiced a 0% congruent Stroop task. Here, overlearning of the task goal in the prior context might make goal maintenance in the 75% congruent condition less necessary. And, in fact, low spans and high spans showed equivalent (and low) error rates in the 75% conditions here, in addition to showing equivalent response-time facilitation effects. High and low spans did differ, however, in response-time interference, suggesting to us that low spans were responding according to goal, but they were slower to resolve the competition between color and word than high spans.

Our Stroop and antisaccade findings generally indicate that high and low WMC subjects differ not only in higher order, complex cognitive tasks, but also in relatively "lower order," simple attention tasks. Specifically, when powerful habits, prepotencies, or reflexes must be held in abeyance in order to satisfy current goals, high spans more effectively exert executive control than low spans. Moreover, our view is that such executive control reflects a synergy of "memorial" and "attentional" processes. Active maintenance of goals, a memory phenomenon, allows the resolution of response competition to occur; without effective goal maintenance, automated routines will control behavior in the face of conflict. However, even when goal maintenance is successful, the attentional implementation of blocking or inhibitory processes may sometimes fail, or at least they may be slow to resolve the competition that is present. It is our view that both of these control processes rely on WMC.

VII. Implementation of WMC in the Brain

We have so far discussed our dual-process view of executive control as if it was entirely new, but this is not really the case. The behavioral and neuroscience research programs of both John Duncan and Jonathan Cohen have heavily influenced our thinking about WMC and executive attention, at least insofar as they relate to the idea of goal maintenance. These views also provide suggestions for how our ideas might be mechanistically implemented in the wetware of the brain. Duncan (1993, 1995) has argued that in novel contexts, or in those that afford multiple actions, attention-control processes somehow weight a hierarchical organization of goal abstractions, and this weighting serves to bias the system toward goal attainment. Important to our perspective, Duncan argues that such attentional, controlled goal weighting is strongly associated with gF and relies heavily on prefrontal cortex circuitry. Evidence for Duncan's ideas come from studies showing that dual-task conditions, low fluid intelligence, and prefrontal cortex damage lead to high rates of "goal neglect" in novel tasks, even when subjects can faithfully report what the goal of the task actually is (probably based on LTM retrieval; Duncan, Burgess, & Emslie, 1995; Duncan et al., 1996). By our view that WMC, attention control, fluid intelligence, and prefrontal cortex functioning are largely overlapping constructs (Engle, Kane, & Tuholski, 1999; Engle & Oransky, 1999; Kane & Engle, 2002), this confluence of influences on goal neglect indicates the centrality of WMC to goal maintenance, and the importance of such maintenance for complex, intentional behavior.

Cohen's research on the Stroop task and on the cognitive neuroscience of executive control also suggests a link between goal maintenance and prefrontal cortex functioning. In essence, Cohen's connectionist models and imaging research suggest that the dorsolateral area of the prefrontal cortex is particularly involved in the on-line maintenance of "task demand," or contextual information that keeps behavior yoked to goals (Braver & Cohen, 2000; Cohen & Servan-Schreiber, 1992; O'Reilly, Braver, & Cohen, 1999). For example, Cohen models the Stroop deficits seen in schizophrenics by reducing the activity of task-demand context nodes (*"name the color"*). This reduction in activity represents in the model schizophrenics' decreased dopaminergic activity in prefrontal cortex circuitry. When these task-demand nodes operate effectively, in a healthy brain, they block activity of pathways associated with the environmentally elicited, but incorrect, response. When "damaged" by schizophrenia, prefrontal cortex damage, or presumably, low WMC, however, these task-demand representations of goal states can no longer block the dominant, prepotent response, leading to exaggerated Stroop interference effects. Mechanistically, then, the executive control of behavior is implemented via the active maintenance of goals (Braver & Cohen, 2000; O'Reilly, Braver, & Cohen, 1999).

A particularly compelling empirical confirmation of Cohen's ideas was reported recently by MacDonald, Cohen, Stenger, & Carter (2000). Under fMRI, subjects completed a 50%-congruent Stroop task in which the instructions to read the word or name the color were presented 11 s before each stimulus. On color-naming trials, where active goal maintenance would seem most necessary, prefrontal cortex activity increased steadily over the 11s delay. On the more automatic word-reading trials, however, no such increase in activity was observed. Thus, prefrontal cortex activity seems to have reflected a mounting preparation to respond according to the novel goal to *"name the color, not the word."* This interpretation is bolstered by the additional finding that delay-period prefrontal activity was negatively correlated with Stroop interference ($r = -0.63$). That is, the more active prefrontal cortex was before the Stroop stimulus arrived, the less Stroop interference was elicited. Related findings have been reported by West and Alain (2000), who used event-related potentials to isolate a slow wave originating in prefrontal cortex that predicts, in advance, when a Stroop error is about to be committed. Specifically, this wave begins 400 to 800 ms before the error-eliciting stimulus is presented, and it is significantly larger in high-congruency than in low-congruency Stroop tasks. Given our findings of WMC differences in error interference under high-congruency conditions, the imaging findings discussed here strongly suggest that WMC differences in executive control are linked to individual differences in prefrontal cortex activity corresponding to active goal maintenance.

The second component of our theory involves differences in the resolution of conflict, evident in antisaccade and Stroop tasks as slower responding for low spans when faced with competition, even when they appear to have acted according to goal. Our interpretation of the memory interference and retrieval inhibition findings that we discussed in the preceding text also would suggest response competition or conflict as the likely culprit responsible for the differences between high and low WMC subjects. For example, in the Rosen and Engle (1998) interference study, once a person has learned to give "*bath*" in response to "*bird*," then during the period when the subject must learn to give "*dawn*" to "*bird*," we believe that high and low WMC subjects differ in their ability to detect and resolve the conflict arising from the retrieval of "*bath*" to "*bird*." High spans appear to be able to suppress the inappropriate retrieval better than the lows.

The detection and resolution of conflict appears to rely on anterior cingulate, as also indicated by recent work from Jonathan Cohen's group (Botvinick et al., 2001; see also MacLeod & MacDonald, 2000). They also reported two computational modeling studies supporting that view. The argument is that the anterior cingulate detects overall conflict in the system and, through a feedback loop, causes increased activity in other regions, such as the prefrontal cortex. That, in turn, would lead to better maintenance of novel connections, task goals, and productions. This neural interaction of competition detection/resolution and goal maintenance seems a likely mechanism by which individual differences of the kinds we have described here could be implemented in the nervous system.

VIII. Conclusions

Measures of STM such as digit and word span correlate very poorly with real-world cognitive tasks but measures of WMC correlate with a wide array of such tasks. Measures of WMC are highly reliable and highly valid indicators of some construct of clear relevance to feral cognition. Our macroanalytic studies have demonstrated that the construct reflected by WMC tasks has a strong relationship with gF above and beyond what these tasks share with simple span tasks. Further, this construct is domain-free and general, and is common to complex span tasks both verbal and spatial in nature. Our microanalytic studies provide evidence that the construct reflects the ability to control attention, particularly when other elements of the internal and external environment serve to capture attention away from the currently relevant task. We have referred to this as executive attention and define it as the ability to maintain stimulus and response elements in active memory, particularly in the presence of events that would capture attention away from that enterprise. We proposed a two-factor model by which individual differences in WMC or executive attention leads to performance differences. We argued that executive attention is important for maintaining information in active memory and secondly is important in the resolution of conflict resulting from competition between task-appropriate responses and prepotent but inappropriate responses. The conflict might also arise from stimulus representations of competing strength. This two-factor model fits with current thinking about the role of two brain structures: the prefrontal cortex as important to the maintenance of information in an active and easily accessible state and the anterior cingulate as important to the detection and resolution of conflict.

Acknowledgments

Address correspondence to: Randall Engle, School of Psychology, Georgia Institute of Technology, 654 Cherry Street, Atlanta, GA 30332-0170. Email requests to randall.engle@psych.gatech.edu.

References

Ackerman, P. L., Beier, M. E., & Perdue, M. B. (2002). Individual differences in working memory within a nomological network of cognitive and perceptual speed abilities. *Journal of Experimental Psychology: General, 131,* 567–589.

Allport, D. A., Styles, E. A., & Hsieh, S. (1994). Shifting attentional set: Exploring the dynamic control of tasks. In C. Umilta & M. Moscovitch (Eds.), *Attention and Performance XV.* (pp. 421–452). Hillsdale, NJ: Erlbaum.

Arnett, P. A., Higgenson, C. I., Voss, W. D., Bender, W. I., Wurst, J. M., & Tippin, J. M. (1999). Depression in multiple sclerosis: Relationship to working memory capacity. *Neuropsychology, 13,* 546–556.

Anderson, J. R. (1983). *The architecture of cognition.* Cambridge, MA: Harvard University Press.

Atkinson, R. C., & Shiffrin, R. M. (1968). Human memory: A proposed system and its control processes. In K. W. Spence & J. T. Spence (Eds.), *The Psychology of Learning and Motivation.* Vol. 2. (pp. 89–95). New York: Academic Press.

Baddeley, A. D. (1986). *Working memory.* London/New York: Oxford University Press.

Baddeley, A. D. (1996). Exploring the central executive. *Quarterly Journal of Experimental Psychology, 49A,* 5–28.

Baddeley, A. D. (2000). The episodic buffer: A new component of working memory? *Trends in Cognitive Sciences, 4,* 417–423.

Baddeley, A. D., & Hitch, G. (1974). Working memory. In G. A. Bower (Ed.), *The Psychology of Learning and Motivation.* Vol. 8. (pp. 47–89). New York: Academic Press.

Baddeley, A. D., & Hitch, G. (1977). Recency re-examined. In S. Dornic (Ed). *Attention and Performance VI.* (pp. 647–667). Hillsdale, NJ: Erlbaum.

Baddeley, A. D., & Logie, R. (1999). Working memory: The multiple component model. In A. Miyake & P. Shah (Eds.), *Models of working memory: Mechanisms of active maintenance and executive control.* (pp. 28–61). New York: Cambridge University Press.

Baddeley, A. D., Gathercole, S., & Papagno, C. (1998). The phonological loop as a language learning device. *Psychologial Review, 105*, 158–173.

Barch, D. M., Sheline, Y. I., Csernansky, J. G., & Snyder, A. Z. (2003). Working memory and prefrontal cortex dysfunction: Specificity to schizophrenia compared with major depression. *Biological Psychiatry, 53*, 376–384.

Barrouillet, P. (1996). Transitive inferences from set-inclusion relations and working memory. *Journal of Experimental Psychology: Learning, Memory, and Cognition, 22*, 1408–1422.

Benton, S. L., Kraft, R. G., Glover, J. A., & Plake, B. S. (1984). Cognitive capacity differences among writers. *Journal of Educational Psychology, 76*, 820–834.

Botvinick, M. M., Braver, T. S., Barch, D. M., Carter, C. S., & Cohen, J. D. (2001). Conflict monitoring and cognitive control. *Psychological Review, 108*, 624–652.

Braver, T. S., & Cohen, J. D. (2000). On the control of control: The role of dompamine in regulating prefrontal function and working memory. In S. Monsell & J. Driver (Eds.), *Attention and Performance XVIII: Control of Cognitive Processes.* (pp. 713–737). Cambridge, MA: MIT Press.

Brewin, C. R., & Beaton, A. (2002). Thought suppression, intelligence, and working memory capacity. *Behavior Research and Therapy, 40*, 923–930.

Brooks, L.R. (1967). The suppression of visualization by reading. *Quarterly Journal of Experimental Psychology, 19*, 289–299.

Bunting, M. F., Conway, A. R. A., & Heitz, R. P. (2003). *Individual differences in the fan effect and working memory capacity.* Unpublished manuscript.

Cantor, J., & Engle, R. W. (1993). Working-memory capacity as long-term memory activation: An individual-differences approach. *Journal of Experimental Psychology, Learning, Memory, and Cognition, 19*, 1101–1114.

Cantor, J., Engle, R. W., & Hamilton, G. (1991). Short-term memory, working memory, and verbal abilities: How do they relate? *Intelligence, 15*, 229–246.

Caplan, D., & Waters, G. S. (1999). Verbal working memory and sentence comprehension. *Behavioral and Brain Sciences, 22*, 77–126.

Carpenter, P. A., & Just, M. A. (1988). The role of working memory in language comprehension. In D. Klahr & K. Kotovsky (Eds.), *Complex information processing: The impact of Herbert A. Simon.* (pp. 31–68). Hillsdale, NJ: Erlbaum.

Case, R. (1985). *Intellectual development: Birth to adulthood.* New York: Academic Press.

Cattell, R. B. (1973). *Measuring intelligence with the Culture Fair tests.* Champaigne, IL: Institute for Personality and Ability Testing.

Clark, C. R., McFarlane, A. C., Morris, P., Weber, D. L., Sonkkilla, C., Shaw, M., Marcina, J., Tochon-Danguy, H. J., & Egan, G. F. (2003). Cerebral function in posttraumatic stress disorder during verbal working memory updating: A positron emission tomography study. *Biological Psychiatry, 53*, 474–481.

Clarkson-Smith, L., & Hartley, A. A. (1990). The game of bridge as an exercise in working memory and reasoning. *Journal of Gerontology, 45*, P233–P238.

Conway, A. R. A., & Engle, R. W. (1994). Working memory and retrieval: A resource-dependent inhibition model. *Journal of Experimental Psychology: General, 123*, 354–373.

Conway, A. R. A., Cowan, N., & Bunting, M. F. (2001). The cocktail party phenomenon revisited: The importance of working memory capacity. *Psychonomic Bulletin and Review, 8*, 331–335.

Conway, A. R. A., Cowan, N., Bunting, M. F., Therriault, D., & Minkoff, S. (2002). A latent variable analysis of working memory capacity, short term memory capacity, processing speed, and general fluid intelligence. *Intelligence, 30*, 163–183.

Conway, A. R. A., Tuholski, S. W., Shisler, R. J., & Engle, R. W. (1999). The effect of memory load on negative priming: An individual differences investigation. *Memory & Cognition, 27*, 1042–1050.

Conway, A. R. A., Kane, M. J., & Engle, R. W. (1999). Is Spearman's g determined by speed or working memory capacity? Book review of Jensen on Intelligence-g-Factor. *Psycoloquy, 10*(074), article 16.

Cowan, N. (1995). *Attention and memory: An integrated framework*. Oxford: Oxford University Press.

Cowan, N. (1999). An embedded-process model of working memory. In A. Miyake & P. Shah (Eds.), *Models of working memory: Mechanisms of active maintenance and executive control.* (pp. 62–101). New York: Cambridge University Press.

Craik, F. I. M., & Watkins, M. J. (1973). The role of rehearsal in short-term memory. *Journal of Verbal Learning and Verbal Behavior, 12*, 599–607.

Cronbach, L. J. (1957). The two disciplines of scientific psychology. *American Psychologist, 12*, 671–684.

Crowder, R. G. (1982). The demise of short-term memory. *Acta Psychologica, 50*, 291–323.

Daneman, M., & Carpenter, P. A. (1980). Individual differences in working memory and reading. *Journal of Verbal Learning and Verbal Behavior, 19*, 450–466.

Daneman, M., & Carpenter, P. A. (1983). Individual differences in integrating information between and within sentences. *Journal of Experimental Psychology: Learning, Memory, and Cognition, 9*, 561–584.

Daneman, M., & Green, I. (1986). Individual differences in comprehending and producing words in context. *Journal of Memory and Language, 25*, 1–18.

Daneman, M., & Merikle, P. M. (1996). Working memory and language comprehension: A meta-analysis. *Psychonomic Bulletin & Review, 3*, 422–433.

Daneman, M., & Tardif, T. (1987). Working memory and reading skill reexamined. In M. Coltheart (Ed.), *Attention and performance XII: The psychology of reading.*(pp. 491–508). Hove, UK: Erlbaum.

Dempster, F. N. (1981). Memory span: Sources of individual and developmental differences. *Psychological Bulletin, 89*, 63–100.

Duncan, J. (1993). Selection of input and goal in the control of behavior. In A. Baddeley & L. Weiskrantz (Eds.), *Attention: Selection, awareness and control.* (pp. 53–71). Oxford: Oxford University Press.

Duncan, J. (1995). Attention, intelligence, and the frontal lobes. In M. Gazzaniga (Ed.), *The cognitive neurosciences.* (pp. 721–733). Cambridge, MA: MIT Press.

Duncan, J., Burgess, P., & Emslie, H. (1995). Fluid intelligence after frontal lobe lesions. *Neuropsychologia, 33*, 261–268.

Duncan, J., Emslie, H., Williams, P., Johnson, R., & Freer, C. (1996). Intelligence and the frontal lobe: The organization of goal-directed behavior. *Cognitive Psychology, 30*, 257–303.

Engle, R. W., & Conway, A. R. A. (1998). Comprehension and working memory. In R. H. Logie & K. J. Gilhooly (Eds.), *Working memory and thinking.* (pp. 67–91). Hillsdale, NJ: Erlbaum.

Engle, R. W., & Oransky, N. (1999). The evolution from short-term to working memory: Multistore to dynamic models of temporary storage. In R. J. Sternberg (Ed.), *The nature of cognition.* (pp. 515–555). Cambridge, MA: MIT Press.

Engle, R. W., Cantor, J., & Carullo, J. J. (1992). Individual differences in working memory and comprehension: A test of four hypotheses. *Journal of Experimental Psychology: Learning, Memory, and Cognition, 18*, 972–992.

Engle, R. W., Carullo, J. J., & Collins, K. W. (1991). Individual differences in working memory for comprehension and following directions. *Journal of Educational Research, 84,* 253–262.

Engle, R. W., Conway, A. R. A., Tuholski, S. W., & Shisler, R. J. (1995). A resource account of inhibition. *Psychological Science, 6,* 122–125.

Engle, R. W., Kane, M. J., & Tuholski, S. W. (1999). Individual differences in working memory capacity and what they tell us about controlled attention, general fluid intelligence and functions of the prefrontal cortex. In A. Miyake & P. Shah (Eds.), *Models of working memory: Mechanisms of active maintenance and executive control.* (pp. 102–134). New York: Cambridge University Press.

Engle, R. W., Nations, J. K., & Cantor, J. (1990). Is "working memory capacity" just another name for word knowledge? *Journal of Educational Psychology, 82,* 799–804.

Engle, R. W., Tuholski, S. W., Laughlin, J. E., & Conway, A. R. A. (1999). Working memory, short-term memory and general fluid intelligence: A latent variable approach. *Journal of Experimental Psychology: General, 128,* 309–331.

Feldman-Barrett, L., Tugade, M. M., & Engle, R. W. (in press). Individual differences in working memory capacity and dual-process theories of the mind. *Psychological Bulletin,* in press.

Finn, P. R. (2002). Motivation, working memory, and decision making: A cognitive-motivational theory of personality vulnerability to alcoholism. *Behavioral & Cognitive Neuroscience Reviews, 3,* 183–205.

Friedman, N. P., & Miyake, A. (2000). Differential roles for visuospatial and verbal working memory in situation model construction. *Journal of Experimental Psychology: General, 129,* 61–83.

Garner, W. R., Hake, H. W., & Eriksen, C. W. (1956). Operationism and the concept of perception. *Psychological Review, 63,* 149–159.

Goldinger, S. D., Kleider, H. M., Azuma, T., & Beike, D. R. (2003). "Blaming the victim" under memory load. *Psychological Science, 14,* 81–85.

Hambrick, D. Z., & Engle, R. W. (2002). Effects of domain knowledge, working memory capacity, and age on cognitive performance: An investigation of the knowledge-is-power hypothesis. *Cognitive Psychology, 44,* 339–384.

Hambrick, D. Z., Kane, M. J., & Engle, R. W. (in press). The role of working memory in higher-level cognition: Domain-specific versus domain-general perspectives. To appear in R. Sternberg & J. Pretz (Eds.), *Cognition and Intelligence.* New York: Cambridge University Press.

Handley, S. J., Capon, A., Copp, C., & Harper, C. (2002). Conditional reasoning and the Tower of Hanoi: The role of spatial and verbal working memory. *British Journal of Psychology, 93,* 501–518.

Heitz, R.P., Unsworth, N, & Engle, R.W. (in press). Working memory capacity, attention, and fluid intelligence. In O. Wilhelm & R.W. Engle (Eds.), *Handbook on measuring and understanding intelligence.* Sage Press.

Hyde, T. S., & Jenkins, J. J. (1973). Recall of words as a function of semantic, graphic, and syntactic orienting tasks. *Journal of Verbal Learning and Verbal Behavior, 12,* 471–480.

Institute for Personality and Ability Testing(1973). *Measuring intelligence with culture fair tests.* Champaign, IL: Institute for Personality and Ability Testing.

Jensen, A. R. (1982). The chronometry of intelligence. In R. J. Sternberg (Ed.), *Advances in the psychology of human intelligence.* (pp. 255–310). Hillsdale, NJ: Lawrence Erlbaum Associates.

Jensen, A. R. (1998). *The g factor: The science of mental ability.* Westport, CT: Praeger.

Jonides, J., & Smith, E. E. (1997). The architecture of working memory. In M. D. Rugg (Ed.), *Cognitive neuroscience. Studies in cognition.* (pp. 243–276). Cambridge, MA: MIT Press.

Kahneman, D., & Beatty, J. (1966). Pupil Diameter and load on memory. *Science, 154*, 1583–1585.
Kail, R., & Salthouse, T. (1994). Processing speed as a mental capacity. *Acta Psychologica, 86*, 199–225.
Kane, M. J., & Engle, R. W. (2000). Working memory capacity, proactive interference, and divided attention: Limits on long-term memory retrieval. *Journal of Experimental Psychology: Learning, Memory, and Cognition, 26*, 333–358.
Kane, M. J., & Engle, R. W. (2002). The role of prefrontal cortex in working-memory capacity, executive attention, and general fluid intelligence: An individual-differences perspective. *Psychonomic Bulletin and Review, 9*, 637–671.
Kane, M. J., & Engle, R. W. (2003a). *A role for working-memory capacity in task switching?* Unpublished manuscript.
Kane, M. J., & Engle, R. W. (2003b). Working-memory capacity and the control of attention: The contributions of goal neglect, response competition, and task set to Stroop interference. *Journal of Experimental Psychology: General, 132*, 47–70.
Kane, M. J., Bleckley, M. K., Conway, A. R. A., & Engle, R. W. (2001). A controlled-attention view of working-memory capacity. *Journal of Experimental Psychology: General, 130*, 169–183.
Kane, M. J., Hambrick, D. Z., Tuholski, S. W., Wilhelm, O., Payne, T. W., & Engle, R. W. (2003). *The generality of working memory capacity: A latent-variable approach to verbal and visuo-spatial memory span and reasoning.* Manuscript under review.
Kane, M. J., Poole, B., Tuholski, S. W., & Engle, R. W. (2003). *Working-memory capacity and the executive control of visual search and enumeration.* Unpublished manuscript.
Kiewra, K. A., & Benton, S. L. (1988). The relationship between information processing ability and notetaking. *Contemporary Educational Psychology, 13*, 33–44.
King, J., & Just, M. A. (1991). Individual differences in syntactic processing: The role of working memory. *Journal of Memory and Language, 30*, 580–602.
Klein, K., & Fiss, W. H. (1999). The reliability and stability of the Turner and Engle working memory task. *Behavior Research Methods, Instruments and Computers, 31*, 429–432.
Kosslyn, S. M., Cacciopo, J. T., Davidson, R. J., Hugdahl, K., Lovallo, W. R., Spiegel, W. R., & Rose, R. (2002). Bridging psychology and biology: The analysis of individuals in groups. *American Psychologist, 57*, 341–341.
Kyllonen, P. C. (1993). Aptitude testing inspired by information processing: A test of the four-sources model. *Journal of General Psychology, 120*, 375–405.
Kyllonen, P. C., & Christal, R. E. (1990). Reasoning ability is (little more than) working-memory capacity? *Intelligence, 14*, 389–433.
Kyllonen, P. C., & Stephens, D. L. (1990). Cognitive abilities as determinants of success in acquiring logic skill. *Learning and Individual Differences, 2*, 129–160.
Law, D. J., Morrin, K. A., & Pellegrino, J. W. (1995). Training effects and working memory contributions to skill acquisition in a complex coordination task. *Learning and Individual Differences, 7*, 207–234.
Logie, R. H. (1995). *Visuo-spatial working memory.* Hillsdale, NJ: Erlbaum.
Long, D. L., & Prat, C. S. (2002). Working memory and Stroop interference: An individual differences investigation. *Memory & Cognition, 3*, 294–301.
MacDonald, A. W., III, Cohen, J. D., Stenger, V. A., & Carter, C. S. (2000). Dissociating the role of the dorsolateral prefrontal and anterior cingulate cortex in cognitive control. *Science, 288*, 1835–1838.
MacLeod, C. M. (1998). Training on integrated versus separated Stroop tasks: The progression of interference and facilitation. *Memory & Cognition, 26*, 201–211.
MacLeod, C. M., & MacDonald, P. A. (2000). Interdimensional interference in the Stroop effect: Uncovering the cognitive and neural anatomy of attention. *Trends in Cognitive Sciences, 4*, 383–391.

MacLeod, C. M., Dodd, M. D., Sheard, E. D., Wilson, D. E. & Bibi, U. (in press). In opposition to inhibition. To appear in B. Ross (Ed.), *The Psychology of Learning and Motivation*. New York: Academic Press.

MacLeod, C. M., Dodd, M. D., Sheard, E.D., Wilson, D. E., & Bibi, U. (in press). In opposition to inhibition. In B. Ross, (Ed.), *The Psychology of Learning and Motivation*, Volume 43, Elsevier.

McNamara, D. S., & Scott, J. L. (2001). Working memory capacity and strategy use. *Memory & Cognition, 29*, 10–17.

Miyake, A., Friedman, N. P., Rettinger, D. A., Shah, P., & Hegarty, M. (2001). How are visuospatial working memory, executive functioning, and spatial abilities related? A latent-variable analysis. *Journal of Experimental Psychology: General, 130*, 621–640.

Morrell, R. W., & Park, D. C. (1993). The effects of age, illustrations, and task variables on the performance of procedural assembly tasks. *Psychology and Aging, 8*, 389–399.

Norman, D. A., & Shallice, T. (1986). Attention to action: Willed and automatic control of behavior. In R. J. Davidson, G. E. Schwartz, & D. Shapiro (Eds.), *Consciousness and self-regulation: Advances in research and theory.* Vol. 4. (pp. 1–18). New York: Plenum Press.

O'Reilly, R. C., Braver, T. S., & Cohen, J. D. (1997, July). *A biologically-based computational model of working memory*. Paper presented at the "Models of Working Memory" Symposium, Boulder, CO.

O'Reilly, R.C., Braver, T.S, & Cohen, J.D. (1999). A biologically based computational model of working memory. In A. Miyake (Eds.), *Models of working memory: Mechanisms of active maintenance and executive control.* (pp. 375–411). New York, NY, US: Cambridge University Press.

Oberauer, K. (1993). Die Koordination kognitiver Operationen. Eine Studie zum Zusammenhang von 'working memory' und Intelligenz [The coordination of cognitive operations. A study of the relationship of working memory and intelligence]. *Zeitschrift für Psychologie, 201*, 57–84.

Oberauer, K., Süß, H.-M., Schulze, R., Wilhelm, O., & Wittmann, W. W. (2000). Working memory capacity—Facets of a cognitive ability construct. *Personality and Individual Differences, 29*, 1017–1045.

Oberauer, K., Süß, H.-M., Wilhelm, O., & Wittmann, W. W. (2003). The multiple faces of working memory: Storage, processing, supervision, and coordination. *Intelligence, 31*, 167–193.

Park, D. C., Lautenschlager, G., Hedden, T., Davidson, N., Smith, A. D., & Smith, P. K. (2002). Models of visuospatial and verbal memory across the adult lifespan. *Psychology and Aging, 17*, 299–320.

Perfetti, C. A., & Lesgold, A. M. (1977). Discourse comprehension and sources of individual differences. In M. A. Just & P. A. Carpenter (Eds.), *Cognitive processes in comprehension.* (pp. 141–183). Hillsdale, NJ: Lawrence Erlbaum Associates.

Postman, L., Stark, K., & Fraser, J. (1968). Temporal changes in interference. *Journal of Verbal Learning and Verbal Behavior, 7*, 672–694.

Pressley, M., Cariglia-Bull, T., Deane, S., & Schneider, W. (1987). Short-term memory, verbal competence, and age as predictors of imagery instructional effectiveness. *Journal of Experimental Child Psychology, 43*, 194–211.

Raven, J. C., Raven, J. E., & Court, J. H. (1998). *Progressive Matrices*. Oxford, England: Oxford Psychologists Press.

Richeson, J. A., & Shelton, J. N. (2003). When prejudice does not pay: Effects of interracial contact on executive function. *Psychological Science, 14*, 287–291.

Roberts, R. J., Jr., Hager, L. D., & Heron, C. (1994). Prefrontal cognitive processes: Working memory and inhibition in the antisaccade task. *Journal of Experimental Psychology: General, 123*, 374–393.

Roediger, H. L., III, & Crowder, R. G. (1976). A serial position effect in recall of United States presidents. *Bulletin of the Psychonomic Society, 8*, 275–278.

Rogers, R. D., & Monsell, S. (1995). The cost of a predictable switch between simple cognitive tasks. *Journal of Experimental Psychology: General, 124*, 207–231.

Rosen, V. M., & Engle, R. W. (1997). The role of working memory capacity in retrieval. *Journal of Experimental Psychology: General, 126*, 211–227.

Rosen, V. M., & Engle, R. W. (1998). Working memory capacity and suppression. *Journal of Memory and Language, 39*, 418–436.

Rosen, V. M., Bergeson, J. L., Putnam, K., Harwell, A., & Sunderland, T. (2002). Working memory and apolipoprotein E: What's the connection? *Neuropsychologia, 40*, 2226–2233.

Salthouse, T. A. (1995). Differential age-related influences on memory for verbal-symbolic and visual-spatial information? *Journal of Gerontology: Psychological Sciences, 50B*, P193–P201.

Salthouse, T. A. (1996). The processing speed theory of adult age differences in cognition. *Psychological Review, 103*, 403–428.

Salthouse, T. A. (2001). A research strategy for investigating group differences in a cognitive construct: Application to ageing and executive processes. *European Journal of Cognitive Psychology, 13*, 29–46.

Salthouse, T., & Meinz, E. J. (1995). Aging, inhibition, working memory, and speed. *Journals of Gerontology: Series B: Psychological & Social Sciences, 50B*, 297–306.

Schmader, T., & Johns, M. (2003). Converging evidence that stereotype threat reduces working memory capacity. *Journal of Personality and Social Psychology, 85*, 440–452.

Shah, P., & Miyake, A. (1996). The separability of working memory resources for spatial thinking and language processing: An individual differences approach. *Journal of Experimental Psychology: General, 125*, 4–27.

Shute, V. J. (1991). Who is likely to acquire programming skills? *Journal of Educational Computing Research, 7*, 1–24.

Stroop, J. R. (1935). Studies of interference in serial verbal reactions. *Journal of Experimental Psychology, 18*, 643–662.

Süß, H.-M., Oberauer, K., Wittman, W. W., Wilhelm, O., & Schulze, R. (2002). Working-memory capacity explains reasoning ability—and a little bit more. *Intelligence, 30*, 261–288.

Swanson, H. L. (1996). Individual and age-related differences in children's working memory. *Memory & Cognition, 24*, 70–82.

Tuholski, S. W., Engle, R. W., & Baylis, G. C. (2001). Individual differences in working memory capacity and enumeration. *Memory & Cognition, 29*, 484–492.

Turley-Ames, K. J., & Whitfield, M. M. (2003). *Strategy training and working memory task performance.* Manuscript submitted for publication.

Turner, M. L., & Engle, R. W. (1989). Is working memory capacity task dependent? *Journal of Memory and Language, 28*, 127–154.

Underwood, B. J. (1975). Individual differences as a crucible in theory construction. *American Psychologist, 30*, 128–134.

Unsworth, N., Heitz, R. P., & Engle, R. W. Working memory capacity and the control of attention. In R. W. Engle, G. Sedek, U. Hecker, & D. N. McIntosh (Eds.), *Cognitive limitations in aging and psychopathology: Attention, working memory, and executive functions.* NY: Oxford University Press.

West, R., & Alain, C. (2000b). Evidence for the transient nature of a neural system supporting goal-directed action. *Cerebral Cortex, 10*, 748–752.

Wilson, K. M., & Swanson, H. L. (2001). Are mathematics disabilities due to a domain-general or a domain-specific working memory deficit? *Journal of Learning Disabilities, 34*, 237–248.

RELATIONAL PERCEPTION AND COGNITION: IMPLICATIONS FOR COGNITIVE ARCHITECTURE AND THE PERCEPTUAL–COGNITIVE INTERFACE

Collin Green and John E. Hummel

I. Introduction

A fundamental aspect of human intelligence is the ability to represent and reason about relations. Examples of relational thinking include our ability to appreciate analogies between different objects or events (Gentner, 1983; Holyoak & Thagard, 1995); our ability to apply abstract rules in novel situations (e.g., Smith, Langston, & Nisbett, 1992); our ability to understand and learn language (e.g., Kim, Pinker, Prince, & Prasada, 1991); our ability to learn and use categories (Ross, 1987); and even our ability to appreciate perceptual similarities (e.g., Palmer, 1978; Goldstone, Medin, & Gentner, 1991; Hummel, 2000; Hummel & Stankiewicz, 1996a).

Relational inferences and generalizations are so commonplace that it is tempting to assume that the psychological mechanisms underlying them are relatively simple, but this would be a mistake. The capacity to form and manipulate explicit relational (i.e., symbolic) representations appears to be a late evolutionary development (Robin & Holyoak, 1994), closely tied to the substantial increase in the size and complexity of the frontal cortex in the brains of higher primates, most notably humans (Stuss & Benson, 1987).

A review of computational models of perception and cognition also suggests that the question of how we represent and reason about relations is nontrivial (Hummel & Holyoak, 1997, 2003): traditional symbolic models of cognition (e.g., Anderson, Libiere, Lovett, & Reder, 1998; Anderson, 1990; Falkenhainer, Forbus, & Gentner, 1989) simply *assume* relations as a given, making no attempt to understand the origins or detailed nature of these representations in the neural substrate; and traditional connectionist/neural networks models (e.g., Edelman & Intrator, 2003; St. John & McClelland, 1990; O'Reilly & Rudy, 2001; Riesenhuber & Poggio, 1999) fail to represent relations at all. Indeed, the proponents of such models typically reject the idea that the human cognitive apparatus is capable of representing relations explicitly (see Hummel, 2000; Hummel & Holyoak, 1997, 2003, for reviews). Comparatively few models have attempted to address the question of how a neural architecture can represent and process relational structures, or the related question of how early, non-relational representations and processes, for example in early vision, make contact with later, more explicit relational/symbolic representations (e.g., as underlie reasoning; see Gasser & Colunga, 2001; Hummel & Biederman, 1992; Hummel & Holyoak, 1997, 2002; Shastri & Ajjenagadde, 1993; Strong & Whitehead, 1989).

II. Bridging the Gaps: Relating Symbols to Neurons and Cognition to Perception

This trend reflects, in large part, a tendency for researchers to focus on their domain of interest to the exclusion of related domains: as a practical matter, it is simply not possible to take the entire cognitive architecture into account in an attempt to understand, for example, reasoning or object recognition. In the domain of reasoning, and higher cognition generally, this tendency often manifests itself in the starting assumption: "Given that knowledge is represented in a symbolic format that is roughly isomorphic to propositional notation" (e.g., Anderson, 1990; Falkenhainer, Forbus, & Gentner, 1989; Newell & Simon, 1976). Rarely do such models pose the question of where the proposed representations originate from, or how they relate to the outputs of basic perceptual processes. In the domain of visual processing the starting assumption is typically the opposite (for a review and critique, see Hummel, 2000). For example, the goal of most models of object recognition is strictly *recognition* (e.g., Edelman, 1998; Edelman & Intrator, 2002, 2003; Poggio & Edelman, 1990; Tarr & Bülthoff, 1995; Ullman & Basri, 1991). Often, a second goal is to describe the resulting models as much as possible in terms of the properties of visual neurons (e.g., Edelman & Intrator, 2003; Reisenhuber & Poggio, 1999). Nowhere in the vast majority of these models is there any attempt to specify how the visual system might deliver *descriptions* of object shape or arrangements of objects in a scene that might be useful to later cognitive processes; indeed, such representations are often explicitly eschewed as unnecessary (see, e.g., Edelman & Intrator, 2003): It is as though once an object has been recognized, there is nothing else left to do (cf. Hummel, 2000, 2003).

The result is a sharp divide between researchers who assume symbolic representations as a given, and researchers who assume symbolic representations are fiction. One seeming exception to this divide appears in the form of distributed connectionist models of cognition (e.g., Elman, 1990; Kruschke, 1992, 2001; McClelland, McNaughton, & O'Reilly, 1995; McClelland & Rumelhart, 1981) and other models that represent concepts as vectors of features (e.g., Nosofsky, 1987; Shiffrin & Styvers, 1997). To the extent that (a) such vectors are reasonable approximations of symbolic representations and (b) basic perceptual processes can be viewed as delivering them as output, these models could serve both as an account of the interface between perception and cognition and as a bridge between neural and symbolic accounts of knowledge representation. And it is convenient—and tempting—to view them as such. However, as detailed in the following, the outputs of perceptual processes are not well modeled as lists of features (i.e., (b) is false; Hummel & Biederman, 1992; Hummel, 2000, 2003); and even if they were, list of features are entirely inadequate as approximations of symbolic representations (i.e., (a) is false; Hummel & Holyoak, 1997, 2003). Therefore, it is necessary to look elsewhere for principles that can serve as an interface between perception and cognition on the one hand, and between neural and symbolic accounts of mental representation on the other.

This chapter reviews our recent and ongoing work toward understanding this interface. We begin by reviewing the role of relational processing in perception and higher cognition, with an emphasis on the implications of relational processing for mental representation and cognitive architecture more broadly. Next, we consider how the visual system might deliver such representations to cognition. Finally, we discuss how relational representations may be used as a basis for scene recognition and comprehension—a process that lies squarely at the interface of perception and cognition.

III. Relational Perception and Thinking

Imagine finding yourself in need of a hammer, and discovering that your children have placed your hammer in the configuration illustrated in Fig. 1. Rather than simply grabbing the hammer, you would first remove the wine glasses from the top of the box, then lift the box out of the way, supporting

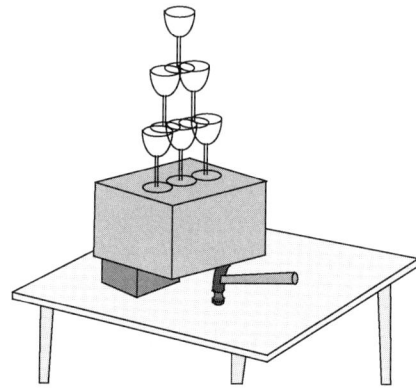

Fig. 1. Illustration of a hammer that it is best not to move.

the hammer with the other hand. This response to the situation in Figure 1, obvious as it seems, illustrates several important facts about our ability to comprehend novel visual scenes.

First, the inference that you should not simply grab the hammer depends on the ability to relate general knowledge (e.g., an understanding of support relations, of what happens to wine glasses that fall, etc.) to specific knowledge about the situation at hand. Second, most of the relevant knowledge, both the background knowledge and the understanding of the situation at hand, is specifically *relational*: It is not particularly relevant that the objects involved are wine glasses, boxes, and a hammer; what matters is that a desired object is supporting a second object that is supporting something fragile. Third, these relations are delivered by the visual system: Without the ability to perceive the relations among the objects, it would be impossible to reason about them, or even to notice that there was anything that required reasoning. Finally, these abilities must be generic enough to work in situations that are completely novel (as the scene in Fig. 1 presumably is). If the hammer were replaced by an unfamiliar widget, the widget's novelty would not render the scene incomprehensible.

The kind of reasoning that the hammer scene invokes is both commonplace and illustrative of relational reasoning more generally. *Relational inferences* are inferences that are constrained by the relational roles that objects play, rather than by the identities or features of the objects themselves: It is not the hammer's identity as a hammer that prevents you from moving it, but its role as *object that supports the object that supports the fragile objects*. The capacity to make relational inferences depends on the ability to represent relational roles explicitly, as entities in their own right. In turn, doing so means representing those roles independently of their arguments (Hummel & Biederman, 1992; Hummel & Holyoak, 1997, 2003): If the representation of the *supports* relation varied as a function of what was supporting what, then there would be little or no basis for generalizing anything learned about support relations in one context (e.g., the context of a pillow supporting a fishbowl) to novel contexts (e.g., a hammer supporting a box supporting wine glasses). It would be as though the two situations were simply *different*, with little or nothing in common.

Representing roles and fillers independently means having one set of units (e.g., neurons) represent relational roles, and a separate set represent the objects that can be bound to those roles. (The units do not need to be physically segregated in the network; they only need to be different units.) By keeping the units separate, any learning that pertains to a relation can be instantiated as connections to and from the units representing the relational roles. Since the connections refer to the roles only, whatever learning they embody (e.g., "if *supports* [x, y] and *fragile* [y], then *must-precede* [*remove-from* [y, x], *move* [x]") will generalize automatically to any new fillers of those roles (Hummel & Holyoak, 1997, 2003).

Representing relational roles independently of their fillers make it necessary to specify which fillers happen to be bound to which roles at a given time (i.e., to *dynamically* bind roles to their fillers). One way to bind roles to their fillers dynamically is to exploit synchrony of firing (e.g., Hummel & Biederman, 1992; Hummel & Holyoak, 1997, 2003; Shastri & Ajjenagadde, 1993; Strong & Whitehead, 1989; von der Malsburg, 1981/1994). The basic idea is that units representing bound roles and fillers fire *in* synchrony with one another and *out* of synchrony with other role-filler bindings. For example, to represent *supports* (box, wine-glasses), units representing *supporter* would fire in synchrony with units representing the box, while units representing *supported* fire in synchrony with units representing the wine glasses; the *supporter*+box set would fire out of synchrony with the *supported*+glasses set. It is possible to imagine other dynamic binding codes. What is critical is that the binding code, whatever it is, must be independent of the signal that codes a unit's degree of certainty in the hypothesis to which it corresponds (e.g., its activation; Hummel & Biederman, 1992). At present, however, synchrony is the only proposed dynamic binding code with neurophysiological support (see Singer & Gray, 1995, for a review).

Dynamic role-filler binding is crucial for binding roles to fillers in working memory (WM), but it is also necessary to: (a) store specific role-filler conjunctions (e.g., describing previously encountered relations between specific objects) in long-term memory (LTM); and (b) form localist tokens of role-filler conjunctions in WM. For both these purposes, conjunctive binding by localist units (i.e., units dedicated to specific role-filler conjunctions) is necessary (Hummel & Holyoak, 2003; see also Hummel & Biederman, 1992; Page, 2000).

In summary, representing relational (i.e., symbolic) structures in a neural architecture is not trivial, and requires a neural/cognitive architecture that is capable of meeting some very specific requirements. In the very least, it must: (1) represent roles independently of their fillers; (2) be able to bind these representations together dynamically in WM; and (3) bind them conjunctively as tokens in both WM and LTM (see Hummel & Holyoak, 2003, for a more complete list of requirements).

Scene comprehension is a problem at the interface of perception and cognition. To the extent that scene comprehension is a case of relational reasoning, it must rest on independent representations of objects and their relational roles; and to the extent that it depends on the outputs of perceptual processing, it also depends on the kinds of objects and relations perception is capable of delivering as output. Together, these considerations suggest that perception delivers to cognition (minimally) a representation of the objects in a scene in terms of their spatial relations to one another (there is evidence that it delivers a great deal more, including specification, for each object, of the relations among the object's parts; see Hummel, 2000). But the perceptual system starts with a representation that does not even specify the identities or locations of objects, much less their relations to one another (namely, the retinal image; and even the representation of local contour elements and "features" in V1 and V2). What does it take to go from a representation of the local features, such as lines and vertices, in an image to a specification of the objects in the scene in terms of their spatial relations to one another?

IV. From Images to Objects in Relations

Deriving an explicit description of the relations among the objects in a scene from the information in an early visual representation of that scene (e.g., as available in visual area V1) entails solving several problems, some of which, such as image segmentation, still elude satisfactory solutions in the computational literature (which is not to say they are unsolvable; it is just that we do not yet fully understand how the mind solves them; see Hummel, 2000): Starting with a representation of the locations of various "features" such as edges and vertices in an image, the visual system must: (a) segment the image into discrete objects, (b) recognize those objects, (c) compute the spatial relations among those objects, (d) form tokens of the objects, their locations, interrelations, etc., as elaborated in the following, and (e) make inferences from the objects and their interrelations to likely interpretations of the meaning of the scene.

These requirements are complicated by the fact that an analogous set of operations characterizes the recognition of individual objects (at least attended objects; Hummel, 2001; Stankiewicz, Hummel, & Cooper, 1998): The visual system must: (a) segment the object's image into parts (e.g., geons; Biederman, 1987), (b) characterize those parts in terms of their abstract shape attributes, (c) calculate the spatial relations among the parts, and (d) match the resulting descriptions to LTM (Hummel & Biederman, 1992). Moreover, as elaborated later, objects within a scene may be organized into *functional groups*—groups of objects that function together in the service of a goal (such as a table and chairs in a dining room)—but which do not typically constitute an entire scene in themselves. That is, scenes are deeply hierarchical, making it necessary both to represent the various levels of the hierarchy and to relate the levels to one another (e.g., parts to objects, objects to functional groups, and functional groups to scenes). In the following, we describe how Hummel and Biederman's (1992) JIM[1] model of object recognition solves some of these problems—and how it fails to solve others—in order to clarify the problems involved in mapping from an unstructured representation of a visual image (e.g., as in V1) to a structured (i.e., explicitly relational) representation of a visual scene.

A. IMAGE SEGMENTATION

Segmenting an image means figuring out *what goes with what*: which features belong to the same object part, which parts belong to the same object, and which objects belong to the same functional group. Simple perceptual properties such as collinearity and cotermination of visual image features, many of which were noted by the Gestaltists, serve to inform the grouping of basic features into objects or object parts (e.g., geons). JIM exploits these principles to group local image features into sets corresponding to geons. Specifically, it uses them to get features of the same geon firing in synchrony with one another and out of synchrony with the features of other geons.

The Gestaltist principles JIM uses to group image features into geons are useful but by no means complete (see Hummel and Biederman, 1992; Hummel & Stankiewicz, 1996b, for discussions of several situations in which they fail). Many of the failures stem from the fact that Gestalt principles are all *local*, in the sense that they refer to the relations between individual (local) image elements (e.g., the collinearity of individual line segments) without regard for the figure to which the features belong as a whole.

[1] John and Irv's Model (see Hummel & Biederman, 1992).

Conspicuously absent are top-down constraints based on knowledge of the various global shapes individual elements can form. By contrast, all other things being equal, the human visual system seems to prefer perceptual groupings that result in familiar objects over those that do not (see, e.g., Peterson & Gibson, 1994). For the same reason, Gestalt principles—and local grouping cues more generally—are poorly equipped to address the grouping of parts into objects or objects into functional groups. One exception may be the local cue of connectedness, which plays a role in determining whether the visual system interprets separate parts as belonging to the same object (Palmer & Rock, 1994; Saiki & Hummel, 1996, 1998a, 1998b).

B. INTERPRETATION OF VISUAL PROPERTIES

Whatever the complete set of cues to perceptual grouping turns out to be, the *results* of perceptual grouping are of paramount importance. The result of JIM's grouping of image features into parts is that JIM knows which image features refer to the same part, and which refer to different parts (subject to the limitations of its grouping algorithm). This knowledge is tremendously valuable because it allows the model to ignore details such as *where* individual features are located in the visual field for the purposes of figuring out what geon they collectively form (based on their identities), and to ignore *what* the features are for the purposes of figuring out where the geon is located in the visual field (how big it is, etc.). In other words, the ability of JIM to solve the binding problem at the level of image features allows it to selectively ignore various properties of those features in order to make inferences based on their *other* properties (Hummel & Biederman, 1992). Solving the binding problem makes it possible to treat different sources of information *independently* (see also Hummel & Holyoak, 1997, 2003).

The general principle is that any system that can bind information together dynamically is free to tear it apart (i.e., treat it independently) at will. The ability to do so is perhaps the single most important difference between symbolic cognition and the cognitive capabilities of purely associationist systems, such as traditional connectionist systems (see Hummel & Holyoak, 2003) and view-based approaches to shape perception (see Hummel, 2000, 2003). Such systems are unable to bind information together dynamically, so they are never at liberty to tear it apart when necessary.

1. The Importance of Keeping Separate Things Separate

This point bears elaborating, as it is both a central theme of this chapter and important to understanding mental representations generally. A local feature detector is a unit (e.g., neuron, symbol, etc.) that responds to a particular visual feature at a particular location in the visual field (a particular size, orientation, etc.). In other words, it represents a *conjunction* of several different visual properties. Neurons in visual areas V1 and V2 are examples of local feature detectors (or, equivalently for the purposes of the current discussion, local *filters*). It is possible to build detectors for geons, or even complete objects, simply by connecting geon or object units directly to collections of local feature detectors, and this is exactly how view-based ("appearance–based") models of object recognition operate: a "view" is an object detector that is connected directly to a set of local feature detectors. The resulting unit can detect its preferred geon or object (or "fragment"; Edelman & Intrator, 2003) when the corresponding local features are present in the image. But because such a unit takes its input from a specific set of local feature detectors, it, like the feature detectors, is only able to recognize its preferred object at a particular location, size, and orientation in the image (with the right algorithm for matching features to stored views, such detectors are capable of modest generalization across rotation in depth; see e.g., Tarr & Bülthoff, 1995).

At the other extreme, it is possible to imagine a model that simply lists all the features in an image without any regard for their locations (e.g., Mel, 1997; Mel & Fiser 2000). The advantage of this approach is that it permits recognition of the geon (or object), regardless of where it appears in the image. The limitation is that, although the model knows *which* features are in the image, it has no idea where they are relative to one another: If the features of an object are all scattered about the image but not in the right relations to form the object, then the model will spuriously "recognize" the object even though it is not present. This problem can be alleviated somewhat by positing detectors for conjunctions of features in the right relations (e.g., A-connected-to-B, A-connected-to-C, etc.; Mel & Fiser, 2000). However, this approach only pushes the problem back one level: Now it is possible to fool the model with an A connected to a B in one place, an A connected to a C in another, and so on.

The deep problem with both of these approaches is that they either use all the information in the image in a conjunctive fashion (as in the case of view-based models), or simply discard information about feature location altogether (as in the feature-based approach) (see Fig. 2). A better approach is simply to *separate* the feature ("what") information from the location ("where") information and use each for the tasks to which it is relevant (see Hummel & Biederman, 1992). There is evidence for this kind of separation of information at a gross level in mammalian visual systems (i.e., in the functions of the ventral ["what"] and dorsal ["where" or "how"] cortical visual processing streams; see, e.g., Goodale et al., 1991; Mishkin & Ungerleider, 1982).

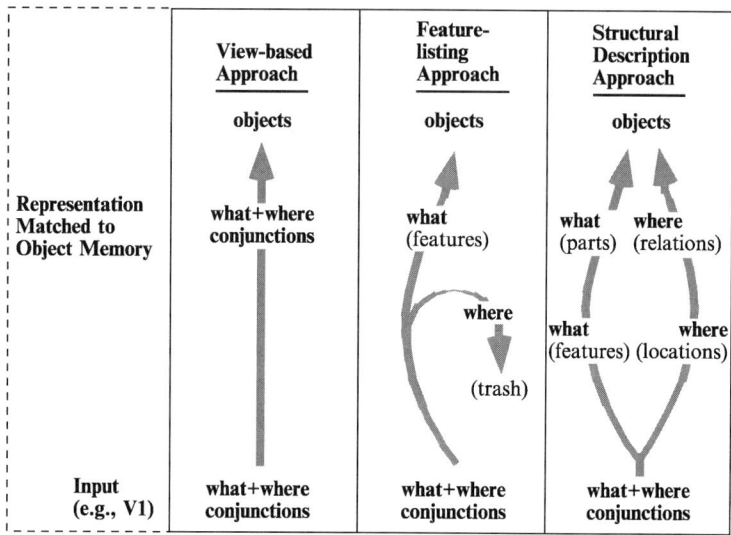

Fig. 2. Three approaches to the use of feature and location information in object recognition. Only structural description models separate feature and location information while preserving both.

This kind of separation of "what" from "where" is also essential within the "what" stream (and probably within the "where/how" stream as well). Like a feature-based model, JIM ignores the locations of a geon's features' for the purposes of inferring the shape attributes of the geon they form. That is, it uses the "what," ignoring the "where." But in contrast to a feature-based model, JIM is not fooled by a collection of unrelated geon features. The reason is that, due to the perceptual grouping of features into geon-based sets, features will only fire in synchrony with one another and, therefore, be interpreted as belonging to the same geon, if they belong to the same geon. And while one processing stream in JIM is busy inferring the shape of a geon from its local features, a *separate* processing stream is using the features' locations to infer the geon's location, size, orientation, and so on. This metric information, which is represented independently of (i.e., on separate units than) the geon's shape, is then used by routines that compute the relations between geons.

C. Computing Relations

The "heavy lifting" of generating a structural description is separating the "what" from the "where," a function made possible by the dynamic binding of features into parts-based sets. Once this separation is accomplished, using the "what" information to compute geon shape attributes and the "where" information to compute relations (such as relative location, relative size, and relative orientation) is relatively straightforward (see Hummel & Biederman, 1992; Hummel, 2001). The latter can be accomplished by simple comparator circuits composed of neural-like units. For example, consider a comparator for *relative location in the vertical dimension* that receives a signal indicating *vertical location 3* (i.e., input from a unit that responds whenever a geon is located at coordinate 3 on the vertical axis) at time $t = 1$, and a signal indicating *vertical location 5* as input at $t = 2$. These inputs indicate that whatever fired at time 1 is below (lower in the visual field than) whatever fired at time 2, and serve as a natural basis for computing that relation (e.g., by serving as inputs to a matrix of units that effectively perform subtraction). The next time it gets *vertical location 3* as input (say, at $t = 3$), the comparator need only activate a unit for *below* (i.e., the result of the "subtraction" $3 - 5$) as output; and the next time it gets *vertical location 5* as input (at $t = 4$), it need only activate a unit for *above* as output (the result of the subtraction $5 - 3$). As long as the units representing the shape of the geon at location 3 are firing in synchrony with the representation of location 3 (which, in JIM, they will be), activating *below* in synchrony with *location 3* not only specifies that the geon at location 3 is below something, but it also binds the representation of the relational role to the representation of the geon's shape. That is, the same simple operations both calculate the relations and, as a natural side effect, bind them to the appropriate geons (see Hummel & Biederman, 1992).

Analogous operations can be used to compute the spatial relations between whole objects for the purposes of scene perception and comprehension. The primary difference is that the arguments of the relations (and thus the inputs to the relation-computing machinery) are descriptions of complete objects rather than object parts.

D. TOKEN FORMATION

The geons and relations comprising an object fire in geon-based sets with separate geons firing out of synchrony with one another, so the final stages of object recognition in JIM are performed by two layers of units (Fig. 3). In the first of these layers, which happens to be the 6th layer of units in JIM, units learn to respond in a localist fashion (i.e., with one unit per pattern) to specific geons in specific relations. For example, a coffee mug would be represented by two such units, one that responds to curved cylinders beside and smaller than other parts (the handle), and one that responds to straight vertical cylinders beside and larger than other parts (the body of the mug). (Simply coding the relations as "beside" and "larger" or "smaller" is admittedly simplified. In particular, specification of their connectedness

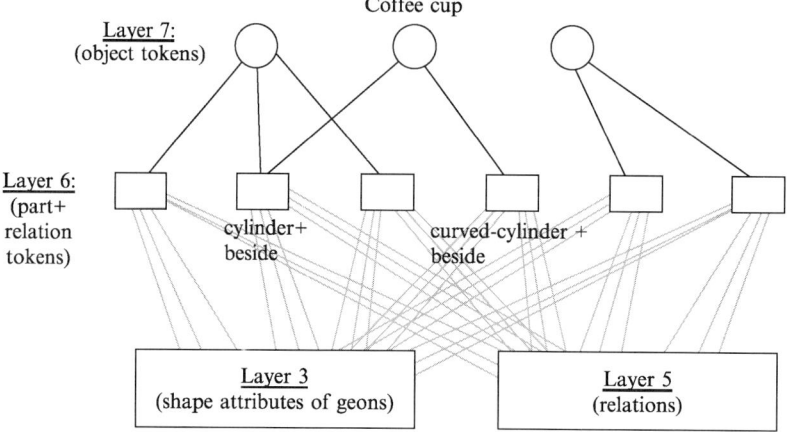

Fig. 3. The upper two layers of the JIM model. Units in Layer 6 respond to specific conjunctions of part attributes and relations. Units in Layer 7 integrate their inputs over time to respond to collections of Layer 6 units, i.e., to complete objects.

relations is conspicuously absent.) In the second recognition layer (JIM's 7th layer), units integrate their inputs over time (i.e., in order to pool the outputs of multiple layer 6 units, which are all firing out of synchrony with one another) to learn to respond to specific combinations of part-relation conjunctions (i.e., to whole objects). Like the layer 6 units, the units in layer 7 respond to their preferred patterns in a localist fashion, with one unit for each object.

The localist nature of these representations is no accident. In addition to making the representation unambiguous with regard to which part(s) and object(s) are present in the image (see Page, 2000, for a discussion of the utility of localist representations), the localist nature of these units also allows them to act as explicit *tokens* of (or "pointers to") the things they represent. As elaborated in the next section, tokens play an essential role in relational reasoning (Hummel & Holyoak, 2003), including scene comprehension.

1. A Case Study in the Importance of Tokens

In the context of object recognition, the importance of tokens for specific part-relation conjunctions—and conjunctions of part-relations conjunctions, and conjunctions of *those* conjunctions—is illustrated by one of the most important and severe limitations of Hummel and Biederman's 1992 version of JIM. Recall that each unit in JIM's layer 6 represents a conjunction of: (a) the shape attributes defining a single geon (e.g., with units for *curved cross section, curved major axis* and *parallel sides* together representing a curved cylinder); and (b) that geon's relations to the other geon(s) in the object. What is not specified by this representation is the other geon(s) to which the relations refer: The curved cylinder is beside and smaller than *something*, but what? When an object has only two parts, as in the case of the mug, the resulting representation is unambiguous. But when an object has more than two parts, the representation can quickly become ambiguous.

Consider, for example, the "totem pole" objects in Figure 4, along with the schematic depictions of JIM's representation of them in its layers 6 and 7 in Figure 5A. To JIM, objects (a) and (b) are identical: they both consist of a crescent that is below something, a circle and a triangle that are both above and below something, and a square that is above something. Hummel and Biederman (1992) noted that this limitation constitutes a novel prediction: JIM predicts that (a) and (b) ought to be more confusable with one another than either is with (c), in which the rectangle changes places with the circle (changing which relations are bound to which parts). Logan (1994) tested and falsified this and related predictions, thereby falsifying Hummel & Biederman's (1992) original version of JIM. (see Hummel & Stankiewicz, 1996b; Hummel, 2001; and Stankiewicz, Hummel, & Cooper, 1998, for reviews of empirical phenomena that reveal other limitations of the original formulation of JIM.).

Logan's (1994) falsification of Hummel and Biederman's (1992) JIM suggests that the architecture of JIM's layers 6 and 7 does not adequately capture an object's structure. But as pointed out by Logan, they do not falsify its general approach to structural description, based on dynamic binding of independent shape attributes and relations. Indeed, there is substantial empirical support for the general approach (see Hummel, 1994,

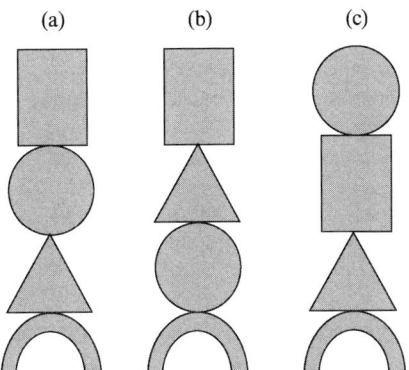

Fig. 4. Three "totem pole" objects. Hummel and Biederman's (1992) JIM model of object recognition predicts that (a) and (b) should be more confusable than either is with (c).

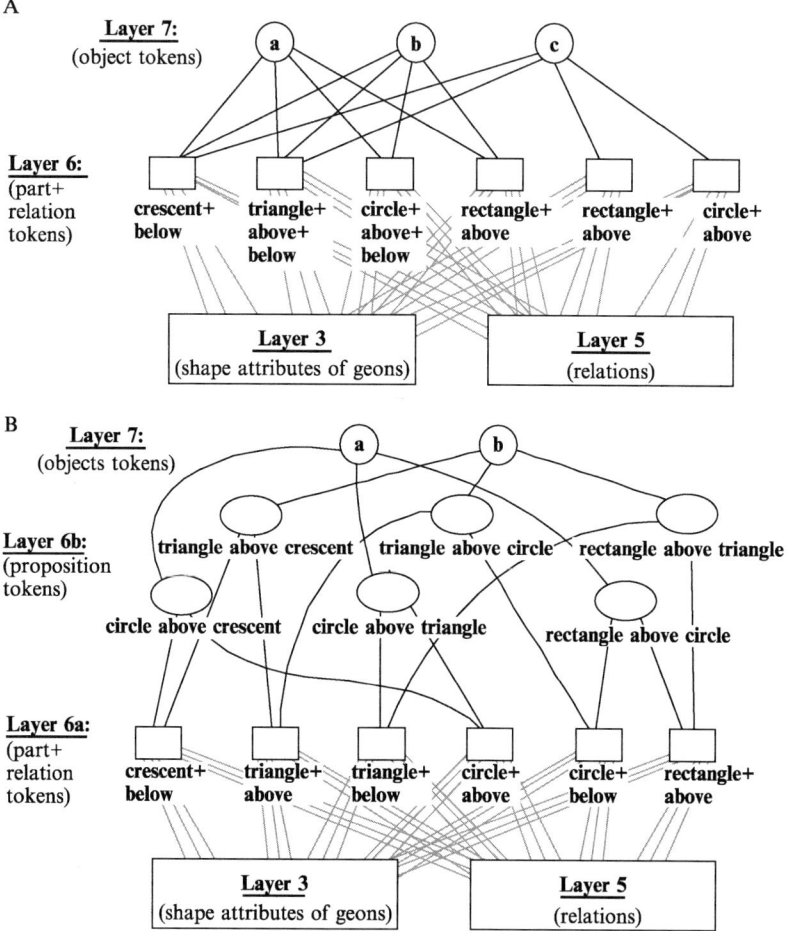

Fig. 5. Structural description of objects without (A) and with (B) proper token formation. JIM's (Hummel & Biederman, 1992) representations are like those in (A), but the representations in (B) are better suited to general object recognition.

2000, 2001; Hummel & Stankiewicz, 1996a, 1996b; Kurbat, 1994; Logan, 1994; Saiki & Hummel, 1998a, 1998b; Stankiewicz & Hummel, 2002; Stankiewicz, Hummel, & Cooper, 1998). Instead, Logan's findings underscore the hierarchical nature of object shape, and the importance of representing each level of this hierarchy explicitly—a task for which JIM's 6th and 7th layers are inadequate.

To elaborate, consider the augmented version of JIM's upper layers depicted in Figure 5B. This representation codes the relations between *pairs* of geons: rather than coding a geon's relations to all other geons in the same unit (as in JIM's 6th layer), units in layer 6a code a geon's shape attributes and its relations to *one* other geon. Although not shown in the figure, these units may code multiple relations (e.g., relative location, relative size, etc.) as long as all those relations refer to the same geon. Units in layer 6b code for pairs of units in layer 6a (e.g., *triangle+below* and *circle+above*) and represent complete propositions expressing the relations between two (and only two) geons (e.g., *above* [circle, triangle], or *above-and-smaller* [circle, triangle]). Layer 7 takes its input from layer 6b, and responds to complete objects (like layer 7 in JIM). The resulting augmented representation, like Logan's (1994) subjects but unlike the original JIM, easily distinguishes objects (a) and (b). Importantly, its ability to do so stems from the fact that it forms explicit tokens for elements at every level of part-relation hierarchy.

One final extension of the Hummel & Biederman (1992) representation is worth noting. In the original JIM, the outputs of units representing a geon's shape and relations to other geons fed directly into units in layer 6 representing part-relation conjunctions (rectangles in Fig. 5A and 5B). If, instead, we allow the outputs of units representing aspects of a geon's shape to feed into one set of units (circles in layer 5b of Fig. 6A), and aspects of its relation(s) to other geons feed into a *separate* set of units (triangles in layer 5b of Fig. 6A) before shape and relation information is combined in layer 6a, then arrive at the situation depicted in Figure 6A: a geon's shape is represented by one token in layer 5b and its relations to one other geon are represented by a separate token.

The resulting representation is isomorphic with the representational scheme Hummel and Holyoak's (1997, 2003) LISA (Learning and Inference with Schemas and Analogies) model uses to code propositions for relational reasoning (Fig. 6B): although Figure 6A illustrates a hierarchy of tokens for representing structural descriptions of object shape, the very same hierarchy can be used to represent and reason about propositions describing *any* relational structure. For example, Figure 6B illustrates how LISA uses this hierarchy to represent the proposition "the café sells coffee." At the bottom of the hierarchy, relational roles (e.g., *seller* and *sold*) and their arguments (*café* and *coffee*) are represented as patterns of activation distributed over units that code their semantic content. Localist tokens for individual roles (triangles in Fig. 6) share bidirectional excitatory connections with the semantic features of those roles, and tokens for objects (circles in layer 5b of Fig. 6) share connections with the semantic features of those objects. *Sub-proposition* (*SP*) units serve as tokens for specific roll-filler bindings (such as the binding of *café* to the *seller* role; rectangles in Fig. 6), and share bidirectional excitatory connections with the corresponding role and filler

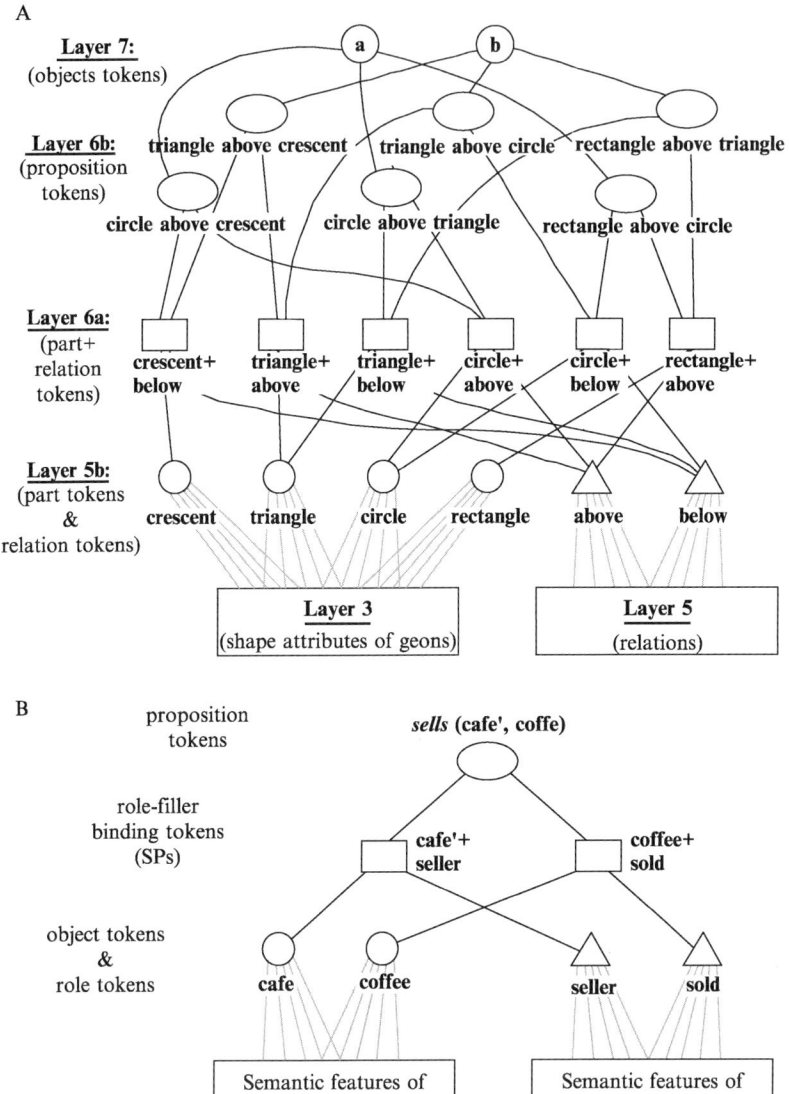

Fig. 6. A representational scheme for recognizing multiple objects simultaneously (A) would serve as a basis for constructing abstract relational descriptions of visual scenes (B). SP = sub-proposition.

units. SPs are connected to P units, which serve as tokens for complete propositions. Not shown in Figure 6B are units that code for *groups* of related propositions (analogous to the object units in layer 7 of Fig. 6A), which share excitatory connections with the corresponding P units. The important point is that the representation depicted in Figure 6A, which is a straightforward extension of the representations JIM generates in response to an object's image, has been shown to serve a basis for relational reasoning and, thus, is a suitable starting point for a model of scene comprehension.

V. Toward a Model of Scene Comprehension

The representational scheme illustrated in Figure 6 is a "missing link" between models of perception on the one hand and models of cognition on the other: given a retinotopically-mapped representation of a visual scene as input, it is possible to generate the representation in Figure 6 using visual routines such as those embodied in JIM (both the original 1992 version, and more recent versions; Hummel & Stankiewicz, 1996a, 1998; Hummel, 2001); the resulting representation serves as a natural basis for relational reasoning (Hummel & Holyoak, 1997; 2003). It is worthwhile to note that the construction of properly tokenized, abstract, structural representations of the environment is decidedly non-trivial. A number of difficult obstacles are yet to be overcome in solving this problem. However, JIM serves as an excellent starting point from which to address the construction of more complex and abstract structural descriptions. We next consider, in a bit more detail, how a representational scheme such as the one depicted in Figure 6 can serve as the basis for recognizing visual scenes and reasoning about their properties.

Object recognition is undoubtedly useful for scene recognition (e.g., seeing coffee makers, cash registers, tables and chairs suggests that one may be in a café), but it is neither necessary nor sufficient. Biederman (1987) demonstrated that it is possible to recognize otherwise ambiguous objects based strictly on their locations in a scene. In such cases, scene recognition precedes and supports object recognition, rather than the reverse. That object recognition is not sufficient for scene recognition is illustrated by the fact that identifying a collection of objects as tables, chairs, coffee makers, etc., is not sufficient to distinguish a café from a café supply warehouse. In order to distinguish a café from a café supply warehouse, it is necessary to understand the relations among the objects. In addition, a number of results suggest that top-down influences on scene perception are substantial. Change detection (Werner & Thies, 2000), eye movements (Hollingworth & Henderson, 2000; Henderson, Weeks, & Hollingworth, 1999; Loftus & Mackworth, 1978), and object detection (Moores, Laiti, &

Chelazzi, 2003) are all influenced by semantic knowledge about visual scenes and objects.

Scenes, composed of objects in particular relations, are thus analogous to objects, composed of parts in particular relations (Biederman, 1987). However, there is an important difference The spatial relations among the parts of an object are fairly tightly constrained. For example, the handles of various mugs may vary in their exact size, shape, and location, but they will almost always be attached to the sides of the mugs' bodies. By contrast, the spatial relations among the objects in a scene are free to vary widely. What is it about the spatial relations among the objects in a scene that determines whether they form a café or a café supply warehouse?

A. The FUNCTIONAL RELATIONS HYPOTHESIS

One intuitive hypothesis is that *functional* relations, rather than specific *spatial* relations, are what distinguish one category of scenes from another. A scene is a café if and only if the objects in the scene are arranged in a way that supports making, buying, and drinking coffee. (This hypothesis is closely related to Gibson's [1950, 1979] notion of *affordances*: A scene is a café if and only if it *affords* these functions.) Although this idea is intuitive, it underscores the abstract relational nature of visual scene recognition. It implies that, not only is it not good enough to be able to recognize the objects in a scene, it is also not good enough to know where the objects are located, or even to know where they are located relative to one another. Instead, it is necessary to be able to compute, from their spatial relations, their functional relations. Doing so requires knowledge of things such as goals and ways to satisfy those goals. It is in this sense that scene recognition is a task at the interface of perception and cognition.

One implication of the functional relations hypothesis is that the meaning (semantics) of a scene is more than the sum of the semantic properties of its constituent objects: Scenes are defined by semantics that reflect the functional relations among their constituent objects. In the limit, the objects themselves can become nearly irrelevant: Along with some basis for making coffee and collecting money, a collection of appropriately arranged rocks or logs could form a perfectly fine café. Or, as illustrated by Biederman (1987), an array of appropriately arranged abstract shapes can form a perfectly fine office, thereby disambiguating the identities of its constituent objects.

Another implication of the functional relations hypothesis is that *functional groups*—groups of objects in spatial relations that satisfy various functional relations—form an explicit intermediate level of representation between objects and complete scenes. A single scene will typically contain multiple functional groups. In the case of a café, for example, there would be groups for sitting and drinking coffee, groups for preparing coffee, and groups for purchasing coffee. Different scenes may share many of the same functional groups. For example, a restaurant will share many functional groups with a café, and a wood shop may share many groups with a metal shop or a laboratory. A key prediction of the functional relations hypothesis is that scenes and scene categories should be confusable to the extent that they share functional groups, even controlling for the absolute number of shared objects and spatial relations.

1. Functional Groups in the Recognition of Familiar Scenes

Biederman (1987) proposed that scenes may be recognized on the basis of *geon clusters*—collections of abstract, coarsely-coded shapes corresponding to complete objects, but perceptually coded, at least initially, as simple geons, in particular relations. For example, a brick-like shape with a roughly vertical slab-like shape behind it would form a geon cluster for a desk and chair. The presence of such a cluster could provide a useful basis for recognizing the scene as an office.

We hypothesize that, based on the statistics of the arrangements of objects in familiar scenes, geon clusters are likely to correspond, not to whole scenes, but to functional groups within scenes. For example, across the population of various kitchens, refrigerators are unlikely to appear in any particular location relative to sinks, since a refrigerator and a sink are unlikely to form a functional group. By contrast, sinks, counters, and dish drains do form a functional group (e.g., "dish-washing station") and, therefore, are likely to appear in regular spatial relations to one another across scenes (e.g., *beside* [counter, sink], *beside* [dish drain, sink] and *on-top* [dish drain, counter]). If so, then experience with a few typical kitchens could provide ample opportunity to learn a geon cluster for the functional group "dish-washing station." Similar statistical regularities would provide opportunities to learn geon clusters for functional groupings of cutting boards and knives, pots and stoves, and so on. Once learned, such geon clusters could provide a rapid route to the recognition of scenes in familiar arrangements, even before the objects within the clusters/groups are visually recognized (as observed by Biederman).

2. Functional Groups in Scene Comprehension and Novel Scene Recognition

Geon clusters for familiar functional groups may provide a fast route for the recognition of scenes with objects in familiar configurations, and functional groups as a more general construct (i.e., as groups of objects in spatial relations that afford particular functions) may also provide a basis for scene recognition and comprehension even in the absence of familiar geon clusters.

An extreme example was given in Figure 1: The spatial relations among of the hammer, boxes, and wine glasses is unlikely to activate any familiar geon cluster, but based on one's knowledge of functional relations (such as support) it is straightforward to comprehend what the scene "means." A less extreme example would be a kitchen in which the table is adorned with beakers, test tubes, and a scale. This scene contains an unfamiliar geon cluster (the table and chairs with scientific instruments) that is nonetheless interpretable as "a kitchen table that is (probably temporarily) being used as some kind of laboratory." As in the hammer and wine glass example, it is the functional relations among the table and the instruments, rather than the familiarity of the particular geon cluster, that suggests the "kitchen laboratory" interpretation.

B. From Spatial Relations to Functional Inferences: The Cognitive Side of the Perceptual–Cognitive Interface

Central to the functional relations hypothesis is the idea that objects in spatial relations activate representations of the objects' functional relations. This hypothesis raises the question of how we know which spatial relations afford which functional relations. Although the question of which functional affordances/relations are learned versus innate is well beyond the scope of this chapter, it seems uncontroversial that at least some functional affordances must be learned. For example, most people would probably agree that the fact that the shifter in a car affords changing the ratio of the rate of revolution of the engine to the rate of revolution of the wheels is most likely learned, rather than innate.

Everyday experience provides ample opportunity to observe patterns of covariation between spatial relations and functional relations, so it is tempting to assume that learning to map from one to the other is a simple matter of learning to associate them. And to a first approximation, this is probably correct. However, the learning is complicated by the fact that the "associations" in question are not simple associations between objects or features, but rather between abstract relations, which themselves can take variable arguments. As a result, traditional connectionist learning algorithms (e.g., Rumelhart, Hinton, & Williams, 1986; O'Reilly and Rudy, 2002) are fundamentally ill-suited to the task; these architectures cannot represent relational structures (see Hummel and Holyoak, 1997, 2003; Marcus, 1998), so they are unable to learn associations between them; a model cannot learn to associate that which it cannot represent.

By contrast, Hummel and Holyoak's (1997, 2003) LISA model of relational learning and reasoning provides an ideal platform to simulate this kind of learning. As noted previously, LISA operates on representations of relations and their arguments (i.e., propositions) like those illustrated in Figure 6—representations that, at least in the domain of spatial relations, can be generated by visual routines embodied in a system such as JIM. Although LISA's operation is too complicated to describe here in detail, it is sufficient to note that LISA is able to learn abstract relations among propositions (e.g., that one relation causes or affords another), and to use its knowledge of familiar situations—both in the form of specific examples, and in the form of abstract schemas or rules—to infer new facts about analogous novel situations. For example, given a description of the spatial relations among some tables and chairs, e.g., as delivered by JIM, and given similar descriptions, along with descriptions of the functional relations among those objects in LTM, LISA can use its knowledge of the familiar situations to infer the (as yet unstated) functional relations among the tables and chairs in the new situation (see Hummel & Holyoak, 2003).

C. Open Questions and Future Directions

Many problems remain to be solved before the general ideas presented here can be turned into a working model of scene recognition and comprehension. We shall briefly mention only a few of the problematic issues.

Some of the most difficult problems surround the hierarchical nature of visual scenes. Scenes are composed of functional groups, which are composed of objects in specific relations, and objects consist of parts in specific relations. The image segmentation routines described by Hummel and Biederman (1992) are designed to take an image of a single object and decompose that object into its constituent parts. The model does not address the problem of segmenting an object from a complex background (the familiar figure-ground segregation problem), or the related problem of knowing which object parts in a multi-object display belong to the same object and which belong to different objects (but see Saiki & Hummel, 1996, 1998a, 1998b, for some progress in this direction). A related problem is that, in a multi-object display, the number of separate object parts will quickly exceed the capacity of visual WM (which capacity is approximately four discrete units, e.g., objects or object parts; Luck & Vogel, 1999). For example, a scene with 4 objects, each with 4 parts, contains 16 parts, for a total of 120 non-redundant sets of inter-part relations. Clearly, it is neither possible nor desirable for the visual system to compute all sets of pairwise relations between all parts in an object image.

In order to deal with the hierarchical nature of visual scenes, a model of scene perception will need, among other things, intelligent routines for directing attention between levels of the hierarchy, and for relating elements at one level to elements at other levels. The representational format illustrated in Figure 6 is one step in the direction of specifying how elements at different levels of the visual hierarchy are related, but it is by no means sufficient. Among other limitations, this representational scheme assumes, at least tacitly, that every object in a scene is represented in terms of its complete parts structure. However, to the extent that Biederman's (1987) idea of geon clusters is correct, "objects" in a cluster may act more like geons (small circles in layer 5b of Fig. 6A) than like complete objects (layer 7 of Fig. 6A). Similarly, there is evidence that we can recognize objects in familiar views without first decomposing them into their parts (Stankiewicz, Hummel, & Cooper, 1998; Stankiewicz & Hummel, 2002; see also Hummel & Stankiewicz, 1996b; Hummel, 2001). These facts could either simplify the problem of representing scenes hierarchically by obviating the need to represent every part of every object explicitly, or they could complicate it by making it unclear at which level of the hierarchy the representation of an object qua element in a cluster should reside. Is such an object an "object" that should reside at layer 7, or a part that should reside at layer 5b? It seems likely that an adequate solution to the hierarchical representation problem will make the latter part of this problem ("is this an object or a part?") simply "go away." But it is difficult to know for sure until we see what that solution looks like.

Implementing a model of scene comprehension will entail solving several other more minor problems as well. And although the general framework presented here arguably raises more questions about scene recognition and comprehension than it answers, we are encouraged that it provides a framework for posing the questions at all.

VI. Conclusions

Scene recognition and comprehension provide an excellent platform for thinking about problems at the perceptual–cognitive interface, as they depend jointly on perceptual input and existing functional and relational knowledge. The problem of scene comprehension—of making the connection between representations given by the visual system and the conceptual knowledge structures that underlie relational reasoning—underscores the importance of developing models of perception that can deliver representations that are useful to the rest of cognition on the one hand, and developing models of cognition whose basic representations and operations can be grounded in the outputs of perceptual processing on the other. Cognitive science is still far from being able to connect a camera to a computer and have the computer make intelligent inferences about the objects in a scene and the actions that can be performed there. Many technical and theoretical problems must be solved before we will be able to fully automate scene comprehension in this way. But one of the most important and basic of those problems is to elucidate the nature of the perceptual–cognitive interface. In turn, one of the most important abilities at the interface of perception and cognition is the ability to tear information apart (e.g., about the identities and locations of features, parts, and objects), to put it back together as needed, and to form and manipulate tokens representing the resulting visual and cognitive entities and their relations.

Acknowledgments

The authors would like to thank Irving Biederman, Steve Engel, Keith Holyoak, Zili Liu, and the members of the LISA lab and the CogFog group for valuable comments and discussion related to the issues presented in this chapter. Preparation of this chapter was supported in part by NIH NRSA F31-NS43892-01. Address correspondence to: Collin Green, Department of Psychology, University of California - Los Angeles, 1285 Franz Hall, Box 951563, Los Angeles, CA 90095-1563 (email: CBGreen@ucla.edu).

References

Anderson, J. R. (1990). *The adaptive character of thought*. Hillsdale, NJ: Erlbaum.
Anderson, J. R., Libiere, C., Lovett, M. C., & Reder, L. M. (1998). ACT-R: A higher-level account of processing capacity. *Behavioral & Brain Sciences, 21*, 831–832.
Biederman, I. (1987). Recognition-by-components: A theory of human image understanding. *Psychological Review, 94*, 115–147.
Edelman, S. (1998). Representation is representation of similarities. *Behavioral & Brain Sciences, 21*, 449–498.
Edelman, S., & Intrator, N. (2002). Models of perceptual learning. In M. Fahle & T. Poggio (Eds.), *Perceptual Learning*. (pp. 337–353). Cambridge, MA: MIT Press.
Edelman, S., & Intrator, N. (2003). Towards structural systematicity in distributed, statically bound visual representations. *Cognitive Science, 27*, 73–109.
Elman, J. L. (1990). Finding structure in time. *Cognitive Science, 14*, 179–211.
Falkenhainer, B., Forbus, K. D., & Gentner, D. (1989). The structure-mapping engine: Algorithm and examples. *Artificial Intelligence, 41*, 1–63.
Gasser, M., & Colunga, E. (2001). Learning relational correlations. In E. M. Altmann & A. Cleeremans (Eds.), *Proceedings of the 2001 Fourth International Conference on Cognitive Modeling*. (pp. 91–96). Mahwah, NJ: Lawrence Erlbaum Associates, Publishers.
Gentner, D. (1983). Structure-mapping: A theoretical framework for analogy. *Cognitive Science, 7*, 155–170.
Gibson, J. J. (1950). *The perception of the visual world*. Oxford, England: Houghton Mifflin.
Gibson, J. J. (1979). *The ecological approach to visual perception*. Boston, MA: Houghton Mifflin.
Goldstone, R. L., Medin, D. L., & Gentner, D. (1991). Relational similarity and the nonindependence of features in similarity judgments. *Cognitive Psychology, 23*, 222–262.
Goodale, M. A., Milner, D. A., Jakobson, L. S., & Carey, D. P. (1991). A neurological dissociation between perceiving objects and grasping them. *Nature, 349*, 154–156.

Henderson, J. M., Weeks, P. A., & Hollingworth, A. (1999). The effects of semantic consistency on eye movements during complex scene viewing. *Journal of Experimental Psychology: Human Perception & Performance, 25*, 210–228.

Hollingworth, A., & Henderson, J. M. (2000). Semantic informativeness mediates the detection of changes in natural scenes. *Visual Cognition, 7*, 213–235.

Holyoak, K. J., & Thagard, P. (1995). *Mental leaps: Analogy in creative thought.* Cambridge, MA: MIT Press.

Hummel, J. E. (1994). Reference frames and relations in computational models of object recognition. *Current Directions in Psychological Science, 3*, 111–116.

Hummel, J. E. (2000). Where view-based theories break down: The role of structure in shape perception and object recognition. In E. Dietrich & A. Markman (Eds.), *Cognitive Dynamics: Conceptual Change in Humans and Machines.* (pp. 157–185). Hillsdale, NJ: Erlbaum.

Hummel, J. E. (2001). Complementary solutions to the binding problem in vision: Implications for shape perception and object recognition. *Visual Cognition, 8*, 489–517.

Hummel, J. E. (2003). "Effective systematicity" in, "effective systematicity" out: A reply to Edelman & Intrator (2003). *Cognitive Science, 27*, 327–329.

Hummel, J. E., & Biederman, I. (1992). Dynamic binding in a neural network for shape recognition. *Psychological Review, 99*, 480–517.

Hummel, J. E., & Holyoak, K. J. (1997). Distributed representations of structure: A theory of analogical access and mapping. *Psychological Review, 104*, 427–466.

Hummel, J. E., & Holyoak, K. J. (2003). A symbolic-connectionist theory of relational inference and generalization. *Psychological Review, 110*, 220–264.

Hummel, J. E., & Stankiewicz, B. J. (1996a). Categorical relations in shape perception. *Spatial Vision, 10*, 201–236.

Hummel, J. E., & Stankiewicz, B. J. (1996b). An architecture for rapid, hierarchical structural description. In T. Inui & J. McClelland (Eds.), *Attention and Performance XVI: Information Integration in Perception and Communication.* (pp. 93–121). Cambridge, MA: MIT Press.

Kim, J. J., Pinker, S., Prince, A., & Prasada, S. (1991). Why no mere mortal has ever flown out to center field. *Cognitive Science, 15*, 173–218.

Kruschke, J. K. (1992). ALCOVE: An examplar-based connectionist model of category learning. *Psychological Review, 99*, 22–44.

Kruschke, J. K. (2001). Toward a unified model of attention in associative learning. *Journal of Mathematical Psychology, 45*, 812–863.

Kurbat, M. A. (1994). Structural description theories: Is RBC/JIM a general-purpose theory of human entry-level object recognition? *Perception, 23*, 1339–1368.

Logan, G. D. (1994). Spatial attention and the apprehension of spatial relations. *Journal of Experimental Psychology: Human Perception and Performance, 20*, 1015–1036.

Loftus, G. R., & Mackworth, N. H. (1978). Cognitive determinants of fixation location during picture viewing. *Journal of Experimental Psychology: Human Perception & Performance, 4*, 565–572.

Luck, S. J., & Vogel, E. K. (1997). The capacity of visual working memory for features and conjunctions. *Nature, 390*, 279–281.

Marcus, G. F. (1998). Rethinking eliminative connectionism. *Cognitive Psychology, 37*, 243–282.

McClelland, J. L., McNaughton, B. L., & O'Reilly, R. C. (1995). Why there are complementary learning systems in the hippocampus and neocortex: Insights from the successes and failures of connectionist models of learning and memory. *Psychological Review, 102*, 419–437.

McClelland, J. L., & Rumelhart, D. E. (1981). An interactive activation model of context effects in letter perception: Part 1. An account of basic findings. *Psychological Review, 88*, 375–407.

Mel, B. (1997). SEEMORE: Combining color, shape, and texture histogramming in a neurally-inspired approach to visual object recognition. *Neural Computation, 9*, 777–804.

Mel, B., & Fiser, J. (2000). Minimizing binding errors using learned conjunctive features. *Neural Computation, 12*, 247–278.

Mishkin, M., & Ungerleider, L. G. (1982). Contribution of striate inputs to the visuospatial functions of parieto-preoccipital cortex in monkeys. *Behavioural Brain Research, 6*, 57–77.

Moores, E., Laiti, L., & Chelazzi, L. (2003). Associative knowledge controls deployment of visual selective attention. *Nature Neuroscience, 6*, 182–189.

Newell, A., & Simon, H. A. (1976). Computer science as empirical inquiry: Symbols and search. *Communications of the ACM, 19*, 113–126.

Nosofsky, R. M. (1987). Attention and learning processes in the identification and categorization of integral stimuli. *Journal of Experimental Psychology: Learning, Memory, & Cognition, 13*, 87–108.

O'Reilly, R. C., & Rudy, J. W. (2001). Conjunctive representations in learning and memory: Principles of cortical and hippocampal function. *Psychological Review, 108*, 311–345.

Page, M. (2000). Connectionist modeling in psychology: A localist manifesto. *Behavioural & Brain Sciences, 23*, 443–512.

Palmer, S. E. (1978). Structural aspects of similarity. *Memory and Cognition, 6*, 91–97.

Palmer, S. E., & Rock, I. (1994). Rethinking perceptual organization: The role of uniform connectedness. *Psychonomic Bulletin & Review, 1*, 29–55.

Peterson, M. A., & Gibson, B. S. (1994). Must figure-ground organization precede object recognition? An assumption in peril *Psychological Science, 5*, 253–259.

Poggio, T., & Edelman, S. (1990). A neural network that learns to recognize three-dimensional objects. *Nature, 343*, 263–266.

Riesenhuber, M., & Poggio, T. (1999). Hierarchical models of object recognition in cortex. *Nature Neuroscience, 11*, 1019–1025.

Robin, N., & Holyoak, K. J. (1994). Relational complexity and the functions of prefrontal cortex. In M. S. Gazzaniga (Ed.), *The Cognitive Neurosciences.* (pp. 987–997). Cambridge, MA: MIT Press.

Ross, B. (1987). This is like that: The use of earlier problems and the separation of similarity effects. *Journal of Experimental Psychology: Learning, Memory, and Cognition, 13*, 629–639.

Rumelhart, D. E., Hinton, G. E., & Williams, R. J. (1986). Learning internal representations by error propagation. In D. E. Rumelhart, J. L. McClelland, & the PDP Research Group (Eds.), *Parallel distributed processing: Explorations in the microstructure of cognition (Vol 1).* (pp. 318–362). Cambridge, MA: MIT Press.

Saiki, J., & Hummel, J. E. (1996). Attribute conjunctions and the part configuration advantage in object category learning. *Journal of Experimental Psychology: Learning, Memory, and Cognition, 22*, 1002–1019.

Saiki, J., & Hummel, J. E. (1998a). Connectedness and the integration of parts with relations in shape perception. *Journal of Experimental Psychology: Human Perception and Performance, 24*, 227–251.

Saiki, J., & Hummel, J. E. (1998b). Connectedness and part-relation integration in shape category learning. *Memory and Cognition, 26*, 1138–1156.

Shastri, L., & Ajjanagadde, V. (1993). From simple associations to systematic reasoning: A connectionist representation of rules, variables and dynamic bindings. *Behavioral and Brain Sciences, 16*, 417–494.

Shiffrin, R. M., & Styvers, M. (1997). A model for recognition memory: REM–retrieving effectively from memory. *Psychonomic Bulletin & Review, 4*, 145–166.

Singer, W., & Gray, C. M. (1995). Visual feature integration and the temporal correlation hypothesis. *Annual Review of Neuroscience, 18*, 555–586.

Smith, E. E., Langston, C., & Nisbett, R. E. (1992). The case for rules in reasoning. *Cognitive Science, 16*, 1–40.

St. John, M. F., & McClelland, J. L. (1990). Learning and applying contextual constraints in sentence comprehension. *Artificial Intelligence, 46*, 217–257.

Stankiewicz, B. J., & Hummel, J. E. (2002). The role of attention in scale- and translation-invariant object recognition. *Visual Cognition, 9*, 719–739.

Stankiewicz, B. J., Hummel, J. E., & Cooper, E. E. (1998). The role of attention in priming for left-right reflections of object images: Evidence for a dual representation of object shape. *Journal of Experimental Psychology: Human Perception and Performance, 24*, 732–744.

Strong, G. W., & Whitehead, B. A. (1989). A solution to the tag-assignment problem for neural networks. *Behavioral and Brain Sciences, 12*, 381–433.

Stuss, D. T., & Benson, D. F. (1987). The frontal lobes and control of cognition and memory. In E. Perecman (Ed.), *The Frontal Lobes Revisited.* (pp. 141–158). New York, NY: The IRBN Press.

Tarr, M. J., & Bülthoff, H. H. (1995). Is human object recognition better described by geon structural descriptions or by multiple views? Comment on Biederman and Gerhardstein (1993) *Journal of Experimental Psychology: Human Perception and Performance, 21*, 1494–1505.

Ullman, S., & Basri, R. (1991). Recognition by linear combinations of models. *IEEE Transactions on Pattern Analysis and Machine Intelligence, 13*, 992–1006.

von der Malsburg, C. (1981/1994). The correlation theory of brain function (1994 reprint of a report originally published in 1981). In E. Domany, J. L. van Hemmen, & K. Schulten (Eds.), *Models of neural networks II.* (pp. 95–119). Berlin: Springer.

Werner, S., & Thies, B. (2000). Is "change blindness" attenuated by domain-specific expertise? An expert-novice comparison of change detection in football images *Visual Cognition, 7*, 163–173.

AN EXEMPLAR MODEL FOR PERCEPTUAL CATEGORIZATION OF EVENTS

Koen Lamberts

I. Introduction

Perceptual categorization is the process of assigning a category label to a perceived object. It is an essential component of numerous cognitive tasks, including object naming and recognition, perceptual learning, inductive and deductive reasoning about objects, and so forth. When a familiar object is presented, humans are able to categorize the object with remarkable accuracy in about <350 ms (Lamberts, 1995). Understanding this ability is clearly essential for a general theory of cognition.

Considering the general importance of perceptual categorization in cognition, it is somewhat surprising that current theories of categorization fail to address how people categorize things that change. Earlier studies have taken perceptual features to be static object properties, and the formal models that successfully describe perceptual categorization do not incorporate processes that can handle objects that change. Yet, many objects in the world have properties that are dynamic. The perceptual features of objects may be subject to constant or intermittent change on many different timescales. In vision research, perception of dynamic objects and events is a central topic (Nakayama, 1998; Smith & Snowden, 1994). Motion perception in particular has been widely studied, and many aspects of perception of rigid and non-rigid object motion are well understood. However, this work has not had much influence on categorization research.

It is important to make a clear distinction between categorization of dynamic objects and categorization of events. Events are episodes in the existence of objects, with well-defined temporal boundaries. Events can also involve static objects, and the same dynamic object can occur in different events. In this article, the main concern is with categorization of events. The purpose of the research was to develop a framework for perceptual categorization that can be used to study the basic processes and mechanisms that underlie the perceptual categorization of *all* events, regardless of whether they involve static or dynamic objects.

Categorization of objects that change and the events they define is likely to involve processes that are not used in categorization of static objects. For instance, categorizing a flying bird, with its changing shape and position, is a very different task from categorizing a static image of the same animal. There is no shortage of studies to suggest that dynamic cues can be used in categorization. People and animals can be identified or categorized on the basis of very impoverished information, if dynamic cues are present. For instance, a large number of studies have shown that properties of actions and actors can be identified from dynamic point-light displays, which only show the motion of the joints (e.g., Brownlow, Dixon, Egbert, & Radcliffe, 1997; Dittrich, Troscianko, Lea, & Morgan, 1996; Johansson, 1973; Mather & Murdoch, 1994; Montepare & Zebrowitz, 1993; Pollick et al., 2001, 2002). In point-light displays, shape information is absent. Static point-light displays may be impossible to identify or categorize, because a particular configuration of points may be compatible with many different shapes. However, in animated point-light displays, the dynamic information provides a stimulus that is sufficiently rich to be categorized without much effort.

Developmental studies provide further evidence for the importance of dynamic object properties in categorization. In a study with four- and seven-year-old children, Mak and Vera (1999) pitted motion against shape as a cue for categorization. The children were first shown two animated objects that differed in shape and motion (e.g., a walking horse and a jumping antelope). Next, they were shown a test object that was similar in shape to one of the study items, but moved in the same way as the other study item (e.g., a jumping donkey). The children were more likely to draw inferences about the test item on the basis of dynamic correspondence with a study item than on shape correspondence. Such findings suggest that the use of dynamic features in the context of object categorization is a primary skill. In another study, Opfer (2002) showed that the nature of movement (aimless vs. apparently goal-directed) can form the basis of judgments about whether objects are alive or not, even in five-year-old children. Arterberry and Bornstein (2002; also see Arterberry & Bornstein, 2001) used a habituation paradigm to demonstrate that six-month-old children can categorize objects on the basis of static and dynamic cues.

The perceptual and development studies that were cited suggest that event classification (which is usually implied in dynamic object classification) is a basic cognitive skill. To understand its properties, two central issues need to be addressed. These issues are not unique to an account of event categorization; they arise in any theory of perceptual categorization. First, we need to determine how events are to be represented. I will propose a representation scheme that covers both static objects and events. Second, we have to specify the mechanisms that support classification of represented events. In line with current theories of perceptual categorization, I will suggest that event classification depends on *similarity* to stored exemplars.

II. Representation of Events

The first issue that must be addressed in any formal theory of categorization is how objects are represented. Although objects can be represented in many different ways, it seems sensible to start from a very general scheme that has proved its value in numerous studies of perceptual classification of static objects. In this scheme, objects are defined as points in a multidimensional psychological space (Nosofsky, 1986). The dimensions of the space correspond to psychological or perceived stimulus dimensions, and the values on the dimensions are features. Thus, each static object corresponds to a feature list, which can be expressed formally as a vector. For instance, rectangles can be defined as points in a two-dimensional space, with perceived height and width as orthogonal dimensions.

To represent events, this framework can be adapted in two different ways. The first possibility maintains the assumption that objects correspond to single points in a multidimensional space. The space itself is defined in such a way that at least one of the dimensions represents change (or rate of change) in one or more of the other dimensions. For instance, suppose that we want to represent an event involving an object that moves from point A in a straight line to point B with a constant velocity. This event corresponds to a point in the three-dimensional space that has start position, end position, and velocity (i.e., rate of change in position) as dimensions. The obvious advantage of such a representation is that it is entirely equivalent to the standard spatial representation of static objects—only the meaning of the stimulus dimensions has changed. The main drawback of this scheme is that it can only be used for events with well understood dynamic regularities.

Such events can be described using linear or non-linear differential equations or difference equations, which define the dimensions that characterize change. However, a description in terms of differential expressions is often not feasible for everyday objects, which may exhibit staggeringly complex dynamic behavior. For instance, it is practically impossible to characterize the motion of a leaf falling from a tree with a simple set of difference equations. A point representation of such an event would require a prohibitively large and complex psychological space (unless a great deal of information about the event is lost).

The second approach abandons the assumption that objects must correspond to single points in the psychological space. Whereas the point assumption is still maintained for static objects, dynamic objects are represented by an ordered sequence of points (or a *trajectory*) in the feature space. As a simple example, consider the two-dimensional space that characterizes the perceived horizontal (X) and vertical (Y) position of a leaf falling from a tree (Fig. 1). The trajectory completely defines the event. In the example, measurement of time and position is continuous, but by quantizing time and plotting markers at regular time intervals the dynamic object can be represented at any desired level of precision. This representation scheme has the advantage that it is a simple extension of the scheme for static objects, and that it does not require the inclusion of difference or rate variables in the psychological space. It includes events that involve static objects as special cases, with a trajectory length of zero. The representation can be applied to any event, regardless of whether an analytic description of the event's

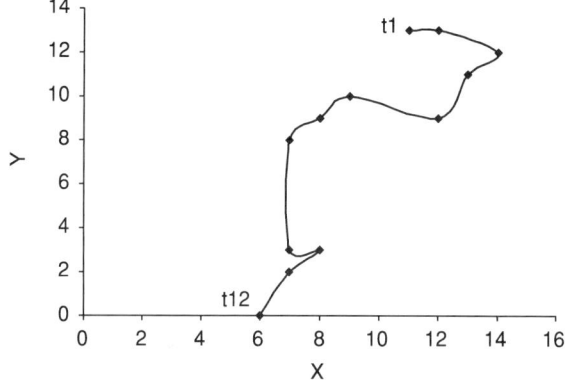

Fig. 1. Trajectory of a falling leaf in two-dimensional feature space. The starting position of the object is indicated by *t1*, and the end position by *t12*. X and Y refer to perceived horizontal and vertical position, respectively.

dynamics is available. For these reasons, I will adopt the trajectory scheme for representing events in this article.

III. Similarity of Events

The notion of similarity plays an essential part in many theories of perceptual categorization, and it is a particularly important concept in exemplar theories of categorization (e.g., Nosofsky, 1986). Exemplar models of categorization assume that learning involves the storage of specific instances or exemplars in memory. Subsequent categorization of an object is then based on the similarity of the object to the instances in memory. Exemplar models have been very successful in explaining perceptual categorization, identification, and recognition (e.g., Estes, 1994; Lamberts, 1995, 1998, 2000; Lamberts, Brockdorff, & Heit, 2002; Medin & Shaffer, 1978; Nosofsky, 1986, 1992; Nosofsky & Palmeri, 1997). For static objects, similarity can be defined as a decreasing function of the generalized Minkowski distance between points that represent stimuli in the psychological space. The distance equation is:

$$d_{ij} = \left(\sum_{p=1}^{P} w_p |x_{ip} - x_{jp}|^r \right)^{1/r} \quad (1)$$

in which P is the total number of stimulus dimensions, w_p is the weight of dimension p, x_{ip} and x_{jp} are the values of stimulus i and exemplar j on dimension p, and r defines the distance metric that applies ($r = 2$ for Euclidean distance, and $r = 1$ for city-block distance). Distance is converted to similarity using an exponential function:

$$\eta_{ij} = \exp(-c \cdot d_{ij}) \quad (2)$$

in which c is a discriminability index ($c \geq 0$). This geometric similarity definition forms the cornerstone of Nosofsky's (1986) Generalized Context Model (GCM), and of several models that have been derived from the GCM (e.g., Lamberts, 1995, 1998, 2000; Nosofsky & Palmeri, 1997). The similarity notion of the GCM applies to a wide range of tasks and stimuli (Nosofsky, 1992), and thereby offers a parsimonious principle for unification and integration of seemingly disparate findings.

The similarity definition of the GCM only applies to point representations of objects and cannot be used directly for objects that are represented as trajectories. However, it is not difficult to extend the definition to trajectories (and hence to events), in a manner that is intuitively straightforward.

The general idea is that similarity between trajectories should be a decreasing function of the total distance between the trajectories. This distance can be obtained by integration over time of the point distance function in Equation 1:

$$d_{ij} = \int_0^T \left(\sum_{p=1}^P w_p |x_{ipt} - x_{jpt}|^r \right)^{1/r} dt \qquad (3)$$

Because the analytical forms of the trajectories are usually not known, explicit calculation of this integral is usually not feasible. In those cases, a numerical approximation must be used. A convenient method uses the so-called midpoint rule, in which the integration interval is partitioned into a number of intervals of equal size. The function is evaluated at the midpoint of each interval. Summation of the products of interval size with function value at each midpoint yields an approximation of the integral. The quality of the approximation depends on the number of intervals. The larger the number of intervals, the better the approximation. This yields the following discrete expression for trajectory distance:

$$d_{ij} = \sum_{t=1}^T \left(\sum_{p=1}^P w_p |x_{ipt} - x_{jpt}|^r \right)^{1/r} \Delta t \qquad (4)$$

in which T is now the total number of discrete, equally-spaced interval midpoints, Δt is the interval size, and all the other symbols have the same meaning as before (but note that the stimulus co-ordinates are now calculated at the interval midpoints). In all the modeling in this article, the discrete distance function was used. Fig. 2 provides an illustration of the midpoint rule. The figure shows the trajectories for two events. The dashed lines show the (Euclidean) distance between the events at a number of time points. The total distance between the events is the sum of all the dashed line lengths, multiplied by the size of the interval between successive measurement points.

IV. Categorization of Events

The assignment of a perceptual event to a category is assumed to depend on similarity. Specifically, it is assumed that the observer has stored instances of events in memory, and that the similarity of a perceived event to those stored instances determines category judgments. The probability that stimulus i is

An Exemplar Model for Perceptual Categorization of Events

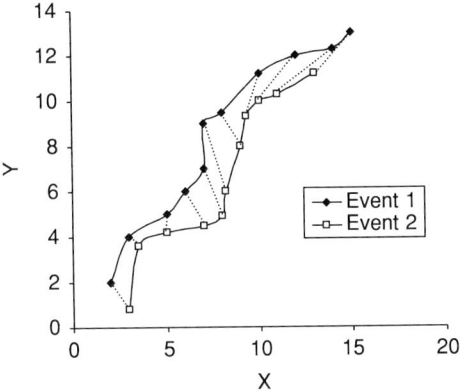

Fig. 2. Calculation of distance between two event trajectories.

assigned to category J is given by a modified version of Luce's (1963) choice rule:

$$P(R_J|S_i) = \frac{b_J \left(\sum_{j \in C_J} \eta_{ij} \right)^\gamma}{\sum_{K=1}^m b_K \left(\sum_{k \in C_K} \eta_{ik} \right)^\gamma} \quad (5)$$

in which η_{ij} is the similarity between stimulus i and stored exemplar j, m is the number of categories, b_J represents the bias for making response J ($\Sigma b = 1$), and the index $j \in C_J$ refers to all stored exemplars that belong to category J. The γ parameter, which is not part of the original choice rule in the GCM, reflects the level of determinism in responding (e.g., Lamberts, 2000; Maddox & Ashby, 1993; McKinley & Nosofsky, 1995). The original choice rule of the GCM works very well for predicting choice proportions averaged across individuals (e.g. Nosofsky, 1987). It has been shown, however, that averaging across individuals can provide misleading information about model validity. In the worst possible case, average data can support a model that does not apply to any of the individuals in the group. Therefore, averaging can make an incorrect model appear correct—it can produce spurious regularity (e.g., Estes, 1956). Generally, averaging is not acceptable in conditions where it affects the underlying structure of the data (Luce, 1997; Maddox, 1999; Myung, Kim, & Pitt, 2000). For this reason, the model will only be applied to data from individual subjects. It has been shown that inclusion of the γ parameter greatly improves the model predictions for data from individual subjects (Maddox & Ashby, 1993; McKinley & Nosofsky, 1995).

The model that I proposed is a general one, in the sense that it can be applied to any type of event, and that it includes static objects as a special case. The dimensions of the perceptual space define the types of events that can be represented, and these dimensions can represent any perceptual quantity or its derivatives. The model can be applied just as well to events that are characterized by object motion as to events that involve a change in luminance or shape of an object, for instance.

Despite its generality, the model does contain testable assumptions about event categorization. The first assumption is that event categorization depends on similarity to stored instances. This makes the model a true exemplar model of categorization, with all the associated benefits (and drawbacks). Without attempting to review the evidence for and against exemplar models of categorization, it is probably fair to state that exemplar models are among the most successful models of perceptual categorization. They have accounted for a truly impressive range of empirical findings, and they have provided a unified theoretical framework for understanding performance in a wide range of tasks (including categorization, but also perceptual identification, recognition memory, and perceptual matching).

The second strong assumption in the model concerns the role of time. Time determines how events are compared. Because events are intrinsically extended in time, it seems natural to assume that time provides the reference frame within which they are encoded. This is by no means the only possibility, and some events may well be encoded differently. Events that involve motion, for instance, might just as well be encoded in a spatial reference frame (Bingham, 1995). However, not all events that are encompassed by the model have a spatial extension. Given the general scope of the model, time is the only dimension that all events must have in common and, therefore, it offers a universally applicable reference frame.

Effective use of a temporal reference frame requires good timekeeping abilities. If two successive but otherwise identical events are encoded using a timekeeping process that drifts, the encoded events will be misaligned and will not be perceived as identical. However, there is no evidence that humans possess universal perceptual timing abilities (e.g., Port, Cummins, & McAuley, 1995). It is clearly naive to assume that we have an internal clock that runs like a perpetual millisecond timer, which can be used as an absolute reference basis for event encoding. In many cases, the ability to identify events is not negatively affected by variations in the overall duration of events, or by differences in their precise time course (e.g., Hill & Pollick, 2000). And yet, people often do encode more than just the serial order of the elements that constitute an event. If a movie is fast-forwarded at twice the normal speed, the result looks very odd indeed (although people will still be able to categorize the events that occur). People can also discriminate between events that differ only in rate of change, and this requires at least interval-level timekeeping. Runeson (1974), for instance, demonstrated that people can distinguish between linear motion paths that have constant velocity and paths that show constant acceleration or deceleration.

Given this confusing state of affairs, how should we see the role of time and of temporal reference frames in the model of event similarity and categorization? The proposal is that events are initially aligned on the basis of non-temporal information. This information can be extrinsic or intrinsic to the event itself. An intrinsic point of alignment could be some qualitative aspect of the event. For example, if the event is the motion pattern of a swinging pendulum over some time period, a natural point of alignment would be the moment at which the velocity of the pendulum is zero. It is further assumed that timekeeping within the event can be accurate relative to the point of alignment, but with the possibility of adjustment in response to further alignment opportunities afforded by qualitative event characteristics. This could even mean that time measurement is relative to overall event duration, or to duration of event segments. For instance, people would have no difficulties aligning the trajectories of fast-swinging and slow-swinging pendulums, because they offer clear alignment points (e.g., points of minimal angular velocity), and because a simple adjustment of the timing unit within each event can produce perfect correspondence. So, the notion of psychological time that is used here can be highly relative and context-dependent. How time is represented and used in a given setting is essentially an empirical issue.

This notion of time relative to points of (re-)alignment is compatible with recent data on the recognition of movement patterns with exaggerated temporal differences (Hill & Pollick, 2000). The participants in Hill and Pollick's (2000) experiment first learned to identify six actors from point-light displays of a simple arm movement. The displays were then modified by dividing the action sequences into segments and scaling the durations of the segments relative to average values. In the positive exaggeration conditions, segments that had a short duration (relative to the average segment duration) were made even shorter, whereas long-lasting segments were made to last relatively longer. The segmentation was based on the stationary points that occurred between periods of movement (these stationary points offer natural points of alignment). The spatial properties of the stimuli were preserved throughout. The results showed that exaggerating temporal differences improved performance on the task, regardless of whether total duration of the stimuli was normalized or not. These results conclusively rule out absolute duration of segments (or of entire events) as the critical cue for event identification, and they are not compatible with a model in which time provides an absolute basis for event encoding. However, they do suggest that relative duration of segments is an important cue. So, whatever representation was used by the observers, it must have preserved some temporal information. Because it is not clear what psychological dimensions were used to represent the stimuli (point-light displays of real actions are highly complex), it is difficult to be more specific about how the trajectory distance model could explain Hill and Pollick's results. Interestingly, Hill and Pollick (2000) suggest that an exemplar-based account might be best suited as an explanation of the exaggeration effects. In any case, their results show that psychological time cannot be seen as absolute time in theories of event perception and categorization.

Following the assumptions about similarity and the role of time, the third assumption of the model is that event categorization involves accumulation and integration of information over time. This assumption implies that people categorize events on the basis of entire trajectories, and not just on the basis of one (or a few) point measurements made along each trajectory. Bingham (1987, 1995) has argued that the structure of various motion events can only be understood from information contained in time-extended trajectories, and not from the limited information available in instantaneous representations (such as vector fields) or in representations based on two or three snapshots along a trajectory. The proposal that trajectory form is critical for event recognition was tested by Bingham, Schmidt, and Rosenblum (1995). They recorded patch-light displays for a number of different events, some of which were inanimate (not the result of human intervention) and some of which were animate (generated by humans). The inanimate displays showed events such as a falling and bouncing spring, a swinging pendulum, or a rolling ball. The animate events were generated by manual control of the same objects. An actor would move the spring or pendulum by hand in an attempt to mimic the inanimate event as closely as possible. The inanimate and animate versions of the same events were carefully synchronized using a metronome. As a result, the inanimate and animate events had the same period and amplitude. However, because the actors failed to replicate the inanimate events perfectly, there were fairly subtle differences in overall trajectory form between the two types of events. Observers were asked to describe the events (in Experiment 1), or to judge whether events were natural or whether the objects were moved by hand (in Experiment 2). The results showed that the observers were generally able to discriminate free motion from hand-guided motion, which points to the importance of trajectory form in event identification.

Muchisky and Bingham (2002) extended these findings using simulated events. In the first three experiments in Muchisky and Bingham (2002), the participants had to perform a forced choice between two displays, one of which contained a simulated free-swinging pendulum, while the other contained a perturbed pendulum. The trajectory form of both stimuli in a trial was similar, and the level of distortion was manipulated. The results indicated that observers could identify the perturbed pendulum, and that they were able to compare trajectory forms. Interestingly, Muchisky and Bingham (2002) showed that the probability of identifying the perturbed stimulus was related to a measure of dissimilarity between trajectories that is similar to the integrated distance measure that I proposed. The measure they used is the mean velocity Weber fraction, which they defined as:

$$MVW = \frac{\sum_{t=1}^{T}\left[\frac{V_P - V_S}{V_S}\right]}{T} \quad (6)$$

in which T is the number of time frames in the event, and V_P and V_S refer to the normalized velocity (calculated at t) in the perturbed and the standard event, respectively. Note that this measure does not crucially depend on the use of velocity as a stimulus dimension; a similar ratio could be calculated for size, luminance, or position, or whichever other dimension would be used to encode a stimulus. The use of velocity as a primary stimulus dimension is appropriate, because a large number of studies have indicated that velocity is detected directly by the visual system (e.g., Lappin, Bell, Harm, & Kohas, 1975; Orban, DeWolf, & Maes, 1984; Rosenbaum, 1975). Like the distance measure that I proposed, the MVW ratio involves comparisons between stimulus values at equivalent time points, and a summation of differences along the trajectories. Although the MVW has a solid psychophysical basis (at least for velocity as a stimulus dimension), it has the drawback that it does not apply to multidimensional stimuli. In that sense, the distance measure that I proposed is more general. Note also that the Weber ratio calculation, which may be appropriate for some dimensions, can be accommodated in the standard model by appropriate scaling of the stimulus values. In any case, the predictive validity of this measure for trajectory dissimilarity confirms that observers integrate information over time in judgments about events.

Muchisky and Bingham (2002) also report an interesting fourth experiment, in which a categorization task was used. Events had to be categorized into one of four different types, distinguished by their trajectory form. The participants were able to perform this task well above the chance level, lending further support to the assumption that trajectory information forms the basis of event discrimination and categorization.

The sensitivity to trajectory form appears to develop early in infancy. Spitz, Stiles, and Siegel (1993) showed that seven-month-old infants could detect the difference between a set of point lights that moved coherently (as if they were all attached to a rigid object) and a set of lights that moved incoherently. The incoherent lights individually followed the same trajectories as the choerent lights, but the relation between the incoherent lights varied. Kim and Spelke (1992) found that seven-month-old infants were sensitive to the effects of gravity on acceleration of a rolling ball, which also indicates that they were able to use trajectory forms. Wickelgren and Bingham (2001) used a habituation paradigm to show that eight-month-old infants are sensitive to trajectory forms. They used three events: (1) a ball that rolled back and forth, (2) a splash of water, and (3) an occlusion event in which a ball swung out from behind a screen and back. After the infants were habituated to one version of an event, they were shown the same event played backwards. Significant dishabituation occurred, which indicates that the infants were sensitive to trajectory forms.

A fourth assumption of the model is that similarity between events can be dependent on the scale of non-temporal variables. If two events have the same duration and the same general trajectory form, but the trajectories differ in size, their similarity will be <1. This assumption appears to contradict empirical results, which suggest that event discrimination and recognition tends to be scale-invariant (Bingham, 1995; Muchisky & Bingham, 2002). For instance, Muchisky and Bingham (2002) varied the amplitude of the motion of standard and perturbed pendulum displays, and found that amplitude had little effect on the ability to discriminate between these two types of event (which is the reason why they used normalized velocities in their Weber fraction measure of trajectory dissimilarity). It is certainly true that scale is often irrelevant for event identification or categorization. People of different height or weight may step at different amplitudes, but we would have no difficulty identifying a gait pattern from the dynamic information that is present. Amplitudes of events that involve motion also vary with viewing distance, which is usually not relevant for event identification. Therefore, it seems sensible to have a similarity notion that is scale invariant, unlike the notion used in the model that I proposed. However, there is no evidence to suggest that scale invariance *always* holds in event recognition or categorization. The fact that scale is often irrelevant does not imply that it should be ignored altogether. People can almost certainly learn to categorize events on the basis of the spatial scale on which they occur, if that is appropriate in some context. For instance, there is some evidence that people can use time to derive spatial scale information. McConnell, Muchisky, and Bingham (1998) found that observers could judge object size in event displays that eliminated all information except time and trajectory forms, suggesting a general sensitivity to scale information. In any case, scale invariance can be built into the model, if necessary, by standardizing the dimensions of the psychological stimulus space.

Having outlined the principles of the model (which I will call the integrator model) and its main assumptions, in the remainder of this article I will review a number of experiments that aimed at testing the model's main principles.

V. Initial Tests of Event Similarity

Perceptual similarity can be measured in many different ways. For instance, participants can be asked to compare two stimuli, and their response times can be taken as an index of stimulus similarity. Perhaps the most direct measurement of similarity is obtained by simply asking participants to rate the similarity of two stimuli that are presented in succession. Although such ratings can be unreliable (because the task leaves room for all kinds of strategic effects and response biases), previous work has demonstrated that direct ratings can provide an excellent basis for predicting subsequent categorization (e.g., Nosofsky & Palmeri, 1997). Therefore, direct ratings seemed to offer a good starting point for an empirical test of the dynamic similarity model.

The purpose of the two similarity-rating experiments that I review here was to test the dynamic similarity notion with relatively simple stimuli. On each trial in the experiments, the participants observed two successive events, and rated their similarity on a scale from 1 to 9. To obtain a reasonably critical test of the model, the stimuli had to be multidimensional. In order to avoid alignment issues, stimuli were needed that differed somewhat in trajectory form, but that had the same duration and did not show any major qualitative differences. Moreover, the stimuli had to be unfamiliar in order to avoid effects of previous knowledge (which is particularly important in the categorization experiments that follow).

In Experiment 1, each event consisted of a single dot that moved from the top left hand corner of the computer screen to the bottom right-hand corner. Only one dot was presented at a time. The events differed in their trajectories. Figure 3 gives an overview of the trajectories that were used in the experiment, plotting horizontal and vertical position over time. All trajectories had exactly the same duration (2,500 ms), with identical start and end points.

The trajectories were generated by cubic Bézier curves, which are determined by four control points in the plane. The curve starts at the position of the first control point, then roughly heads towards the positions of the two middle points, and terminates at the position of the fourth control point. The first control point in this experiment was always in the top left-hand corner, and the fourth control point was in the bottom right-hand corner. The positions of the two intermediary control points were varied. The resulting

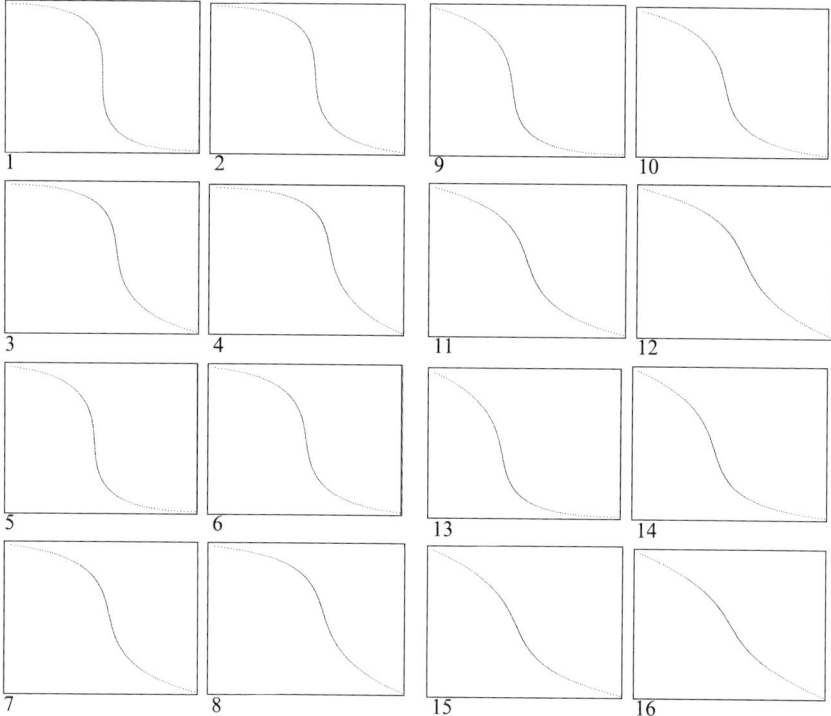

Fig. 3. Stimulus trajectories in Experiment 1.

trajectories were monotonic over time in both dimensions. The velocity of the moving dot was not constant throughout a trajectory. On a trial, the dot would sweep in from top left, then decelerate on its way to the central region of the screen, and finally accelerate away again. Although the resulting trajectories looked smooth and natural, they were unfamiliar. A total of 16 different stimuli were used in the experiment, in which three participants took part. A trial contained two sequentially presented stimuli. All possible ordered stimulus pairs were presented four times in total (pairs with identical stimuli were not presented). After the presentation of a stimulus pair, the participants rated the similarity of the stimuli on a scale from 1 (most dissimilar) to 9 (most similar).

The data from each participant were analyzed separately. The integrator model was applied to the 120 mean ratings from each participant. In the modeling, it was assumed that the observed ratings were linearly related to the similarity values predicted by the model:

An Exemplar Model for Perceptual Categorization of Events 241

$$\rho_{ij} = \alpha + \beta \cdot \eta_{ij} \tag{7}$$

in which ρ_{ij} is the observed similarity rating for stimulus pair (i, j), η_{ij} is the similarity value generated by the model, and α and β are free model parameters. The psychological stimulus space was assumed to have two dimensions, corresponding to horizontal position and vertical position. In calculating the similarity values, it was assumed that both stimulus dimensions were equally weighted, which left only one parameter, c, the discriminability index (see Equation 2), to be estimated. The parameters were estimated using a least-squares criterion.

The results of the model-fitting procedure are shown in Fig. 4. Although the model was fitted to the 120 mean ratings for each participant, the observed and predicted values in Fig. 4 were obtained by further averaging across stimulus pairs for which the model made similar predictions. This procedure made it easier to notice meaningful, qualitative deviations between model predictions and observed data. The averages were obtained by sorting the 120 stimulus pairs according to their predicted rating, and by grouping them into bins of 10 stimulus pairs each. Fig. 4 plots the observed and predicted mean ratings in each bin.

Although absolute model fits have very little meaning (e.g., Pitt, Myung, & Zhang, 2002), the model fits from the three participants do show that the integrator model managed to explain some of the variation in the similarity judgments (note also that these fits were achieved with a single effective parameter, because α and β only served as scaling parameters). This does not mean that the model is correct, of course. In fact, there are strong indications that the integrator model failed to capture significant aspects of the similarity data. It turns out that the model tended to make similar prediction errors for the three participants, as indicated by significantly correlated residuals.

A detailed analysis of the similarity ratings for the different stimulus pairs suggested that the participants did not treat all the temporal segments of the stimuli as equally important. To explore this possibility, a modified version of the integrator model was applied, in which distances between stimuli trajectories were calculated at points that were 250 ms apart (because all trajectories had the same start and end positions, only nine points were relevant). Although this nine-point calculation offered only a fairly crude approximation of the continuous integrator model, it did permit estimation of the relative contribution of the distance at each time point to the total distance between the trajectories, without having to rely on an excessive number of estimated parameters. The modified integrator model had the same three parameters as the standard model, plus nine parameters that served as weights for the distances at the corresponding time points.

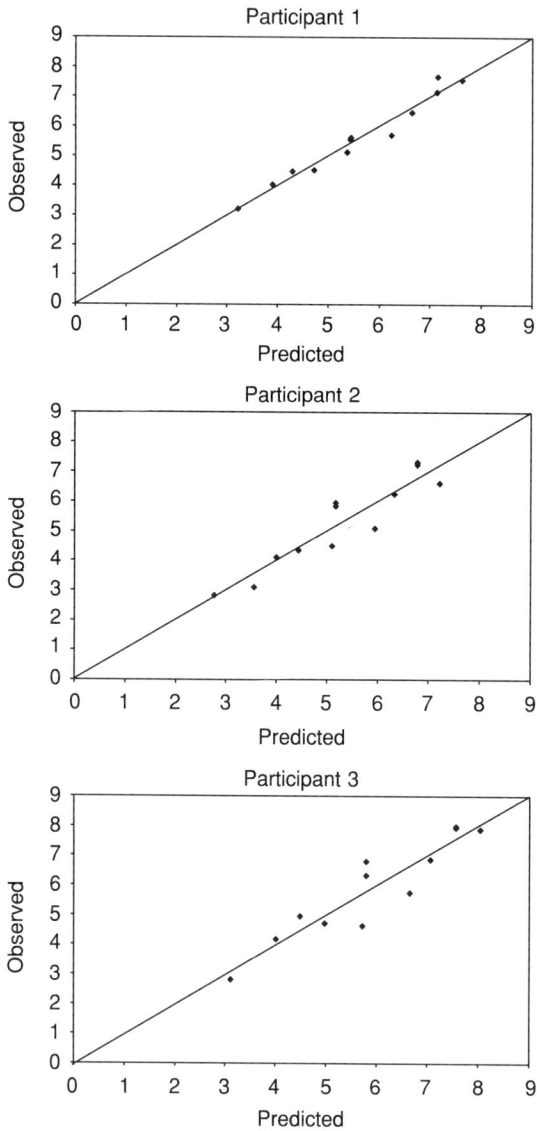

Fig. 4. Observed and predicted mean similarity ratings in Experiment 1. The predictions were generated by the integrator model.

The modification greatly improved the fit of the model for each participant. Figure 5 shows the estimated weights of the different time points in the distance calculation. The three participants all relied heavily on the start and end

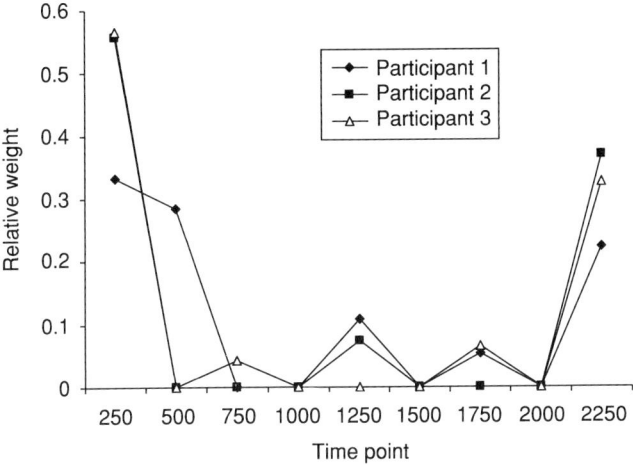

Fig. 5. Estimated weights of different time points in the trajectory distance calculation, Experiment 1.

segments of the trajectories, and they largely ignored the middle of the trajectories. The predictions from the modified model are shown in Figure 6.

It is not clear whether the time-point weightings have any special significance. The fact that they were so similar across the three participants does suggest that they are not just the result of an arbitrary choice. It would be reasonable to assume that the participants assigned most importance to those segments on which the stimuli tended to vary most, because that would make the similarity assessment relatively easy. However, if the average distance between all the trajectories in the experiment is plotted as a function of time, it is clear that the largest differences occurred in the middle segments, and that the stimuli were on average quite close together in the segments that were most heavily weighted (Fig. 7). It is possible that the participants found it easier to determine the location of the dot when it was closest to the reference rectangle that bordered the screen, but this explanation is unlikely to be correct. The distances between stimuli near the center of the screen were so large that even inaccurate position measurement could differentiate between the stimuli. Another possible explanation is that the weightings reflect the inaccuracy of timekeeping within the stimulus presentation interval. If the participants were aware of their inability to keep accurate time, a sensible strategy would be to emphasize the initial trajectory segments more than later segments. However, this does not explain why the latest segments were also heavily weighted.

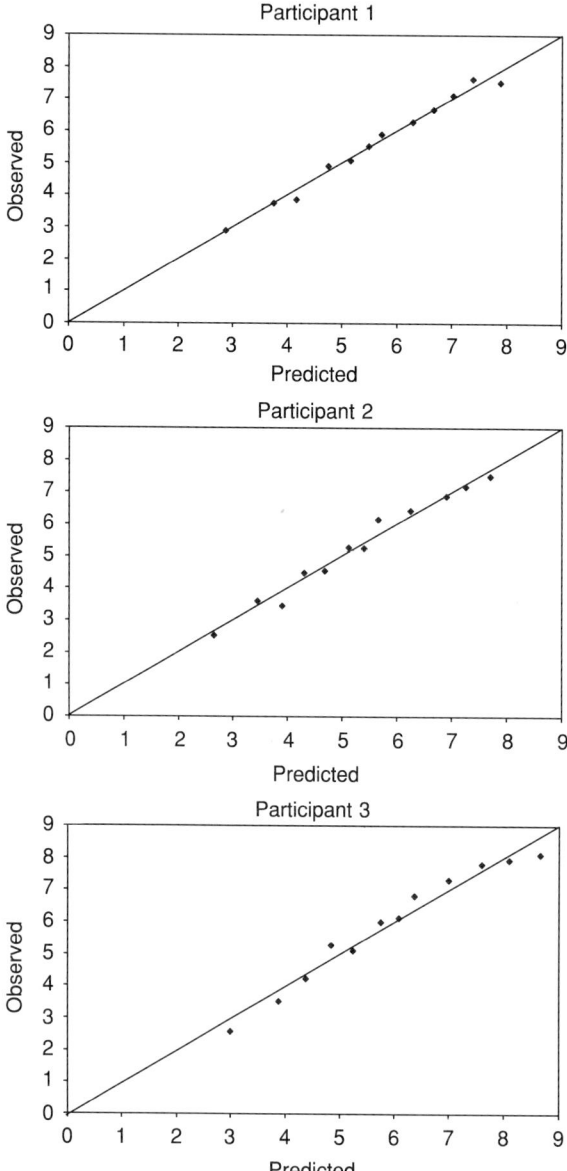

Fig. 6. Observed and predicted mean similarity ratings in Experiment 1. The predictions were generated by the weighted integrator model.

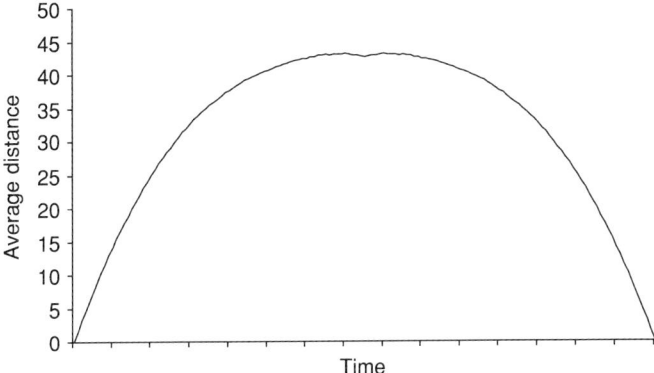

Fig. 7. Average distance between trajectories in Experiment 1 as a function of time.

In an attempt to clarify this issue further, several alternative stimulus representations were explored. Model versions in which velocity was a stimulus dimension did not fit the data better than the standard model, so there was no evidence that velocity was encoded and used directly. Inclusion of acceleration or trajectory curvature as dimensions did not improve matters either. Altogether, there did not seem to be an obvious alternative to stimulus representation in terms of horizontal and vertical position, combined with differential weighting of different trajectory segments. The reason for the differential weighting remains unclear.

What are the implications of these results for the integrator model? The similarity rating data indicate that the standard version of the integrator model is incorrect for the stimuli used in the experiment. However, the modified version that included segment weights for the trajectories performed well, suggesting that a limited integration process did occur. I experimented with alternative models that did not involve information accumulation or integration over time, but these models invariably performed worse than the weighted integration model. For instance, the similarity ratings were not predicted by the maximum Euclidean distance between the trajectories at any point in time, by maximum curvature difference, or by the maximum velocity difference between trajectories. It seems unlikely that the participants based their judgments on just a single point measurement of some basic or derived stimulus property.

The purpose of Experiment 2 was to establish the generality of these findings by using stimuli that had an entirely different surface appearance from the stimuli in Experiment 1. If the participants used trajectory information in their similarity assessments, only the underlying kinetic structure of the stimuli should be important, not their surface appearance. Instead of a moving dot, the stimuli were now pie slices that varied in radius and angle within an event (Fig. 8). The values of these two dimensions were determined by the same Bezier functions that generated the horizontal and vertical position of the dots in Experiment 1, so the underlying structure of the stimulus set was identical in both experiments. The stimuli all had the same start and end values on both dimensions. The starting angle was 5° and the end angle was 315°. The radius changed from 33 pixels to 148 pixels. Each event lasted for 2,500 ms (150 frames). The experiment had two participants, and the procedure was identical to that in Experiment 1.

Again, the mean similarity ratings were analyzed with the same two models that were applied in the first experiment. For both participants, the integrator model fitted the data much worse than the weighted integrator model, so I will focus only on the results from the weighted integrator model. The model predictions are plotted against observed values in Figure 9. For both participants, there were no systematic deviations between observed and predicted values. Figure 10 shows the estimated relative weights of different trajectory segments. The pattern that emerged was very similar to that from the first experiment. Again, the segments near the start and near the end of the trajectories were weighted more heavily than the segments near the middle of the trajectories.

The conclusion from Experiment 2 was that the standard integrator model performed poorly, while the weighted integrator model provided an excellent account of the similarity ratings. The new surface structure of the stimuli (pie slices instead of moving dots) did not appear to affect the results, compared to Experiment 1. This correspondence in response patterns for stimuli with very different appearances confirmed the importance of trajectory information in similarity assessment.

Fig. 8. Snapshot of stimulus in Experiment 2.

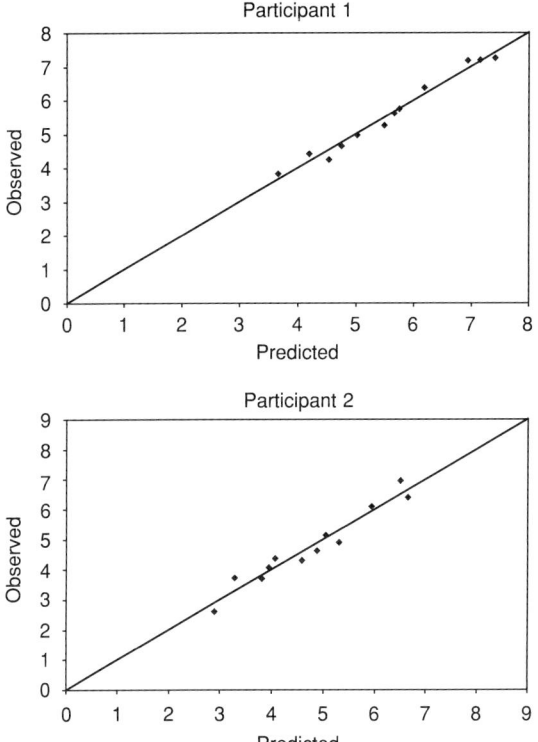

Fig. 9. Observed and predicted mean similarity ratings in Experiment 2. The predictions were generated by the weighted integrator model.

VI. Trajectories as a Basis for Event Categorization

The previous experiments have demonstrated that the dynamic similarity notion of the integrator model provided a good account of explicit similarity ratings, if initial and final trajectory segments were weighted more heavily. The aim of the next two experiments was to investigate whether trajectory similarity can form the basis of categorization of events. The experiments were designed as standard categorization experiments (e.g., Medin & Schaffer, 1978), in which the participants first learned to assign a small number of stimuli to one of two categories. In the subsequent transfer task, the same stimuli were presented for categorization again, as well as a set of new stimuli. The choice proportions in the transfer stage were of primary interest.

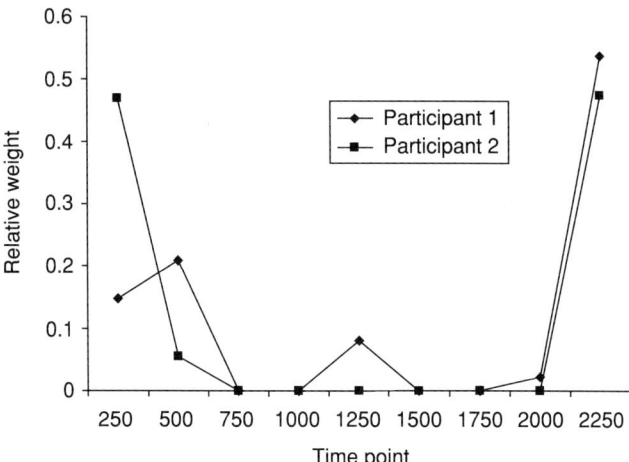

Fig. 10. Estimated weights of different time points in the trajectory distance calculation, Experiment 2.

In Experiment 3, the stimuli were identical to those in Experiment 1 (moving dots with trajectories generated by Bezier functions). The experiment consisted of training and transfer stages. In the training stages, the participants learned to categorize six stimuli into two categories. Three stimuli belonged to category A (numbers 2, 4, and 5 in Fig. 3), and three to category B (numbers 11, 13 and 14 in Fig. 3). On each training trial, a randomly chosen training stimulus was presented, and the participant gave an A or B response by pressing the appropriate button. Immediately after the response, correct–incorrect feedback was given. In the transfer stages, the sixteen stimuli in Figure 3 were presented repeatedly for categorization, in random order, without response feedback. In the instructions, a cover story was presented which explained that the participants had to learn to discriminate between two types of fundamental particle, moving through a magnetic field. The participants were told that the behavior of these particles was highly complex, and they were instructed to try and remember each trajectory as well as they could.

The results from the transfer task are presented in Table I. For each of the four participants, the stimuli appeared to cluster into four groups, according to the proportion of category A responses that were given. Stimuli 1 to 4 generally yielded proportions of category A responses that were close to 1. Responses to stimuli 5 to 8 were predominantly in category A (82% overall), but less consistently so than on stimuli 1 to 4. Stimuli 9 to 12 produced a majority (72% overall) of category B responses, and stimuli 13 to 16 produced

TABLE I
PROPORTIONS OF CATEGORY A RESPONSES IN EXPERIMENT 3

	Participant			
Stimulus	1	2	3	4
1	0.97	1.00	1.00	1.00
2A	0.97	1.00	1.00	1.00
3	0.98	0.97	1.00	1.00
4A	0.98	0.97	0.98	0.98
5A	0.95	0.90	0.77	0.88
6	0.82	0.85	0.83	0.88
7	0.60	0.90	0.77	0.75
8	0.58	0.90	0.82	0.93
9	0.42	0.38	0.40	0.23
10	0.22	0.25	0.25	0.23
11B	0.10	0.27	0.27	0.32
12	0.03	0.28	0.37	0.47
13B	0.03	0.07	0.08	0.00
14B	0.02	0.03	0.02	0.05
15	0.02	0.02	0.03	0.07
16	0.02	0.00	0.03	0.00

consistent category B responses (97%). Note that these clusters do not coincide with the sets of old and new stimuli. Stimuli 1, 3, 15, and 16 were never presented in training, and yet they produced responses that were as consistent as those to stimuli 2, 4, 13, or 14 (which were part of the training set). Stimuli 5 and 11 were presented in training, but were classified less consistently than the other training stimuli.

A. THE INTEGRATOR MODEL

The integrator model, which assumes that similarity between two dynamic stimuli depends on the integration of the distance between the trajectories along the entire duration of the event, was applied to the data from each participant. For each data set, three parameters were estimated: (1) c, the discriminability index; (2) b, the response bias; and (3) γ, the consistency parameter. The best-fitting parameter values were determined using a maximum-likelihood criterion, assuming that choice proportions had a joint binomial distribution. Table II presents the overall goodness-of-fit in terms of log-likelihood and explained variance. Figure 11 summarizes the observed and predicted choice proportions, averaged across participants. Although the overall goodness-of-fit was reasonable for each participant, there were

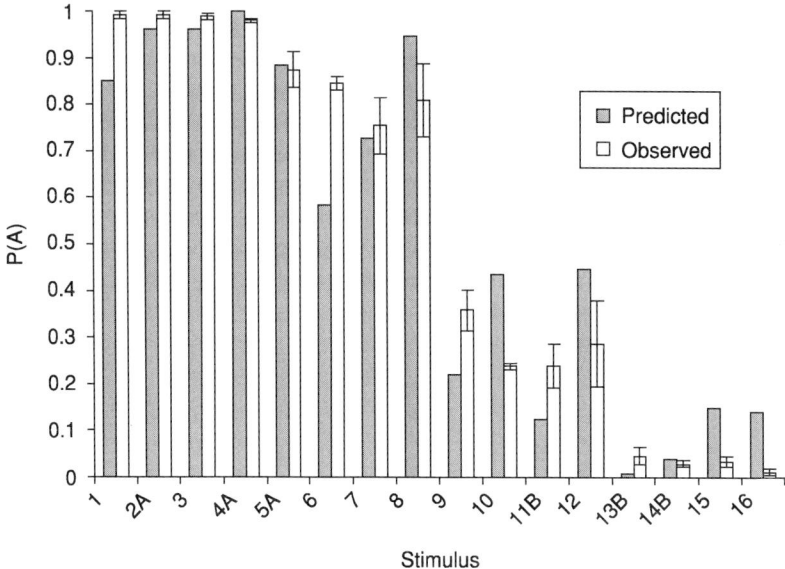

Fig. 11. Observed and predicted proportions of category A responses in Experiment 3. The predictions were generated by the integrator model. The error bars show 95% confidence intervals.

several reliable discrepancies between observed and predicted choice proportions. For instance, the integrator model completely failed to account for the relatively high proportion of category A responses to stimulus 6. The model certainly captured a considerable part of the variance in the proportions, but its systematic failures on several stimuli do raise questions about its validity.

B. THE WEIGHTED INTEGRATOR MODEL

The weighted integrator model was also applied to the data from each participant individually. Because there were only 16 data points per participant, it was not meaningful to add 9 weight parameters to the model. Therefore, the segment weights estimated from Experiment 1 (Fig. 5) were used in the model,

TABLE II

GOODNESS-OF-FIT STATISTICS FOR THE INTEGRATOR MODEL: EXPERIMENT 3

Measure	Participant 1	Participant 2	Participant 3	Participant 4
ln L	−108.747	−90.309	−85.784	−65.907
R^2	0.83	0.89	0.89	0.93

TABLE III

GOODNESS-OF-FIT STATISTICS FOR THE WEIGHTED INTEGRATOR MODEL: EXPERIMENT 3

Measure	Participant 1	Participant 2	Participant 3	Participant 4
ln L	−43.623	−45.633	−45.297	−38.335
R^2	0.97	0.98	0.97	0.98

leaving the same three estimated parameters as in the standard integrator model. The goodness-of-fit statistics of the weighted model are shown in Table. III. The model predictions (averaged across participants) are shown in Figure 12. For every participant, the weighted integrator model fitted the data much better than the standard model. The averages in Fig. 12 reflect this.

In many categorization studies, it has been found that observers can allocate attention to stimulus dimensions in such a way that categorization performance is optimal (e.g., Kruschke, 1992; Lamberts, 1995, 1998; Nosofsky, 1986). This result may have an interesting equivalent in event

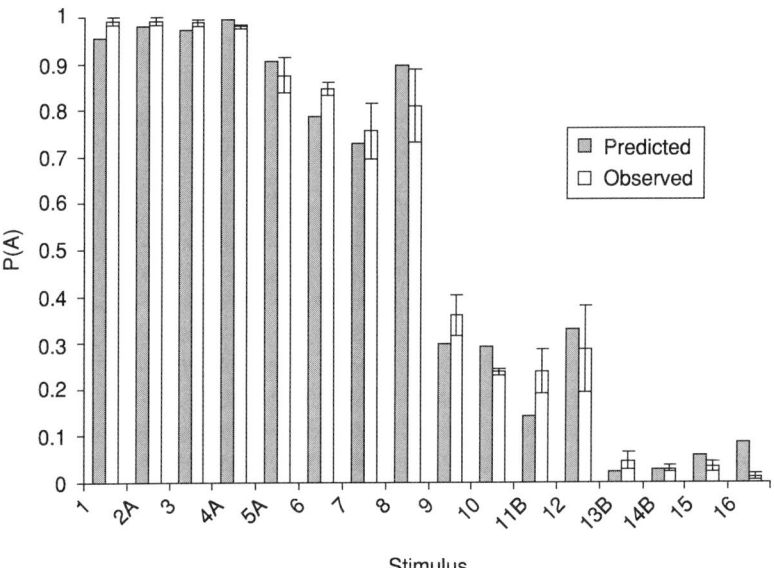

Fig. 12. Observed and predicted proportions of category A responses in Experiment 3. The predictions were generated by the weighted integrator model. The error bars show 95% confidence intervals.

categorization. Both stimulus dimensions (i.e., horizontal and vertical position) were essential for classification of the events in Experiment 3, so selective weighting of these dimensions did not offer any benefits. This was confirmed by separate model applications, in which dimension weights were added as parameters. The increase in goodness-of-fit compared to the model with equal weights for both dimensions was negligible for all participants. However, it is possible that the participants weighted trajectory segments according to their diagnostic relevance. The results from the similarity rating tasks in Experiments 1 and 2 did suggest that the segment weightings were not optimal for the task at hand, but the hypothesis might still hold for the current categorization experiment. Ideal segment weightings can be determined by estimating the weights that optimize categorization of the training stimuli in the experiment, for a given value of c, and assuming that there is no response bias. Figure 13 shows the optimal weights for the categorization task, estimated for nine discrete segments (using the same segmentation principle that was applied in the first two experiments). However, a modified integrator model with these optimal segment weights performed worse for all participants than the weighted integrator model with the weights estimated from the similarity rating task, indicating that the participants did not use optimal segment weights in their category judgments.

The main conclusion from Experiment 3 is that the weighted integrator model provided a good account of the category choice data. The model correctly predicted how the participants generalized what they had learned from the training stimuli to the transfer set, which included previously

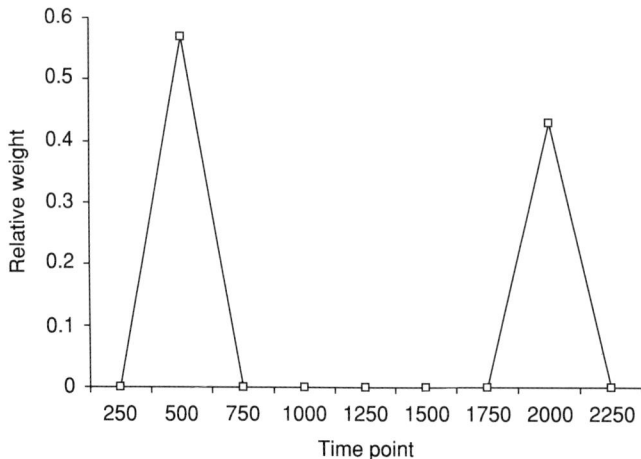

Fig. 13. Optimal weights of different time points in the trajectory distance calculation, Experiment 3.

TABLE IV
PROPORTIONS OF CATEGORY A RESPONSES IN EXPERIMENT 4

	Participant	
Stimulus	1	2
1	0.87	0.98
2A	0.93	0.96
3	0.87	0.89
4A	0.80	0.93
5A	0.73	0.84
6	0.89	0.71
7	0.67	0.47
8	0.69	0.64
9	0.44	0.56
10	0.36	0.42
11B	0.18	0.24
12	0.40	0.33
13B	0.20	0.07
14B	0.22	0.09
15	0.20	0.04
16	0.16	0.00

unseen stimuli. The segment weights estimated from the similarity ratings made a significant contribution to the model's ability to account for the categorization data.

The purpose of Experiment 4 was to replicate Experiment 3, using the stimuli from Experiment 2 (pie slices instead of moving dots). In all other respects, the experiment was identical to Experiment 3. Table IV shows the mean response proportions for the two participants in the experiment. The proportions of category A responses were quite similar to those from the previous experiment. Again, the stimuli appeared to form four clusters.

First, the standard integrator model with three parameters was applied to the data from each participant. Table V shows the goodness-of-fit statistics for this model. The predicted choice proportions are shown in Figure 14. The

TABLE V
GOODNESS-OF-FIT STATISTICS FOR THE INTEGRATOR MODEL: EXPERIMENT 4

Measure	Participant 1	Participant 2
$\ln L$	−68.757	−73.359
R^2	0.78	0.84

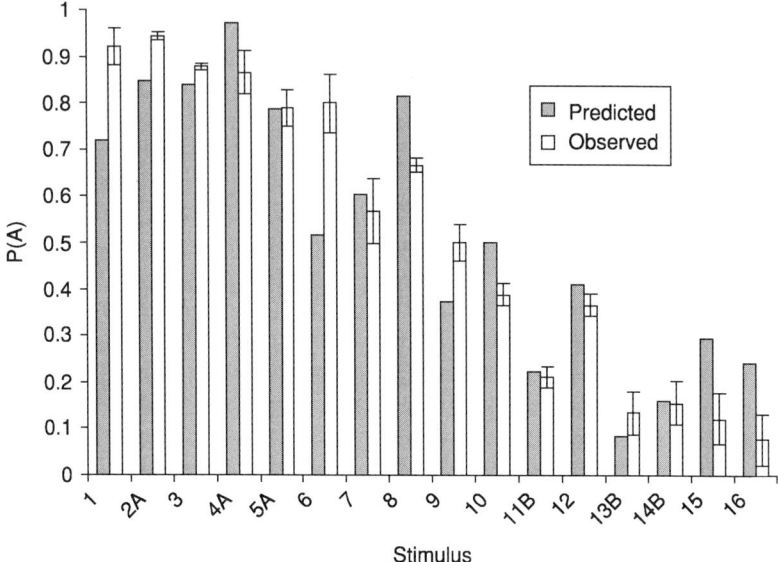

Fig. 14. Observed and predicted proportions of category A responses in Experiment 4. The predictions were generated by the integrator model. The error bars show 95% confidence intervals.

model predictions were not very accurate, which is confirmed by the relatively poor goodness-of-fit values in Table V. The integrator model did provide reasonable predictions for the six training stimuli (2, 4, 5, 11, 13, and 14), but the model did not predict transfer to new test stimuli very well. For instance, the integrator model significantly underestimated the proportions of category A responses for stimulus 6 (as it did in Experiment 3).

The weighted integrator model was applied with the average segment weightings from Experiment 2. The goodness-of-fit statistics are shown in Table VI, and the model's predictions (averaged across participants) can be found in Figure 15. Again, the weighted integrator model fit the data considerably

TABLE VI

Goodness-of-Fit Statistics for the Weighted Integrator Model: Experiment 4

Measure	Participant 1	Participant 2
ln L	−48.576	−47.570
R^2	0.91	0.95

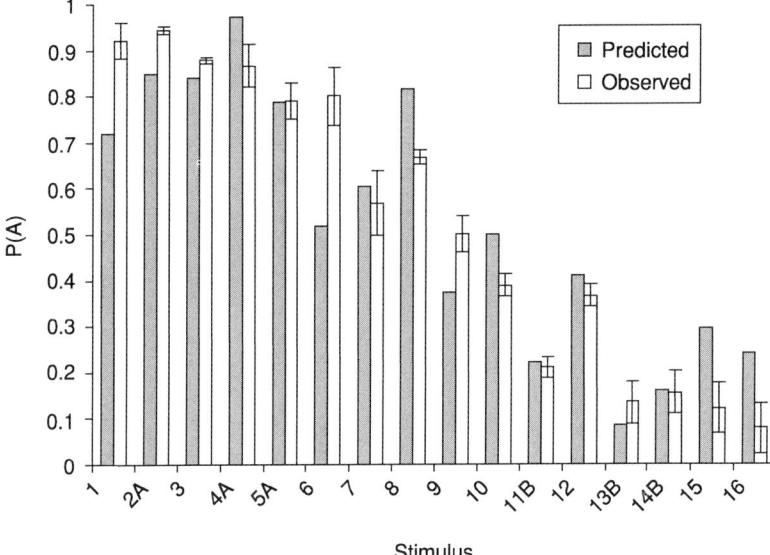

Fig. 15. Observed and predicted proportions of category A responses in Experiment 4. The predictions were generated by the weighted integrator model. The error bars show 95% confidence intervals.

better than the standard model. The goodness-of-fit values were somewhat worse than those in the previous experiment, but the model still explained the most significant trends in the data. The surface appearance of the stimuli (pie slices instead of moving dots) appeared to have had little effect on the way in which the stimuli were categorized.

VII. Conclusions

Dynamic stimuli and events have been neglected in perceptual categorization research. The experiments and the modelling that were presented in this article should be seen as a first step towards the inclusion of dynamic objects and events in mainstream theories of perceptual categorization. The starting point of the research was a direct generalization of the context model of classification. In the integrator model, events are represented as trajectories in a multidimensional stimulus space. Similarity between events is assumed to be a decreasing function of the total distance between the trajectories, using time as an index. The integrator model has the advantage that it includes the context model for static stimuli as a special case. Many assumptions of the model are compatible with previous results on event perception and recognition.

The standard integrator model did not provide a good account of the similarity ratings and categorization data in the four experiments, suggesting that participants did not simply integrate trajectory information over time. However, a weighted integrator model, in which different trajectory segments were allowed to contribute differently to the overall distance computation, provided a good account of the main trends in the similarity ratings and categorization data. The general conclusion from the research was that the integrator model appeared to offer a useful starting point for a theory of perceptual categorization of dynamic objects and events. Although the basic version of the model failed to explain many aspects of the data, the framework proved sufficiently flexible to accommodate discrepancies in the data with a simple modification. Of course, this flexibility may make the model difficult to falsify, and further research will be needed to establish the exact scope and potential of the model.

One important restriction of the experiments was that they all involved events that were qualitatively similar. We have carried out several experiments (not reported here) with events that were qualitatively different. For instance, in one categorization experiment, we used rectangles of varying height and width as stimuli. Within an event, the changes in height and width could generate a number of qualitatively different trajectories (the trajectories could be linear or curvilinear, could contain loops, and varied in orientation and time course). The results from this experiment (and from other experiments with similar stimuli), demonstrated that people have an overwhelming tendency to rely exclusively on qualitative aspects of the stimuli, if the task permits. Generalization patterns in the transfer task depended almost entirely on qualitative stimulus aspects. For instance, if the participants had previously observed a rectangle that shrunk in width but grew in height as a member of one category, they would categorize transfer stimuli with the same qualitative properties in that category, regardless of the precise quantitative characteristics of the trajectories. Not surprisingly, the integrator model had nothing to say about the results from these experiments.

This tendency to rely on qualitative aspects of events wherever possible is in itself quite intriguing, and could have a number of possible causes. If categories can be learned by simply assigning a verbal label to each stimulus according to some easily detected qualitative event property, storage and processing requirements are minimal, so this could be a rational strategy. Of course, the strategy can only work if boundaries between event classes coincide with qualitative differences between events. Perhaps event categories in daily life are often structured along qualitative boundaries. This might even help to explain why people can have such poor conceptual representations of quantitative aspects of natural events (e.g., Hecht & Bertamini, 2000; McCloskey & Kohl, 1983).

The experiments in this article not only involved stimuli with qualitatively similar trajectories, the stimuli were also very simple (with only two dimensions). The simplicity of the stimuli was useful, because it supported modelling with minimal assumptions (and with relatively few free model parameters). However, the question remains whether the integrator model can be applied to events that involve complex stimuli with more dimensions. This issue was addressed in a separate series of experiments, in which point-light displays of actions were used as the stimuli (Lamberts & Seabrook, 2003). The displays were obtained by intrapolation and extrapolation of original point-light recordings, and by morphing recordings from different actors. The participants first learned to categorize a set of displays, and then carried out a transfer task that involved categorization of previously unseen displays. Although some participants were able to rely on subtle qualitative aspects of the stimuli to perform the task, other participants did seem to integrate trajectory information across a number of stimulus dimensions, and their choices were well explained by the integrator model.

Although the integrator model provides a starting point for understanding event categorization, there are clearly numerous issues that need to be resolved before we could hope to develop a general theory of categorization that covers both static objects and events. Compared to categorization of static objects, event categorization is considerably more complex, and it is far from certain that a framework such as the one that I proposed will be sufficient to make real progress. The only way to find out, of course, is to test the limits of the theory in the widest possible range of settings. This promises to be a challenging project.

Acknowledgments

The research in this article was supported by a ROPA research grant from the Economic and Social Research Council (ESRC), reference R022250200. I would like to thank Noellie Brockdorff, Gordon Brown, Andrew Cohen, and Evan Heit for helpful suggestions. Address correspondence to: Koen Lamberts, Department of Psychology, University of Warwick, Coventry CV4 7AL, United kingdom (email: K.lamberts@warwick.ac.uk).

References

Arterberry, M. E., & Bornstein, M. H. (2001). Three-month-old infants' categorization of animals and vehicles based on static and dynamic attributes. *Journal of Experimental Child Psychology, 80*, 333–346.

Arterberry, M. E., & Bornstein, M. H. (2002). Infant perceptual and conceptual categorization: The roles of static and dynamic stimulus attributes. *Cognition, 86*, 1–24.

Bingham, G. P. (1987). Kinematic form and scaling: Further investigations on the visual perception of lifted weight. *Journal of Experimental Psychology: Human Perception & Performance, 13*, 155–177.

Bingham, G. P. (1995). Dynamics and the problem of visual event recognition. In R. F. Port & T. Van Gelder (Eds.), *Mind as motion: Dynamics, behavior and cognition.* (pp. 403–448). Cambridge, MA: MIT Press.

Bingham, G. P., Schmidt, R. C., & Rosenblum, L. D. (1995). Dynamics and the orientation of kinematic forms in visual event recognition. *Journal of Experimental Psychology: Human Perception & Performance, 21*, 1473–1493.

Blake, R. (1993). Cats perceive biological motion. *Psychological Science, 4*, 54–57.

Brownlow, S., Dixon, A. R., Egbert, C. A., & Radcliffe, R. D. (1997). Perception of movement and dancer characteristics from point-light displays of dance. *Psychological Record, 47*, 411–421.

Dittrich, W. H., Troscianko, T., Lea, S. E. G., & Morgan, D. (1996). Perception of emotion from dynamic pointlight displays represented in dance. *Perception, 25*, 727–738.

Estes, W. K. (1956). The problem of inference from curves based on group data. *Psychological Review, 53*, 134–140.

Estes, W. K. (1994). *Classification and cognition.* New York: Oxford University Press.

Fox, R., & McDaniel, C. (1982). The perception of biological motion by human infants. *Science, 218*, 486–487.

Hecht, H., & Bertamini, M. (2000). Understanding projectile acceleration. *Journal of Experimental Psychology-Human Perception and Performance, 26*, 730–746.

Hill, H., & Pollick, F. E. (2000). Exaggerating temporal differences enhances recognition of individuals from point light displays. *Psychological Science, 11*, 223–228.

Johansson, G. (1973). Visual perception of biological motion and a model for its analysis. *Perception and Psychophysics, 14*, 201–211.

Kim, I. K., & Spelke, E. S. (1992). Infants: Sensitivity to effects of gravity on visible object motion. *Journal of Experimental Psychology: Human Perception and Performance, 18*, 385–393.

Kruschke, J. K. (1992). ALCOVE: An exemplar-based connectionist model of category learning. *Psychological Review, 99*, 22–44.

Lamberts, K. (1995). Categorization under time pressure. *Journal of Experimental Psychology: General, 124*, 161–180.

Lamberts, K. (1998). The time course of categorization. *Journal of Experimental Psychology: Learning, Memory, and Cognition, 24*, 695–711.

Lamberts, K. (2000). Information-accumulation theory of speeded categorization. *Psychological Review, 107*, 227–260.

Lamberts, K., Brockdorff, N., & Heit, E. (2002). Perceptual processes in matching and recognition of complex pictures. *Journal of Experimental Psychology: Human Perception and Performance, 28*, 1176–1191.

Lamberts, K., & Seabrook, R. (2003). *Perceptual categorization of action events.* Manuscript submitted for publication.

Lappin, J. S., Bell, H. H., Harm, O. J., & Kottas, B. (1975). On the relation between time and space in the visual discrimination of velocity. *Journal of Experimental Psychology: Human Perception and Performance, 1*, 383–394.

Luce, R. D. (1963). Detection and recognition. In R. D. Luce, R. R. Bush, & E. Galanter (Eds.), *Handbook of mathematical psychology.* (pp. 103–189). New York: Wiley.

Luce, R. D. (1997). Several unresolved conceptual problems of mathematical psychology. *Journal of Mathematical Psychology, 47*, 79–87.

Maddox, W. T. (1999). On the dangers of averaging across observers when comparing decision bound models and generalized context models of categorization. *Perception & Psychophysics, 61*, 354–374.

Maddox, W. T., & Ashby, F. G. (1993). Comparing decision bound and exemplar models of categorization. *Perception & Psychophysics, 53*, 49–70.

Mak, B. S., & Vera, A. H. (1999). The role of motion in children's categorization of objects. *Cognition, 71*, 11–21.

Mather, G., & Murdoch, L. (1994). Gender discrimination in biological motion displays based on dynamic cues. *Proceedings of the Royal Society of London, 258*, 273–279.

McCloskey, M., & Kohl, D. (1983). Naive physics: The curvilinear impetus principle and its role in interactions with moving objects. *Journal of Experimental Psychology: Learning Memory and Cognition, 9*, 146–156.

McConnell, D. S., Muchisky, M. M., & Bingham, G. P. (1998). The use of time and trajectory forms as visual information about spatial scale in events. *Perception & Psychophysics, 60*, 1175–1187.

McKinley, S. C., & Nosofsky, R. M. (1995). Investigations of exemplar and decision bound models in large, ill-defined category structures. *Journal of Experimental Psychology: Human Perception and Performance, 21*, 128–148.

Medin, D. L., & Schaffer, M. M. (1978). Context theory of classification learning. *Psychological Review, 85*, 207–238.

Montepare, J. M., & Zebrowitz, L. A. (1993). A cross-cultural comparison of impressions created by age-related variations in gait. *Journal of Nonverbal Behavior, 17*, 55–68.

Muchisky, M. M., & Bingham, J. P. (2002). Trajectory forms as a source of information about events. *Perception & Psychophysics, 64*, 15–31.

Myung, I. J., Kim, C., & Pitt, M. A. (2000). Toward an explanation of the power law artifact: Insights from response surface analysis. *Memory & Cognition, 28*, 832–840.

Nakayama T. (Ed.) (1998). *High-level motion processing.* Cambridge, MA: MIT Press.

Nosofsky, R. M. (1986). Attention, similarity, and the identification-categorization relationship. *Journal of Experimental Psychology: General, 115*, 39–57.

Nosofsky, R. M. (1987). Attention and learning processes in the identification and categorization of integral stimuli. *Journal of Experimental Psychology: Learning, Memory, and Cognition, 13*, 87–109.

Nosofsky, R. M. (1992). Similarity scaling and cognitive process models. *Annual Review of Psychology, 43*, 25–53.

Nosofsky, R. M., & Palmeri, T. J. (1997). An exemplar-based random walk model of speeded classification. *Psychological Review, 104*, 266–300.

Opfer, J. E. (2002). Identifying living and sentient kinds from dynamic information: The case of goal-directed versus aimless autonomous movement in conceptual change. *Cognition, 86*, 97–122.

Orban, G. A., De Wolf, J., & Maes, H. (1984). Factors influencing velocity coding in the human visual system. *Vision Research, 24*, 33–39.

Pitt, M. A., Myung, I. J., & Zhang, S. (2002). Toward a method of selecting among computational models of cognition. *Psychological Review, 109*, 472–491.

Pollick, F. E., Lestou, V., Ryu, J., & Cho, S. B. (2002). Estimating the efficiency of recognizing gender and affect from biological motion. *Vision Research, 42*, 2345–2355.

Pollick, F. E., Paterson, H. M., Bruderlin, A., & Sanford, A. J. (2001). Perceiving affect from arm movement. *Cognition, 82*, B51–B61.

Port, R. F., Cummins, F., & McAuley, J. D. (1995). Naïve time, temporal patterns, and human audition. In R. F. Port & T. Van Gelder (Eds.), *Mind as motion: Dynamics, behavior and cognition.* (pp. 339–372). Cambridge, MA: MIT Press.

Rosenbaum, D. A. (1975). Perception and extrapolation of velocity and acceleration. *Journal of Experimental Psychology: Human Perception and Performance, 1*, 395–403.

Runeson, S. (1974). Constant velocity — not perceived as such. *Psychological Research, 37*, 3–23.

Smith, A. T., Snowden, R. J. (Eds.) (1994). *Visual detection of motion.* London: Academic Press London.

Spitz, R. V., Stiles, J., & Siegel, R. M. (1993). Infant use of relative motion as information for form: Evidence for spatiotemporal integration of complex motion displays. *Perception & Psychophysics, 53*, 190–199.

Wickelgren, E. A., & Bingham, J. P. (2001). Infant sensitivity to trajectory forms. *Journal of Experimental Psychology: Human Perception and Performance, 27*, 942–952.

ON THE PERCEPTION OF CONSISTENCY

Yaakov Kareev

I. Introduction

There is ample evidence to suggest that people perceive the world around them as more consistent than it really is. As long ago as 1620, Francis Bacon, describing the "idols"—the bad habits of mind that cause people to fall into error—noted that people expect more order in natural phenomena than there actually exists: "The human understanding is of its own nature prone to suppose the existence of more order and regularity than it finds" (Bacon, 1620/1905). More recent research indicates that Bacon's observation is indeed accurate. One well-known example is the fundamental attribution error—people seeing greater consistency (i.e., less variance) in other people's behavior than there actually is (Gilbert & Malone, 1995; Ross, 1977). Moreover, not only do people judge others to behave more consistently than they do, they also ascribe that consistency to the operation of stable personality characteristics (Mischel, 1968). Put differently, variance in the behavior of others is perceived as smaller than it actually is. Another set of well-known examples includes the illusion of control (Langer, 1975) and the perception of illusory correlations (Hamilton & Guiford, 1976; Hamilton & Sherman, 1989). There, people find relationships between actions and outcomes, or between pairs of variables, where little or no correlation exists. With respect to correlations and contingencies, people tend to see them as stronger than they really are. Perceiving variance as smaller and correlations as stronger than they are, are the two sides of the same coin: both indicate that the world is perceived as more consistent—less variable, more predictable—than it actually is.

Inaccuracies, let alone systematic biases, in the perception of the environment are of great interest to psychologists. On the rarely stated but straightforward assumption that the more accurate the perception of the environment the better the functioning, every systematic bias in perception poses a challenge and demands an explanation.

Classically, biases have been explained, or rather, explained away, in one of two nonexclusive ways. One line of explanation, motivational in nature, tends to see biases as the result of some activity in the service of the self. People are viewed as acting in ways that preserve or bolster their self image or sense of integrity. Selective or even distorted encoding, processing, and retrieval of information have often been invoked to explain misperceptions of reality. The other line of explanation, cognitive rather than motivational in nature, views biases as a necessary evil—the unavoidable companions of efficient, although at times inaccurate, heuristics. These heuristics have evolved to provide fast (and typically correct) decisions and assessments of reality, but along with savings in time and computational resources they also lead, in some (by now quite famous) cases, to inaccurate estimates and biases. The heuristics and biases approach to judgment under uncertainty (Tversky & Kahneman, 1974; Kahneman, Slovic, & Tversky, 1982) is the major example of this line of explanation.

Both lines of explanation of biases in the perception of reality—motivational and cognitive—share the assumption that the data available are unbiased. Accordingly, any distortions or systematic biases found in behavior must result from the operation of the mental system—from selective attention, from decisions (conscious or not) as to what to encode, from the way information is processed, or from the way information is retrieved. In what follows, I present a different thesis. I suggest that with respect to the perception of consistency, the data available to us are systematically biased, that we indeed see, on average, a world more consistent than it really is. Consequently, the systematic biases often evident in people's perception of consistency may reflect the *accurate* processing of *systematically biased* data, rather than the *biased* processing of *unbiased* data.

The argument rests on the assumption that when observing their environment people must rely on samples. The reasons for having to make do with sample data—with only a partial picture of the world—are numerous: at times, only a few data points may be available; at others, time pressure may dictate an early termination of data collection or retrieval; finally, working memory capacity, a structural characteristic of the cognitive system, severely constrains the number of items that can be considered simultaneously (originally estimated at about seven items, Miller, 1956; recent estimates put the number as low as four, Cowan, 2001). Thus, notions about characteristics of the environment are often based on small-sample statistics.

It is a statistical fact—a fact whose psychological implications have hardly been considered—that the sampling distributions of variance and correlation are severely skewed: the values likely to be observed in samples attenuate variance and amplify correlation. In other words, sample statistics provide biased estimates of these two parameters. The bias is stronger when the sample is smaller; as shown in the following text, the bias strength is substantial for samples of the size likely to be considered by humans.[1]

It should be emphasized that the present argument invokes neither biased sampling from the environment or memory, nor biased encounters with the environment such that similar items are experienced in spatio-temporal contiguity. It is true that the associative structure of memory and the tendency of "birds of feather to flock together" may also increase apparent consistency. However, the present argument does not invoke biased sampling or the correlational structure of the environment, as it rests on the statistical fact that the expected value of a randomly drawn sample provides a biased estimate of both variability and correlation.

The rest of the paper is organized as follows: First, the statistical argument concerning the sampling distributions of measures of variance and of correlation is presented in some detail. Then, evidence is presented to the effect that, with respect to measures of variability and correlation, people: (a) tend to rely on samples when the amount of data available exceeds their working memory capacity; and (b) do not correct for the biased values likely to be observed in small samples. Thus, people are shown to rely on biased estimates of variability and correlations. Finally, the implications of such biases are discussed.

II. The Statistical Argument

It is a well-known statistical fact that the sampling distributions of variance and correlation are highly skewed and the more so, the smaller the sample size (e.g., Hays, 1963). Consequently, central values of the sampling distributions of those parameters are biased. To provide unbiased estimates

---

[1] Variance and correlation differ from measures of central tendency, for which sample data provide unbiased estimates. Also, recall that the variance of the sampling distribution of all parameters, indicating the expected inaccuracy, not bias, in a sample statistic is *larger*, the smaller the sample size.

of the population parameters a correction, taking into account sample size, has to be applied.

A. VARIANCE

The variance of a sample, drawn at random from a population whose values are normally distributed, provides a biased estimate of the population variance. The biasing factor is $(N-1)/N$, for a sample of size N. Clearly, the attenuation decreases as N increases, but for $N = 7$, the sample size likely to be considered by an average adult, its value is 0.86, resulting in a considerable attenuation. Another way to appreciate the bias is to note that the variance of a sample of seven items, randomly drawn from a normal distribution, is smaller than the variance of that distribution in about 0.65 of the cases. Thus, for sample sizes likely to be considered by people, sample statistics for variance are considerably attenuated. To be sure, I do not claim that it is variance, as defined by statisticians (the mean of the squared deviations from the arithmetic mean), that people use as their measure of variability; but other measures of variability—measures that people may be more likely to use (such as the range, the interquartile range, or the mean absolute deviation)—are all highly correlated with variance, and their sample-based estimates all suffer from a similar attenuation. Moreover, earlier research has indicated that subjective estimates of variability are strongly correlated with variance (for reviews, see Peterson & Beach, 1967, Pollard, 1984). At the same time, the measures employed in the studies mentioned were such that they could not be used to assess if, and to what extent, the perception of variability is biased.

B. CORRELATION

The sampling distribution of r_{xy}, Pearson's product–moment correlation, is also skewed, and the more so the smaller the sample size. To illustrate, Fig. 1 (derived from the tables by David, 1954) shows the sampling distribution of r_{xy}, in a population in which the correlation is 0.50, for sample sizes of 4, 7, and 10. Not only is the skew evident in the shape of the distributions, but the medians of the three distributions are 0.594, 0.538, and 0.524, respectively, clearly showing the increased chance of observing a correlation more extreme than that of the population, and the relationship of that chance to sample size.

C. IMPLICATIONS OF THE STATISTICAL FACTS

If people, when assessing variability or correlation, draw a random sample from the environment or from memory to calculate the statistic in question, more often than not the value in the sample would indicate greater

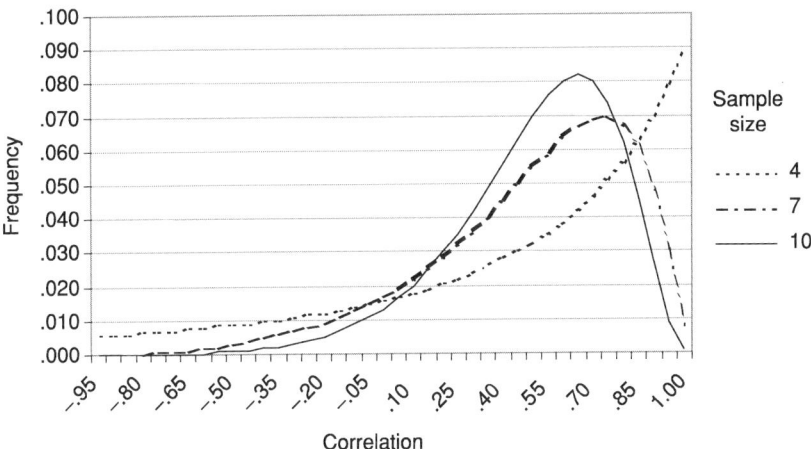

Fig. 1. Sampling distributions of r_{xy} when $\rho_{xy} = 0.50$, for samples of sizes 4, 7, and 10.

consistency than that existing in the population from which the sample was drawn. Furthermore, if the size of the sample considered is close to people's working memory capacity, the incidence of such misperceptions would be quite high. Unless some correction for sample size is applied, an accurate calculation of the sample statistic, and use of its value as the estimate of the parameter in the population, would most often result in the world being seen as more consistent than it is: Variability would seem smaller, and a correlation would seem stronger than it actually is.

Much of the present argument rests on the assumption that initial samples strongly affect people's impressions. Surely people retrieve, or are exposed to, additional data at later stages. Still, people are known to have much confidence in small-sample data (Tversky & Kahneman, 1971) and to exhibit strong primacy effects (e.g., Hogarth & Einhorn, 1992). Once an impression sets in, future data are encoded and interpreted in the light of that original impression. Thus, the data most likely to be encountered first point at what the subsequent (and the eventual) estimate might be.

III. Experimental Evidence

People surely have intuitive notions of variability and correlation, but there is no reason to expect that these notions match any of the statistical measures developed to capture those values. As a result there is no simple way to uncover a bias in perception, even if one exists. The mismatch posed no problem for earlier studies of the perception of variability and correlation, since they aimed at the correspondence between "objective" consistency—as captured by variance and the product–moment correlation—and its perception (i.e., subjective estimates; for reviews, see, e.g., Allan, 1993; Alloy & Tabachnik, 1984; Beyth-Marom, 1982; Peterson & Beach, 1967; Pollard, 1984). Participants in such studies are typically asked to estimate variance or correlation on some arbitrary scale (e.g., a number between −100 and +100, or between 0 and 100 for correlation; a number between 0 and 100 for variance). Responses on such scales are then used to chart the correspondence between objective values and subjective perception. Such subjective measures, however, cannot capture systematic shifts relative to the actual values and, therefore, are useless for the present purposes.

Consequently, instead of attempting to measure absolute levels of perceived consistency, we have designed tasks in which participants compared or chose between populations. Typically these populations did not differ in their objective degree of consistency, but would be perceived as different if judged on the basis of samples differing in size without applying a correction. Since the degree of the bias is related to sample size, judgments of populations with identical characteristics—but viewed under conditions likely to result in samples of different size—can be used to test the present hypothesis. In all situations studied, if a sample-related bias did not exist or was corrected for, behavior would be unrelated to the experimental manipulation. In contrast, if a sample-induced bias did operate, judgments in the different conditions were expected to differ in systematic ways. As described in greater detail in the following text, sample sizes were manipulated in a number of ways: At times participants compared populations in front of them to populations that had been removed from view, or to populations from which only a sample was available. In other cases, we capitalized on individual differences and compared the behavior of people differing in their working memory capacity. Finally, on occasion we manipulated the size of the sample available to the participants. It should be emphasized that there could be numerous reasons why behavior would *not* differ in the conditions compared in the studies. If people are either unaware of the parameters in question, unable to assess them, or have learned to correct for sample-related biases, one would expect no effect of the manipulations. In contrast, if people are sensitive to the values of the parameters in question, assess their value on the basis of a small number of items, and do not correct for the biases, behavior in the compared conditions should differ.

The stimuli used in all the studies to be reported consisted of concrete everyday materials. The use of such tangible materials ruled out the possibility that the items presented were conditional on participants' earlier responses—a concern often expressed in computer-controlled experiments. In all experiments it was obvious that the experimenter could neither modify the makeup of the population considered, nor affect the choice of items to be viewed or their order.

In addition, participants were unlikely to have any prior expectations about the materials used. We consider this an important feature of our studies, since meaningful materials for which prior notions exist and expectations for particular values operate might hopelessly confound our results.

A. THE PERCEPTION OF VARIABILITY

With respect to the perception of the variability of a population, one should start by asking whether people are at all sensitive to the variance of a distribution. Only if they are could one ask if that perception is veridical or biased and, if the latter is the case, whether the bias is related to the size of the sample likely observed. The following experiments (described in greater detail by Kareev, Arnon, and Horwitz-Zeliger, 2002) constitute an attempt to answer these questions.

1. *Experiment 1: Similarity Judgments of Populations in Full View and Out of View*

Experiment 1 was designed to answer two questions: (1) Do people note the variability of a population even when attention is not drawn to it? (2) If variability is noticed, is it remembered veridically or is it distorted in some manner? To answer these questions participants first viewed a group of items that was then removed. They then indicated which of two new groups, in full view at the time of decision, better resembled the original one. Participants were not aware that one of the two new groups was identical to the original, while the other was either less or more variable.

The study allowed for a stringent test of our question: If people perceive and remember the variance of a population and do so accurately—either because they use the whole population to estimate it, or because they use sample variability but correct it for the bias due to sample size—they should be as good at choosing the identical comparison group over both the less and the more variable one. However, if people infer the variance of the out-of-view population on the basis of a sample retrieved from memory and do not correct for sample size, their estimate of that variance would be attenuated downward. In that case, people would easily reject the more variable comparison group but would find it difficult to choose correctly between the identical population and the one of lower variability. Needless to say, if people are insensitive to variability, they would be unable to distinguish between the two comparison populations and perform the task at chance level in both conditions.

As mentioned in the preceding text, one of the two comparison groups was identical to the original, item for item. The comparison group that was not identical to the original differed in variability such that its variance was either 6/7 or 7/6 of the variance of the original group. The values of the items comprising the group were either continuous or discrete (and binary). For the continuous values, the original population consisted of 28 paper cylinders colored up to a certain height with the colored sections normally distributed. The non-identical comparison groups had the same mean, but differed in their standard deviations. For the discrete values the original population consisted of 19 small discs marked with the letter L and 9 discs marked with the letter T. The non-identical groups had either a 21–7 or a 15–13 division. The variability of the non-identical comparison population was manipulated independently of the type of variable. Ninety six students participated in the experiment for a monetary reward.

Participants first observed two groups of items (one for each type of variable), one after the other. They then compared one pair of populations for each original group, indicating which of the two better resembled the corresponding original population. All boxes were shaken before being opened for inspection; this not only assured a different arrangement of the items, but also implied that the spatial arrangement of the items was immaterial for the judgment.

Choices were scored to reflect not their accuracy, but rather the tendency to judge the less variable population as more similar to the original. This, in turn, reflects the degree of support for the prediction that people would perceive variability derived from memory as smaller than that of a population in full view. The mean score was 0.33, and differed significantly from 0 ($p = 0.020$). Importantly, the type of variable did not have a significant effect on the choices ($F < 1$). This is of interest since, for the discrete variable, the change in variability also involved a change in the central value (the proportion). The similar effect observed for both types of variable rules out an explanation based on sensitivity to a change in proportion, rather than to a change in variability. A breakdown of the participants' choices revealed that the identical comparison box was judged as more similar to the original box in only 0.49 of the cases when compared with that of the smaller variability, but in fully 0.66 of the cases when the comparison box had the larger variability. As reasoned in the preceding text, such a result could not be obtained if people either assess variability correctly or do not notice it at all. On the contrary, these findings are compatible with the claim that people, when retrieving a population from memory, indeed conceive of its variability as smaller than it actually is.

2. Experiment 2: Effects of Partial Versus Full Information on Comparisons and Choices

Experiment 1 established that people are sensitive to the variability of a distribution, but perceive it as smaller when derived from memory. Use of a sample, retrieved from memory without correction for sample size, was implicated as the mechanism causing that attenuation. Experiment 2 was designed to further explore the role of sampling in the perception of variability. In the experiment, participants judged two pairs of populations. Unbeknownst to the participants, the two populations within a pair were identical. Every participant performed two judgment tasks, each involving a pair of populations. In the first task, participants responded to a direct question as to which of the pair of populations. In the first task, participants responded to a direct question as to which of the pair of populations was more (or less) homogenous. In the second task, participants chose one of two populations from which two items would later be drawn. Reward depended on the similarity between the two drawn items (i.e., the chances for a reward were inversely related to the variability of the population).

The main manipulation in the study was viewing condition: for each pair of populations, one of them was in full view at the time a judgment was made, whereas the other was not. Information about that population of the pair that was not in full view at the time of judgment was gleaned in one of two ways: (1) in the "Out-of-Sight" condition, the population had been seen in its entirety, but was removed at the time of judgment; and (2) in the "Sample-Only" condition, what participants knew of the population was based on a sample of 7 items drawn out of the 28 items comprising that population. The sample itself was in view at the time of judgment. Viewing condition was manipulated between participants. "Type of Task" (direct question or choice) and "Type of Variable" (binary or continuous) were manipulated within participants, with each participant performing two of the four combinations of the two within-participant variables.

Each population consisted of 28 items, a number far exceeding working memory capacity. We assumed that, for the population that was "Out-of-Sight" participants would have to rely on a sample drawn from their memory. As such, it should seem less variable than the population in full view if no correction were applied. Regarding the "Sample-Only" condition, the availability of only a sample was highly prominent. If people had any inkling of the effects of samples, their attempts to correct for them should be evident there. Here too, if people are unaware of variability, incapable of assessing its value, or aware of the consequences of having to rely on sample data, there would be no preference of one population over the other. In contrast, if people are sensitive to variability, but unaware of the consequences of relying on a sample, then the population out of view, or that from which a sample had been seen, would be judged as the less variable of the two.

One hundred and forty four students participated in the study for payment. For the continuous variable items, both populations consisted of 28 paper cylinders, identical to those employed in the original distribution of Experiment 1. For the binary variable items, the populations consisted of 28 uniformly colored pieces of wood, 18 of which were of one color, and the remaining 10 of another color.

For the direct-question task, participants were either asked in which of the two populations the distribution of values was more homogeneous (continuous variable) or which population had a split of colors closer to 0.5/0.5 (binary variable). Note that, for the direct-question response task, a response bias to choose always the population in one viewing condition over the other would have the opposite effect for the two types of variables. For the choice task, the participants were rewarded if the pair of items drawn from the chosen population fell within a certain range (for the continuous variable) or were identical in color (for the binary variable). Since the chance of winning the reward is greater, the smaller the variability of the population from which items are to be drawn, we took the participants' choice as an indication of which population they believed had smaller variability. All combinations of Task and Type of Variable were equally frequent, the order of presentation being fully counterbalanced within each viewing condition.

A judgment was scored '1' if it was in line with our hypothesis, that is, if the Out-of-Sight or the Sample-Only population was considered less variable. A judgment was scored '0' if the population in full view was considered to be the less variable. An analysis of variance of these data revealed that the only significant effect was the deviation of the overall mean, whose value was 0.577, from the value of 0.5 expected by chance ($p = 0.013$). Thus, the results indicate that when a population is out of sight or when only a sample of it is available, its variability is perceived to be smaller than that of an identical population but in full view at the time of judgment. Since in real-life situations a complete population is rarely available, these results imply that variability is usually attenuated.

It is worth noting that the overall effect was identical under both viewing conditions. This further suggests that, when a population is out of sight its parameters are estimated by recalling a sample. It should also be noted that the overall proportion of cases in which the variability of the population in full view was judged as larger was 0.577. Although this value is significantly greater than chance, it is still lower than the 0.65 or so expected if people correctly judge the variability of a population in full view and compare it to a population from which only a sample of 7 is available (whether by the experimental manipulation or by retrieving samples of that size from memory). One possible explanation of the difference is that people partially correct for the bias induced by small-sample data. Another possibility is that, even for populations in full view, variability is assessed on the basis of sampling (even if more than one sample), resulting in slightly biased perception and in a smaller difference between it and the other population than that predicted by theory. To anticipate, the results of Experiment 3 favor the latter explanation.

3. Experiment 3: Working Memory Capacity and the Perception of Variability

Experiment 3 was designed to explore the relationship between individual differences in working memory capacity and the perception of variability. If people indeed sample data to infer population characteristics when the amount of data is large, working memory capacity could be a factor limiting the size of such samples. If this is the case and no correction for sample size is applied, people with smaller working memory capacity would be expected to perceive variability as lower than would people with larger capacity. This hypothesis was tested in an experiment in which participants first observed a population consisting of 28 items—a number far exceeding working memory capacity—and then predicted the makeup of a sample of 7 items to be drawn, without replacement, from that population. Participants then drew a sample and were rewarded according to the degree of correspondence between their prediction and the actually drawn sample. We compared the predictions of participants differing in their working memory capacity, expecting predictions made by participants with lower capacity to be less variable than those made by participants with larger capacity.

Each participant performed the task four times—twice for populations that were fully in view at the time of prediction and twice for populations seen shortly before prediction but out of sight at the time of prediction. Type of variable was manipulated within each viewing condition, such that one population involved a continuous variable and the other, a binary-valued variable. Participants' working memory capacity was estimated by their performance in a standard digit-span task. The participants were 59 Hebrew University undergraduate students. The materials employed in the study were the same paper cylinders and pieces of wood used in Experiment 2. Different colors were used for the two continuous and the two binary populations.

The items were stored in opaque boxes. In the out-of-sight condition, the lid of the box was raised for 10 secs and then closed; for the full-view condition, the lid was raised and remained open. The out-of-sight boxes were presented before the full-view boxes, with predictions for all four boxes made after all of them had been seen, but before any drawing began. For the binary-valued box, the participants predicted the number of items of each color out of the 7 items of the sample to be drawn. For the continuous variable, they predicted the number of items that would be colored above or below a reference height (that created the same 18–10 split of the 28 items as in the case of the binary variable). After all predictions had been made, the open boxes were closed and the participants drew a sample of 7 items without replacement from each of the four boxes. The participants were rewarded 4 IS (about $1 at the time) when their prediction exactly matched the makeup of the sample, and 2 IS when it deviated by 1.

An extreme group design, comparing participants who had a digit span of < 6 ($N = 21$) with those whose digit span exceeded 6 ($N = 24$), revealed that, as expected, sample makeups predicted by participants with smaller capacity were significantly less variable than those made by participants with larger capacity ($p = 0.041$). Capacity also interacted with Viewing Condition ($p = 0.016$): the two groups did not differ in the out-of-sight condition, but did differ in the full-view condition. Finally, predicted sample makeups were less variable for the binary than for the continuous variable ($p = 0.014$). The main effect of Capacity indicates that people with smaller working memory capacity exhibit smaller variability in their products than do people with larger capacity. As reasoned in the preceding text, such a difference could occur if, even when more data were available, the participants relied on samples whose size corresponded to their working memory capacity, without correcting their estimates of variability for sample size.

While the main effect of Capacity was in line with our predictions, the significant interaction between Capacity and Viewing Condition was unexpected, as the difference between the two groups was expected to be larger in the out-of-sight rather than in the full-view condition. Furthermore, the results of Experiment 2 led us to expect a main effect of Viewing Condition, but none was obtained. In light of the unexpected interaction between Capacity and Viewing Condition, we looked for another way to test the hypotheses that people, in making predictions, rely on limited samples commensurate with their working memory capacity, and more so in the out-of-sight than in the full-view condition. The setup of the experiment provided us with such another way of testing both hypotheses. Since the variability of a sampling distribution is larger, the smaller the sample on which it is based, if people with smaller capacity use smaller samples to estimate variability, the overall distribution of their answers should be more variable. Similarly, if the use of sample data is more prevalent in the out-of-sight condition, one expects larger variability in answers there than in the full-view condition. A comparison of the within-group variance of the predictions made by members of the low-capacity group to that of members in the high-capacity group revealed that, across all four tasks, the variance of the former was significantly larger than that of the latter ($p = 0.036$, one-tailed)—another indication that people use sample data in their assessment of variability. The same kind of analysis was also employed to compare performance in the two viewing conditions. If people use sample data, sample size (or number of samples considered) would be smaller when the population is out of sight than when it is in full view. Indeed, the variance of the predictions made in the out-of-sight condition was significantly larger than that in the full-view condition ($p = 0.048$, one-tailed). Taken together with the main effect of Capacity reported in the preceding text, these two findings support the claim that people use samples to infer population variability, with people with smaller capacity apparently using smaller samples than do people with larger capacity.

The results of Experiment 3 also help address an issue left unsettled in Experiment 2. There, the overall proportion of cases in which the out-of-sight or the sample-only population was judged to be of smaller variability was significantly greater than chance, but smaller than that expected if no sampling had occurred for the population in full view (while samples of size 7 were used for the others). It was argued there that such a discrepancy could have resulted either from partial correction for sample size, or from the use of samples even for the population in full view (in which case the number of samples or the size of the sample was larger). The data observed in Experiment 3 favor the latter explanation: the significant difference in the overall variance of the answers provided by the low-capacity and high-capacity groups persisted, even when only cases in full view were considered ($p = 0.0037$, one-tailed). Thus, it seems that the use of small-sample data to infer population statistics is prevalent, when the amount of available data exceeds working memory capacity.

4. Experiment 4: Determinants of Choices and Confidence

Variability should affect the confidence with which one can choose one of two populations on the basis of the difference between their means. Obviously, the population whose mean is estimated to have the more desirable value should be preferred over the other; at the same time, the likely accuracy of the estimate of the mean, and hence the likelihood of an error, is indicated by the variability within each population. In other words, normatively, in making such a choice, variability should be noted and taken into account, with larger variability reducing one's confidence in the decision. Experiment 4 was designed to establish (a) if people take variability into account when choosing between two populations with different means, and if they do, (b) whether it is sample variability, as observed, or sample variability corrected for sample size that better predicts choices and confidence in these choices.

The task was performed with a pair of distinct populations, stored together in a big box. Each population consisted of 50 matchboxes containing a few matches. The two populations differed in their mean number of matches but had either the same or very similar variance. As explained in more detail in the following text, participants drew several matchboxes of each type and noted the number of matches in each. They then chose the type of matchbox which they believed had a higher number of matches, and placed a monetary bid that indicated their confidence in their choice. Characteristics of the samples viewed by the participants were then used in a multiple regression analysis to find out what statistics best predicted choices and bids. In particular we were interested in determining if variability was at all taken into account, and if it was, whether it was sample variability, as observed, or sample variability corrected for sample size that better predicted the decisions made.

Since our analysis was to relate participants' performance to characteristics of the samples they *actually* drew from the pair of populations, it was necessary to ensure a wide range of sample values. Therefore, we used eight pairs of populations in all. One of the two populations in every big box—the "standard population"—always had the same characteristics: a mean of 5.0 and a standard deviation of 1.92. The mean number of matches of the other population in a pair was larger than that of the standard by 1.5, 2, 2.5, or 3 matches. Of the eight pairs of populations, there were two pairs for each of the four possible differences in means. In addition, we manipulated the size of the sample participants drew from each population; sample sizes were always different for the two pairs of populations with the same difference in means. It should be noted that changes in sample size affect the expected values of inferential statistics and their significance, but not estimates of differences between means or effect sizes. The characteristics of the various populations are described in detail in Kareev et al. (2002).

In performing the task, the participants first sampled the specified number of boxes with replacement, opening and noting the number of matches in each of the sampled boxes. Sampling was self-paced and the order in which boxes were sampled was at the participant's discretion. When the predetermined sample size was reached for the matchboxes of both types, the participant was told that two additional boxes, one of each color, would be drawn later; he or she was then asked to bet on which type would contain more matches, placing a bid on the difference in number of matches between them. To calculate the reward (positive, zero, or negative), the bid was to be multiplied by the difference in the number of matches between the two boxes actually drawn.

The task was performed three times by each participant, with a different pair of populations used each time. The participants were 80 students, each paid for participation, plus a reward calculated as described in the preceding text.

Correlations were calculated to determine which statistics of the actually observed samples best accounted for participants' choices and bids. Choices were scored 1 when the population with the higher mean was chosen, and 0 when the other was.[2] The following statistics were derived from the samples actually observed, and correlated with choices and bids: (a) difference between sample means; (b) variances (actual sample variance; and estimated population variance based on sample variance, corrected for sample size); (c) ratio between the variances of the samples; (d) sample sizes; (e) point–biserial correlation and point–biserial correlation squared, both serving as estimates of the effect size of the difference between the two populations (each of these was calculated twice, once with the actual sample variance and once with sample variance corrected for sample size); (f) Z and t inferential statistics for the difference between the two means (recall that the value for Z uses actual sample variances divided by sample sizes, and that for t uses estimates, employing a correction for sample sizes); and (g) significance of the Z and t statistics. Thus, the analysis included measures that do and do not have variance as one of their components, and juxtaposed the predictive power of measures that use actual sample variance and measures that use estimates of population variance (derived from sample variance corrected for sample size). Our main objective was to determine which of the sample statistics was *the best* predictor of behavior, and to find out: (a) whether it was one having a measure of variance as one of its terms; and, if it did, (b) whether that term reflected sample variance, as observed, or sample variance corrected for sample size. Since many of the predictive measures compared had common components, the correlation between them was very high, and there was no point in testing for the significance of the difference between correlation coefficients. Instead, the measure of interest was the rank order of those correlations. As it turned out, the best single predictor of the participants' choices was the significance of the Z-test—a measure which is affected not only by the difference between the two means, but also by their (actual) variances and by the sample size: its correlation with choice was $r = 0.522$ ($p < 0.001$). The best single predictor of the bids was the uncorrected estimate of effect size—a

---

[2] Another possible scoring of choices would be to score a choice as 1 when that population having the higher sample mean was preferred over the other. Due to the large differences between population means, the difference between sample means was in the same direction as that between population means in most cases (229 out of 240, with 3 other cases of identical sample means), rendering the distinction unimportant. Indeed, for both choices and bids, the same measures turned out to be the best predictors for either scoring systems.

measure that takes into account the difference between the two means and the variance in the combined samples, without correcting it for sample size. Its correlation with bid size was $r = 0.302$ ($p < 0.001$). When individual differences in bid size were taken into account, by subtracting each individual's mean bid from each of his or her bids, that same measure remained the best single predictor, with prediction improving ($r = 0.387, p < 0.001$).

Most important from the present perspective are the findings that, for choices and bids alike: (a) variability was a component of the best predictors of behavior (i.e., people were taking not only the means but also variability into account), and (b) the best predictors included a measure of variability that was based on actual sample variance, not on estimates of variance corrected for sample size. It is also of interest that the best predictor of choices (the significance of Z) also reflects the sizes of the samples considered. It is not contended, of course, that in making choices or bids people calculate the significance of a Z-test or effect size. Rather, we see the current findings as an indication that, in making decisions people use some measure that *does* take variability into account; at the same time, it is the variability of the sample, as observed, rather than an estimate of population variability corrected for sample size that is used in that measure. As pointed out in the introduction, the sample variability is, on average, downward attenuated, and the more so, the smaller the sample. Such attenuation does not affect the choice itself, which depends on the difference between the means, but increases the confidence with which the choice is made.

5. Experiment 5: A Primacy Effect in Sampling

With the former experiments already establishing people's use of sample statistics, without correcting for sample size in tasks involving variability, Experiment 5 was designed to explore what part of the data available constitutes the sample considered by the participants. The participants first drew samples from two populations, then chose one of them to be used in a subsequent prediction task, and finally predicted—for a reward—the value of 20 items, drawn one at a time, with replacement, from the population of their choice. With the items in this experiment presented sequentially and their total number exceeding working memory capacity, the study enabled us to check for primacy and recency effects, as well as to estimate the size of the sample considered. The experiment was also used to find out, once more, if people take note of variability when choosing the more homogenous population and, therefore, increase their chances for reward.

Type of Variable and Total Number of Sampling Trials were manipulated between participants. First, the items constituting each pair of populations had either one of two values (binary populations) or one of five values (multi-valued populations). Second, the total number of sampling trials (for both populations combined) was either 13 or 19. These numbers ensured that samples drawn from the two populations were of unequal size. The total sample size was announced in advance, rendering the eventual difference in sample size highly prominent. Tall, opaque urns with an opening wide enough to insert a hand but not to see the contents were used to store the 36 items comprising each population. For the binary-valued populations, the items were beads—24 of one color and 12 of another. The beads in one urn were red and green, and the beads in the other were blue and yellow. For the multi-valued populations, the items were playing cards with face values ranging from 6 to 10, with frequencies of 4, 8, 12, 8, and 4, for the five values, respectively. The cards in one urn were from the red suits, and the cards in the other were from the black suits. Participants were 160 students who participated to fulfill a course requirement or for payment. They also received a reward reflecting their success in the prediction phase.

As items were drawn sequentially, and with the samples drawn from each urn in a pair always differing in size and almost always in variability, we could use multiple regression analysis to assess the degree to which characteristics of the actually drawn samples (or parts of them) accounted for the participants' choices.

Following the sampling stage, the participants chose which urn to use in the subsequent prediction phase, in which they predicted for each of 20 trials the value of an item to be drawn from the chosen urn. For the beads, a correct prediction was rewarded 0.5 IS (about $0.12). For the cards, a correct prediction was rewarded 0.6 IS, and a prediction deviating by 1 from the value drawn was rewarded 0.3 IS. This scheme resulted in an expected reward of 1/3 IS at each trial, to participants who predicted the more frequent value of the beads or the mean value of the cards. During prediction, items were also drawn with replacement.

Our analyses revealed that people are apparently aware that predictions based on larger samples are more reliable than those based on smaller samples, and that they were sensitive to differences in variability. On average, the urn from which a larger sample had been drawn was chosen in 0.63 of the cases, and the urn with the smaller sample variance was chosen in 0.54 of the cases; when one of the urns was both the one from which a larger sample had been drawn and the one with the smaller sample variance, the proportion with which it was chosen was 0.69. A multiple regression analysis using the stepwise method revealed that for all four conditions combined (with sample sizes and variances standardized within condition), the best combination of predictors involved the difference between sample sizes (whose correlation with choice was $r = 0.341$, $p < 0.001$) and the difference between the two standard deviations ($r = -0.169$, $p = 0.033$); with these, the multiple regression reached a value of $R = 0.418$ ($p < 0.001$).

More important to the specific question of the experiment, the data were analyzed to determine if all the available data or only a sub-sample of them best predicted people's choices. Given the large body of literature on primacy and recency effects (e.g., Hogarth & Einhorn, 1992), we analyzed the quality of prediction using sub-samples taken either from the beginning or from the end of the actual sample. The size of the sub-samples varied from 6 to 13, in steps of 1. As it turned out, for each of the four conditions, it was possible to identify a subset whose data better predicted the participants' choices than did the sample as a whole. That subset tended to include the first items and its median size was 10. Across all four conditions combined, the use of the first 10 items to predict choices not only did not impair our ability to predict participants' choices correctly, but in fact slightly improved it. The value of R was 0.434, and the proportion of correct predictions rose from 0.675, when all data were used, to 0.688, when data from only the first 10 items were used. The results of this analysis indicate that people are indeed restricted in the size of the sample they consider when the total number of available items exceeds their capacity. With a total of 10 items considered, an average of 5 items from each population were used—a value commensurate with estimates of working memory capacity when data can be assigned to different categories (Mandler, 1967). The analysis also reveals that the first items encountered are the ones more likely to be taken into account (i.e., a primacy effect), a finding in line with results reported in other studies comparing the strength of primacy and recency effects (Hogarth & Einhorn, 1992).

6. Summary of Variability Experiments

The five experiments dealing with the perception of variability lead to a number of conclusions. First, people are sensitive to variability, and take it into account (as they should) in tasks in which it is of consequence, such as predicting a value from a single population or estimating the difference between two population means. Second, people use sample data to assess variability, without correcting for the bias likely to be brought about by the use of such data. As a result, perceived variability is downward attenuated: people regard the world as less variable than it really is. More general implications of that attenuation will be discussed in the following text.

B. THE PERCEPTION OF CORRELATIONS

In studying people's perception of correlation, our approach was similar to that employed in the studies on the perception of variability. Here too, people faced tasks in which noticing the parameter of interest and acting upon it increased their chances of obtaining a monetary reward. As before, participants were not asked directly about the parameter of interest; instead, the perceived correlation was inferred from participants' predictions. Since the skew (and hence, the bias) in the sampling distribution of a correlation is greater, the smaller the sample, we compared the behavior of participants likely to differ in the size of the sample they considered. Experiment 6 compared the behavior of participants differing in their working memory capacity, whereas Experiment 7 manipulated the number of items presented. In both experiments, if people are unaware of the correlations in the population, remember and use all items available (rather than a sample) to assess correlations, or if using a sample, correct for the bias that a sample of that size is likely to cause, the groups of participants compared should not differ in their behavior. In contrast, if people use only a small number of items even when more are available, and if they do not correct for the biasing effect of small samples, then the groups of participants compared would differ, with the groups likely to use smaller samples perceiving correlations as stronger. The arguments and the experimental findings are described in greater detail in Kareev (1995b) and in Kareev, Lieberman, & Lev (1997). The special case of a contingency between two binary variables and its relation to sample size is further discussed in Kareev (2000). Yet another bias in the perception of correlation (and randomness, as a special case) is discussed in Kareev (1992, 1995a).

1. Experiment 6: Working Memory Capacity and the Perception of Correlation

The task involved the correlation between two binary variables. Each participant was presented with a large, opaque bag containing 128 small envelopes. Each envelope was red or green, and contained a coin marked with an X or O. The participant drew one envelope at a time and predicted the mark on the coin. The envelope was then opened and if the prediction was right, the participant earned the coin.

Effects of the marginal distribution of the two variables, strength of the relationship between them, and working memory capacity were studied in a three-way, between-participants factorial design. The values of both variables were divided either evenly (64-64) or unevenly (80-48), the strength of the correlation varied in steps of 0.20 in the range of −0.60 to +0.60[3],

---

[3] The correlation was regarded as positive when the more common values of one variable were associated with the more common values of the other; it was regarded as negative when the more common values of one variable were associated with the less common values of the other. A detailed discussion of this point appears in Kareev (1995a).

and participants were designated as having either low or high working memory capacity. The task was self-paced, and rarely lasted more than 40 minutes. One hundred and twelve students participated in the experiment for payment.

One analysis of the data involved perceived correlation, a measure that was derived from the 2×2 contingency table relating envelope color and the participant's predictions. A three-way analysis of variance revealed that perceived correlation corresponded closely to actual correlation ($p < 0.001$, for the linear contrast testing the correspondence between actual and perceived correlation). More importantly, there was a significant interaction between correlation and working memory capacity ($p = 0.002$), with participants with lower capacity perceiving positive correlations as more positive and negative correlations as more negative than did participants with higher capacity. Another analysis, in which a perceived correlation more extreme than the actual one was scored 1 and less extreme was scored 0 (with participants in the condition of no correlation excluded), replicated the result, with the proportion of more extreme perceived correlations being 0.64 for the low capacity group and only 0.36 for the high capacity group ($p = 0.005$). It should be noted that, while low capacity people perceived the correlations as more extreme, their perceived correlations were no less (and probably more) accurate than those of the high capacity group (Kareev, Lieberman, & Lev, 1997).

Correlations are useful to the extent that they improve predictions. A second analysis was carried out to find if, and to what extent, the differences in perceived correlations were also reflected in the accuracy of the predictions (and, hence, in participants' rewards). A three-way analysis of the number of correct predictions revealed a significant main effect of all three variables, as well as a significant interaction between Correlation and Marginal Distribution. The linear effect of Correlation ($p < 0.001$) was due to the fact that the number of correct predictions corresponded directly to the absolute strength of the correlation. The effect of Marginal Distribution ($p = 0.017$) was due to the fact that the number of correct predictions in the asymmetric distributions (76.05) was larger than that for the symmetric distributions (72.48). The significant difference reflects sensitivity also to the marginal distributions of the values. The interaction between Marginal Distribution and Correlation was due to the fact that the advantage of the asymmetrical distributions was more pronounced, the more positive correlation ($p = 0.017$). This relationship is another manifestation of the positive bias discussed in Kareev (1995a). Most important from the present standpoint was the main effect of working memory capacity ($p = 0.014$). Participants with lower capacity outperformed those with higher capacity (76.11 vs. 72.43 correct responses, respectively).

The results reveal an overall sensitivity to correlation and other statistical characteristics of the population in question. Furthermore, as predicted, people with smaller working memory capacity, and hence likely to consider smaller samples, perceived the correlations as more extreme than did people with larger capacity. Such a difference rules out the possibility that a correction for the bias likely to result from the sample size is applied.

2. Experiment 7: Sample Size and the Perception of Correlation

In Experiment 6, it was individual differences in working memory capacity that led to presumed differences in sample size. In Experiment 7, sample size was experimentally manipulated. As before, if people are unaware of the correlation or apply a correction of sample statistics, performance should not differ systematically with different sample sizes.

Participants in the experiment drew a single sample out of a population consisting of 100 items, whose values varied along two continuous variables. They then were provided with the value of one of the variables of one additional item, and asked to predict the value of the other variable of that item. Sample size was manipulated by having the number of items drawn be smaller by, equal to, or larger by two than the participant's working memory capacity. Viewing condition was also manipulated, with one-half of the participants having the sample in full view at the time of prediction, whereas the other one-half saw one item at a time with none in front of them at the time of prediction. The population consisted of 100 plain index cards, each bearing a drawing of a small circle with two lines emanating from it. One of the lines was always parallel to the top edges of the card, and could vary in length. The other line, always of the same length, could vary in its angle, relative to the horizontal. The correlation between the length of the first line and the angle of the second was 0.70. After having drawn the specified number of cards (and either turning each of them face down after having seen it or keeping it face up), the participant drew one more card and handed it, face down, to the experimenter. The experimenter covered one of the two lines with a piece of paper, and handed the card back to the participant, who had to predict the value of the hidden line by drawing it on the piece of paper covering it. The prediction was then compared to the actual value, and rewarded in line with its accuracy. The variable to be predicted—length of the horizontal line or angle of the equal-length line—was balanced between participants in the three sample-size conditions. One hundred and forty four students participated in the experiment.

Since participants in the study made a single prediction, it was impossible to calculate their perceived correlation. Instead we calculated the absolute difference between the standard score of the predictor (the exposed line) and the standard score of the predicted value. Both scores were computed relative to the sample that the participant had actually seen. For this measure, the smaller the value, the stronger the perceived correlation. When the sample was out of view, the values of that measure were 1.30, 1.78, and 1.83, for the conditions in which sample size was smaller by, the same as, or larger by 2 than working memory capacity, respectively. When the sample remained in full view, the pattern was reversed, with the corresponding values being 2.87, 1.05, and 0.63, respectively. The interaction between the two variables was significant ($p < 0.001$). Clearly, when the sample was out of view, the smaller the sample the greater the perceived correspondence between the standard scores of the predictor and the criterion. In contrast, when the sample remained in full view, the opposite effect was evident.

Another analysis involved the proportion of times the standard scores of the predictor and the criterion had the same sign (indicating that the perceived correlation was in the same direction as that in the population). That proportion was 0.63, 0.48, and 0.29 for the -2, 0, and $+2$ sample groups when the sample was out of view, and 0.50, 0.64, and 0.75 for the same sample groups when the sample remained in full view. The pattern of the interaction indicates that the correlation was more accurately perceived for a sample out of sight when the sample itself was smaller, not larger; as before, the opposite effect was observed for participants for whom the sample remained in full view ($p = 0.005$). Interestingly, performance by participants whose sample remained in full view was overall better ($p = 0.044$).

A final analysis involved errors in prediction. For that analysis we calculated the absolute difference between the standard scores of the predicted and the actual value of the criterion. Here the differences were 0.87, 1.71, and 1.70 for the -2, 0, and $+2$ groups in the out-of-view condition, and 2.16, 1.05, and 0.79 in the full-view condition. Here too, the interaction was significant ($p < 0.001$).

The repeating pattern of significant interactions clearly indicates that, for the more common case in which the sample is only available from memory, smaller samples lead to perception of the correlation as stronger, to greater sensitivity in the detection of the direction of the correlation, and to higher accuracy in predictions. The opposite pattern was observed when the sample remained in full view, indicating that when more data are available, people are capable of using the extra information provided to them.

3. Summary of Correlation Experiments

The two experiments dealing with the perception of correlation indicate that, both for binary and continuous variables, the use of small-sample data results in the perception of a correlation as stronger than it is perceived to be when assessed on the basis of a larger sample. In other words, when a correlation exists, the use of smaller samples serves to amplify that correlation, relative to how it is perceived when more data have been available. To the extent that the immediate concern of the cognitive system involves the detection of correlations, rather than the accurate assessment of their value, having less time, data, or storage capacity available may help, rather than hinder, the achievement of that goal.

IV. Summary and Implications

As noted in the introduction, observers of human behavior have long suspected that the perception of consistency is persistently biased in such a way that the world is perceived as less variable and more regular than it actually is. This paper offers an explanation of this misperception. Of necessity—due to paucity of data, time pressure, or working memory limitations—people have to infer characteristics of the environment from sample data. In other words, they see the world around them through a narrow window. Given that people indeed use sample data to assess the degree of variability or the strength of a correlation, the statistical nature of the sampling distributions of these variables would lead to such misperception: since sample variance tends to be smaller and sample correlation tends to be more extreme than their corresponding population parameters, people would see a world that is more consistent than it really is. It follows that the fault for the bias in the perception of consistency need not be faulty information processing, as hitherto assumed. Rather than the *inaccurate* processing of *unbiased* data, the reason for the misperception of consistency could be the *accurate* processing of *biased* data. No biased processing needs to be postulated for the bias to emerge: accurate processing of well-sampled data leads to such a distorted view.

The present set of studies tested whether people use all the data when many data points are available, and whether they do or do not correct for the bias likely to result, when only a small number data points are used. The results indicate that although people are sensitive to variability and correlation, they use only a small number of data points even when more are available. Furthermore, people do not (at least not fully) correct for the bias resulting from such use. Working memory capacity was implicated as a major factor limiting the size of the sample considered, and hence of the bias resulting from the use of small-sample data.

Seeing the world as more consistent than it actually is has some obvious implications: if variances around a central value are small and if correlations are strong, confidence in one's ability to make accurate predictions and good choices between alternatives is bound to increase. Such increase in confidence will increase optimism and might even affect one's sense of well-being.

Our results also suggest that, while all people view the world through a narrow window, people viewing the world through an even narrower window—children (whose working memory capacity is smaller than that of adults, e.g., Huttenlocer & Burke, 1976), people under stress (cognitive load decreases available capacity, e.g., Gilbert, Pelham, & Krull, 1988), and less intelligent people (working memory capacity is related to intelligence, e.g., de-Jong & Das-Smaal, 1995, Engle, 2002, Jurden, 1995)—will see the world around them as even more consistent than others. For them, there will be even fewer shades of gray, and wider areas of black and white; although their estimates of central values and differences between them will be, on average, less accurate, their confidence in their estimates and decisions will typically be higher.

Francis Bacon pointed out people's tendency to see too much regularity in the world around them and lamented it. The present findings prove his observation to be correct. The prevalence of the misperception could indicate, however, that it is not as dysfunctional as his lament implies.

Acknowledgments

This project was partly funded by the Israel Science Foundation (Grant No. 712/98). Address correspondence to: Yaakov Kareev, School of Education, The Hebrew University, Jerusalem, Israel (email: Kareev @ vms.huji.ac.il).

References

Allan, L. G. (1993). Human contingency judgments: Rule based or associative? *Psychological Bulletin, 114*, 435–448.

Alloy, L. B., & Tabachnik, N. (1984). Assessment of covariation by humans and animals: The joint influence of prior expectations and current situational information. *Psychological Review, 91*, 112–149.

Bacon, F. (1620/1905). *Novum Organum* (trans. R. L. Ellis & J. Spedding, edited by J. M. Robertson). London: George Routledge and Sons.

Beyth-Marom, R. (1982). Perception of correlation reexamined. *Memory & Cognition, 10*, 511–519.

Cowan, N. (2001). The magical number 4 in short-term memory: A consideration of mental storage capacity. *Behavioral and Brain Sciences, 24*, 87–185.

David, F. N. (1954). *Tables of the correlation coefficient.* Cambridge, England: Cambridge University Press.

de-Jong, P. F., & Das-Smaal, E. A. (1995). Attention and intelligence: The validity of the Star Counting Test. *Journal of Educational Psychology, 87*, 80–92.

Engle, R. W. (2002). Working memory capacity as executive attention. *Current Directions in Psychological Science, 11*, 19–23.

Gilbert, D. T., & Malone, P. S. (1995). The correspondence bias. *Psychological Bulletin, 117,* 21–38.
Gilbert, D. T., Pelham, B. W., & Krull, D. S. (1988). On cognitive busyness: When person perceivers meet persons perceived. *Journal of Personality and Social Psychology, 54,* 733–740.
Hamilton, D. L., & Guiford, R. (1976). Illusory correlation in interpersonal perception: A cognitive basis of stereotypic judgments. *Journal of Experimental Social Psychology, 12,* 392–407.
Hamilton, D. L., & Sherman, S. J. (1989). Illusory correlations: Implications for stereotype theory and research. In D. Bar-Tal, C. F. Graumann, A. W. Kruglanski, & W. Stroebe (Eds.), *Stereotyping and prejudice: Changing conceptions.* (pp. 59–82). New York: Springer-Verlag.
Hays, W. L. (1963). *Statistics for psychologists.* New York: Holt, Rinehart, & Winston.
Hogarth, R. M., & Einhorn, H. J. (1992). Order effects in belief updating: The belief-adjustment model. *Cognitive Psychology, 24,* 1–55.
Huttenlocher, J., & Burke, D. (1976). Why does memory span increase with age? *Cognitive Psychology, 8,* 1–31.
Jurden, F. H. (1995). Individual differences in working memory and complex cognition. *Journal of Educational Psychology, 87,* 93–102.
Kahneman, D., Slovic, P., & Tversky, A. (1982). *Judgment under uncertainty: Heuristics and biases.* Cambridge, England: Cambridge University Press.
Kareev, Y. (1992). Not that bad after all: Generation of random sequences. *Journal of Experimental Psychology: Human Perception and Performance, 18,* 1189–1194.
Kareev, Y. (1995a). Positive bias in the perception of covariation. *Psychological Review, 102,* 490–502.
Kareev, Y. (1995b). Through a narrow window: Working memory capacity and the detection of covariation. *Cognition, 56,* 263–269.
Kareev, Y. (2000). Seven (indeed, plus or minus two) and the detection of correlation. *Psychological Review, 107,* 397–402.
Kareev, Y., Arnon, S., & Horwitz-Zeliger, R. (2002). On the misperception of variability. *Journal of Experimental Psychology: General, 131,* 287–297.
Kareev, Y., Lieberman, I., & Lev, M. (1997). Through a narrow window: Sample size and the perception of correlation. *Journal of Experimental Psychology: General, 126,* 278–287.
Langer, E. J. (1975). The illusion of control. *Journal of Personality and Social Psychology, 32,* 311–328.
Mandler, G. (1967). Organization and Memory. In K. W. Spence & J. T. Spence (Eds.), *The psychology of learning and motivation,* Vol. 1. (pp. 328–372). New York: Academic Press.
Miller, G. A. (1956). The magical number seven, plus or minus two: Some limits on our capacity for processing information. *Psychological Review, 63,* 81–97.
Mischel, W. (1968). *Personality and assessment.* New York: Wiley.
Peterson, C. R., & Beach, L. F. (1967). Man as an intuitive statistician. *Psychological Bulletin, 68,* 29–46.
Pollard, P. (1984). Intuitive judgments of proportions, means, and variances: A review. *Current Psychological Research and Review, 3,* 5–18.
Ross, L. (1977). The intuitive psychologist and his shortcomings. In L. Berkowitz (Ed.), *Advances in experimental social psychology, 10,* 173–220. SanDiego: Academic Press.
Tversky, A., & Kahneman, D. (1971). Belief in the law of small numbers. *Psychological Bulletin, 76,* 105–110.
Tversky, A., & Kahneman, D. (1974). Judgment under uncertainty: Heuristics and biases. *Science, 185,* 1124–1131.

CAUSAL INVARIANCE IN REASONING AND LEARNING

Steven Sloman and David A. Lagnado

I. The Information Is in the Invariants

Cognition depends on that which does not change. Perception involves discovering the cues that consistently signal things of interest and distinguishing them from noise. Prediction requires identifying the variables whose behavior is constant over time so that their future behavior can be derived from their present values. Explanation involves assimilating an observation or phenomenon to a process or representation that applies to a wider, more inclusive class that emanates from or instantiates relations that are regular. Perhaps most important, control requires knowing the systematic relations between actions and their outcomes, so the right action can be chosen at the right time. In all of these cases, the secret is to identify and use invariance—the constant, regular, systematic relations that hold between the objects, events, and symbols that concern cognition.

A. IN THE DOMAIN OF EVENTS, CAUSAL RELATIONS ARE THE FUNDAMENTAL INVARIANTS

The world is full of change. Patterns of light and sound change continuously and relatively quickly. Life forms change, both the forms themselves over evolutionary time and (sadly) individuals over lifetimes. The sun has even set on the British empire by some accounts. Everything that has a physical realization is transient. In the domain of objects and events, delimited as they are in space and time, the search for invariance must go beyond the physical.

The hypothesis we pursue here is that the invariant which guides human reasoning and learning about events is causal structure. Causal relations hold across space, time, and individuals; the logic of causality guides prediction, explanation, and action; and people are designed to learn causal models. It is no surprise that causal relations are invariant. After all, much of science is devoted to discovering and representing invariant causal structure (e.g., force changes acceleration, demand increases price, structure determines function, interference causes forgetting, representativeness influences probability judgment). The causal principles that govern mechanisms are generally assumed to hold across the entire reference class that the principle applies to. Every physical body in the universe is subject to inertia and every living organism with a memory has been and will always be subject to interference.

Causal mechanisms themselves are decidedly not invariant. A car engine is a causal mechanism that is designed to be reliable but, as we all know, that is a pipedream. Shadows are cast by objects that block a light source like the sun, but the manifest form of such a mechanism may change continuously as the earth rotates and clouds shift. The invariant is not the mechanism itself but the principles that govern its operation, the function relating torque to force or light, objects, and shadow. Causal principles that govern how events affect other events are the carriers of information. They are the most reliable bases for judgment and action available.

One might argue, along with philosophers like Russell (1912), that invariant laws are not causal at all, but rather mathematical. Metaphysically, this may indeed be correct. But the brunt of the argument we will make is that the laws that people rely on in their thinking about events are not merely mathematical (or logical or probabilistic), but causal. The best evidence is that causal knowledge is not grounded in mathematical knowledge. On the contrary, mathematical knowledge is sometimes a representation of causal knowledge (Sherin, 2001). Mochon and Sloman (2003) demonstrate that people can select the causal versions of equations, and that their selections predict which versions of equations they consider most understandable and how people expect the variables in the equation to influence one another. Moreover, when asked to write down equations, people have a strong preference for the version that matches their causal understanding. We probably have several tricks for coming to grips with mathematical relations. Causal structure, in contrast, is part of the fundamental cognitive machinery.

B. Not All Invariance is Causal

Propositional logic and set theory describe invariant relations that are not necessarily causal. The relations among, for example, parts and wholes (e.g., how objects relate to scenes), classes (e.g., how the class of humans relates to the class of animals), or syntactic elements in language are not causal. However, propositional logic is severely limited in what it can represent. It is known to be unable to describe the meaning of certain linguistic constructions, like conditionals (statements with the form "if p, then q"). Few uses of "if" in everyday discourse have much to do with material implication (Edgington, 1995). The problem for propositional logic arises because the meaning of a conditional is not truth-functional; it cannot be expressed as the truth of any particular proposition (Lewis, 1976). It depends on whether q would hold if p did, whether or not they happen to be true in the actual world and whether or not q would hold if p did not. We would probably all agree with the statement that "if Shakespeare did not write all those plays, then somebody else did" even though both the antecedent ("if") clause and the consequent ("then") clause are unknown and probably unknowable with any certainty. The representation of whether something *would* hold is just not in the domain of propositional logic, which is concerned with whether propositions are true or false. Many statements are not about what is true. They might be imperatives or performatives, about who to blame, about subjective states or moral preferences, or about what the world would be like if things were different.

"If" generally restricts attention to the cases where the antecedent (like "Shakespeare did not write all those plays") holds or would hold in some other possible world. The possible world analysis of counterfactual if-constructions states that people imagine the closest possible world in which the antecedent is true and look to see if the consequent holds in that world (Stalnaker, 1968). This analysis goes a long way but it requires an analysis of the "closest possible world," and one that does not depend on the meaning of "if." We will explain in the following how Pearl (2000) provides an elegant solution to this problem using causal analysis. This is a natural domain for causal analysis because its central concern is not truth, not an assignment of propositions to values indicating their correspondence to the state of the world, but rather how the world works, what the mechanisms are that generate the dynamics we observe whether or not they have actually operated to construct a particular state. A toaster is a causal mechanism whose causal properties can be explained even if it is off and not generating events whose descriptions have truth values.

Probability theory also captures invariance. But, for the most part, the invariance it describes results from the operation of causal mechanisms. The reason that the probability of rolling double-six with two fair dice is 1/36 has to do with counting the possible causal outcomes of rolling the dice separately. The reason that the weather forecaster predicts rain with a probability of 0.7 in most cases has to do with a causal model that predicts future weather outcomes by extrapolating from the current conditions. The reason that the conditional probability is high that the ground is wet given that it has rained is that the former is a causal effect of the latter. Not all probability relations have a causal basis; quantum effects may not and some subjective probabilities may not. My degree of belief that the ancient Sabines comprised a powerful city state reflects confidence, not causality, although even my confidence has causal determinants.

In general then, causal relations are not the only kind of invariance useful for representing the world. There are various kinds of mathematical representations, as well as logical and probabilistic representations. But noncausal forms of invariance are less useful than causality for describing relations among events because they do not naturally describe the processes that generate structure over time and, they fail to support key forms of counterfactual inference as directly as causal models do.

C. Our Claim is Empirical

We propose that people use causal models more than other sorts of models when learning and reasoning about events (c.f. Andersson, 1986; diSessa, 1993; Driver, Guesne, & Tiberghien, 1993; Hunt & Minstrell, 1994; Reif & Allen, 1992; Reiner, Slotta, Chi, & Resnick, 2000; Waldmann, 1996; White, 1993). One type of evidence consistent with this view comes from the series of experiments demonstrating that causal explanations quickly become independent of the data from which they are derived. A range of experiments have revealed belief perseveration in the face of discredited evidence (reviewed in Ross & Anderson, 1982). An example pertinent here comes from Anderson, Lepper, and Ross (1980). In one case, they presented participants with a pair of firefighters, one of whom was successful and who was classified as a risk taker, the other unsuccessful and risk averse. After explaining the correlation between performance as a firefighter and risk preference, participants were informed that an error had been made, that in fact the pairings had been reversed and the true correlation was opposite to that explained. Nevertheless, participants persevered in their beliefs; they continued to assert the relation they had causally explained regardless of the updated information. Causal beliefs shape our thinking to such an extent that they dominate thought and judgment even when they are known to be divorced from observation. In such cases, they can result in biased judgment.

Experiments on belief perservation call for causal explanation. That is, people answer the question "why?" by explicitly distinguishing causes from effects and stating or implying that the effect would have been different if the cause had been different. Explanations in the physical and social domains tend to be causal of course, but note that they do not have to be. In principle, one could appeal to a class inclusion hierarchy (e.g., the reason that this rodent uses norepinephrine as a neurotransmitter is that it is a mammal) or to a mathematical theorem. But causal explanation is often the most natural form of explanation.

II. What Is a Cause?

The claim that causal relations are important has substance only if causal relations are distinct from other kinds of relations. First, note that causal relations obtain between events or classes of events, they occur in space and time and are generally thought to be constrained in these dimensions. One very general temporal constraint is that effects cannot precede their causes. Sometimes we talk in a non-spatiotemporally bounded way as if abstract properties can be causes and effects (increases in pressure cause increases in temperature, love causes beauty). But even here, the actual causes and effects as they manifest themselves in the world are physical entities that obtain for periods of time (sometimes very long or very short). Spatiotemporal boundedness distinguishes causal relations from definitions. A definitional relation identifies a predicate with a set of necessary and sufficient conditions; it is not a spatiotemporally-constrained relation among classes of events.

Causal relations also imply certain counterfactuals. To say that A causes B is to say that, if event B were to have no other sufficient causes at the moment, then if event A had not occurred, B would not have occurred. This distinguishes causes from co-occurrences. A causal relation does not merely say that events go together but that there is some generating mechanism that produces an event of one type when engaged by an event of another type. As a result, if the mechanism had not been engaged by the cause (counterfactually), the effect would not have resulted (Mackie, 1980; Pearl, 2000).

A. Causal Models

A formal framework has recently been developed based on Bayesian graphical probability models to reason about causal systems (Spirtes, Glymour, & Scheines, 1993; reviewed in Pearl, 2000). In this formalism, a directed graph is used to represent the causal structure of a system, with nodes corresponding to system variables, and direct links between nodes corresponding to causal relations (see example in Fig. 1).

Each node is accompanied by a set of parameters (conditional probabilities of the value of the node given its direct causes) that specify the function that describes the mechanism relating a set of causes to an effect. Causes might be conceived of as direct causes, or enabling or disabling conditions. They might produce the effect jointly or individually. The functional relation might be deterministic or probabilistic (due either to the incompleteness of

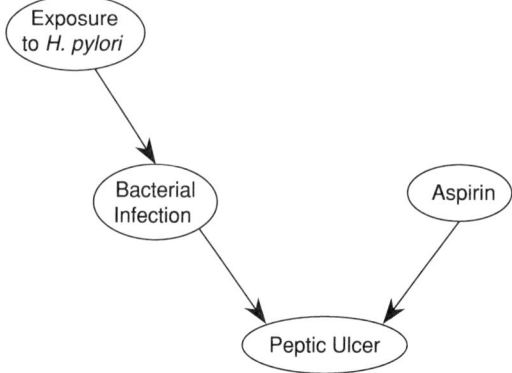

Fig. 1. A simplified causal graph of the potential causes of peptic ulcers.

the graph or to genuine noise in the system). The causal modeling framework allows all of these possibilities (and more).

The precise nature of the functional relation determining each effect can be expressed using a different but isomorphic representational scheme called structural equation modeling. Each effect can be associated with a function expressing exactly how it is produced by its causes. For example, if a spark, oxygen, and a source of energy are required to produce fire, the following equation could represent a causal mechanism:

Fire = f(spark, oxygen, energy, noise)

where f indicates conjunction (all causes are required) and noise means that there are sources of randomness that make the relation probabilistic. Sometimes sources of randomness can be reduced to other causal mechanisms (e.g., the wind) and noise variables may not be necessary even in probabilistic systems (Spirtes, Glymour, & Scheines, 1993). Causal graphs are good for expressing a complex system of causal relations; structural equations are good for expressing the specific function relating a set of causes to their effect.

One of the central ideas of the causal modeling framework is that stable probabilistic relations between the observed variables of a system are generated by an underlying causal structure. Thus, given a particular structure, one can expect certain conditional and unconditional dependencies in the data we observe; certain variables should be related, others should not, and all the relations will sometimes depend on the values of other variables. In the simplest case, if no pathway exists in a causal graph between two variables, those two variables should be statistically independent. In the case of a causal chain:

A→B→C

A and C should be correlated unless the value of B is fixed, in which case they should be independent (because A tells us nothing about C when we already know the value of B). This is just one example of a Markov condition, or what psychologists tend to call the "screening-off property" of causal graphs (for an easy-to-read introduction to Markov conditions, see Glymour, 2001).

Conversely, given the observation of certain dependencies in the world, one can infer something about the underlying causal structure, and in some cases identify it uniquely. For example, if you know that A and C are correlated but independent given the value of B, then only three causal models that include only A, B, and C are possible:

A→B→C   C→B→A   A→B→C

These are called Markov-equivalent. Making inferences from dependencies in the world (i.e., in data) to causal structure requires two assumptions concerning the relation between a causal graph and the probabilistic patterns of data it generates. One of these, the *causal Markov condition*, states that the direct causes of a variable render it probabilistically independent of any other system variables except its direct or indirect effects. This condition will hold so long as a causal graph explicitly represents any variable that is a cause of two or more variables in the graph. The second of these, the *stability assumption*, stipulates that any probabilistic independencies in the data should arise solely because of causal structure and not spuriously. The claim here is that *stable* independencies arise from the structure of a causal model. Two variables are expected to be unrelated, for example, if no causal path between them exists. In contrast, *unstable* independencies arise from some coincidental set of values of the conditional probabilities in the model. Situations can arise where two variables satisfy the definition of probabilistic independence and yet are causally related. Such situations are unstable in the sense that the apparent independence disappears as soon as the conditional probability given any value of the other variable changes. The assumption that such situations are not affecting inference has analogs in models of vision. There, one often assumes that if you see one person, then you should assume that there is only one person present; you should not assume that there is another person behind the first in exactly the position that would obscure them. The probability of two (or three or four...) people when all you see is one is so low that it should be neglected. The causal model analog is that we should assume that the independencies we observe arise from actual causal mechanisms and not from highly unlikely coincidences. The assumption derives from the desire to pick out stable mechanisms rather than transitory events.

B. MAKING INFERENCES GIVEN NEW INFORMATION

The structure of a causal graph, in combination with the probability distribution across its nodes, determines what inferences we can make on the basis of new information. When this information takes the form of an observation, then Bayesian updating tells us how we ought to modify our probabilities to incorporate the new data, to learn. For example, given the causal model in Fig. 1, if we find out that an individual has an *H. pylori* bacterial infection, we should increase (to a degree that depends on the relevant conditional probabilities) both the probability that the person has been exposed to the *H. pylori* bacteria and the probability that they have (or will develop) peptic ulcers.

However, what if we eradicate the bacterial infection by giving them an appropriate course of antibiotics? That is, what if instead of merely observing the causal system, we intervene on it through action? Such an action warrants a change in our belief that the person will develop peptic ulcers, but does not warrant a change in the probability that they were exposed to the bacteria. More generally, the probabilistic inferences that we are licensed to draw after observing a particular value of a variable may not be the same as those that we are licensed to draw after intervening to set the variable to that same value. Bayesian updating fails to recognize this difference. It does not differentiate between *observing* and *acting*. That is, the same conditional probability $P(X|Y)$ is used to represent the probability of X given that Y *is observed*, and the probability of X given that Y *is intentionally set*. But these can be quite different, as our example illustrates—the probability of exposure given the absence of an infection is quite distinct from the probability of exposure given that we eradicate the infection.

C. THE REPRESENTATION OF ACTION

One of the innovative features of the causal model framework is that it proposes a normative account for the representation of interventions, and for the inferences that they license. In so doing, it formalizes the difference between observation and intervention. Pearl (2000) achieves this through the introduction of the "*do( )*" operator. In short, the *do* operator represents an action through two effects on the state of a causal model. First, it sets the value of a variable to a specific value: $do(X = x)$ sets the variable X to the value x. Second, it entails a small modification of the causal graph: X is disconnected from its causes. Pearl calls this a surgery. The idea is that an agent is acting to determine the value of X, therefore, the normal causes of X have no influence on it. The action overrides the causes of X, rendering them irrelevant. Otherwise, the graph remains the same. The effects of the intervention are then computable through Bayesian updating on this 'mutilated' graph.

To illustrate using the graph in Figure 1, consider an intervention (e.g., use of antibiotics) that sets the *infection* variable to absent. This leads to the modified graph in Figure 2: The directed link from *exposure* to *infection* is deleted and the links from *infection* to *peptic ulcers* and from *aspirin* to *peptic ulcers* are left unchanged. In effect the intervention amounts to placing the variable *infection* under the influence of a new mechanism that sets its value to absent.

This account provides a normative model for the representation of both actual and imagined interventions (like representations of counterfactuals), and tells us how these interventions will (or would) affect the values of the other variables in the system. In particular, it dictates what probabilistic inferences we are entitled to make. Thus, the modified graph in Figure 2 permits us to infer that the probability of *peptic ulcer* is reduced, but not to infer any change in the probability of *exposure*. The latter prohibition captures the basic asymmetry of the cause-effect relation: manipulating a cause can change an effect but not vice-versa.[1]

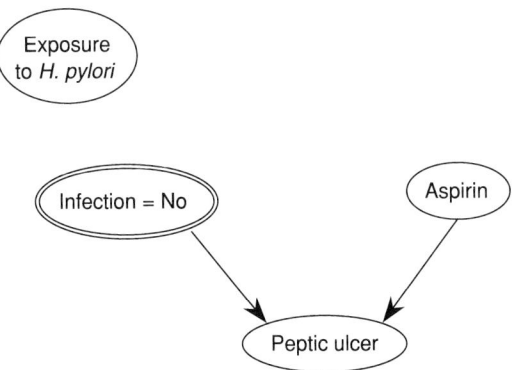

Fig. 2. Causal graph after an intervention to eradicate the bacterial infection.

---

[1] Some caveats (due to Clark Glymour): (1) an intervention on a variable can impose a new probability distribution rather than setting a determinate value; (2) causal relations between events are always asymmetric but causal relations among variables can be symmetric (e.g., turning the pedals of a bike turns the rear wheel, but turning the rear wheel can also turn the pedals); and (3) for cyclic graphs, the *do* operator is not always appropriate.

This conception of intervention draws on the idea that the directed links in a causal graph represent local, autonomous, and stable mechanisms: intervening to set a variable to a fixed value only disrupts those mechanisms that previously controlled that variable, but leaves all other mechanisms intact. Further, it formalizes the intuitive notion that X causes Y (directly or indirectly) if some subset of interventions to change X *would* lead to a change in Y. It is this synergy of the concepts of causal link, mechanism, and intervention that gives the causal model framework its originality and power.

D. COUNTERFACTUALS UNDERSTOOD IN TERMS OF POSSIBLE WORLDS

One standard way of interpreting counterfactuals is in terms of possible worlds (Lewis, 1973, 1986; Stalnaker, 1968). The idea is that the truth of a counterfactual is determined by consideration of the possible worlds that result from slight modifications to the actual world, sufficient to make the antecedent of the counterfactual true. For example, consider the counterfactual question 'If there had not been excessive heat, would the device still have failed?' To determine the answer one must imagine a possible world very similar to the actual one, but in which the device is not exposed to excessive heat. One then looks in that 'closest' possible world (or a set of such worlds) to see if the device fails or not.

But how do we determine which possible world is closest? What similarity metric should we use? Pearl's analysis is that the closest possible world is the one described by our causal model of this world, but simplified using the *do* operator. Specifically, take your causal model of this world, find the variables in it that correspond to the antecedent of the 'if' clause, and use the do operator to set them according to the values specified by the 'if' clause. At the same time, simplify the model by disconnecting the variables from their normal causes. We find this analysis appealing for the case of causal counterfactuals. Counterfactuals that have noncausal conceptual bases, like "if it has three sides, then it is a triangle," are unlikely to be explicated in terms of causal models.

E. LEVELS OF CAUSALITY

A causal graph represents a causal system at a particular level of granularity. Causal systems afford multiple descriptions, each at its own level. The human body can be described coarsely, in terms of its physiological systems (nervous system, cardiovascular, etc.) and how they interrelate, or more finely, for example each physiological system could be decomposed into its parts. Clearly, this could be done at multiple levels of precision. The most specific level describes a particular causal event in terms of all of its contingent subevents, all relevant variables and their interactions and effects. According to Pearl (2000), a causal analysis at this level is deterministic because it describes every condition leaving no uncertainty (for the sake of discussion, we leave aside quantum indeterminism as it probably has little to do with everyday causal models). Of course, descriptions this precise may not be possible and so such deterministic models may be merely ideals. As soon as variables are ignored, descriptions become more coarse; and we almost always do ignore variables. If we ask whether smoking causes cancer, and certainly if we do so in a non-scientific context, we tend to ignore other factors, such as contaminants in the environment, what people are eating, and the shape of a person's lungs, all of which could well contribute to cancer and to smoking's effect on cancer. This does not necessarily render our analysis worthless, because these other variables can potentially be treated as a source of noise. In other words, whenever we ignore variables and operate with coarse models, and we do all the time, causality becomes probabilistic.

Causal analyses are hierarchical in another sense as well, in terms of their level of abstraction. A particular causal relation at its most specific level of description is a realized mechanism, at its most general it is a causal principle for generating mechanisms. For example, a guillotine is a specific causal mechanism. The mechanism depends on some abstract causal principles, one being that gravity causes acceleration. Note that general principles apply at every level of granularity and, in this sense, these two kinds of hierarchy are independent. A plausible psychological hypothesis is that people store relatively few causal models, and certainly few at a detailed level of analysis. Instead, people may store causal principles that allow them to construct causal models—and thus explanations for events—on the fly.

III. Counterfactual and Probabilistic Judgment

A. Causal Models Can Be Used to Predict Base-Rate Neglect

One way to tell that people use causal models to reason is from evidence showing that causal models mediate judgments of probability (Tversky & Kahneman, 1980). We can distinguish two types of evidence relevant to making a judgment of the probability of a unique event: (1) class data and (2) case data (see Tversky & Kahneman, 1982). Class data refers to evidence about the event emanating from its type; case data concern the specific event itself. Tversky and Kahneman argue that evidence specific to the case at hand overwhelms the field; class data can be treated as background and, therefore, is sometimes neglected. They make the point with the following problem:

A cab was involved in a hit-run accident at night. Two cab companies, the Green and the Blue, operate in the city. Imagine you are given the following information.

85% of the cabs in the city are Green and 15% are Blue.

A witness identified the cab as a Blue cab. The court tested his ability to identify cabs under the appropriate visibility conditions. When presented with a sample of cabs (half of which were Blue and half of which were Green) the witness made correct identifications in 80% of the cases and erred in 20% of the cases.

What is the probability that the cab involved in this accident was Blue rather than Green?

Tversky and Kahneman report a median response of 0.80. A Bayesian analysis however distinguishes four variables: W (the witness's report that the cab was blue); B (the event that cab involved in the accident was blue); G (the event that cab was green); and R (the base rate of blue cabs). The question asks for

$$P(B|W \& R) = \frac{P(W|B \& R) \bullet P(B|R)}{P(W|B \& R) \bullet P(B|R) + P(W|G \& R) \bullet P(G|R)} = 0.41$$

assuming the observed cab was randomly drawn from the population of cabs and the witness's report was randomly drawn from an appropriate population of judgments. On this analysis, the cab is more likely to be green than blue despite the witness's report because of the high base rate of green cabs. Yet, people tended to be guided solely by the witness's report. One condition that elicited responses closer to the Bayesian conclusion was inspired by Ajzen (1977). Tversky and Kahneman (1982) ran a version of the problem in which they replaced the statement of base rates (the second paragraph of the problem) with one that made the base rates appear to be causally relevant to the incident:

Causal version:
Although the two companies are of roughly equal in size, 85% of the total accidents in the city involve Green cabs, and 15% involve Blue cabs.

In this case, participants took base rates into some account. The median response was 0.60.

We hypothesize that, in a causal context like a car accident, people tend to evaluate causal effects by constructing a causal model and reasoning from it (Sloman, 2003). They do not reason about probabilities per se. The implication is that evidence—even probabilistically relevant evidence—that is not part of a causal structure can be neglected. In particular, evidence that is taxonomically but not causally related to the object of judgment, like the number of cabs in a city, will tend to be neglected.

Such reasoning is not probabilistically sound but can be justifiable. It is generally unfair to blame someone or find them guilty because of their background or their prior conduct. The crimes of your father, of members of your state or race, or even your own previous bad behavior surely can carry information about the probability of your guilt. But if it is not tied to a specific causal story about the misdeed at hand, it can be legally and morally irrelevant (for data corroborating the judged irrelevance of merely statistical evidence, see Wells, 1992).

Sloman (2003) tested the hypothesis that base-rate neglect in the cab problem results from participants who do not perceive the base rate to be causally relevant to the judged outcome. Participants were given the cab problem as well as a series of questions intended to reveal their individual causal models of the problem. The causal models were used to fit individuals' responses to the cab problem. Overall, a lot of base-rate neglect was observed: 32% of participants in the causal condition and 38% in the noncausal condition gave the witness's credibility (80%) as their response. However, the difference between the two conditions was small and failed to replicate Tversky and Kahneman (1982).

The causal model questions asked the participant whether a functional relation connected one variable to another. For example, to assess the causal relation from the base rate (percentage of green vs. blue cabs) to the judged event (cab involved was green vs. blue), participants were asked if a change in the former would change their belief in the latter. Answers were used to derive a causal model for each participant. To illustrate, someone who responded "yes" only to the question about the effect of a change in the witness's report on belief that the cab was blue, would be assigned the model:

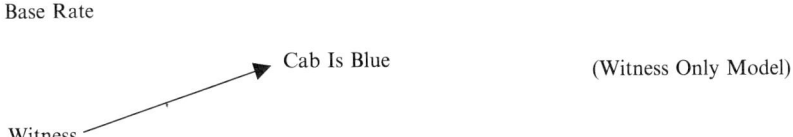

This is the simplest model consistent with Tversky and Kahneman's claim that people believe that the witness's credibility was relevant to their judgment but the base rate was not. It was the model most frequently generated in both the causal and noncausal conditions. The next most frequent model in both conditions was the simplest one consistent with the Bayesian response. It stated the relevance to the judgment of both the base rate and the witness's testimony:

(Bayesian Model)

No other model was generated with any regularity.

Variability in the choice of models was considerable, nevertheless models can be divided into two main types using the screening-off property: (1) those consistent with the witness-only model, and (2) those consistent with the Bayesian model. These causal model classifications were used to predict people's responses to the cab problem. In accordance with the causal modeling hypothesis, participants who endorsed a witness-only model type were more likely to neglect the base rate and those who endorsed a Bayesian model type were more likely to give a judgment closer to the Bayesian response that takes both witness and base rate information into account. Moreover, participants were marginally more likely to report that the base rate was causally relevant when it was presented in causal terms.

Although the restriction to causally relevant evidence has a convincing normative justification in the determination of guilt and blame (one should not be accountable for thy father's sins), morally (and legally) ambiguous cases certainly exist. Should police be allowed to detain those who fit a racial or ethnic profile for a crime even without direct evidence causally linking the individual to the crime? Such detention can be discriminatory and violate individual rights; of course, if the profile is statistically valid, it can also help deter crime. Wells (1992) found that even base rates concerning the proportions of accidents caused by vehicles of a certain type were deemed insufficient by his American student participants to conclude guilt for an accident. Our interpretation is that people have a higher threshold for using causally relevant evidence to convict than for using it to determine the probability of guilt.

B. Explanation Discounting

Consider an effect that has two possible causal explanations. For example, the effect might be Jim's belief that everyone's talking about him and it could be caused either by Jim's paranoia or by the fact that everyone is indeed talking about him. Here's a causal model to describe such a situation:

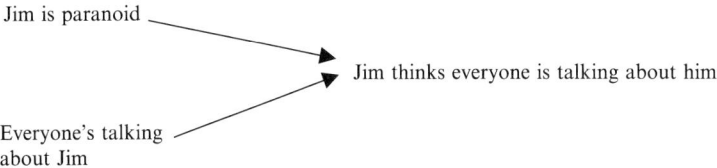

This causal model assumes that the two causes are marginally independent. However, a ubiquitous assumption in the Bayes' net literature is that individually sufficient causes in such a model are not *conditionally* independent. If you know that the effect has occurred, and you have no other relevant information, then that raises the probability of both causes. The effect is diagnostic of their causes. However, the knowledge that one of the causes occurred (e.g., Jim is diagnosed as paranoid) makes it less likely that the other cause is the reason for the effect (it is less likely that everyone is in fact talking about him). In other words, even though

Pr(cause2|cause 1) = Pr(cause 2),

i.e., marginal independence of the two causes,

Pr(cause2|cause 1, effect) <Pr(cause2|effect),

i.e., dependence conditional on the effect. This is known as "explaining away" because it reflects the fact that if you know that an effect occurred, knowing one cause occurred makes it less likely that the other cause did.

Psychologists have known for some time that people are sensitive to this relation among explanations for an effect, at least in the social domain. The social psychology literature reports many examples of what is called "discounting." That literature focuses on people's explanations of other people's behavior and notes that people tend to put less weight on an individual's disposition as an explanation of their behavior if they construe the situation that they are in as also being a sufficient cause. The most celebrated instance of this is Jones and Harris's (1967) attribution study. Participants read pro- or anti-Castro essays written by students. Some participants were informed that the students were told what to write; others were told that students chose their own position. Participants then judged the essay writer as pro- or anti-Castro. Although judgments were biased in the direction of the essay in both cases, judgments were attenuated when the student had been told to write the essay. The presence of a situational explanation (what the students were told to do) attenuated the dispositional attribution (their attitude to Castro).

Morris and Larrick (1995) show both normatively and empirically that explanation discounting depends on the correlation between causes. They found that discounting did not occur when causes were positively correlated. Causal model theory offers a more general and precise way to determine the conditions for explanation discounting: it should depend on the causal model that people bring to their understanding of the situation.

In attribution experiments, explanation discounting reflects the difference between two judgments: first, the degree-of-belief that an individual is behaving as they do by virtue of their dispositions or attitude:

Pr(attitude X|behavior Y)

and second, the degree-of-belief that the person has such an attitude given that you also know of some situational explanation for their behavior:

Pr(attitude X|behavior Y, situational explanation for Y)

If the attitudinal and situational causes of the behavior are independent, in analogy to the paranoia diagram in the preceding text, then explaining away predicts that this second probability should be lower than the first, in line with the phenomenon of discounting. But if the causes are dependent, then this prediction does not hold. For example, if the situation is the following:

Attitude X → Situational explanation for Y → Behavior Y

the dispositional and situational causes should be correlated. Such a structure implies that knowledge that the situation holds should *increase* belief that the individual has the requisite attitude (and knowing the attitude should also increase belief in the situational explanation).[2]

---

[2] Here's a proof developed with the aid of Sean Stromsten based on the assumption that causes increase the probability of their direct effects (e.g., the P(behavior|explanation) > P(behavior)). Let A be the individual's attitude, B be the situation, and C be the behavior.

Step 1. P(B|A) > P(B) if and only if P(A|B) > P(A) (by Bayes' theorem) if and only if P(A|B) > P(A|~B) [because P(A) = P(A|B)P(B) + P(A|~B)P(~B)], where n means negation.

Step 2. P(A|C) = P(A|B)P(B|C) + P(A|~B)P(~B|C) (by definition of the chain structure). P(A|B) = P(A|B)P(B|C) + P(A|B)P(~B|C). Therefore, P(A|B) > P(A|C) (because of the result in Step 1).

Step 3. P(A|B) = P(A|B,C) (this is the screening-off property of the chain structure). Therefore, P(A|B,C) > P(A|C) (from result of Step 2).

Step 4. P(B|A,C) = P(A|B,C)P(B|C)/P(A|C) (Bayes' theorem). Therefore, P(B|A,C) > P(B|C) (by Step 3). This shows that, for the chain model with strengthening causes, conditionalizing on the second variable increases the probability relative to conditionalizing on just one.

C. THE LOGIC OF DOING

The causal modeling framework is distinguished from other kinds of logic by the *do* operator. This is the concept that distinguishes observation from intervention and what gives the framework the ability to represent both action (intervention in the world) and imagination (intervention in the mind). The *do* operator makes a distinct claim about the structure of reasoning, a claim that distinguishes it from standard probability and logical calculi. Namely, it predicts that effects are not always diagnostic of their causes. In particular, when an effect is physically or mentally manipulated, it gives no information about its normal causes.

Consider the following causal problem from Sloman and Lagnado (2002):

There are three billiard balls on a table that act in the following way:

If ball 1 moves, then ball 2 moves. If ball 2 moves, then ball 3 moves.

(1) Suppose that someone held ball 2 so that it could not move, would ball 1 still move?

(2) Suppose that someone held ball 2 so that it could not move, would ball 3 still move?

The causal model underlying this scenario looks like this:

Ball1 → Ball2 → Ball3

The causal modeling framework represents the two questions as:

(1) Pr(Ball 1 moves|*do* and Ball 2 does not move)

(2) Pr(Ball 3 moves|*do* and Ball 2 does not move)

To evaluate these entities, we must assume that Ball 2 does not move. According to the logic of *do*, we must also simplify the causal model by removing any links into Ball 2 (because we are setting its value, its causes are not):

Ball 1   Ball 2 → Ball 3

It is immediately apparent that the value of Ball 1 is no longer affected by Ball 2 and, therefore, the model predicts the "undoing effect," that the lack of movement of Ball 2 is not diagnostic of its normal cause, Ball 1. In other words, people should respond "yes" to the first question. Because Ball 2 remains the cause of movement of Ball 3, we expect a response of "no" to the second question. This prediction is directly contrary to the prediction of standard probability theory which does not have the *do* operator at its disposal. All it can do is use a standard conditional probability to model the questions:

(1)′ Pr(Ball 1 moves|Ball 2 does not move)

(2)′ Pr(Ball 3 moves|Ball 2 does not move)

While there is no difference between (2)′ and (2), (1)′ should be low, unlike (1). It reflects the observational probability of Ball 1 moving if Ball 2 does not. In the normal course of events, Ball 1 does not move when Ball 2 doesnot. The standard logical inference is a special case of this probabilistic inference. A conventional logical analysis of the problem would use the following Modus Tollens schema that is normally valid:

If Ball 1 moves, then Ball 2 moves.
Ball 2 does not move
Therefore, Ball 1 does not move.

What do people actually say in this context? In Sloman and Lagnado (2002), the vast majority responded "yes" to the question about Ball 1 and "no" to the question about Ball 3, thus validating the causal model prediction and contradicting the probabilistic/logical one. People agreed with us that if Ball 2 is prevented from moving, then that has no implications for Ball 1 and that should be reflected in the operative causal model. Sloman and Lagnado provide a number of replications of this basic effect using a range of abstract and concrete contexts, various causal models, and probabilistic as well as deterministic causal relations. They also show that the results depend on a causal interpretation of the conditional ("if") statements. Presenting arguments in "if...then..." form without contextual support indicating that they are to be understood as expressing causal relations is not sufficient to get the effect.

One might argue that our logical analysis is not valid because it treats the lack of movement of Ball 2 as an observation, a state of affairs in the world, neglecting its counterfactual character (that we *suppose* that someone prevents it from moving when in fact no one did). But this is precisely the limitation of standard logic, that it has no means of expressing counterfactuals or action of any sort.

D. CONCLUSIONS

Causal modeling seems to play a central role in the process of judgment when the object of judgment can be construed as a causal effect. Such a construal is almost always appropriate in the legal domain as well as in scientific domains (modulo atomic physics perhaps), indeed in any domain in which physical, social, or abstract events cause other events. Causal models may well be the primary determinant of what is considered relevant when reasoning, when making judgments and predictions, and when taking action within such domains.

IV. Language Use

Language often concerns causal structure in an explicit way: we talk about causal structure all the time. What is it about my football team that is going to cause them to beat your football team? Which causal model of history explains the current tension in the Middle East? What is causing Bob and Sue's marriage to fall apart?

But causal structure also plays a less obvious role in the way we use language to refer. For example, pronoun reference is sometimes determined by agency (Brown & Fish, 1983; Hoffman & Tchir, 1990). Consider:

(1) Steven admires Brian because *he* is so candid.

(2) Steven annoys Brian because *he* is so candid.

In (1), *he* refers to Brian but in (2) *he* refers to Steven. The reason is that in both cases *he* refers to the agent of the preceding verb (Brian is the cause of admiration but Steven is the cause of annoyance). More generally, nouns often achieve reference by indexing causal structure. The goodness of a word for an object is often determined by the degree to which the object satisfies the set of causal relations picked out by the word.

Since the seminal conceptual analysis of Wittgenstein (1953) and empirical analysis of Rosch (1973), almost all psychologists have given up on the idea that determining whether a word refers to an object involves matching the object to a set of necessary and sufficient conditions (c.f. Smith & Medin, 1981). Various alternative conceptions have been offered: naming involves determining the similarity of an object to a set of exemplars (Nosofsky, 1984) or to a prototype; and naming involves the elicitation of a shared cognitive schema grounded in bodily experience (Lakoff, 1987) or merely a pointer to a substance (Millikan, 1998).

But all theories are faced with explaining a ubiquitous fact about how people choose names: that unobservable properties are often given more weight in a naming decision than observable properties (studies particularly relevant to causal models include Gopnik, Glymour, Sobel, Schulz, Kushnir, & Danks, in press; Gopnik, Sobel, Schulz, & Glymour, 2001). In some cases, when dealing with artifacts—human-made objects—the function of the object is given more weight than its physical appearance, even by young children. Kemler Nelson, Russell, Duke, and Jones (2000) showed children a named object and then had them choose between an object similar in function but dissimilar in form and one similar in form but without the function as another instance of the name category. The children tended to choose objects that preserved the function of the original when the function had been tied to the physical features. Sometimes it is the intended function that is given more weight (Matan & Carey, 2001; Rips, 1989). Sometimes it is the creator's intention that matters. In one experiment, Bloom and Markson (1998) had three- and four-year-olds draw pictures of a lollipop, a balloon, the experimenter, and themselves. The pictures of lollipops and balloons were indistinguishable as were the pictures of the experimenter and the child, yet, when asked what the drawing was a picture of, the children named the pictures according to their original intentions. In the domain of living things, unobservable properties like parentage and what is inside are given more weight, at least after a certain age (Keil, 1989; Simons & Keil, 1995). In all these cases, unobservable properties are given priority over observable ones. The general rules mentioned are far from hard and fast (see Sloman & Malt, in press, for review and discussion), but nevertheless such cases exist and warrant explanation.

A closely related problem is that what we call things, at least natural kinds, must obey certain *modal* constraints (Rips, 2001). A natural kind label must refer not merely to a set of objects in the world but to a set of possibilities. Otherwise, there would be no way to explain how to generalize names to novel instances or how to analyze counterfactual conditionals (if Leo were a lion, he would have a mane). The close relation that exists between causal relations and possible worlds already gives a hint that causal relations might be critical for these kinds of phenomena.

A common approach to these problems is to assume that naming decisions are governed by a belief about the to-be-named object's *essence* or true, underlying nature (e.g., Gelman & Hirschfeld, 1999; Keil, 1995). Objects that are judged to have the essence are members of the name category; objects that do not are not. The essence is unobservable, reflecting as it does the object's deeper nature. The essence is assumed to be the fundamental cause of the object's observable properties and derives in the case of living things from genetic structure (or life force in some cultures), in the case of artifacts from intended function or the creator's intention (Diesendruck, Markson, & Bloom, 2003), in the case of social kinds from social role, and so on. So this view is quite compatible with the idea that what we see in the world around us—observables—are not the critical determinant of naming. What matters is the essence that we infer and attribute to an object or simply assume to exist even if we know nothing about it. And this essence can assign category membership to a possibility as easily as it can to an actual object.

However, Rips (2001) points out that this is not the only account of natural kind naming that can explain why unobservables matter so much and how modal constraints come into play. Another is what he calls the "extrinsic view," that names are not governed by an intrinsic essence but by a set of extrinsic causal laws. An object warrants a name if it can participate in the events that objects of that type participate in. Something is named "water" if it freezes, evaporates, quenches thirst, flows through hydroelectric dams, etc., if in general it is governed by the causal laws that things of that type are governed by. An object could satisfy this definition without having any particular essence; indeed, an object might satisfy different causal laws for different reasons (water quenches thirst and reflects light for different reasons) and some of those reasons might even be superficial and reflect observables. Strevens (2001) makes a complementary argument against essentialism, arguing that essences are gratuitous; the work of categorization is done by causal knowledge.

Why do Rips and Strevens allude to causal knowledge as opposed to any other type of knowledge? After all, not all knowledge is causal, some of it concerns part-whole relations, other class inclusion relations, and so on. A part of the answer is that people are not always able to make as much use of noncausal forms of knowledge. Several studies have examined the relative impact on naming of features depending on their causal status. Ahn (1998) found that causes are treated as more important in category membership judgments than effects. Ahn, Kim, Lassaline, and Dennis (2000) specified a chain of causal relations among three features of a set of named objects. Test objects were missing one of the features and participants judged how likely the objects were as examples of the named category. Likelihood judgments were proportional to the causal depth of the feature. Rehder and Hastie (2001) presented people with information about the attributes of various artifacts (cars and computers). Some participants were also given information about causal relations among the attributes. At test, participants were asked if new objects were members of the learned category or not. Attributes mattered in proportion to the number of causal relations they participated in.

In contrast to this strong evidence for the importance of causal relations in category judgments, there is strong evidence against the use of class inclusion relations (Hampton, 1982; Markman, Horton, & McLanahan, 1980; Sloman, 1998). Part-whole knowledge, however, does play a large role in structuring our knowledge of categories (Tversky & Hemenway, 1984; Morris & Murphy, 1990). For example, to know what a bicycle is, is to know, in part, that it has wheels and a handlebar. Of course, what ties the parts of an object together into a whole are causal mechanisms. Bicycles have the parts that let them serve their function, the bodies of living things have parts that afford the causal powers for survival, decorative parts attract other agents, and so on. So causal knowledge is in this sense the most fundamental.

Causal knowledge takes a particular form. It relates properties to one another, it does not relate objects per se. Causal laws describe how changes in one property lead to changes in other properties (e.g., changes in pressure cause changes in temperature, changes in intentions cause changes in behavior). So, to the extent that knowledge is causal, it forces a knowledge representation that does not organize objects into categories (subordinate and superordinate, cross-cutting, or whatever). Rather, it organizes objects into sets of properties and relates those properties to one another (see Sloman & Malt, in press, for further discussion).

In conclusion, people do not treat category features as independent. Instead they try to understand the relation of features to one another, and they consider how this relation relates to that of typical objects associated with a name. Categories emerge in order to describe the conditions required of a particular causal relation (e.g., things that are round and fuzzy and smell nice will cause the desire to stroke or embrace). This conclusion converges with Ross's (1999; Ross & Murphy, 1999) demonstrations that categories are formed in a way that depends on their use. Categories formed in the course of solving a problem retain properties specific to that problem. It also converges with recent models describing performance on various categorization tasks as depending on featural relations (Rehder & Hastie, 2001; Sloman, Love, & Ahn, 1998).

V. Induction

A. INDUCTION AND CAUSAL MODELS

Induction is the process by which we reason from observations about the world to general conclusions, from particulars to universal. Such universal conclusions are necessarily uncertain as there is no way to prove a universal from any finite set of particular facts. This is one of the conclusions drawn by Hume (1748) in his seminal work on how people make inductive inferences and how they can be justified. No matter how many times we see the sun rise in the morning, we cannot know for sure that it will rise *every* morning. Our belief that the sun will rise tomorrow is to some extent guesswork.

Hume argued that all inductive inference depends on relations of cause and effect. Although this view waned for a time in philosophical discussion of induction, it has been staging a comeback (Lipton, 1991; Miller, 1987). The idea can be construed this way: any general conclusion we derive from particular facts is mediated by the construction of a causal model to explain the facts. The general conclusion is just a description of the causal model, or (more often) some causal relation embedded in it. For example, the regular rising of the sun led people to the conclusion that the sun and the earth are circling one another (it required observations of the movements of other celestial objects and many years of thought, discussion, and battle to decide which was circling which). So an early causal model of the solar system came into being that supported many general statements about the planets and their relative distances. One of the model's predictions is that the sun will continue to rise every morning. The causal model has of course changed over the years as new facts have been collected and inconsistencies discovered. Unfortunately, the most recent causal model predicts that the sun will only continue to rise for a finite number of years due to its limited energy. Fortunately, you have plenty of time to finish reading this paper.

B. ARGUMENT STRENGTH MEDIATED BY CAUSAL KNOWLEDGE

This theory of induction helps us to understand certain phenomena of inductive inference. Medin, Coley, Storms, and Hayes (2003) have demonstrated several phenomena that depend on causal knowledge about why a category might have a property. They found, for example, that both Americans and Australians judged the argument.

> Bananas have property X12, therefore, monkeys have property X12.

to be stronger than the argument

> Mice have property X12, therefore, monkeys have property X12.

even though mice and monkeys are more similar than bananas and monkeys. Presumably the first argument is stronger because it is easy to imagine a causal model in which the property is transferred from bananas to monkeys. The causal model would derive from the general causal principle:

> Ingesting X → Have X

No such causal principle normally transfers properties directly from mice to monkeys.

Heit and Rubinstein (1994) asked people to evaluate the strength of arguments like the following:

> 1a. Chickens have a liver with two chambers, therefore, hawks have a liver with two chambers.
>
> 1b. Tigers have a liver with two chambers, therefore, hawks have a liver with two chambers.

2a. Chickens prefer to feed at night, therefore, hawks prefer to feed at night.

2b. Tigers prefer to feed at night, therefore, hawks prefer to feed at night.

People found 1a stronger than 1b, i.e., the inference about anatomy from chickens to hawks was stronger than the inference from tigers to hawks. But 2b was stronger than 2a, the inference about feeding behavior was stronger from tigers than from chickens. Presumably, these results obtained because people generated a causal model of the anatomical structure of hawks that is more similar to that of chickens than to that of tigers. Because most people do not know a lot of specifics about the anatomical structure of hawks and tigers, they had to infer it from causal principles (termed "overhypotheses" by Goodman, 1955; c.f. Shipley, 1993) about the origin of anatomical structure like the following:

Having the genetic code of species X ➔ Anatomical structure Y

In contrast, both tigers and hawks are known to be predators, and chickens are not, so causal knowledge about feeding habits

Hunting for food ➔ Behaviors effective for hunting. led to the opposite similarity relations.

Where do these causal models that are supposed to explain the observed facts come from? This is a question we will address in the next part of this paper where we confront the question of learning. What the current analysis shows is that the principles for generating causal models are generally more important for making inductions than causal models per se. Causal models are not necessarily waiting like ripe cherries to be picked; they generally have to be constructed for a particular purpose. The availability of abstract causal relations that can be applied to a variety of different cases is what allows us to do so.

Sloman (1994) found that statements increased belief in another statement if they shared an explanation. For example, telling people that boxers are not eligible for most health insurance plans increased their judgment of the probability that asbestos removers are not eligible either. The common explanation depended on the causal relations:

Increased health risk ➔ Cost to health insurers ➔ Denial of coverage

In contrast, telling people that boxers are more likely than average to develop a neurological disorder decreased their judged probability that asbestos removers are more likely than average to develop neurological disorders. For this predicate, the causal model for boxers (having to do with being struck on the head frequently) is different than the causal model for asbestos removers (having to do with inhaling a dangerous substance). The availability of a nonmatching explanation seemed to lead people to discount the plausibility of a statement (see also Sloman, 1997). More generally, the willingness to affirm a statement in these studies is influenced, if not governed, by the construction of a causal model in an attempt to explain the statement and thus determine its viability.

Notice how quickly and easily causal explanations come to mind in all these studies. A priori, constructing a causal explanation is far from trivial. It requires retrieving causal relations from a vast warehouse of facts in memory and stringing them together in a plausible way. The ease people exhibit in doing so suggests that the construction of causal models is a basic cognitive process.

C. CAUSAL ANALYSIS VERSUS COUNTING INSTANCES: THE INSIDE VERSUS THE OUTSIDE

Properties that vary less within a category should be more projectible within the category—induction should be more likely—than properties that are more variable. If you know one or more members of a category have a property and that the property does not vary much, then you can conclude that another instance of the category is likely to have it. Nisbett, Krantz, Jepson, and Kunda (1983) have shown that people are sensitive to this fact. They asked participants about the likelihood that all natives of a Pacific island are overweight given that one native is overweight. They also asked about the likelihood that all natives have dark skin given that one does. Presumably skin color is less variable than degree of obesity and, therefore, one would expect less induction (lower likelihood judgments) for weight than for skin color. This is just what they found.

But sensitivity to variability does not imply that participants represent variability directly. Information about variability could be implicit in a causal model. Namely, properties may be central to the degree that they participate in causal relations and centrality can serve as a proxy for variability. Properties that are causes of others must be less variable if their variation causes variation in those others. In the Nisbett et al. (1983) study, skin color may have been understood to be more closely regulated by causal relations than obesity because it is more closely tied to obligatory gene expression and less to optional eating habits. Therefore, skin color is more central and judged more projectible. Hadjichristidis, Sloman, Stevenson, and Over (1999) have shown that people are more willing to project a property that is more central over a less central property even when the properties are controlled for variability. An inside view of a category via an analysis of causal structure is sufficient and indeed more general than an outside view of a category via consideration of instances and how they differ.

D. CONCLUSIONS

Like some philosophers, some psychologists have returned to the view that induction is mediated by causal models, which are often generated online through the application of causal principles and abstract causal relations that have general applicability. Such causal models help to explain how people make inductive inferences when the inference can be conceived as a causal effect. In other cases, inference involves analogy: A predicate is applied to one category because it is known to apply to an analogous category. In such cases, the analogy seems to be between causal structures. Finally, causal models give a psychologically plausible way to think about why people sometimes show sensitivity to statistical information. Instead of assuming that people calculate statistics like measures of the variability of a property, the requisite information can be interpreted as a property's centrality in a causal model.

VI. Learning

In order to attain knowledge of the invariant structure of the world, we must decipher the ever-changing perceptual experience it gives rise to. As Mill (1843) presciently argued, we find order in the chaos of nature by attending to its variation. Speaking of our perception of the world, rather than our inferences about its causal structure, Gibson (1979) summarizes this view: "What is invariant does not emerge unequivocally except with a flux. The essentials become evident in the context of changing nonessentials." In the case of causality, the "changing nonessentials" are the patterns of observations, what is invariant is the causal structure. But how do we pass from this flux of perception to the invariants that underlie it?

A. COVARIATION-BASED THEORIES OF CAUSAL LEARNING

The common approach to this question is to present people with a learning problem where event types are pre-sorted into potential causes and effects, and to investigate how the strengths of putative cause-effect links are estimated. Most psychological models of causal learning, whether associative (e.g., Shanks & Dickinson, 1987; Shanks, 1995; Van Hamme & Wasserman, 1994) or rule-based (e.g., Allan, 1993; Cheng, 1997; Catena, Maldonado, & Cándido, 1998), assume that these strengths are computed on the basis of covariation data, but differ with respect to how people integrate the data.

Associative theorists build on the Humean idea that the patterns of regularity we experience lead us to form correspondent mental associations. Rather than simply tracking the constant conjunction of events, however, animals and humans appear to be sensitive to the contingencies between events, the degree to which one event predicts another. In the case of binary events the standard index for such contingencies is ΔP (Allan, 1980), which for cause C and event E is given by equation (1):

$$\Delta P = P(E|C) - P(E|\sim C) \quad (1)$$

A prominent class of associative theories (e.g., Shanks, 1995; Van Hamme & Wasserman, 1994) assume the operation of an error-driven learning mechanism such as the Rescorla–Wagner rule (1972). This incrementally updates associative strengths between event representations, and estimates ΔP at its equilibria (Danks, 2003). It is this strength of association between events that is supposed to determine judgments of the degree to which one event causes another. The associative theory is attractive because of its continuity with animal learning, the provision of a dynamic learning mechanism, and its ability to account for a variety of empirical phenomena (e.g., blocking, predictive validity, and overshadowing). However, while ΔP may be a suitable standard for judgments of contingency between events, it is not always suitable for judgments of causality. Cheng (1997) cites situations in which it is clearly unsuitable, such as ceiling effects where ΔP for a candidate cause is zero because the effect is constantly produced by an alternative cause $[P(E|C) = P(E|\sim C) = 1]$. In such a case, it seems appropriate to suspend judgment about the strength of the cause rather than assign it a value of zero. Furthermore, associative theories cannot account for various empirical phenomena. For example, numerous studies show that causal judgments vary systematically even when ΔP is held constant (Buehner & Cheng, 1997; Lober & Shanks, 2000; Perales & Shanks, 2003).

In contrast to this Humean approach and in response to the need to provide boundary conditions for a covariation model, Cheng (1997) proposed the power PC theory. This is a computational level, rule-based model inspired by philosophers such as Cartwright (1989) and Harre and Madden (1975), who claim that things in the world possess stable capacities or powers. According to the power PC theory, people posit "hidden" causal powers in order to interpret covariational information. Given an appropriate focal set, in which the causal factor to be assessed is independent in probability of other causes, causal power can be estimated via the relative frequencies of observable events. Cheng derives power equations for both generative and preventive causes. For a generative cause C of effect E the power equation is:

$$p = \Delta P/(1 - P(E| \sim C)) \qquad (2)$$

The theory assumes that people encode the appropriate event frequencies, and then compute an estimate of causal strength that approximates power p. As can be seen from equation (2), the power of C to cause E is proportional to ΔP, but normalized by the base rate of the effect $P(E|\sim C)$. This formulation avoids the ceiling and threshold effects that plague the ΔP index. For example, when the base rate of the effect is equal to one, the value of power is undefined, in accordance with the intuition that people suspend judgment in such cases. Formally, causal power corresponds to a particular parameterization of a causal network, a noisy-OR function (Glymour, 2001; Tenenbaum & Griffiths, 2001), that assumes that an effect can be produced by independent causal mechanisms. Novick and Cheng (2003) generalize the model to interactive causes.

Although the intuitions behind causal power are reasonable, and the independence assumptions plausible in many real world situations, the evidence that causal estimates approximate power is mixed. In particular, numerous studies show that when power is held constant, judgments shift with ΔP (Lober & Shanks, 2000; Perales & Shanks, 2003; Vallée-Tourangeau, Murphy, Drew, & Baker 1998). However, more recent experiments suggest that people are sensitive to the precise nature of the judgment question. In particular, a counterfactual probe question promotes responses that conform to power rather than ΔP (Collins & Shanks, 2003). This fits with a derivation of Pearl' (2000) showing that the power equation is a measure of the counterfactual sufficiency of a cause to produce an effect (the probability that an effect would have occurred if the cause had). Moreover, sensitivity to the type of question used to probe causal judgments suggests—contra both associative theory and power PC—that people can flexibly compute different measures of causal strength according to the test question.

In sum, both associative and power PC models focus on learning situations where event types are presorted into potential causes and effects (cf. Gopnik et al., in press; Glymour, 2001). Modulo certain constraints (e.g., on the power PC view alternate causes must be unconfounded), both induce causal strength estimates from covariation data.

B. STRUCTURE BEFORE STRENGTH

Neither approach, however, can fully describe the invariance that people are sensitive to because people know about much more than the causal strength of independent causes. Most importantly, people know a lot about complex causal structure itself. The causal systems that people encounter and understand can involve many variables and can combine in diverse ways. Sets of events can be joint causes of an effect, others can be alternative causes. Some variables might be necessary, others sufficient, some might be enabling conditions, others disabling. In the language of causal modeling theory, there are a wide variety of combination functions that can obtain. Moreover, there are an explosively large number of possible causal structures. So the problem of determining the strength of a particular cause is secondary most of the time, the primary problem is to determine the qualitative relations among variables. It is the structure of the world that must be described before quantitative estimation of particular relations is even attempted.

This is essentially the point made by Tenenbaum and Griffiths (2001) who argue that people's primary task is to detect whether a causal relation exists, and only secondarily to estimate the strength of this relation. Although their analysis concentrates on the question of whether or not a link exists between a potential cause and its effect, their intuition applies equally to the question of which variable is a cause and which an effect. The central point is that structural inferences are logically prior to strength estimations.

C. INSUFFICIENCY OF COVARIATIONAL DATA

Once our focus shifts to the problem of learning causal structure, it becomes apparent that covariational data alone will rarely be sufficient. For one, it will seldom lead to a unique causal model. Thus, on the basis of just covariational information about variables A, B, and C, one cannot distinguish between A → B → C and A ← B ← C because each model predicts that all three variables will be correlated and that A and C will be conditionally independent given B. Secondly, determining causal structure with confidence from correlational data alone typically requires a lot of data; both a large number of correlations to establish the causal structure, as well as a lot of data per correlation to know if the correlation is real or not. Such data are often unavailable, and when they are, people find them hard to process. Cognitive strategies and resource limitations make the data analysis problem difficult if not intractable. And in fact, people do struggle to learn causal structure from correlational data. A variety of studies show that no more than 30% of adult participants are able to learn even simple causal structures from observation of covariational data (Danks & McKenzie, 2003; Lagnado & Sloman, 2002; Sobel, 2003; Steyvers, Tenenbaum, Wagenmakers, & Blum, 2003). Despite these difficulties, people do learn causal structure, often on the basis of a small data set, and sometimes from just a single event.

D. Cues to Causal Structure

How then do people manage to acquire knowledge of causal structure, given that the correlational information supplied by our observations of the world is seldom sufficient? There appear to be several complimentary routes.

1. Prior Knowledge

One critical source of causal knowledge is instruction or education, especially when learning about complex and culturally embedded systems. This may reduce the number and complexity of causal beliefs we must discover ourselves, but it does not solve the basic problem of how we, or our instructors before us, acquire causal knowledge in the first place. Another rich source of causal information is analogy or boot-strapping from prior causal beliefs. We try to understand novel systems in terms of analogies or models drawn from systems we already understand. Again, however, analogy cannot furnish us with primary causal knowledge.

2. Prior Assumptions

Causal model theorists (e.g., Waldmann, 1996; Waldmann & Holyoak, 1992) claim that people make prior assumptions in order to learn from covariational data (see also Cheng, 1997). These include prior beliefs about causal directionality (e.g., which events are causes and which are effects), and prior beliefs about the temporal delays between cause and effect. In spirit this position resembles Kant's response to Hume: that we impose certain a priori constraints on our experience of the world. For example, Waldmann maintains, in opposition to associative theories, that people are sensitive to the causal status of cues and outcomes, and that this explains differences between predictive and diagnostic learning (e.g., Waldmann & Holyoak, 1992; Waldmann, 2000, 2001; but see Cobos, López, Caño, Almaraz, & Shanks, 2002, for an opposing view). Hagmayer and Waldmann (2002) show that the assumptions that people make about the temporal delays between events determine which events they pair together as cause and effect, and what they select as a possible cause.

3. Order of Information Receipt as Cue to Causal Order

In general, the temporal order of events in experience is a highly reliable cue for causal structure in the world because effects never precede causes. This correspondence suggests a useful heuristic: Use experiential order as a proxy for real world order. That is, if you perceive or produce an event, infer that any subsequent correlated changes in the environment are either effects of that cause, or effects of an earlier common cause of that event. Such a heuristic will prove extremely useful, but can also be misleading, for example, when you erroneously infer that you have caused an event just because it occurs immediately after you perform an unconnected action (e.g., the phone rings just as you switch the light on). Repeated trials, however, can usually identify the spurious nature of such associations.

4. Intervention (Experimentation)

Temporal order is an especially effective cue in the case of action because we experience our actions in real time and, therefore, their temporal relations to their effects are almost always veridical. In short, actions precede their effects in experience. When merely observing, causes generally also precede effects, although situations occur when we learn about an effect before we learn about its cause. This is the case whenever we use effects to diagnose causes (as doctors and scientists do frequently). Thus, acting on variables in the world affords us a critical cue to causal status. Further, this ability to exert control over certain variables in our environment permits us to control for possible confounding causes. By wiggling a putative cause and observing subsequent wiggling of an effect, we can rule out the possibility that these are both effects of an unknown common cause (thus performing an informal experiment). For example, a child who sporadically shakes a rattle can infer that it is their action that produces the associated sound. Thus, 'the whimsical nature of free manipulation replaces the statistical notion of randomized experimentation and serves to filter sounds produced by the child's actions from those produced by the uncontrolled environmental factors' (Pearl, 2000).

Intervention can also increase the difficulty of learning. First, it limits learning to the effects of the variables that are intervened on. When learning from observation, one can (at least in principle) learn something about the relations among all variables simultaneously. Second, as we saw in the discussion of the *do* operator, an intervention changes the causal model under investigation (it disconnects the intervened-on variable from its causes). This means that the learner is dealing with a different causal model on each occasion of learning. Third, if a variable value is set through an intervention, then that variable's normal probability of occurrence is hidden from view.

Nevertheless, experiments have demonstrated an advantage of intervention over observation (Lagnado & Sloman, 2002; Sobel, 2003; Steyvers et al., 2003). Lagnado and Sloman (2002) presented people with probabilistic data generated by a three variable causal chain (A → B → C) and asked them to select the correct underlying model from various candidate models. In one scenario people were told that two different chemicals (A and B) were somehow involved in the process of making a perfume C. Their main task was to figure out the causal roles of these two chemicals in the production process— for example, whether A caused both B and C separately, or A and B separately caused C, or B caused A which then caused C, and so on. There were two trial-by-trial learning conditions: participants either observed the values for all three variables, or were able to intervene to set the value for one of the variables (either A or B) prior to seeing the values for the other two. Although people found the task difficult in both conditions, interveners performed much better than observers, with the latter exhibiting a strong bias towards a model with independent causes (A → C ← B). Several recent studies using different paradigms (Sobel, 2003; Steyvers et al., 2003) and with young children (Gopnik et al., in press; Schulz, 2001; Schulz & Gopnik, 2001) have also found an advantage for intervention over observation.

5. Possible Factors Driving the Advantage of Intervention

The question arises why intervention facilitates learning in these experiments. One possibility is that intervention provides a critical temporal cue. But intervention has other potential advantages. For one, interveners can engage in systematic testing, and experimentation allows the generation of data that can discriminate between structures impossible to distinguish by observation alone. For example, observation of a correlation between two variables X and Y is insufficient to determine whether X causes Y or vice-versa. But interventions on these variables can discriminate: if you vary X and Y subsequently varies, then X causes Y; if Y does not vary, than either Y causes X, or they are both caused by an unspecified common cause. This in turn can be decided by varying Y. Another advantage is that the requirement on interveners to decide what intervention to make on each trial may enhance learning by focusing attention.

We ran a further set of studies (Lagnado & Sloman, 2003a) to try to discriminate among these factors. The possibility that the difference between intervention and observation resulted from an informational difference was ruled out by a condition in which observers saw the results of another person's interventions. Despite seeing identical data, this group performed far worse than interveners, and no different from the previous (unyoked) group of observers who had seen a representative sample of the probability distribution. The ability to conduct systematic testing and the need to engage in a decision were ruled out as explanations by the finding that interveners instructed to make prespecified interventions performed no worse than those who chose their own interventions.

6. Intervention Advantage Driven by Temporal Priority Cue

The one factor that can explain the results in all of our studies is the temporal priority cue present in the intervention but not the observation condition. An intervener first selected an intervention, and *then* viewed the values of other variables. People could exploit this cue by assuming that any changes in the values of variables following an intervention were effects of it. This contrasts with the observational case, in which all values were displayed simultaneously.

To test this idea, we ran a study in which the temporal order of information was either consistent (e.g., temporal order A, B, C) or inconsistent (e.g., A and B presented simultaneously, then C) with the correlational data from the correct chain model. Overall, we saw no difference between intervention and observation, but people in the temporally consistent condition outperformed those in the temporally inconsistent one (and performed better than interveners in all previous studies). This supports the idea that temporal cues drive the advantage of intervention. Changes following an intervention are interpreted as effects of the intervention.

7. Learning in a Dynamic Situation

Our findings are consistent with the claim that people struggle to learn complex networks (Waldmann & Martignon, 1998), especially in highly probabilistic environments. In contrast to the discrete trial-based approach paradigmatic in this field, we have also used a novel causal learning paradigm, in which people dynamically manipulated variables online in a causal system. Variables were controlled directly and their effects observed immediately. Even with complex networks people were much better at inferring causal structure when they were able to intervene (Lagnado & Sloman, 2003b). It appears that the dynamic nature of the display and of people's interaction with the system facilitates quick detection of the relevant dependencies. Moreover, once they had established these dependencies, people were able to select additional interventions that allowed them to infer unique structures.

E. CONCLUSIONS

The value of temporal order may have to do with the direct experience of causality. That is, people might learn a lot from the temporal order of cues because it makes their experience at the time of learning isomorphic to the functioning of the actual causal system. Alternatively, temporal order might simply provide a highly informative cue. Knowing that X comes before Y is very suggestive that X causes Y and it is a fact that need only be experienced once or a small number of times (depending on the noise in the system). Temporal information greatly reduces the required sample size to learn. At this point, the experiments have not been run that would decide between these two accounts of learning from temporal data.

VII. Discussion

The human ability to learn to predict and control a range of environments is striking. Prediction and control come from knowing what to manipulate to achieve an effect and how to perform the manipulation. When manipulations are dangerous or consume substantial resources, the ability to perform the manipulation mentally can be invaluable. Causal models are intended to represent the knowledge necessary to perform this function.

We are by no means the first to question the High Church cognitive science view that high-level cognitive capacities like causal reasoning, counterfactual thought, probability judgment, induction, and language can be reduced to abstract logical operations. Our particular contribution to the critique of this view is to show the importance of agency and action in human thought. Our charge has been to show the value of causal modeling in a variety of domains, a form of analysis that depends critically on how people understand the effects of action and on the distinction between action and observation.

If we are right that the major source of invariance in human experience are the causal principles that generate the mechanisms that govern what we observe, then causal structure seems the place to look to discover what people are sensitive to. The existence of a coherent and powerful theoretical framework for causal analysis gives cognitive scientists a foothold on representing that structure.

Acknowledgments

This work was funded by NASA grant NCC2–1217. Clark Glymour and Brian Ross made invaluable comments on a prior draft. Address correspondence to: Steven Sloman, Cognitive and Linguistic Sciences, Brown University, Box 1978, Providence, RI 02912 (email: Steven_Sloman@brown.edu).

References

Ahn, W.-k. (1998). Why are different features central for natural kinds and artifacts? The role of causal status in determining feature centrality. *Cognition, 69*, 135–178.

Ahn, W.-k., Kim, N. S., Lassaline, M. E., & Dennis, M. J. (2000). Causal status as a determinant of feature centrality. *Cognitive Psychology, 41*, 361–416.

Ajzen, I. (1977). Intuitive theories of events and the effects of base-rate information on prediction. *Journal of Personality and Social Psychology, 35*, 303–314.

Allan, L. G. (1980). A note on measurements of contingency between two binary variables in judgment tasks. *Bulletin of the Psychonomic Society, 15*, 147–149.

Allan, L. G. (1993). Human contingency judgments: Rule-based or associative? *Psychological Bulletin, 114*, 435–448.

Anderson, C. A., Lepper, M. R., & Ross, L. (1980). The perseverance of social theories: The role of explanation in the persistence of discredited information. *Journal of Personality & Social Psychology, 39*, 1037–1049.

Andersson, B. (1986). The experiential gestalt of causation: A common core to pupil's preconceptions in science. *European Journal of Scientific Education, 8*, 155–171.

Bloom, P., & Markson, L. (1998). Intention and analogy in children's naming of pictorial representations. *Psychological Science, 9*, 200–204.

Brown, R., & Fish, D. (1983). The psychological causality implicit in language. *Cognition, 14*, 237–273.

Buehner, M. J., & Cheng, P. W. (1997). Causal induction: The power PC theory versus the Rescorla-Wagner theory. In M. G. Shafto & P. Langley (Eds.), *Proceedings of the nineteenth annual conference of the Cognitive Science Society.* (pp. 55–60). Mahwah, NJ: Erlbaum.

Cartwright, N. (1989). *Nature's capacities and their measurement*. Oxford: Clarendon Press.

Catena, A., Maldonado, A., & Cándido, A. (1998). The effect of the frequency of judgment and the type of trials on covariation learning. *Journal of Experimental Psychology: Human Perception and Performance, 24*, 481–495.

Cheng, P. W. (1997). From covariation to causation: A causal power theory. *Psychological Review, 104*, 367–405.

Cobos, P. L., López, F. J., Caño, A., Almaraz, J., & Shanks, D. R. (2002). Mechanisms of predictive and diagnostic causal induction. *Journal of Experimental Psychology: Animal Behavior Processes, 28*, 331–346.

Collins, D. J., & Shanks, D. R. (2003). Conformity to the power PC theory of causal induction depends on type of probe question. Manuscript submitted for publication.

Danks, D. (2003). Equilibria of the Rescorla-Wagner model. *Journal of Mathematical Psychology, 47*, 109–121.

Danks, D., & McKenzie, C. (2003). Learning complex causal structures. *Cognitive Science.* Submitted for publication.

Diesendruck, G., Markson, L., & Bloom, P. (2003). Children's reliance on creator's intent in extending names for artifacts. *Psychological Science, 14*, 164–168.

diSessa, A. A. (1993). Towards an epistemology of physics. *Cognition and Instruction, 10*, 105–225.

Driver, R., Guesne, E., & Tiberghien, A. (1993). Some features of children's ideas and their implications for teaching. In R. Driver, E. Guesne, & A. Tiberghien (Eds.), *Children's ideas in science.* (pp. 193–201). Buckingham, United Kingdom: Open University.

Edgington, D. (1995). On conditionals. *Mind, 104*, 235–329.

Gelman, S. A., & Hirschfeld, L. A. (1999). How biological is essentialism? In D. L. Medin & S. Atran (Eds.), *Folkbiology.* Cambridge, MA: MIT Press.

Gibson, J. J. (1979). *The ecological approach to visual perception*. Boston, MA: Houghton Mifflin.

Glymour, C. (2001). *The mind's arrows.* Cambridge, MA: The MIT Press.

Goodman, N. (1955). *Fact, fiction, and forecast.* Cambridge, MA: Harvard University Press.

Gopnik, A., Glymour, C., Sobel, D. M., Schulz, L. E., Kushnir, T., & Danks, D. (in press). A theory of causal learning in children: Causal maps and Bayes nets. *Psychological Review.*

Gopnik, A., Sobel, D. M., Schulz, L. E., & Glymour, C. (2001). Causal learning mechanisms in very young children: Two, three, and four-year-olds infer causal relations from patterns of variation and covariation. *Developmental Psychology, 37*, 620–629.

Hadjichristidis, C., Sloman, S. A., Stevenson, R. J., & Over, D. E. (1999). "Inside Information" Centrality and Property Induction. *Proceedings of the Twenty-First Annual Conference of the Cognitive Science Society*. Vancouver, Canada.

Hagmayer, Y., & Waldmann, M. R. (2002). How temporal assumptions influence causal judgments. *Memory & Cognition, 30*, 1128–1137.

Hampton, J. A. (1982). A demonstration of intransitivity in natural categories. *Cognition, 12*, 151–164.

Harre, R., & Madden, E. H. (1975). *Causal powers: A theory of natural necessity*. Totwa, NJ: Rowman & Littlefield.

Hoffman, C., & Tchir, M. A. (1990). Interpersonal verbs and dispositional adjectives: The psychology of causality embodied in language. *Journal of Personality and Social Psychology, 58*, 765–778.

Hume, D. (1748). *An enquiry concerning human understanding*. Oxford: Clarendon.

Hunt, E., & Minstrell, J. (1994). A cognitive approach to the teaching of physics. In K. McGilly (Ed.), *Classroom lessons: Integrating cognitive theory and classroom practice*. (pp. 51–74). Cambridge, MA: MIT Press.

Jones, E. E., & Harris, V. A. (1967). The attribution of attitudes. *Journal of Experimental Social Psychology, 3*, 1–24.

Keil, F. C. (1989). *Concepts, kinds, and cognitive development*. Cambridge, MA: MIT Press.

Keil, F. C. (1995). The growth of causal understanding of natural kinds. In D. Sperber, D. Premack, & A. J. Premack (Eds.), *Causal cognition: A multidisciplinary approach*. (pp. 234–262). New York: Oxford University Press.

Kemler Nelson, D. G., Russell, R., Duke, N., & Jones, K. (2000). Two-year olds will name artifacts by their function. *Child Development, 71*, 1271–1288.

Lagnado, D. A., & Sloman, S. A. (2002). Learning causal structure. In W. Gray & C. D. Schunn (Eds.), *Proceedings of the twenty-fourth annual conference of the cognitive science society*. (pp. 560–565). Hillsdale, NJ: Erlbaum.

Lagnado, D. A., & Sloman, S. A. (2003a). The advantages of intervention in causal learning. Manuscript in preparation.

Lagnado, D. A., & Sloman, S. A. (2003b). Dynamic learning of causal structure. Manuscript in preparation.

Lakoff, G. (1987). *Women, fire, and dangerous things: What categories reveal about the mind*. Chicago, IL: University of Chicago Press.

Lewis, D. (1973). *Counterfactuals*. Oxford: Basil Blackwell.

Lewis, D. (1976). Probabilities of conditionals and conditional probabilities. *Philosophical Review, 85*, 297–315.

Lewis D. (1986). *Philosophical papers*. Vol. 2. New York: Oxford University Press.

Lipton, P. (1991). *Inference to the best explanation*. New York: Routledge.

Lober, K., & Shanks, D. R. (2000). Is causal induction based on causal power? Critique of Cheng (1997). *Psychological Review, 107*, 195–212.

Mackie, J. L. (1980). *The cement of the universe: A study of causation*. Oxford: Clarendon.

Markman, E. M., Horton, M. S., & McLanahan, A. G. (1980). Classes and collections: Principles of organization in the learning of hierarchical relations. *Cognition, 8*, 227–241.

Matan, A., & Carey, S. (2001). Developmental changes within the core of artifact concepts. *Cognition, 78*, 1–26.

Medin, D. L., Coley, J. D., Storms, G., & Hayes, B. (2003). A relevance theory of induction. *Psychonomic Bulletin and Review, 10*, 517–532.

Mill, J. S. (1843). *A system of logic, ratiocinative and inductive: Being a connected view of the principles of evidence and the methods of scientific evidence.* New York, NY: Harper.

Miller, R. W. (1987). *Fact and method.* Princeton, NJ: Princeton University Press.

Millikan, R. G. (1998). A common structure for concepts of individuals, stuffs, and real kinds: More Mama, more milk, and more mouse. *Behavioral and Brain Sciences, 9*, 55–100.

Mochon, D., & Sloman, S. A. (2003). Causal models frame interpretation of mathematical equations. Manuscript submitted for publication.

Morris, M. W., & Larrick, R. (1995). When one cause casts doubt on another: A normative analysis of discounting in causal attribution. *Psychological Review, 102*, 331–355.

Morris, M. W., & Murphy, G. (1990). Converging operations on a basic level in event taxonomies. *Memory & Cognition, 18*, 407–418.

Nisbett, R. E., Krantz, D. H., Jepson, D. H., & Kunda, Z. (1983). The use of statistical heuristics in everyday inductive reasoning. *Psychological Review, 90*, 339–363.

Novick, L. R., & Cheng, P. W. (in press). Assessing interactive causal influence. *Psychological Review.*

Nosofsky, R. M. (1984). Choice, similarity, and the context theory of classification. *Journal of Experimental Psychology: Learning, Memory, and Cognition, 10*, 104–114.

Pearl, J. (2000). *Causality: Models, reasoning and inference.* New York: Cambridge University Press.

Perales, J. C., & Shanks, D. R. (2003). Normative and descriptive accounts of the influence of power and contingency on causal judgment. *Quarterly Journal of Experimental Psychology, 56*, 977–1007.

Rehder, B., & Hastie, R. (2001). Causal knowledge and categories: The effects of causal beliefs on categorization, induction, and similarity. *Journal of Experimental Psychology: General, 130*, 323–360.

Reif, F., & Allen, S. (1992). Cognition for interpreting scientific concepts: A study of acceleration. *Cognition and Instruction, 9*, 1–44.

Reiner, M., Slotta, J. D., Chi, M. T. H., & Resnick, L. B. (2000). "Naïve physics reasoning" a commitment to substance-based conceptions. *Cognition and Instruction, 18*, 1–34.

Rescorla, R. A., & Wagner, A. R. (1972). A theory of Pavlovian conditioning: Variations in the effectiveness of reinforcement and nonreinforcement. In A. H. Black & W. F. Prokasy (Eds.), *Classical conditioning II: Current theory and research.* (pp. 64–99). New York: Appleton-Century-Crofts.

Rips, L. J. (1989). Similarity, typically, and categorization. In S. Vosniadou & A. Ortony (Eds.), *Similarity and analogical reasoning.* New York: Cambridge University Press.

Rips, L. (2001). Necessity and natural categories. *Psychological Bulletin, 127*, 827–852.

Rosch, E. (1973). On the internal structure of perceptual and semantic categories. In T. E. Moore (Ed.), *Cognitive development and the acquisition of language.* New York: Academic Press.

Ross, B. H. (1999). Post-classification category use: the effects of learning to use categories after learning to classify. *Journal of Experimental Psychology: Learning, Memory, and Cognition, 25*, 743–757.

Ross, B. H., & Murphy, G. L. (1999). Food for thought: cross-classification and category organization in a complex real-world domain. *Cognitive Psychology, 38*, 495–553.

Ross, L., & Anderson, C. A. (1982). Shortcomings in the attribution process: On the origins and maintenance of erroneous social assessments. In D. Kahneman, P. Slovic, & A. Tversky (Eds.), *Judgment under uncertainty: Heuristics and biases.* Cambridge, MA: Cambridge University Press.

Russell, B. (1912). On the notion of cause. *Proceedings of the Aristotelian Society, 13*, 1–26.

Schulz, L. (2001). Do-calculus: Inferring causal relations from observations and interventions. *Paper presented at the Cognitive Development Society Meeting.*

Schulz, L., & Gopnik, A. (2001). Inferring causal relations from observations and interventions. *Paper presented at a Causal Inference Workshop: the Neural Information Processing Systems Meeting,* Whistler, B. C.

Shanks, D. R. (1995). *The psychology of associative learning.* Cambridge, MA: Cambridge University Press.

Shanks, D. R., & Dickinson, A. (1987). Associative accounts of causality judgment. In G. H. Bower (Ed.), *The psychology of learning and motivation: Advances in research and theory, 21,* 229–261. San Diego, CA: Academic Press.

Sherin, B. L. (2001). How students understand physics equations. *Cognition and Instruction, 19,* 479–541.

Shipley, E. F. (1993). Categories, hierarchies, and induction. In D. L. Medin (Ed.), *The psychology of learning and motivation, 30,* 265–301. San Diego, CA: Academic Press.

Simons, D. J., & Keil, F. C. (1995). An abstract to concrete shift in the development of biological thought: The insides story. *Cognition, 56,* 129–163.

Smith, E. E., & Medin, D. L. (1981). *Categories and concepts.* Cambridge, MA: Harvard University Press.

Sloman, S. A. (1994). When explanations compete: The role of explanatory coherence on judgments of likelihood. *Cognition, 52,* 1–21.

Sloman, S. A. (1997). Explanatory coherence and the induction of properties. *Thinking and Reasoning, 3,* 81–110.

Sloman, S. A. (1998). Categorical inference is not a tree: The myth of inheritance hierarchies. *Cognitive Psychology, 35,* 1–33.

Sloman, S. A. (2003). Casual models can be used to predict base-rate neglect. *Proceedings of the Twenty-Fifth Annual Conference of the Cognitive Science Society.* Hillsdale, NJ: Erlbaum.

Sloman, S. A., & Lagnado, D. (2002). Do we "do"? Manuscript submitted for publication.

Sloman, S. A., Love, B. C., & Ahn, W. (1998). Feature centrality and conceptual coherence. *Cognitive Science, 22,* 189–228.

Sloman, S. A., & Malt, B. C. (in press). Artifacts are not ascribed essences, nor are they treated as belonging to kinds. *Language and Cognitive Processes.*

Sobel, D. (2003). Watch it, do it, or watch it done. Manuscript submitted for publication.

Spirtes, P., Glymour, C., & Scheines, R. (1993). *Causation, prediction, and search.* New York: Springer-Verlag.

Stalnaker, R. C. (1968). A theory of conditionals. In N. Rescher (Ed.), *Studies in Logical Theory, American Philosophical Quarterly.* monograph series.

Steyvers, M., Tenenbaum, J. B., Wagenmakers, E. J., & Blum, B. (2003). Inferring causal networks from observations and interventions. Manuscript submitted for publication.

Strevens, M. (2001). The essentialist aspect of naive theories. *Cognition, 74,* 149–175.

Tenenbaum, J. B., & Griffiths, T. L. (2001). Structure learning in human causal induction. In T. K. Leen, T. G. Dietterich, & V. Tresp (Eds.), *Advances in Neural Information Processing Systems. 13.* Cambridge, MA: MIT Press.

Tversky, A., & Kahneman, D. (1980). Causal schemas in judgments under uncertainty. In M. Fishbein (Ed.), *Progress in Social Psychology.* Hillsdale, NJ: Lawrence Erlbaum.

Tversky, A., & Kahneman, D. (1982). Evidential impact of base rates. In D. Kahneman, P. Slovic, & A. Tversky (Eds.), *Judgment under uncertainty: Heuristics and biases.* Cambridge, MA: Cambridge University Press.

Tversky, B., & Hemenway, K. (1984). Objects, parts, and categories. *Journal of Experimental Psychology: General, 113,* 169–193.

Vallée-Tourangeau, F., Murphy, R. A., Drew, S., & Baker, A. G. (1998). Judging the importance of constant and variable candidate causes: A test of the Power PC theory. *Quarterly Journal of Experimental Psychology, 51A*, 65–84.

Van Hamme, L. J., & Wasserman, E. A. (1994). Cue competition in causality judgments: The role of nonpresentation of compound stimulus elements. *Learning and Motivation, 25*, 127–151.

Waldmann, M. R. (1996). Knowledge-based causal induction. In D. R. Shanks, K. J. Holyoak, & D. L. Medin (Eds.), *The psychology of learning and motivation, Vol. 34: Causal learning.* (pp. 47–88). San Diego, CA: Academic Press.

Waldmann, M. R. (2000). Competition among causes but not effects in predictive and diagnostic learning. *Journal of Experimental Psychology: Learning, Memory, and Cognition, 26*, 53–76.

Waldmann, M. R. (2001). Predictive versus diagnostic causal learning: Evidence from an overshadowing paradigm. *Psychonomic Bulletin & Review, 8*, 600–608.

Waldmann, M. R., & Holyoak, K. J. (1992). Predictive and diagnostic learning within causal models: Asymmetries in cue competition. *Journal of Experimental Psychology: General, 121*, 222–236.

Waldmann, M. R., & Martignon, L. (1998). A Bayesian network model of causal learning. In M. A. Gernsbacher & S. J. Derry (Eds.), *Proceedings of the Twentieth Annual Conference of the Cognitive Science Society.* (pp. 1102–1107). Mahwah, NJ: Erlbaum.

Wells, G. L. (1992). Naked statistical evidence of liability: Is subjective probability enough? *Journal of Personality and Social Psychology, 62*, 739–752.

White, B. Y. (1993). Thinkertools: Causal models, conceptual change, and science education. *Cognition and Instruction, 10*, 1–100.

Wittgenstein, L. (1953). *Philosophical investigations.* New York: Macmillan.

INDEX

A

Accessibility, 18–25, 21f, 23f, 25f
Activation, 36, 38–40, 57–58
   aphasia and, 80–88, 83t, 85f, 86f, 87f
   interactions and, 70–72
   lexical access and, 67–70, 77–80, 88–90, 89t
   lexical bias effect and, 72–74
   malapropisms and, 74–77
   mixed-error effect and, 74–77
Adjectives, 45, 62
Affordances, 217–218
Agrammatism, 91–92, 92n5
Agreement(s), 109–110, 139–140. *See also* Marking; Meaning; Morphing
   controllers, 124–125
   distributivity/semantic integration in, 116–119, 117f
   extrinsic/intrinsic control in, 119–122
   kinds of, 114–116
   notional numbers and, 126–28, 126t, 127f
   plural, 119
   reaching, 114–116
   representation and, 130–133
   targets, 116, 122–123
Alzheimer's disease, 154
Amodal propositions, 36–37, 56–57
Amygdala, 52
Analogy, 8
"The analysis of sentence production," 63
Analysis of variance (ANOVA), 15–18, 18f, 20, 21f, 24–25
Anophor resolution, 5–6, 58
Aphasia
   activation and, 80–88, 83t, 85f, 86f, 87f
   agrammatic, 91–92, 92n5
   anomic, 92
   errors, 80–81
   interactive two-step model and, 80–88, 82n3, 83t, 85f, 86f, 87f
   lexical-phonological feedback and, 80–88, 83t, 85f, 86f, 87f
Aristotle, 49
Arterberry, M. E., 229
Articles, 51, 65
Articulation, 40–41, 64
Associative network theory. *See* Network theory, associative
Associative theory, 313–314
Assumptions, 229, 291, 314, 316
Atkinson and Shiffrin model, 146
Atkinson, R. C., 146
Attention, 181–182
   executive, 149–150, 163–164, 176–78, 177f
Attentional frames, 40, 41
Attractions, 123–124, 126–128, 126t, 127f
Attributions, 301–302
Averaging, 233

B

Baars, B. J., 72, 73–74
Bacon, Francis, 261, 284
Baddeley, A. D., 146–147
Barsalou, L.W., 6
Behavior, 301–302, 302n2
Beliefs, 288
Bezic curves, 239, 246
Bias, 262–263, 261n1, 283
   factor, 264

Bias (*Continued*)
  response, 249
  sample-related, 266
Biederman, I, 207, 214
Bingham, G. P., 236–237, 238
Bock, J. K., 118, 132, 135
Bornstein, M. H., 229
Brain, 35, 52, 71
  activity, 112
  damage, 82
  hemocynamic responses of, 79
  prefrontal cortex of, 186–187, 190–193
  WMC and, 190–192
Breedin, S. D., 93–94, 94f
Bunting, M. F., 163

C

Cantor, J., 157–158
Capacity Condition, 272
Carpenter, P. A., 150–152, 159
Carreiras, M., 118, 132
Cascading, 79
Cat, 69, 69n1
Categorization
  of events, 228, 232–238, 233f
  models, 231
  of objects, 228
  perceptual, 227
Causal analysis, 311–312
Causal learning
  covariation-based theories of, 312–314, 315
  intervention and, 317–319
  strength/structure in, 314–316
Causal models, 291–293, 292f, 319
  base-rate neglect and, 297–300
  framework of, 303–304
  induction and, 308–312
Causal relations, 287–291, 307–308
Causation, 49
Cause, 50, 301
Change, rate of, 229
Characters, 8
Cheng, P. W., 313
Closed class, 122
Cognition, 208
  complex, 145
  correlation, 156–167, 165f
  higher-order, 158, 203
  models of, 203

perceptions and, 201–203, 219–220
Cohen, Jonathan D., 190, 191, 192
Coley, J. D., 309
Comprehenders, 49, 54–55
Comprehension. *See also* Language comprehension
  amodal models of, 51
  linguistic input and, 56
  measures of, 151
  perceptual representations during, 53–55
  phonological lexical feedback and, 70–71
  scene, 206, 215–222, 216f
  text, 55
Conan, Sir Arthur, 47
Conceptualizations, 64
Concord, 129, 137
Concordance hypothesis, 48, 50
Conflicts, 186, 192
Connectionist learning theory, 64, 102
  learning-based model and, 95–101, 99t
  neuroimaging/neuropsychological evidence and, 91–95, 91n4, 94f
Consistency parameter, 249
Consistency, perception of, 283–284
  choices/comparisons/confidences and, 269–271, 273–276, 275n2
  correlations and, 278–283
  experimental evidence for, 265–283
  populations and, 266, 267–268
  primacy effect and, 276–278
  statistical argument for, 263–265, 263n1, 265f
  variability and, 267–280
  WMC and, 271–273
Consonant exchanges, 72
Construals, 36, 38, 43
  components of, 42–46, 42f, 57–58
  definition of, 40–41
  distributive, 118
  information captured by, 56
  perspective, 44–45
Content items, 91, 93
Continuity Assumption, 48, 56, 82
Control, 181, 287
  executive, 185–190, 188f
  extrinsic/intrinsic, 119–122
Controllers, 124–125. *See also* Morphing
Conway, A. R. A., 163, 180–181
Correlations, 263–265, 263n1, 265f, 283
  cognition and, 156–167, 165f
  perception of, 278–283

product-moment, 266
  sampling size and, 281–283
  WMC and, 279–281, 279n3
Counterfactuals, 291, 295–296
  probabilistic judgment and, 297–305
Cowan, N., 163
Crowder, R. G., 146
Cue(s), 228
  competition, 97, 98
  lexical/syntactic, 51
  linguistic, 48, 51
Curiel, J. M., 29
Cuttell Culture Fair Test, 168
Cutting, J. C., 135

D

Dahan, D., 53
Daneman, M., 150–152
Dell, G. S., 72, 95–97, 96f, 99–101, 99t
Delta rule, 97
Depression, 153
Derivative hypothesis, 27
Dimensions, vertical, 211
Discrete model, 68–69, 75–76
  two-step, 77–78, 78f
Dis-integration, 138–139, 138n1
Distance, 44
  equation, 231
  Euclidean, 245
  event categorization and, 247–255, 248f, 249t, 250f, 250t, 251f, 251t, 252f, 253t, 254f, 254t, 255f
  Minkowski, 231
  trajectories, 232, 233f, 239–240, 240f
Distance, spatial, 6–8, 7f
  semantic association and, 16–18, 18f
  situation models and, 12–16, 15f, 26
Distractors, 53, 183
Distributivity, 116–119, 117f
Dutch language, 131, 137, 138
  agreements in, 117–118
  numbers in, 121, 133

E

Editing, 74
Editors, 72
Effects, 50
Emotions, 52

Encoding, 262
Engle, R. W., 152, 157, 180–183, 187
English language, 110, 111, 140
  agreements in, 117–118, 139
  numbers in, 121
  syntax, 139
ERP. *See* Event-related brain potentials
Errors
  exchange, 73
  mixed, 74–77
  naming, 83t, 84, 86–87, 86f, 87f
  occurrence of, 82
  patient, 82
  semantic, 76, 76n2
  of speakers, 82
  word, 86
Essentialism, 307
Event-related brain potentials (ERP), 79–80, 94
Events, 54, 256–257
  amplitudes of, 238
  categorization of, 228, 233–238, 233f, 247–255, 248f, 249t, 250f, 250t, 251f, 251t, 252f, 253t, 254f, 254t, 255f
  identify, 234–235
  representation of, 229–231, 230f
  segments and, 235
  similarity of, 231–232, 239–247, 240f, 242f, 243f, 244f, 245f, 246f, 247f
  variables and, 238
Exchanging, 67
Exec-Attn factor, 175–176, 177f
Experiencer, 35
Explaining away, 301
Explanations, 287, 300–302
Eye, 41, 44, 52, 166–167

F

Fan effect, 180
Feature detector, 208–209
Fixating, 47
fMRI. *See* Functional magnetic resonance imaging
Focal entity, 49
Force dynamics, theory of, 57
Formulations, 64
French language, 121
Functional magnetic resonance imaging (fMRI), 79–80, 95
Functional webs, 38–39, 40–41

Function-content hypothesis, 64–67, 102
  learning-based model and, 95–101, 99t
  neuroimaging/neuropsychological evidence and, 91–95, 91n4, 94f
Functions, 91, 93, 93n6, 305–306

G

Garrett, Merrill, 63–65, 67, 101–102
GCM. *See* Generalized Context of Model
Gender
  grammatical, 79, 133, 137
  in languages, 119–122
  of nouns, 129
General fluid intelligence (gF), 168, 177, 178–179
Generalizations, 201, 256
Generalized Context of Model (GCM), 231–232, 232
Geons, 211, 212, 214
German language, 121
Gestaltists, 207–208
gF. *See* General fluid intelligence
Gibson, J. J., 312
Glenberg, A. M., 52
Glymour, Clark, 295n1
Goal(s), 29
  active, 8–9, 18–25, 21f, 23f, 25f
  completed, 9, 18–25, 21f, 23f, 25f
  considered-but-postponed, 19
  failed, 9
  momentary, 10, 18
  postponed, 9, 18–25, 21f, 23f, 25f
  protoganist, 9
  relevance, 11t, 12–18, 15f, 18f, 26
  top level, 19
Goodness-of-fit statistics, 250t, 251t, 253t
Gordon, J. K., 95–97, 96f, 99–101, 99t
Graesser, A. C., 29
Grammar, 113
Grammatical affixes, 65
Grammatical agreement, 109
Grammatical functions, 64–65
Grammatical plurality, 125
Griffiths, T. L., 315
Groups, functional, 207, 218

H

Harris, V. A., 301
Hartsuiker, R. J., 115–116
Haskell, T. R., 131

Havinga, J., 69
Hayes, B., 309
Head rotations, 44
Hill, H., 235–236
Hilliard, H. E., 29
Hitch, G., 146–147
Holyoak, K. J., 220
The Hound of the Baskervilles (Conan), 47
Huijbers, P., 68
Hume, D., 307
Humean idea, 313
Hummel, J. E., 207, 214, 220
Humphreys, K. R., 74

I

Ideomotor theory of action, 50
Immersed Experiencer Framework (IEF)
  empirical evidence consistent with, 51–55
  language comprehension and, 36–37, 45, 49, 57–58
Independencies, stable/unstable, 293
Independent-levels hypothesis, 64–67
Induction, 306–310
Inferences, 10–12, 11t
  learning and, 294
  reasoning and, 294
  relational, 204–205
Inhibitions, 183–184
Integration, 36, 38
  definition of, 46
  distance and, 230
  factors influencing, 48–51, 57–58
  human experience and, 48–49
  linguistic cues and, 51
  overlap and, 49–50
  predictability and, 50–51
  of time, 236
  transition types and, 46–48
Integrator model, 241, 249–250, 250f, 250t, 255
  modified, 242–243, 242f, 243f
  standard, 246, 256
  weighted, 243–246, 244f, 245f, 246f, 247f, 250–255, 251f, 251t, 252f, 253t, 254f, 255f, 256
Interactions
  activation and, 70–72
  lexical access and, 90–91
  lexical-phonological feedback and, 68f, 72–73
  pattern of, 282

Interactive feedback, 70–72
Interactive two-step model, 68, 71–72, 75
   aphasia and, 80–88, 82n3, 83t, 85f, 86f, 87f
Interference
   conditions, 183–184
   proactive/reactive, 164
   retrieval, 180–182
Interventions, 294–295, 295f, 295n1, 317–319
Intonation units, 40
Intuitions, 314
Italian language, 117–118

J

Japanese language, 114, 139
Jepson, D. H., 311
JIM model of object recognition, 207, 208, 210, 213–214, 213f
Jones, E. E., 301
Judgments, 228–229, 262
   likelihood, 307
   object of, 298
   partial *vs.* full information on, 269–270
   of populations, 267–269
   probabilistic, 297–305
Just, M. A., 159

K

Kahneman, D., 297–298
Kane, M. J., 181–182, 186–187
Kareev, Y., 274, 279, 280
Kaschak, M. P., 52
Kempen, G., 68
Kintsch, W., 38, 49
Kintsch's construction-integration model, 40
Knowledge, 204, 312, 316
Krantz, D. H., 311
Kunda, Z., 311

L

Lagnado, D., 303, 317–318
Lakoff, G., 57
Langacker, R. W., 48
Langston, M. C., 3, 29
Language(s), 48, 57, 137
   acquisition, 63
   definition of, 36
   distributivity and, 117–119
   elements, 288–289

   gender in, 119–122
   morphology and, 118
   performance, 122
   situations and, 41
Language comprehension, 63. *See also* Activation; Construals; Integration
   action's role in, 52–53
   activation and, 36, 38–40
   difficulty, 51
   findings, 35–37
   IEF and, 36–37, 38–39, 38t
   other frameworks of, 37–38
   process, 38–39, 38t, 57–58
   violations of, 110
Language production, 63. *See also* Activation; Lexical-phonological feedback
   connectionist learning theory and, 91–95, 94f
   function-content and, 91–95, 94f
   production/speech errors and, 64–67
Larrick, R., 302
Learning, 319–320
   casualty levels and, 296–297
   causal, 311–320
   causal invariance in, 287–291
   causal models and, 289–294, 292f
   counterfactual/probabilistic judgment and, 297–305
   error-based, 96–97
   explanation discounting and, 300–302
   induction and, 308–312
   inferences and, 294
   language use and, 305–312
   meaning of numbers in, 111
   representation and, 294–296, 295f
Learning and Motivation (Garrett), 63, 102
Lemma, 69, 101–102
   access, 68, 68f, 81, 84–85, 85f
   errors, 76, 76n2
   target, 81
Levelt, W. J. M., 69
Lexical acces
   interaction and, 90–91
   learning-based model of, 95–101, 99t
   phonological neighborhoods, 88–91, 89t
   time-course studies of, 77–80, 78f
   two-step theories of, 67–69, 68f
Lexical bias effect, 72–74
Lexical-phonological feedback, 67
   aphasia and, 80–88, 83t, 85f, 86f, 87f

Lexical-phonological feedback (*Continued*)
  interaction and, 68f, 72–73
  lexical bias effect and, 72–74, 82
  malapropisms and, 74–77
  mixed-error effect and, 74–77
Linguists, cognitive, 51
LISA model, 215, 216f
Location, 48–49, 211
Logic, 301–302
  propositional, 288–289
Long-term memory. *See* Memory, long-term
LTM. *See* Memory, long-term

M

MacDonald, M. C., 128, 131
MacKay, D. G., 72, 73–74
Magliano, J. P., 3, 29
Magneto-encephalography (MEG), 79–80, 95
Mak, B. S., 228
Malapropisms, 74
  lexical-phonological feedback and, 74–77
  occurrence of, 75–77, 79, 81
  syntactic category effects in, 84–88, 85f, 86f, 87f
Marginal Distribution, 280
Markers, grammatical, 45
Marking, 109, 138
  agreement and, 123–129, 126t, 127f
  hypothesis, 125–129, 127f
  meaning to, 112–113
  to morphing, 113–114
  number, 134–135
Marking-and-morphing (M&M) approach, 116, 128, 129
Markov-equivalent, 293
Maximal input hypothesis, 115–116
McConnell, D. S., 238
McNamara, D. S., 161
Mean Velocity Weber (MVW) ratio, 237
Meaning, 109, 138–139
  in agreement, 110–112, 115–123, 117f, 122–123
  to marking, 112–113
  plural, 123–124
Medin, D. L., 309
MEG. *See* Magneto-encephalography
Melton, Arthur, 146
Memory
  active, 186
  immediate, 147
  long-term, 49, 186
  working, 6–8, 7f, 21, 24, 54–55, 57, 146–147, 148f
Memory, long-term (LTM), 146–147, 148f, 206–207
Memory, short-term (STM), 146–147, 148f
  measures of, 168, 169f, 192
  nested models and, 175–176, 176f
  processes, 170
  variances common to, 168–170, 169f
  verbal/spatial, 172–173, 178–179
Memory, working capacity (WMC), 206
  alternative explanations of, 156–167, 165f
  brain and, 190–192
  complex tasks of, 167–168
  confirmatory analyses of, 173–175, 174f
  correlation and, 279–281, 279n3
  executive attention and, 149–150, 163–164, 176–177, 177f
  executive control and, 185–190, 188f
  general hypothesis and, 159
  inhibition/suppression and, 183–184
  low/high, 163, 165, 165f, 182, 187–189, 188f
  macroanalytic approach to, 157, 167–179, 169f, 174f, 176f, 177f
  measurement of, 150–156, 154n1, 168, 169f
  mental effort/motivation and, 164–167, 165f
  microanalytic approach to, 156–157, 180–185, 186f
  nature of, 145–150, 148f
  nested models and, 175–176, 176f
  prepotent responses and, 184–186, 186f
  rehearsal difference hypothesis and, 160–162
  reliability of, 155–156
  retrieval interference and, 180–183
  span tasks of, 145, 150–153
  speed hypothesis and, 162–163
  strategic allocation hypothesis and, 159
  task-specific hypothesis and, 158–159
  validity of, 153–155, 154n1
  variability perception and, 271–273
  variance common to, 168–170, 169f
  verbal/visuo-spatial, 170–173, 178–179
  word knowledge and, 157–158
Mental model. *See* Situation models
Meseguer, E., 118, 132
Meyer, A. S., 69
Mill, J. S., 310
Minimal input hypothesis, 115–116
Minkoff, S., 163

Mixed-error effects, 74–76, 81
Miyake, A., 178
M&M. *See* Marking-and-morphing approach
Mochon, D., 288
Modus Tollens schema, 304
Morphemes, 65
  features of, 130
  function, 67, 91, 93n6
Morphing, 109, 137–138
  marking to, 113–114
  representation and, 130–133
  requirements, 129–130
  scope and, 135–137
  transmission and, 134–135
Morris, M. W., 302
Motivation, 49, 164–167, 165f
Motley, M. T., 72, 73–74
Movements, 226–227
Muchinsky, M. M., 234–235, 236

N

Naming, 305
Naming-in-context deficits, 100
Narratives
  comprehension of, 2–3
  experimental, 11t, 13–15, 17–18
Nations, J. K., 157–158
Nelson-Denny Reading Comprehension Test, 152, 161
Network theory, associative, 6–8, 7f, 27–28, 28f
Neuroimaging
  cognitive psychology and, 64, 71, 91–95, 94f
  connectionist learning theory and, 91–95, 91n4, 94f
  studies, 79–80
Neurons, 71, 202, 209
Nicol, J., 136
Nisbett, R. E., 311
Nonwords, 74
Nosofsky, R. M., 229
Nouns, 64, 84
  count, 21
  head, 121, 129
  local, 123, 127–128, 132
  mass, 123
  non, 86
  plural number on, 113
  scores, 86–87, 86f, 87f
  singular, 132

Nuisance variable, 160
Number(s), 111
  agreement, 117, 138
  grammatical, 120–122, 131–132
  marking, 134–135, 139
  notional, 124–128, 126t, 127f
  plural, 132
  singular, 132
  specification, 132
  verb, 112–113, 116, 118, 122–123

O

Objects, 54, 64, 306
  accessibility of, 18–25, 21f, 23f, 25f
  categorization of, 228
  defined, 229
  dynamic, 228
  JIM model of, 207, 208, 210, 213–215, 213f
  numerosity of, 111
  perceived, 227
  recognition of, 202–203, 209–210, 210f
  single-point correspondence of, 230–231, 230f
  totem pole, 212–215, 212f, 213f
  visual representations of, 35–36
Observations, 292–293
Octigan, E., 118, 132
Opfer, J. E., 228–229
Orientation, 44–45
Out-of-Sight condition, 269–270, 271, 273
Overlap Assumption, 49–50

P

Panning, 47
Parameter, 263–264
  consistency, 249
  values, 249, 250f, 250t
Pearl, J., 289, 294–295
Pechmann, T., 69
Perceptions, 41. *See also* Consistency, perception of
  brain areas and, 52
  cognition and, 201–202, 219–220
  comprehension and, 53–55
  correlations and, 278–283
  functional relations hypothesis and, 217–219
  image segmentation and, 207–208
  motion, 227
  objects/images and, 206–215, 210f, 212f, 213f
  reality and, 262

Perceptions (*Continued*)
  relational, 203–206, 204f, 210–211, 212f
  scene comprehension and, 206, 215–222, 216f
  theories of, 72
  token formation and, 211–215, 212f, 216f
  visual properties and, 208–210, 210f
Perceptual categorizations, 227, 239, 255.
    See also Events
Perspectives, 43
  distance/location of, 44
  orientation and, 44–45
PET. *See* Positron emission tomography
Peterson, R. R., 77
Philadelphia Naming Test, 82, 83t
Phonological access, 81–82
Phonological information, 77–78, 78f
Phonological neighborhoods, 88–91, 89t
Point-light displays, 228, 235–236
Pollick, F. E., 235–236
Population(s)
  full view, 267–269, 271–273
  multi-valued, 277
  out-of-view, 267–269
  parameter, 264
Positional frames, 65
Positron emission tomography (PET), 79–80
Power PC theory, 313–314
Predicates, 128
Predictability, 48, 50–51
Predictions, 277–278, 283–284, 287, 320
  base-rate neglect and, 297–299
Prepositions, 91, 91n4
Primacy effect, 276–278
Priming, 8, 80
  negative, 183
  semantic, 54
  spatial, 5, 26
  structural, 93
Probability
  Bayesian graphical, 291, 298, 300
  theory, 289–290
Probe(s)
  experimental conditions for, 17
  goal-related, 10, 11t
  mediated, 78
  protagonist, 14–15
  reaction times, 5, 20–21, 21f, 22, 23f
  relevant-object, 18
  text, 11, 11t, 14
  word responses, 55

Production, 137
  components of, 64, 93
  deficits, 71, 101
  distinctions, 67
  phonological lexical feedback and, 70–71
  theories, 80
Pronoun(s), 91, 91n4
  behavior of, 124–128, 126t, 127f, 136, 140
  morphing and, 129–130, 133
  number, 122–123
  personal, 109
  target, 136
Propositional findings, 55–57
Propositional phrases, 40, 45
Propositions, 51, 55–56
Psycholinguistics, 63, 101, 137
Psychology, 2, 50, 262, 301
  perspectives in, 45
  social/emotional, 153
Psychology, cognitive, 3. *See also*
    Connectionist learning theory
  neuroimaging/neuropsychological data and,
    64, 71, 91–95, 94f
Psychopathology, 153, 154
Pulvermüller, F., 38

R

Radvansky, G. A., 29, 49
Randomness, 277, 292
Ravens Progressive Matrices, 168
Readers, 8
  attention of, 3
  comprehension of, 3, 152, 158
  good, 152
  object inferences of, 10–12, 11t
Reading, 1, 24
  rate, 41
  span tasks, 150–151
  words and, 38
Reasoning, 201, 320
  casualty levels and, 296–297
  causal analysis and, 311–312
  causal invariance in, 287–291
  causal models and, 291–294, 292f
  counterfactual/probabilistic judgment and,
    297–305
  explanation discounting and, 300–302
  induction and, 308–312
  inferences and, 294

language use and, 305–312
  representation and, 294–296, 295f
Recognition
  object, 202–203, 209–210, 210f
  phonological lexical feedback and, 70–71
Regency effect, 276–278
Rehearsals, 160–162
Reliability, 155–156
Representation, 35–36
  of action, 294–296, 295f
  agreement and, 130–133
  of events, 229–231, 230f
  functional, 64–65
  Hebbian model of, 38
  learning and, 294–296, 295f
  lexical, 64–65
  morphing and, 130–133
  point, 231–232
  positional, 64–66
  visual, 35, 206–207
Response(s)
  bias, 249
  competition, 186–187
  comprehenders and, 54–55
  hemocynamic, 79
  prepotent, 184–186, 186f
  probe-word, 55
  time facilitation, 188–189
Response time (RT), 163
Retention, 168
Richeson, J. A., 154
Rips, L., 307
Roles, 203
Rosch, E., 305
Rosen, V. M., 182–183
Rosenblum, L. D., 236
RT. See Response time
Russell, B., 288

S

Saffran, E. M., 93–94, 94f
Sample-Only condition, 269–270
Sampling, 274–275
  initial, 265
  primacy effect in, 276–278
  random, 264
  size, 281–282
SAT. See Scholastic Aptitude Test
Savoy, P., 77

Scanning, 47
Scenes, 47
  comprehension, 206, 215–222, 216f
  functional relations hypothesis and, 217–219
  recognition of familiar, 218–219, 220–222
Schizophrenics, 191–192
Schmidt, R. C., 236
Scholastic Aptitude Test (SAT), 152, 157
Schriefers, H., 69
Schwartz, M. F., 93–94, 94f
Scott, J. L., 161
Segments, 236
Semantic association, 16–18, 18f
Semantic informations, 77–78, 78f
Semantic integration, 116, 119
Semantic representations, Hebbian model of, 38
Semantic substitutions, 66, 81, 88
Semantics, 218
Sentence(s), 13, 17. See also Lemma
  comprehension, 35–36
  constraint in, 40
  fragment completion, 114
  intervening, 25
  movement, 4
  passive, 128
  processing, 70
  production, 95–101, 99t
  structure, 55–56
  target, 96
Sequences, action, 47
Shah, P., 178
Shakespeare, William, 289
Shelton, J. N., 154
Shiffrin, R. M., 146
Shifting, 67
Short-term memory. See Memory, short-term
Siegel, R. M., 237–238
Similarity
  assumptions, 236
  of events, 231–232
  stored instances and, 234
Situation models, 1
  activation in, 12–16, 15f
  experiments, 3–6, 4f, 9–12, 11t
  focal attention in, 3–6, 4f
  narrative components of, 2
  objects' goal activation in, 8
  previous relevant research in, 9
Sloman, S. A., 288, 299, 303, 310, 317–318

SOA. *See* Stimulus-onset-asynchrony
Software, RSVP, 13
Sound
 exchanges, 65–66
 speech, 75
Space, 49
Spanish language, 117–118
Speaking, 64, 82, 132
Speech, 109
 agrammatic, 91–92, 92n5
 rate, 41
 sounds, 63
Speech errors, 63, 71
 patterns, 91
 production processing levels
  and, 64–68, 68f, 80
 properties of, 65, 101
Speed, processing of, 162–163
Spitz, R. V., 237–238
Stability assumptions, 291
Stanford University, 12, 17, 20, 22, 24
Stiles, J., 237–238
Stimulus, 231, 266–267
 pair of, 240
 perturbed, 237
 representation of, 245
Stimulus-onset-asynchrony (SOA), 77, 78f
STM. *See* Memory, short-term
Storms, G., 309
Stromsten, Sean, 302n2
Stroop tasks, 154, 165–166, 185–186, 191
Subjects, 64, 128
Suh, S. Y., 26
Suppression, 183–184
Syntactic information, 79
Syntactic-sequential states, 95, 97–99, 99t

T

Tanenhaus, M. K., 53
Task(s)
 antisaccade, 164, 184–185, 186f, 191
 categorization, 237, 242, 242f
 context, 187–188, 188f
 direct-question, 270
 prosaccade, 164, 184–185, 186f
 range of, 231
 span, 145, 150–153
 specific hypothesis, 158–159
 Stroop, 154, 165–166, 187, 191

 transfer, 248, 249t
 type of, 269–270
 without recall, 159
Tenebaum, J. B., 315
Text(s). *See also* Situation models
 comprehension, 55
 experimental, 13
 informational levels of, 1, 35–36
 probes, 11, 11t, 14
 propositional base of, 1
 surface structure of, 1
Therriault, D., 163
Thinking, 201, 203–206, 204f
Thornton, R., 128
Time, 49
 integration of, 236
 measurement, 235
 perceptual, 234–235
 points of alignment and, 235–236
 role of, 234–235
Tokens, 211, 212–215, 212f, 213f
Total Number of Sampling Trials, 276–277
Trabasso, T., 3, 26
Trajectories, 232, 233f, 239–240, 240f
Turley-Ames, K.J., 161
Turner, M. L., 152
Tversky, B., 297–298

U

Utterances, 65, 91, 129, 139–140

V

van Dijk, T. A., 38, 49
Vantage point, 48–49
Variable, type of, 269–270, 276
Variances
 LTM/STM, 168–170, 169f
 perceiving, 261–262
 sampling of, 263–265, 263n1, 265f
Velocity, 237, 245
Vera, A. H., 228
Verbal Scholastic Aptitude
 Test (VSAT), 151, 157, 160
Verbs, 64
 behavior of, 125–127, 127f, 136, 140
 difficulty with, 92, 92n5
 heavy, 93–94, 98
 light, 57, 93–94, 94f, 98

morphing and, 129–130
numbers and, 112–113, 116, 118, 122–123
plural-ageeing, 124
replacement of, 84
simple, 93
Viewing Condition, 272
Vigliocco, G., 115–116, 136
Visual processing, 202, 221
Visual properties, 208–210, 210f
Visual representations, 35, 206–207
Visual systems, 206–207
Vitevitch, M.S., 88
Vorberg, D., 69
VSAT. *See* Verbal Scholastic Aptitude Test

W

Waldmann, M. R.
Weber's Law, 81
Weightings, 243–244, 244f, 245f, 246f, 247f
  optimal, 252, 252f
Wernicke's area, 80
Whitfield, M. M., 161
Wickelgren, E. A., 238
Wittgenstein, L., 305
WMC. *See* Memory, working capacity
Word(s)
  brain and, 35, 52
  comprehension, 35
  content, 67, 94, 98
  context conditions, 74
  errors, 86
  exchanges, 65–66

frequency, 71
function, 65–67, 94, 98
functional webs and, 39
interacting, 65–66
knowledge, 157–158
order, 45, 51
outcomes, 74
pairs, 73
picture interference, 80
picture-naming for, 88
probe, 55
processing of, 53–54
production, 89, 89t
reading and, 38
recall, 168
recognition, 70
retrieval, 67
span tasks, 151
superiority effect, 72
target, 74–75
tool, 52
whole, 63
Working capacity memory. *See* Memory,
  working capacity

Y

Yaxley, R. H., 29, 49, 53–54

Z

Zooming, 47
Zwaan, R. A., 29, 49, 53–54

CONTENTS OF RECENT VOLUMES

Volume 30

Perceptual Learning
    Felice Bedford
A Rational-Constructivist Account of Early Learning about Numbers and Objects
    Rochel Gelman
Remembering, Knowing, and Reconstructing the Past
    Henry L. Roediger III, Mark A. Wheeler, and Suparna Rajaram
The Long-Term Retention of Knowledge and Skills
    Alice F. Healy, Deborah M. Clawson, Danielle S. McNamara, William R. Marmie, Vivian I. Schneider, Timothy C. Rickard, Robert J. Crutcher, Cheri L. King, K. Anders Ericsson, and Lyle E. Bourne, Jr.
A Comprehension-Based Approach to Learning and Understanding
    Walter Kintsch, Bruce K. Britton, Charles R. Fletcher, Eileen Kintsch, Suzanne M. Mannes, and Mitchell J. Nathan
Separating Causal Laws from Causal Facts: Pressing the Limits of Statistical Relevance
    Patricia W. Cheng
Categories, Hierarchies, and Induction
    Elizabeth F. Shipley
Index

Volume 31

Associative Representations of Instrumental Contingencies
    Ruth M. Colwill
A Behavioral Analysis of Concepts: Its Application to Pigeons and Children
    Edward A. Wasserman and Suzette L. Astley
The Child's Representation of Human Groups
    Lawrence A. Hirschfeld
Diagnostic Reasoning and Medical Expertise
    Vimla L. Patel, Jos F. Arocha, and David R. Kaufman
Object Shape, Object Name, and Object Kind: Representation and Development
    Barbara Landau
The Ontogeny of Part Representation in Object Concepts
    Philippe G. Schyns and Gregory L. Murphy
Index

Volume 32

Cognitive Approaches to Judgment and Decision Making
    Reid Hastie and Nancy Pennington
And Let Us Not Forget Memory: The Role of Memory Processes and Techniques in the Study of Judgment and Choice
    Elke U. Weber, Wiliam M. Goldstein, and Sema Barlas
Content and Discontent: Indications and Implications of Domain Specificity in Preferential Decision Making
    William M. Goldstein and Elke U. Weber
An Information Processing Perspective on Choice
    John W. Payne, James R. Bettman, Eric J. Johnson, and Mary Frances Luce
Algebra and Process in the Modeling of Risky Choice
    Lola L. Lopes
Utility Invariance Despite Labile Preferences
    Barbara A. Mellers, Elke U. Weber, Lisa D. Ordez, and Alan D. J. Cooke
Compatibility in Cognition and Decision
    Eldar Shafir

Processing Linguistic Probabilities: General
Principles and Empirical Evidence
   David V. Budescu and Thomas S. Wallsten
Compositional Anomalies in the Semantics of
Evidence
   John M. Miyamoto, Richard Gonzalez, and
   Shihfen Tu
Varieties of Confirmation Bias
   Joshua Klayman
Index

Volume 33

Landmark-Based Spatial Memory in the Pigeon
   Ken Cheng
The Acquisition and Structure of Emotional
Response Categories
   Paula M. Niedenthal and Jamin
   B. Halberstadt
Early Symbol Understanding and Use
   Judy S. DeLoache
Mechanisms of Transition: Learning with a
Helping Hand
   Susan Goldin-Meadow and Martha
   Wagner Alibali
The Universal Word Identification Reflex
   Charles A. Perfetti and Sulan Zhang
Prospective Memory: Progress and Processes
   Mark A. McDaniel
Looking for Transfer and Interference
   Nancy Pennington and Bob Rehder
Index

Volume 34

Associative and Normative Models of Causal
Induction: Reacting to versus Understanding
Cause
   A. G. Baker, Robin A. Murphy, and Frdric
   Valle-Tourangeau
Knowledge-Based Causal Induction
   Michael R. Waldmann
A Comparative Analysis of Negative Contingency
Learning in Humans and Nonhumans
   Douglas A. Williams
Animal Analogues of Causal Judgment
   Ralph R. Miller and Helena Matute
Conditionalizing Causality
   Barbara A. Spellman
Causation and Association
   Edward A. Wasserman, Shu-Fang Kao,
   Linda J. Van Hamme, Masayoshi Katagiri,
   and Michael E. Young
Distinguishing Associative and Probabilistic
Contrast Theories of Human Contingency
Judgment
   David R. Shanks, Francisco J. Lopez,
   Richard J. Darby, and Anthony Dickinson
A Causal-Power Theory of Focal Sets
   Patricia W. Cheng, Jooyong Park, Aaron
   S. Yarlas, and Keith J. Holyoak
The Use of Intervening Variables in Causal
Learning
   Jerome R. Busemeyer, Mark A. McDaniel,
   and Eunhee Byun
Structural and Probabilistic Causality
   Judea Pearl
Index

Volume 35

Distance and Location Processes in Memory for
the Times of Past Events
   William J. Friedman
Verbal and Spatial Working Memory in Humans
   John Jonides, Patricia A. Reuter-Lorenz,
   Edward E. Smith, Edward Awh,
   Lisa L. Barnes, Maxwell Drain, Jennifer
   Glass, Erick J. Lauber, Andrea L. Patalano,
   and Eric H. Schumacher
Memory for Asymmetric Events
   John T. Wixted and Deirdra H. Dougherty
The Maintenance of a Complex Knowledge Base
After Seventeen Years
   Marigold Linton
Category Learning As Problem Solving
   Brian H. Ross
Building a Coherent Conception of HIV
Transmission: A New Approach to Aids
Educations
   Terry Kit-fong Au and Laura F. Romo
Spatial Effects in the Partial Report Paradigm: A
Challenge for Theories of Visual Spatial
Attention
   Gordon D. Logan and Claus Bundesen
Structural Biases in Concept Learning: Influences
from Multiple Functions
   Dorrit Billman
Index

Volume 36

Learning to Bridge Between Perception and
Cognition
   Robert L. Goldstone, Philippe G. Schyns, and
   Douglas L. Medin
The Affordances of Perceptual Inquiry: Pictures
Are Learned From the World, and What That
Fact Might Mean About Perception Quite
Generally
   Julian Hochberg

Perceptual Learning of Alphanumeric-Like Characters
  Richard M. Shiffrin and Nancy Lightfoot
Expertise in Object and Face Recognition
  James Tanaka and Isabel Gauthier
Infant Speech Perception: Processing Characteristics, Representational Units, and the Learning of Words
  Peter D. Eimas
Constraints on the Learning of Spatial Terms: A Computational Investigation
  Terry Regier
Learning to Talk About the Properties of Objects: A Network Model of the Development of Dimensions
  Linda B. Smith, Michael Gasser, and Catherine M. Sandhofer
Self-Organization, Plasticity, and Low-Level Visual Phenomena in a Laterally Connected Map Model of the Primary Visual Cortex
  Risto Mikkulainen, James A. Bednar, Yoonsuck Choe, and Joseph Sirosh
Perceptual Learning From Cross-Modal Feedback
  Virginia R. de Sa and Dana H. Ballard
Learning As Extraction of Low-Dimensional Representations
  Shimon Edelman and Nathan Intrator
Index

Volume 37

Object-Based Reasoning
  Miriam Bassok
Encoding Spatial Representation Through Nonvisually Guided Locomotion: Tests of Human Path Integration
  Roberta L. Klatzky, Jack M. Loomis, and Reginald G. Golledge
Production, Evaluation, and Preservation of Experiences: Constructive Processing in Remembering and Performance Tasks
  Bruce W. A. Whittlesea
Goals, Representations, and Strategies in a Concept Attainment Task: The EPAM Model
  Fernand Gobet, Howard Richman, Jim Staszewski, and Herbert A. Simon
Attenuating Interference During Comprehension: The Role of Suppression
  Morton Ann Gernsbacher
Cognitive Processes in Counterfactual Thinking About What Might Have Been
  Ruth M. J. Byrne
Episodic Enhancement of Processing Fluency
  Michael E. J. Masson and Colin M. MacLeod
At a Loss From Words: Verbal Overshadowing of Perceptual Memories
  Jonathan W. Schooler, Stephen M. Fiore, and Maria A. Brandimonte
Index

Volume 38

Transfer-Inappropriate Processing: Negative Priming and Related Phenomena
  W. Trammell Neil and Katherine M. Mathis
Cue Competition in the Absence of Compound Training: Its Relation to Paradigms of Interference Between Outcomes
  Helena Matute and Oskar Pineo
Sooner or Later: The Psychology of Intertemporal Choice
  Gretchen B. Chapman
Strategy Adaptivity and Individual Differences
  Christian D. Schunn and Lynne M. Reder
Going Wild in the Laboratory: Learning About Species Typical Cues
  Michael Domjan
Emotional Memory: The Effects of Stress on "Cool" and "Hot" Memory Systems
  Janet Metcalfe and W. Jake Jacobs
Metacomprehension of Text: Influence of Absolute Confidence Level on Bias and Accuracy
  Ruth H. Maki
Linking Object Categorization and Naming: Early Expectations and the Shaping Role of Language
  Sandra R. Waxman
Index

Volume 39

Infant Memory: Cues, Contexts, Categories, and Lists
  Carolyn Rovee-Collier and Michelle Gulya
The Cognitive-Initiative Account of Depression-Related Impairments in Memory
  Paula T. Hertel
Relational Timing: A Theromorphic Perspective
  J. Gregor Fetterman
The Influence of Goals on Value and Choice
  Arthur B. Markham and C. Miguel Brendl
The Copying Machine Metaphor
  Edward J. Wisniewski
Knowledge Selection in Category Learning
  Evan Heit and Lewis Bott
Index

Volume 40

Different Organization of Concepts and Meaning Systems in the Two Cerebral Hemispheres
  Dahlia W. Zaidel

The Causal Status Effect in Categorization: An Overview
  Woo-kyoung Ahn and Nancy S. Kim
Remembering as a Social Process
  Mary Susan Weldon
Neurocognitive Foundations of Human Memory
  Ken A. Paller
Structural Influences on Implicit and Explicit Sequence Learning
  Tim Curran, Michael D. Smith, Joseph M. DiFranco, and Aaron T. Daggy
Recall Processes in Recognition Memory
  Caren M. Rotello
Reward Learning: Reinforcement, Incentives, and Expectations
  Kent C. Berridge
Spatial Diagrams: Key Instruments in the Toolbox for Thought
  Laura R. Novick
Reinforcement and Punishment in the Prisoner's Dilemma Game
  Howard Rachlin, Jay Brown, and Forest Baker
Index

Volume 41

Categorization and Reasoning in Relation to Culture and Expertise
  Douglas L. Medin, Norbert Ross, Scott Atran, Russell C. Burnett, and Sergey V. Blok
On the Computational basis of Learning and Cognition: Arguments from LSA
  Thomas K. Landauer
Multimedia Learning
  Richard E. Mayer
Memory Systems and Perceptual Categorization
  Thomas J. Palmeri and Marci A. Flanery
Conscious Intentions in the Control of Skilled Mental Activity
  Richard A. Carlson
Brain Imaging Autobiographical Memory
  Martin A. Conway, Christopher W. Pleydell-Pearce, Sharon Whitecross, and Helen Sharpe
The continued Influence of Misinformation in Memory: What makes a Corrections Effective?
  Colleen M. Seifert
Making Sense and Nonsense of Experience: Attributions in Memory and Judgment
  Colleen M. Kelley and Matthew G. Rhodes

Real-World estimation: Estimation Modes and Seeding Effects
  Norman R. Brown
Index

Volume 42

Memory and Learning in Figure–Ground Perception
  Mary A. Peterson and Emily Skow-Grant
Spatial and Visual Working Memory: A Mental Workspace
  Robert H. Logie
Scene Perception and Memory
  Marvin M. Chun
Spatial Representations and Spatial Updating
  Ranxiano Frances Wang
Selective Visual Attention and Visual Search: Behavioral and Neural Mechanisms
  Joy J. Geng and Marlene Behrmann
Categorizing and Perceiving Objects: Exploring a Continuum of Information Use
  Philippe G. Schyns
From Vision to Action and Action to Vision: A Convergent Route Approach to Vision, Action, and Attention
  Glyn W. Humphreys and M. Jane Riddoch
Eye Movements and Visual Cognitive Suppression
  David E. Irwin
What Makes Change Blindness Interesting?
  Daniel J. Simons and Daniel T. Levin
Index

Volume 43

Ecological Validity and the Study of Concepts
  Gregory L. Murphy
Social Embodiment
  Lawrence W. Barsalou, Paula M. Niedenthal, Aron K. Barbey, and Jennifer A. Ruppert
The Body's Contribution to Language
  Arthur M. Glenburg and Michael P. Kaschak
Using Spatial Language
  Laura A. Carlson
In Opposition to Inhibition
  Colin M. MacLeod, Michael D. Dodd, Erin D. Sheard, Daryl E. Wilson, and Uri Bibi
Evolution of Human Cognitive Architecture
  John Sweller
Cognitive Plasticity and Aging
  Arthur F. Kramer and Sherry L. Willis
Index